# Containing Health Care Costs in Japan

# Containing Health Care Costs in Japan

Naoki Ikegami and
John Creighton Campbell,
Editors

Ann Arbor
THE UNIVERSITY OF MICHIGAN PRESS

Copyright © by the University of Michigan 1996
All rights reserved
Published in the United States of America by
The University of Michigan Press
Manufactured in the United States of America
⊗ Printed on acid-free paper

1999   1998   1997   1996      4   3   2   1

*A CIP catalog record for this book is available from the British Library.*


Library of Congress Cataloging-in-Publication Data

Containing health care costs in Japan / edited by Naoki Ikegami and
   John Creighton Campbell.
        p.   cm.
     Includes index.
     ISBN 0–472–10538–8 (hardcover : alk. paper)
     1. Medical care, Cost of—Japan.   I. Ikegami, Naoki, 1949–
II. Campbell, John Creighton.
RA410.55.J3C66   1996
338.4′33621′0952—dc20                                        96–26049
                                                                CIP

NUST

IAEH3658
AHN3122

# Contents

## Section III: Technology and Costs

## Section IV: Institutions and Costs

## Section V: Health Behavior and Attitudes

# Introduction

*Naoki Ikegami and John Creighton Campbell*

As the debate over what to do about health care in the United States develops, Americans have looked overseas for examples of what might work better in providing more coverage and somehow constraining costs. Canada is most often invoked, but its single-payer system, though attractive in its simplicity, appears far too radical a change to seem practical to many experts. Attention has thus also been drawn to Germany, Australia, and other countries that combine a relatively pluralistic health insurance system with universal coverage and at least somewhat effective cost control.

Japan is often mentioned in this context, but it is probably the least well understood major system, even among experts in the field. We believe it deserves more study. Japan is, after all, the second largest economy in the world, its population is unusually healthy (long life-spans, low infant mortality), and its health care costs are roughly half those of the United States in terms of per-capita spending or percentage of national product. Not incidentally, the money that Japan has not had to spend on health care, compared with the United States, has helped it maintain the high rates of investment that lead to rapid economic growth. This factor is probably more important than the oft-cited gap in defense spending in explaining the Japanese edge in our economic competition.

Moreover, at least some aspects of the Japanese approach to health care are potentially quite relevant to the United States.

- The system is based on a fee-for-service provision in which the patient has free choice among doctors and hospitals.
- Most health insurance is employment-related, but nonemployees are also fully covered; the Japanese solution to the difficult problem of covering small-business employees in particular is quite relevant to the United States.
- A variety of cross-subsidization mechanisms bring a remarkable degree of equality of burdens and treatment to patients across different income levels and needs.
- Costs are controlled through a mandatory fee schedule covering virtually all medical goods and services. The schedule is periodically revised in a process that is politically quite efficient, albeit not very "scientific."

- A deliberate policy change on the part of government brought a dramatic leveling off of relative health care expenditures, which actually had been growing at the same rapid rate as in the United States in the 1970s.

Of course, Japanese health care has substantial problems of its own, and no one would argue that the entire system should be imported by the United States. There are, nonetheless, many lessons to be learned about its specific mechanisms as well as the general Japanese approach to health care. It was from that perspective that we conceived a research project to ask two questions: Why are Japanese health care costs low? How did Japan succeed in leveling off growth?

Happily, the creation of the Center for Global Partnership by the Japan Foundation provided a chance for obtaining resources for this project. Center staff in New York was helpful as we worked out our plans. The problem we faced was the lack of infrastructure in health policy research in Japan. Policy research in general is not overwhelmingly popular among Japanese scholars, and the health care field in particular has been avoided by serious researchers because of the difficulties of obtaining data, of remaining objective in a polarized political debate, and of mastering the immense complexities of the subject. Our task was further magnified by the need to explain a very different system—in which even such basic terms as "hospital" or "fee-for-service" have different meanings—in a way that Americans can understand.

Our strategy was to recruit a group of relatively young Japanese specialists on health care, augmented by a few North American Japan specialists whose research had touched on related topics. While we presented a general framework for the project, for the most part we left it to the individual researchers to define their own projects. We then called on some distinguished American health care specialists, most of whom had previously had little contact with Japan, to perform two important roles. First, through a process of dialogue, they could give Japanese researchers some exposure to the international discourse in this field, to the "big questions," and could help ensure rigorous academic standards for our project. Second, they could help interpret our findings about Japan for an American audience, who, of course, would be thinking largely in terms of the debate over health care reform in the United States.

When our proposal was accepted by the Center for Global Partnership, we convened an exploratory conference in Washington, D.C. in March 1992 to talk over the basic framework and provide focus to the individual research projects. The researchers then went to work, and over the next year we did our best to help them by providing statistical and descriptive information on both the Japanese and American systems. The resulting papers were then translated (when necessary) and presented and discussed at a two-day conference at a pleasant hot spring in Izu, outside Tokyo, in March 1993.

The papers were then revised by the authors and underwent some editing in Ann Arbor. We also either wrote or commissioned a few additional papers to fill in some gaps. In addition, each of the experts on American health care wrote up their comments on the papers, and in some cases added additional observations (including material from presentations at a public forum in Tokyo, sponsored and published by the professional magazine *Shakai Hoken Junpô*). The result is the present volume.

We should acknowledge that this book does not purport to be a comprehensive and definitive treatment of the Japanese health care system. Even if such a project were possible, it is certainly well beyond the intellectual, organizational, and financial resources that we could muster. Still, we are confident that these papers throw light on many important aspects of health care in Japan that have never before been treated in English, and often not even in Japanese. Certainly the attention to the key issue of cost containment that runs through most of these papers is nearly unique. We believe the book as a whole is a substantial addition to the existing literature on Japanese health care available to Americans (see such books as Steslicke 1973; Norbeck and Lock 1987; Sonoda 1988; Powell and Anesaki 1990; and Okimoto and Yoshikawa 1993; plus such articles as Fujii and Reich 1988; and Iglehart 1988).

We are also writing a complementary book that draws on the research gathered in this volume as well as additional materials and our own somewhat idiosyncratic perspectives on how health care systems work in general and in Japan. It takes an institutionalist approach in trying to tell the story of how Japan's low-cost, egalitarian health care system works in practice. The topics include actors, arenas, and agendas; health care providers; the health insurance system; the efficacy of the fee schedule in holding down costs from both a macro and a micro perspective; and the problem of quality (Campbell and Ikegami forthcoming).

The present volume is organized around a set of broad themes that are important in understanding the cost-containment mechanisms of the Japanese health care system. Each group of papers is followed by the revised version of the comments by the American experts at the Izu conference. To provide an overview, however, we begin with a short paper by Ikegami that is the only portion of this book to appear separately in English—it was published in *Science,* 23 October 1992, and is reprinted with a few updates.

The first pair of papers analyzes health expenditures from a macro perspective. Yukiko Katsumata addresses the thorny problem of measuring health spending for purposes of cross-national comparison. It turns out that Japanese official statistics do not include some items that are included in American statistics, but adding these only slightly closes the wide gap in spending between the two countries. Ikegami and Yoshinori Hiroi draw on Organization for Economic Cooperation and Development statistics to account for some of the differences in American and Japanese expenditures. William Hsiao's comments point out several methodological pitfalls and add his own perspective on how differences in spending between the United States and Japan break down.

The second section takes up three of the factors that help to explain why Japanese spending is so low. Hiroi's paper is an unusual systematic account by an insider of the mechanisms of Japan's mandatory fee schedule and how they were changed in the early 1980s in a successful attempt to level off expenditure growth. The papers by Koichi Kawabuchi and by Ikegami, Takanori Ishii, and Jay Wolfson focus on where the cost differences between Japan and the United States are most dramatic: hospital physical facilities and administrative spending by payors and hospitals. George Greenberg comments from his perspective as a health planner at the Department of Health and Human Services.

The third group of papers examines how the Japanese system copes with the cost of technological change in the fields of surgery, diagnostic machinery, and pharmaceuticals. Toshihiko Hasegawa points out that the large difference in hospital admissions (and therefore hospital costs) between Japan and the United States is largely due to far lower rates of surgery in Japan. Akinori Hisashige explains how MRI diffused just as rapidly in Japan as in the United States, but at much lower cost due to the fee schedule. Ikegami looks at the actual cost and usage differences in prescription drugs, while Will Mitchell, Thomas Roehl, and John Campbell discuss whether tight controls on pharmaceutical costs had the negative effects on R&D often cautioned by American manufacturers. John Eisenberg's comment addresses the implications of these findings in the broader context of technology assessment and the education of physicians.

The following section returns to the high-cost area of hospital care to examine some micro-level issues of cost containment. Two papers focus on long-term institutional care for the elderly, which in the United States usually takes place in nursing homes, and in Japan, in hospitals. Ikegami's chapter with Yamada contrasts costs and quality in the two systems. Yasuo Takagi assesses the impact of a change from fee-for-service to capitated reimbursement on provider behavior in one geriatric hospital. The other two papers take up acute-care hospitals, one by Ikegami and Shunya Ikeda that presents new data on how long patients have to wait for inpatient care in Japan, and one by Naoko Muramatsu and Jersey Liang that compares the length of stay and total costs for a matched set of heart patients in an American and a Japanese hospital. William Weissert's comment explores the implications of these findings for health reform in the United States.

The penultimate section turns to health behavior by individuals as a potential explanation for why health care costs are so much lower in Japan. Hiroko Akiyama presents data from a comparative U.S.-Japan survey to show that Japanese are more likely to take early action when they feel ill, possibly resulting in lower costs in the long run. Margaret Lock focuses on the quite moderate use of formal medical care by middle-aged women in Japan, due essentially to cultural factors. Ruth Campbell reports on her observations of elderly patients visiting doctors to argue that the celebrated Japanese "three-minute consultation" may have its advantages with this population when it occurs frequently. Eric Feldman looks into the Japanese dilemma of defining brain death for purposes of organ transplantation, and finds that it was a Japanese suspicion of doctors rather than cost-containment motivations that has hampered development in this field. The comment by Arnold Rosoff interprets these observations from an American legal and bioethical perspective.

The last section is about the politics of health care. John Campbell looks at how politics has shaped the fragmented but quite egalitarian health insurance system into an effective mechanism for dampening conflict. He and Mikitaka

Masuyama then deal with the politics of health care provision, centering on the long struggle between the Ministry of Health and Welfare and the Japan Medical Association (JMA), centering on the period of negotiations over the fee schedule. Takagi asks to what extent JMA efforts in fee schedule negotiations actually benefited private practitioners. Ted Marmor finishes with a comment on all these developments from the viewpoint of a political scientist deeply immersed in American efforts to reform health care.

Again, while we make no claim that these papers cover all of the interesting ground of Japanese health care on their subjects, or that they in all cases are completely authoritative treatments of their individual topics, we are confident that they add much new and sound analysis and will serve as a basis for further research.

It remains to thank several institutions and individuals who helped this project to fruition. Campbell is grateful to the Japan-U.S. Educational Commission for the Fulbright fellowship that supported his initial research on health care in Japan, and to the Keio University Faculty of Law and Professor Sone Yoshinori for acting as his host. Ikegami thanks the Wharton School at the University of Pennsylvania for the visiting professorship that allowed the early planning of this project. We are both grateful to the Center for Global Partnership for its generous financial support.

As for individuals, Yamada Takeshi participated ably in our discussions and helped in gathering data as well as in providing administrative support in his capacity as a staff member of the Health Care Science Institute, which took on management of the Japan side of the project. Tominaga Ikuko of the Keio University Hospital helped with the Japanese manuscripts and in preparing graphics. At the University of Michigan, Heidi Tietjen, Assistant Director of the Japan Technology Management Program, expertly managed our finances, and Bruce Willoughby, director of the Center for Japanese Studies Publications Program, supervised preparation of the manuscript through to camera-ready copy, with fine help from copy-editor Carol Shannon and keyboardist Wendy Rose. A variety of research tasks were well carried out by Cathy Peters, Ted Gilman, and Mikitaka Masuyama in Ann Arbor.

Needless to say, none of these individuals and institutions are responsible for errors of fact or interpretation, and indeed all of the authors are speaking for themselves rather than as official spokespeople for their employers.

REFERENCES

Campbell, John Creighton, and Naoki Ikegami. Forthcoming. *The art of balance in health policy: Maintaining Japan's low-cost, egalitarian system.* New York: Cambridge University Press and Tokyo: Chūō Kōron.

Fujii Mitsuru, and Michael Reich. 1988. Rising medical costs and the reform of Japan's health insurance system. *Health Affairs* 9:9–24.

Iglehart, John K. 1988. Health policy report: Japan's medical care system. *The New England Journal of Medicine* 319:12, 17.

Norbeck, Edward, and Margaret Lock, eds. 1987. *Health, illness, and medical care in Japan.* Honolulu: University of Hawaii Press.

Okimoto, Daniel, and Aki Yoshikawa. 1993. *Japan's health system: Efficiency and effectiveness in universal care.* New York: Faulkner & Gray.

Powell, Margaret, and Masahira Anesaki. 1990. *Health care in Japan.* London: Routledge.

Sonoda, Kyoichi. 1988. *Health and illness in changing Japanese society.* Tokyo: Tokyo University Press.

Steslicke, William E. 1973. *Doctors in politics: the political life of the Japan Medical Association.* New York: Praeger.

# Conventions and Usages

Japanese names are given in the Western order, with family name second. Our rule in translating names of Japanese agencies and programs is to follow the Ministry of Health and Welfare's most common usage. The major exception is Kokumin Kenkō Hoken, the health insurance program for the nonemployed, which is usually but misleadingly translated National Health Insurance. We use the term Citizens Health Insurance as a better expression of its nature and a legitimate gloss on the Japanese word Kokumin. We also generally translate *shinryōjo* as "office" rather than "clinic," and *kaigyōi* as "office-based physician."

Conversions of yen figures into dollars are only to give the reader a sense of the order of magnitude of the amount. In general the conversions have been calculated at the rate of $1 = ¥180, as a rough approximation of purchasing power parity (PPP) throughout the period, rounded off to two significant digits. We consider this convention preferable to using annual estimates of PPP, such as those calculated by the Organization for Economic Cooperation and Development (OECD) and used in its Health Data File, because, for example, our procedure does not make a yen amount that has actually been stable to appear to change over time. The exceptions are: chapters 6 and 16, comparing specific costs in a single year between Japan and the United States, in which the OECD estimate of PPP for that year is used; and chapter 11 on pharmaceutical charges, where one table uses the same PPP rate as was employed in the original source.

It should be emphasized that all PPP estimates are always somewhat arbitrary, since the "market basket" of goods and services used for comparison cannot be identical. More generally, quantitative cross-national comparisons should always be viewed with considerable skepticism, since discrepancies in definitions and ways of counting creep in at many points. In this volume we have tried to be realistic about the limitations as well as the considerable payoffs of comparative analysis.

CHAPTER 1

# Overview: Health Care in Japan[1]

*Naoki Ikegami*

SUMMARY    Japan's health care system balances universal coverage at reasonable cost. The government has taken on the responsibility of acting as insurer and subsidizing health care spending for the employees of small enterprises and the self-employed. Despite the fee-for-service form of payment, costs have been contained by the use of a nationally uniform fee schedule that is mandatory for all providers. However, the increasingly affluent and aging population is making new demands on the system that can only be met by a major restructuring.

## Introduction

By the broad measures of performance, the Japan's health care system appears to have achieved a paragon of success. Gross health indices are the best in the world, with an infant mortality rate at 0.46% of live births and a life expectancy at birth of 75.9 years for males and 81.8 years for females (Kōsei Tōkei Kyōkai 1991). There is universal coverage with virtually unlimited access to all health care facilities by every citizen. Moreover, because Japan's per-capita rates of computer-aided tomography (CAT) scans and renal dialysis are among the highest of all nations, there would seem to be no overt signs of rationing.[2] What makes this record even more impressive is that the ratio of the gross domestic product (GDP) devoted to health care is little more than half that of the United States (Organization for Economic Cooperation and Development 1990, 129, 151, 198).

In this article, I briefly describe how the Japanese health care system works in order to provide some general context for international comparison.[3] Is Japan's system really a paragon? In particular, how is equity achieved? Why has it been possible to contain costs under a fee-for-service system? Are there any negative effects coming from cost containment? What are the relationships between cost, access, and quality?

### The Delivery System: Functionally Undifferentiated

About 81% of Japan's hospitals and 94% of its physicians' offices (referred to as clinics) are privately operated (Ministry of Health and Welfare [MHW] 1992a, 35,

8

380–81). Although hospital beds have recently become regulated, there are still no restrictions on any other form of capital investment. However, this entrepreneurism has been permitted only by private practitioners. Investor-owned for-profit hospitals are prohibited, and the hospitals' chief executives must always be physicians. These legal limitations have effectively constrained the development of multihospital systems. Most of the hospitals are small, physician-owned family concerns that have developed from clinics. Few of them have ventured into high-technology medicine because of the restraints posed by the financing system, and thus the high-technology area tends to be dominated by the smaller but more prestigious public sector.

Health care in Japan differs from that in the United States in that the physicians in clinics do not have any access to hospital facilities and therefore must refer to others all patients needing the kind of care that the physicians cannot provide within their own premises. Hospitals, however, employ their physicians on fixed salaries and maintain large outpatient departments from which they admit all their inpatients. Because of this mutually exclusive arrangement, both clinics and hospitals compete for patients who have the freedom to choose the facility that they feel best fits their needs. This situation means that there is little functional differentiation between clinics and hospitals, and their boundary is further blurred because a third of the clinics have a small number of beds (the distinction is primarily legal in that facilities with more than twenty beds are designated as hospitals, whereas those having fewer than twenty are called clinics). There is also not much differentiation between acute and long-term care. Hospitals have taken on the function of nursing homes in Japan, and 45% of the inpatients over the age of sixty-five have been hospitalized for more than six months (MHW 1989, 319).

### The Financing System: Strictly Regulated

In contrast to the basically laissez-faire policy taken toward the delivery system, the financing system is highly regulated. First, although there are multiple payers, consumers have virtually no choice over the selection of their plan. They must join the one statutory plan offered by their employers, or, if they are self-employed, the one administered by their local governments or trade associations. However, the lack of choice does not really affect the consumer because there is very little flexibility. All plans offer basically the same set of comprehensive medical benefits, including medications, long-term care, dental care, and some preventive care.

Second, neither insurers nor providers have the freedom to negotiate individually a different fee schedule. The fee-for-service system operates under a minutely defined price schedule set by the government. All providers are paid exactly the same amount, inclusive of physician's fees, for the same service regardless of the physician's expertise, the facility's characteristics, or its geographical location.

Third, consumers cannot opt out of the statutory system, and private health insurance, which is mainly limited to cash compensations to cover incidental expenses during hospitalizations, remains insignificant. Providers are strictly prohibited from balance billing (charging more than the fee schedule allows). Extra charges are permitted only for private hospital rooms (only 10% of the rooms are of this status in Japan) (Kōsei Tōkei Kyōkai 1991, 67) and for a very restrictive range of new technology, which is still being assessed.

The insurance plans (table 1) can be broadly divided into two categories. The first is the insurance system for employees and their dependents, in which the premiums are generally paid on an equal basis between employer and employee. Together this amounts to about 8.2% of the average monthly wage and is automatically deducted from the paycheck as a Social Security payment. However, because contributions are not made, or are smaller, from the biannual bonuses, which typically total a third of an employee's annual income, premiums amount to only 2.7% of the average employee's total income (Kōsei Tōkei Kyōkai 1991, 66). This system of employer-based insurance can be subdivided into five segments: (1) Government-Managed Health Insurance (GMHI) for workers in small enterprises of more than five but fewer than three hundred employees; (2) Society-Managed Health Insurance (SMHI) (jointly managed by management and labor representatives) for workers in large enterprises (numbering 1,800 societies); (3) the Day Laborers' Insurance (those expected to work for less than two months); (4) the independent Seamen's Insurance; and (5) the Mutual Aid Association Insurance for public-sector employees. For all plans under this system the copayment rate is 10% for employee care, 20% for dependent inpatient care, and 30% for dependent outpatient care.

The second is the insurance system for the self-employed, pensioners, and their dependents. The elderly would be covered by this system unless they are employed or their low income makes them eligible for coverage by their children as dependents. Premiums are calculated on the basis of income, the number of individuals in the insured household, and assets. This category can be divided into the community-based ordinary Citizens Health Insurance (CHI), in which the municipal government acts as insurer, and the CHI associations, which insure members in the same occupation, such as carpenters or barbers. Under this system, the copayment rate is 30% for both inpatient and outpatient care.

Except for the 0.6% on public assistance for health care,[4] it is mandatory that all Japanese be covered by one of these plans. The employer-based plans cover 65% of the population, whereas the plans for the self-employed and their dependents cover the remaining population. The copayment is waived for all the elderly age seventy and over (sixty-five and over for those bedridden), who only have to pay a nominal amount when receiving health care.

### How Equality Is Achieved

Equity is maintained because the regulations described above do not allow providers or insurers the freedom to negotiate for more favorable arrangements regarding cost or quality. The inequities in copayment rates are largely mitigated by the provision that any out-of-pocket copayment faced by a patient in a given

**Table 1. Health insurance plans in Japan**

| Sector | Health plan | Population covered (%) |
|---|---|---|
| Employees | | 64.6 |
| Public and quasi-public | Mutual Aid Associations (MAA) | 9.7 |
| Large firms | Society-Managed Health Insurance (SMHI) | 25.5 |
| Small and medium firms | Government-Managed Health Insurance (GMHI) | 28.9 |
| Other | Seaman's, Day Laborer Health Insurance | 0.5 |
| Nonemployed | | 35.4 |
| Regular | Citizens Health Insurance (CHI)* | 32.1 |
| Associations | CHI associations | 3.3 |
| Total | | 100.0 |

*CHI is Kokumin Kenkō Hoken, often translated by the misleading name National Health Insurance.
Source: Kōsei Tokei Kyōkai 1991, 76–77.

month over the amount of ¥60,000 ($333) (or ¥33,600 [$187] for those with low income) is reimbursed regardless of the plan.[5] Thus, out-of-pocket expenses for copayments amount to only 12% of the total health care expenditure provided under social insurance (Kōsei Tōkei Kyōkai 1991, 237). According to a 1988 survey conducted in Tokyo, neither the utilization rate nor the health care expenditure per person was affected by an individual's income level (Tokyo Metropolitan Government 1989). In a national survey in 1985, of those who had experienced an illness but had not seen a physician, only 0.4% gave economic reasons for not having done so (MHW 1986, 168).

How has it been possible to realize an equitable system within the framework of multiple payers? Even if regulations mandate a uniform fee schedule, plans insuring those with low income would find it difficult to balance their expenditure with their revenue from premiums. The answer lies primarily in the government taking on the responsibility by providing subsidies and managing these plans. In Citizens Health Insurance, which is the insurer for the self-employed and pensioners who tend to be at most risk and have the lowest level of income, the local government acts as the insurer, and the central government provides a direct subsidy amounting to half of total expenditures. For those employed in small enterprises and day laborers, the insurer is the central government, which also provides a subsidy amounting to 14% of total expenditure.

The most expensive component of health care, geriatric care, is paid for by contributions to the pooling fund created by the Health Care for the Elderly Law in 1982, which pays for all health care costs incurred by the elderly, regardless of plan. To this pooling fund each plan must contribute the sum that would have been paid for the health spending of the elderly insured in their plan, but this amount is standardized, so that a plan's ratio of the elderly would become equivalent to the ratio of the whole country. Thus, no plan is penalized or rewarded by the ratio of the elderly they have insured, and the burden becomes equitably redistributed. In addition, the central and local governments contribute 20% and 10%, respectively, of the total expenditure of the pooling fund.

## The Road to Greater Equality

The present level of equity was achieved through a slow process that began by increasing the number of those insured and then by leveling the inequities between the plans. Health insurance in Japan was first made available in 1927 for manual workers employed in large companies by establishing insurance societies. Insurance premiums were paid on an equal basis by employer and employee, but there were no copayments. The government took the lead in introducing this plan, believing that it would contribute to the nation's wealth by providing healthy and productive workers and also that it would preempt the socialist movement. Thus, the benefits focused on the ambulatory care of acute illness and injury, while nursing care continued to be provided by the family. This system was extended to all manual workers belonging to enterprises employing five or more persons in 1935, and to white-collar workers in 1940. A community-based insurance (the precursor of the CHI), which paid half the costs for the self-employed, was first legislated in 1938. The worker's dependents became covered for half their costs in 1940. This rapid expansion owes much to the increasingly strong voice of the army pointing to the need for more healthy soldiers in the war with China (Saguchi 1982).

Although defeat in World War II nearly destroyed the system, it was rapidly rebuilt as a result of a new commitment to establish a welfare state. Under Article 25 of the new constitution enforced from 1947, the government has the responsibility to provide an adequate minimum for realizing a healthy and culturally enriching life. A combination of government subsidies and legislation finally led to universal coverage in 1961 when the last local governments became insurers for their CHI. The subsequent years have witnessed greater equality among the plans. The copayment was decreased from 50% to 30% for the CHI in 1968, and for dependents of those under the employee-based plans, it was decreased to 20% for inpatient care and 30% for outpatient care in 1973. In 1973 the system of reimbursing copayments above a certain amount also was initiated for all plans, and all copayments were waived for the elderly. The recent pressures for cost containment have paradoxically led to a positive effect on equity; in 1984, copayments were introduced for the first time for those employed.

The development of health insurance in Japan shows how systems can be adopted and later changed to suit a country's policy needs. The concept of social insurance came straight from Bismarck's model. However, while in Germany the sickness funds have maintained their autonomy and the people may opt to choose private insurance, the Japanese system has become far more uniform and egalitarian as a result of mandating conformity to the national fee schedule as a precondition for receiving subsidies, and as a result of the system of cross-subsidization for financing geriatric care.

**The Existing Inequities**

Although the government's role in providing subsidizes has narrowed the inequities among the plans, some still do exist. Much attention has been drawn in Japan to premium and copayment rates that differ between the employee-based plans and the CHI. However, although the income of the employed is well known, that of the self-employed is difficult to estimate; therefore, the difference in burden may not be as great as it first appears. To control for these factors, I focus on the differences among the SMHI, which insures those employed in large companies. Looking at the cost side, the total premium rate varies from 5.8% to 9.5% between the highest and lowest insurance societies. This difference is closely related to the average age of the employees. Thus, declining industries such as coal mining, which have an older work force, have to pay higher premiums. Also, in industries where the average wage is low, such as textiles, although the absolute premium amount is low, the premium rate is high. This difference reflects the fact that health care utilization is income inelastic in Japan.

With regard to benefits, individual insurance societies can exercise initiative in three areas. The first is the ratio of premiums paid by employers, which varies from 50% to 80%, with a mean of 56.7%. The second is the ratio allocated to health screening and promotion, which varies from 3.1% to 8.4% of the total expenditure, with a mean of 6.6%. The third is the ratio allocated to additional benefits, consisting mainly of the reimbursement of a patient's copayment. This varies from zero to 4.4%, with a mean of 2.9% (Ikegami 1991).

These inequities have not aroused much public attention because they are essentially marginal. As noted above, insurers cannot negotiate over main benefits because that is strictly controlled by the uniform fee schedule. Moreover, these differences have been historically decided and have rarely been subject to serious negotiations between management and labor. But if one regards equality in health care to be paramount, then the whole system of multiple payers must be dismantled in favor of a single payer, as has been advocated by the Japan Medical Association (JMA). Yet if health care is to be regarded at least partially as a private good, then some degree of flexibility should be allowed. Indeed, it could be argued that the present system is too rigid. The strict regulations have resulted in a small but significant black market for patients wishing to gain access to eminent specialists. This takes the form of a monetary gift to the attending physician in the range of ¥100,000 to ¥300,000 ($550 to $1,600) but is usually limited to patients hospitalized in the private rooms of the university and other prestigious hospitals. The other area where extra payment is made despite official prohibition is in geriatric hospitals. The providers have argued that they are charging for nonprofessional nursing care, diapers, and so forth, which are not, or are inadequately, covered by insurance.[6]

**Mechanism for Cost Containment**

The reason why so much attention has been focused on differences is that Japan has been able to contain costs because the system has been basically egalitarian.

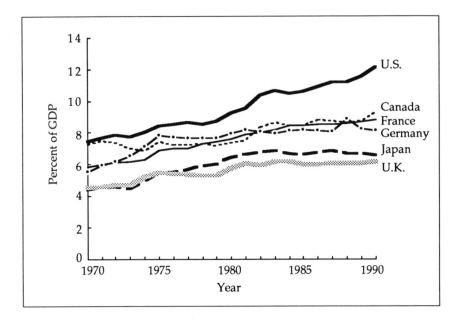

**Figure 1. Total health expenditure as a percent of gross product (GDP) in selected countries, 1970–87**

Under a single-tier system, people's expectations do not become inflated to the level that the most affluent are willing to pay for their health care. More specifically, the uniform fee schedule acts as the primary mechanism for cost containment because it implicitly establishes both the scope and standard of services that can be provided. As has been mentioned, neither providers nor payers can individually negotiate to expand benefits; any such decision must be made by the government. Because any expansion of services or price increase would be applied for all insurers, the government has a strong incentive to constrain the growth of total health expenditures. The incentive derives from the fact that when total health expenditures increase, it will automatically lead to increases in the government subsidies since the plans are subsidized at fixed rate.

Rigorous control over the price and scope of services has been maintained especially since the 1980s as a result of the government's commitment to contain overall public expenditures. In addition to limiting the increase of fees for procedures to a bare minimum, the price of pharmaceuticals has been more than halved and that of laboratory tests decreased by bundling. As figure 1 shows, these measures have been relatively successful. Japan's ratio of health care expenditure to GDP rose as rapidly as in the other countries in the 1970s, but that ratio has leveled off in the 1980s in marked contrast to the United States. Although the ratios in Canada and Germany have also leveled, these countries started at a far higher share of health care costs to GDP. Thus, with the exception of the United Kingdom, Japan has the lowest ratio among the developed countries.

Negotiations for revisions in the fee schedule take place in the Central Social Medical Care Council of the MHW. The council comprises eight representatives from providers (five physicians, two dentists, and one pharmacist), eight from payers (four from insurers, which includes two from the government, and two each from management and labor), and four that represent public interests (three economists and one lawyer). The estimated allowable increase in the total health care expenditure is first decided. This total increase is theoretically based on the periodic survey made every second year on the financial state of hospitals and clinics (the latter being equivalent to a study of physicians' income). However, in point of fact, it is virtually decided by the Ministry of Finance because the government's subsidies must be kept within general budgetary limits. After this amount has been settled, the price revision for each individual item is decided by negotiations among the providers. The net effect of revising the price of each item to the already decided total increase in expenditure is calculated by multiplying the change in each item by its volume as estimated from the national survey of claims data.

**How Volume Is Constrained**

How has it been possible to achieve cost containment when only the price is controlled? If prices are regulated, then volume usually expands. The reasons why this has not occurred to the extent that it would invalidate the estimated growth in expenditure can be ascribed to the following. First, some of the fees are set at such a low level that they would not pay for the provider's cost. In general, hospitals tend to lose money on inpatient service, which they offset by gains on outpatient service. While it is true that hospitals combine the functions of nursing homes in Japan, the average cost per day, inclusive of all services, averages only ¥14,109 ($80) for inpatient care (including physician expenses). In contrast, the average for an outpatient visit is ¥5,078 ($30) (MHW 1992b, 24). There is no separate funding for financing capital investment except in the public sector. As a result, private hospitals have been inhibited from venturing into the field of high-technology medicine. The exceptions are renal dialysis and imaging equipment, the very areas in which Japan has the highest per capita number. In the case of the renal dialysis, a policy decision was made to set initially a high price to speed its adoption. In the case of the imaging equipment, hospitals have felt the need to maintain a competitive position to attract patients and physicians. In addition, the costs of these technologies are relatively low when compared with surgical pro-cedures because they are not labor intensive, and domestic manufacturers have developed and aggressively marketed inexpensive models.

Second, there is a retrospective review of claims sent by providers. Detailed item-by-item claims of the services rendered must be sent by every institution at the beginning of each month to the intermediary payment funds that operate at the prefecture level. These claims are then inspected by the fund's designated panel of physicians. If the panel concludes that excessive numbers of procedures or drugs have been provided, then payment will be denied for those items. In addition, claims over the amount of ¥5 million ($28,000) are subjected to special reviews at the national level. The actual ratio of the claims judged as providing excessive care is less than 1%, but because these are concentrated on the high-cost claims, the review does have some effect. Also, the denials tend to have a sentinel effect on the provider because should they gain a reputation for excessive services, their claims would in the future be subject to a more intense examination.

### Is the System Really a Success?

It could be argued that the excellent health indices and the low costs are a reflection of lifestyle and economic conditions rather than the health care system. This may well be accurate, but universal coverage without overt rationing is in itself a major achievement. The next question may well be, are Japanese health care costs really low? First, it could be argued that the calculation of health care costs has not been sufficiently standardized and, as a result, underestimates Japanese costs. However, even if the ratio were increased by 10%, it would still be below that of the major industrialized countries. Second, the Japanese health care system may have been given a relatively easy task by society. There were only 473 reported cases of AIDS in Japan as of 30 April 1992 (MHW 1992c); the diet is low in fat and total calories; and while 12% of the population is over sixty-five, some 57% of them still live with their children (Bureau of Statistics 1992, 400–1). However, no diet is perfect, and too much salt has led to a high prevalence of stroke (Marmot 1989). Contrary to expectations, the ratio of the elderly in institutions is 6.2%,[7] a figure higher than in the United States. Third, Japan's economic growth may have masked the sharp increase in health care costs. While Japan had very high growth in real per capita health care expenditure from 1960 to 1987, it started from a low baseline of $258 (purchasing power parity) in 1960, and thus much of the increase could be regarded as a reflection of the growing affluence.

However, even if the caveats could be disposed of in the above manner, Japan's method of achieving cost containment does have some serious intrinsic problems. First, there are limits to the fee-scheduling approach, especially in the areas of prescribing drugs and ordering laboratory tests. These areas have been a major problem in Japan because most physicians in clinics do their own dispensing, and hospital-based doctors dispense from the institution's pharmacy. Also, laboratory tests are billed by hospitals and clinics even in cases where they are contracted out. Although periodic surveys of market prices are made by the government, and insurance prices are adjusted accordingly, providers continue to make a profit because competition leads to a new round of price cutting. The providers have maintained that they need this margin to offset the deficit coming from low hospitalization fees. This competition has not necessary led to greater efficiency, however. Despite the downward trend in price, most pharmaceutical companies have managed to survive successfully by continuously introducing marginally improved high-price products that are marketed as major innovations. It is for this reason that Japan's use of third-generation antibiotics is more extensive than anywhere else (Inglehart 1988).

The second problem is rigidity. Within the budgetary limits, both the content and price are determined by political negotiations within the closed ranks of the providers rather than market forces. To minimize conflict, they have pursued an incremental policy of trying to maintain the preexisting relative share of each clinical specialty, and that between hospitals and clinics, and so forth. As a consequence, the share of the traditional ambulatory services mainly in the field of primary care has remained high compared to inpatient services and high-technology medicine. Although this situation has had a positive effect on cost containment, it has also proved difficult to introduce innovative service or to improve the amenity level of hospital services.

The third problem is quality. The price is uniform for all providers based on the assumption that their quality is the same. However, patients are increasingly turning to the university and large public hospitals because of their higher perceived quality. As a result, there are long queues for ambulatory visits and waiting lists for hospitalization. This situation is difficult to reverse because freedom of choice has been regarded as a cardinal principle in the delivery of care in Japan. One solution actively being advocated by the government and the JMA is the development of a referral system. However, clinics and hospitals have basically regarded each other as competitors rather than partners. Moreover, for the system to work effectively, both parties must evaluate the content and quality of their care. Such an evaluation requires information disclosure and a formal system of external audit, concepts that are foreign to Japanese culture, and especially so in health care.

## Closing Remarks

No health care system is perfect because infinite demands must always be met with finite resources. On the criteria of cost, access, and quality, Japan has been relatively successful in the areas of cost and access. This is a remarkable accomplishment as it has been achieved despite the fee-for-service method of payment and the existence of multiple payers. However, while it is true the benefits are essentially the same for all, the uniform fee schedule has served as a rationing mechanism less overt but more rigid than the British system. Because revisions in fees are made by political negotiations within the closed ranks of the stakeholders, the private practitioners providing ambulatory care have managed to maintain their dominant position in the rationing process. However, new demands are being placed on the health care system. On one hand, there is demand for a higher level of professional quality by the increasingly affluent society. On the other hand, the aging population requires a network of care management and better facility standards. A major restructuring of the system is needed before this can be realized. The current concept of equity must be redefined so that the main focus lies not so much in the equality of service provision, but in developing the best mix of public and private sectors in the delivery and financing of health care.

NOTES

1. Slightly revised from *Science* 258 (23 October 1992): 614–18. Reprinted with permission.

2. According to Niki R. (1985, 113), the total of 2,120 CAT scanners in December 1982 already exceeded the per capita number in the United States. The number had increased to 5,902 by October 1990 (MHW 1992a). The number of MRIs at that time was 756. Niki B. (1985, 131–33) has also pointed out that in the same year Japan had the highest per capita number on renal dialysis procedures, with 444 per million. In December 1988 the number was 707 per million (Kōsei Tōkei Kyōkai 1991, 175).

3. For more detailed analysis see Ikegami 1988, 1989, 1991.

4. Kōsei Tōkei Kyōkai 1991, 95–99. Due to some minor duplications in the counting of the number insured, this ratio not covered by health insurance does not come up in table 1.

5. Dollar equivalents at the approximate purchasing power parity (PPP) rate of $1.00 = ¥180.

6. According to Niki's survey (1992), the average monthly out-of-pocket payments amount to about ¥82,422 ($460).

7. Calculated from MHW 1987, 1988.

REFERENCES

Bureau of Statistics. 1992. *1990 Population census of Japan*, vol. 2. Tokyo: Nihon Tōkei Kyōkai.
Iglehart, J. K. 1988. *New England Journal of Medicine* 319: 1,166.
Ikegami, N. 1988. *International Journal of Technological Assess* 4.2: 239.
———. 1989. *International Journal of Health Planning and Management* 4: 181.
———. 1991. *Health Affairs* 10.3: 88.
Kōsei Tōkei Kyōkai. 1991. *Kōsei no shihyō* (Welfare indicators) 38.9: 175, 237, 389, 425, 426; 38.12: 95–99; 38.14: 66, 67.
Marmot, M. G. 1989. *British Medical Journal* 299: 1,547.
Ministry of Health and Welfare (MHW). 1986. *1985 Kokumin kenkō chōsa* (National health survey). Tokyo: Kōsei Tōkei Kyōkai.
———. 1987. *Kanja chōsa* (Patient survey). Tokyo: Kōsei Tōkei Kyōkai.
———. 1988. *1987 Shakaifukushi gyosei gyomuhōkoku* (Report on social welfare administration). Tokyo: Kōsei Tōkei Kyōkai.
———. 1989. *1987 Kanjya chōsa* (Patient survey). Tokyo: Kōsei Tōkei Kyōkai.
———. 1992a. *1990 Iryō shisetu chōsa* (Medical facilities survey). Tokyo: Kōsei Tōkei Kyōkai.
———. 1992b. *1990 Shakai iryō shinryō kōibetsu chōsa hōkoku* (Survey of social medical care by treatment). Tokyo: Kōsei Tōkei Kyōkai.
———. 1992c. *Shukan igakukai shinbun 1* (June 15).
Niki, B. 1985. *Iryōkeizaigaku* (Medical economics). Tokyo: Igakushoin.
Niki, R. 1985. *Social Science Medicine* 12.10: 113.
———. 1992. *Shakaihoken junpō* 1768: 6; 1770: 19.
Organization for Economic Cooperation and Development. 1990. *Health care systems in transition.* Paris: OECD.
Sagouchi, T. 1982. *Socialization of medical care* (Iryō no shakaika). Tokyo: Keisō Shobō.
Tokyo Metropolitan Government. 1989. *Basic study of Tokyo's National Health Insurance.* Tokyo.

CHAPTER 2

# Comparison of Health Expenditure Estimates between Japan and the United States

*Yukiko Katsumata*

SUMMARY   It has often been asserted that Japanese health care expenditure statistics undercount actual spending. This study examines the composition of Japanese expenditure statistics. First, a new estimate of Total Health Expenditure (THE) is calculated, one based on national accounts that is comparable to the data used by the Organization for Economic Cooperation and Development (OECD). Second, estimates of spending on items that are not usually counted in Japan were then added to produce an adjusted THE figure that is comparable to American figures. These adjustments increased the estimate of Japanese spending by about 7%, or about 0.5% of GNP, which narrowed the gap in spending between the two countries by only a small amount.

## Calculating Health Expenditure in Japan

According to the OECD Health Data (1991), the estimated total health expenditure in Japan for the 1990 fiscal year was ¥27.5 trillion. For comparison with U.S. data, this amount can be divided by population (Schieber, Poullier, and Greenwald 1992, 70–71) and then converted into dollars using purchasing power parity (PPP); the result (ibid., 86–87) is a THE per capita of $1,244 for Japan, compared with $3,499 for the United States in 1990. Note that the gap in health spending has widened substantially. In 1980 U.S. THE per capita was 57% greater than in Japan, but in 1990 it was 177% greater.

The question is whether this OECD calculation can be believed. That is, have differences in the method of calculation, such as counting some items in the United States and not in Japan, led to a systematic underestimation of health spending in Japan? To answer this question, we need to take a close look at how health spending statistics are compiled.[1]

In general, there are two approaches to estimating health spending. One is based on national income accounting for the entire economy, as calculated by the U.S. Department of Commerce and the Japanese Economic Planning Agency

**Table 1. Adjustment of health expenditure in Japan, by category**

| Expense and source | 1980 | 1981 |
|---|---|---|
| Selected outlays of general government | | |
| by purpose: Table 7, Line 4. Health | | |
| (7-1) Total fixed capital formation | 418.6 | 461.1 |
| (7-2) Subsidies | 149.8 | 137.8 |
| General government final consumption expenditure according | | |
| to cost-comparison and purpose: Table 8, Line 4. Health | | |
| (8-1) Fixed capital depreciation | 103.6 | 118.2 |
| (8-2) Final consumption expenditure | 908.1 | 1,016.4 |
| Transfers from general government to household | | |
| (social security transfers). Table 9. | | |
| (9) Selected schemes for medical insurance | 10,537.0 | 11,434.4 |
| Final consumption expenditure of households in domestic | | |
| market by object: Table 13, Line 5. Medical and Health Care | | |
| (13) Final consumption expenditure | 13,966.4 | 15,181.1 |
| Final consumption expenditure of private, nonprofit | | |
| institutions serving households according to cost-composition | | |
| and purpose: Table 14, Line 2. Medical care | | |
| (14) Final consumption expenditure | 7.3 | 41.8 |
| | | |
| THE: Total health expenditure | 15,376.6 | 16,720.0 |
| PHE: Public health expenditure | 11,917.2 | 12,973.3 |

Note: THE calculation = (7-1)-(8-1)+(8-2)+(13)+(14); PHE calculation = (7-1)+(7-2)-(8-1)
+(8-2)+(9)+(14).
Sources: Economic Planning Agency, Annual Report on National Accounts; OECD Health
Data 1991.

(EPA). The other approach is to calculate spending from surveys of health care establishments, as carried out by the Health Care Financing Administration (HCFA) in the United States and the Ministry of Health and Welfare (MHW) in Japan. It is sometimes thought that the national account approach is better in theory but that the more specialized agencies may work harder on gathering statistics; in any case, the latter estimates are usually somewhat higher (Huber and Newhouse 1991).

According to staff members, the OECD originally tried to work with U.S. national accounts data but has since come to rely on the HCFA health accounts. For Japan, the OECD bases its estimates on national accounts data. However, these data are not published in disaggregated form. In order to allow systematic

| | | | Fiscal Year | | | | | |
|---|---|---|---|---|---|---|---|---|
| 1982 | 1983 | 1984 | 1985 | 1986 | 1987 | 1988 | 1989 | 1990 |
| 501.1 | 414.2 | 373.8 | 353.0 | 364.7 | 435.2 | 418.6 | 406.5 | 526.5 |
| 151.5 | 158.5 | 150.4 | 164.3 | 166.6 | 172.2 | 185.1 | 189.8 | 214.8 |
| 132.5 | 146.0 | 161.5 | 173.0 | 176.6 | 185.8 | 182.7 | 193.2 | 202.7 |
| 1,046.4 | 1,154.2 | 1,275.8 | 1,212.2 | 1,230.1 | 1,266.7 | 1,361.5 | 1,512.6 | 1,678.1 |
| 12,335.0 | 13,497.4 | 13,953.8 | 14,859.7 | 15,834.5 | 16,814.4 | 17,609.8 | 18,546.5 | 19,635.6 |
| 16,448.1 | 17,405.4 | 17,774.9 | 19,789.5 | 21,142.9 | 22,411.1 | 23,225.2 | 24,483.4 | 25,799.4 |
| -35.7 | 9.2 | 6.9 | -26.7 | -99.3 | 93.8 | -51.7 | -140.2 | -109.5 |
| 17,978.9 | 18,995.5 | 19,420.3 | 21,319.3 | 22,628.4 | 24,005.9 | 24,956.0 | 26,258.9 | 27,906.6 |
| 13,865.8 | 15,087.5 | 15,599.2 | 16,389.5 | 17,320.0 | 18,408.9 | 19,340.6 | 20,322.0 | 21,742.8 |

comparisons with the U.S. data, I therefore calculated THE from the EPA's national account data. The results for 1980–90 are shown in table 1.

Unfortunately, for reasons that are not immediately apparent, these estimates did not turn out to be the same as those of the OECD for Japan's THE. As shown in table 2, the OECD estimate was up to 3% higher than mine for the first half of the decade, but 1% or 2% lower for the second half. The discrepancies for Public Health Expenditure (PHE) are somewhat greater. My estimate is used in this analysis because it is directly derived from published data and its categories are clear.

In any case, in terms of trends in the decade of the 1980s, these estimates do not diverge very much. Table 2 includes the OECD estimates and those calculated by the author from national account data, for both THE and PHE. For reference, the figure most commonly used for medical costs in Japan, "national medical care expenditure," (*kokumin iryōhi*) as calculated by the MHW, is also included in table 2. It includes more than PHE and less than THE (see below), but generally follows the same trends.

**Table 2. New and OECD estimates of Japan's THE and PHE**

| Expense category | 1980 | 1981 | 1982 | 1983 | 1984 | 1985 | 1986 | 1987 | 1988 | 1989 | 1990 |
|---|---|---|---|---|---|---|---|---|---|---|---|
| THE | 15,376.6 | 16,720.0 | 17,978.9 | 18,995.5 | 19,420.3 | 21,319.3 | 22,628.4 | 24,005.9 | 24,956.0 | 26,258.9 | 27,906.6 |
| OECD THE | 15,760.0 | 17,130.0 | 18,463.0 | 19,430.0 | 20,040.0 | 21,040.0 | 22,230.0 | 23,703.0 | 24,930.0 | 26,000.0 | 27,500.0 |
| THE - OECD THE | -383.4 | -410.0 | -484.1 | -434.5 | -619.7 | 279.3 | 396.4 | 302.9 | 26.0 | 258.9 | 406.6 |
| Difference as % of OECD THE | -2.4 | -2.4 | -2.6 | -2.2 | -3.1 | 1.3 | 1.8 | 1.3 | 0.1 | 1.0 | 1.5 |
| PHE | 11,917.2 | 12,973.3 | 13,865.8 | 15,087.5 | 15,599.2 | 16,389.5 | 17,320.0 | 18,408.9 | 19,340.6 | 20,322.0 | 21,742.8 |
| OECD PHE | 11,154.8 | 12,074.0 | 12,987.5 | 14,065.3 | 14,521.1 | 15,283.9 | 16,261.6 | 17,213.6 | 18,043.2 | 19,042.6 | 20,500.0 |
| PHE - OECD PHE | 762.4 | 899.3 | 878.3 | 1,022.2 | 1,078.1 | 1,105.6 | 1,058.4 | 1,195.3 | 1,297.4 | 1,279.4 | 1,242.8 |
| Difference as % of OECD PHE | 6.8 | 7.4 | 6.8 | 7.3 | 7.4 | 7.2 | 6.5 | 6.9 | 7.2 | 6.7 | 6.1 |
| NME by MHW | 11,980.5 | 12,870.9 | 13,865.9 | 14,543.8 | 15,093.2 | 16,015.9 | 17,069.0 | 18,075.9 | 18,755.4 | 19,729.0 | 20,607.4 |

**Technical Definitions**

The calculations in this report follow the definitions in two publications by the OECD: *Public Expenditure on Health* (1977) and *Measuring Health Care 1960–1983* (1985). The first report defined THE as private final consumption expenditure on medical care (CHE) + government final consumption expenditure on health care (GHE) – capital expenditure on health. PHE is defined as GHE + transfers to households earmarked for health services or to nonprofit institutions supplying health services to household (GTHE).

These definitions were modified in the later report, *Measuring Health Care 1960–1983*. THE was defined as National Health Expenditure (NHE) – private investment on health. NHE was a new concept appearing for the first time in this report. It was defined as national consumption on health (NCH) + government investment in hospitals and dispensaries (GIH) + private investment in clinics, laboratories, x-ray centers, and so forth. NCH was also used for the first time here, defined as household final consumption on medical care and health expenditure (HCH) + government final consumption on health (GCH). In the same 1985 report, PHE was defined as GIH + government or social security transfers for medical care (GTH) + GCH.

The definitions in both reports were basically the same, so the 1985 definitions were used here to calculate THE and PHE. Table 1 includes details on which parts of the *Annual Report on National Accounts* were used in these calculations.

We can now examine these components in detail. The subtotals in the *Annual Report* are classified according to economic activities in three categories: industries, governmental service providers, and private, nonprofit organizations. Total health-related consumption is calculated by adding medical- and health-related consumption in these three categories. "General government" is defined as "governmental service providers," and specifically denotes either the central or local government. "Private, nonprofit organizations" include various health-related facilities managed by groups, such as social-insurance-related organizations, the Federation of Citizens Health Insurance Associations, Employees' Pension Fund Association, and the Japan Red Cross. "Industries" include hospitals and clinics that are not included in such nonprofit organizations.

THE is defined as NHE – private investment in health. Because private investment in health is part of NHE, THE can also be defined as NHE – private investment in health. Thus, HCH + GCH combined with GIH becomes THE.

HCH is that part of final consumption expenditure of households in domestic market by object that is spent for health care. This element affects all three of the above-mentioned economic activities. This is because when estimating household final consumption expenditure, HCH is calculated based on payments made by households to hospitals and clinics (i.e., revenues for hospitals and clinics). Hospitals and clinics in this case include those that are managed by both nonprofit and private institutions.

GCH is that part of "final consumption expenditure according to cost-composition and purpose" made by both governments and private, nonprofit institutions serving households that is spent for health care. "Final consumption expenditure" in this case equals the total of "employee income, fixed capital depreciation, interim investment, and indirect tax" minus "household final consumption expenditure." Household final consumption expenditure in this case is for the sale of products and services and specifically includes such items as usage fees and commission revenues. For example, the fees paid by both inpatients and outpatients to national and public hospitals constitute medical revenue, and thus are included in "household final consumption expenditure."

What specifically, then, is final consumption expenditure? "Employee income" is labor cost, "fixed capital depreciation" is depreciation expense, "interim investment" is operating expense, travel expense, and research subcontracting expense, and "indirect tax" is such things as automobile weight tax, consumption tax, and fixed asset tax. If the final consumption expenditure of private, nonprofit organizations is negative, it means that the household final consumption expenditure exceeds the total of employee income, fixed capital depreciation, interim investment, and indirect tax. In other words, private, nonprofit organizations are operating on a sound financial basis. However, the health care component of the "final consumption expenditure of private, nonprofit institutions serving households according to cost-composition and purpose" was not always negative. In the eleven-year period between FY 1980 and FY 1990, it was positive before FY 1984 (except in FY 1982) and has been steadily declining, with some minor fluctuations, since turning negative in FY 1984.

GIH is equivalent to the sum of the "total fixed capital formation" and the "subsidies" components (of the "general government expenditure according to purposes—health") minus the "fixed capital depreciation" component of the health expenditure (of the "general government final consumption expenditure according to cost-composition and purpose—health"). Net capital formation (total capital formation minus the depreciation of durable goods) is calculated by subtracting fixed capital depreciation from total fixed capital formation.

In calculating THE, health expenditure was examined from both the consumptions and output perspectives.

The concept behind the calculation of PHE is basically the same as that used for THE. However, in order to limit health expenditures to public expenditures, PHE in this case includes only that household health expenditure that is based on government fund transfers. That is, PHE is treated as health expenditure in the form of social payments. Because it was decided to base this estimate on EPA's national accounts data, two forms of government payment could not be properly accounted for. The medical component of public assistance is excluded, but portions of workman's compensation that do not really cover medical care (i.e., income replacement for an illness or disability) are included. However, these amounts are not large enough to make a significant difference in estimating PHE.

## Total Health Expenditure and National Medical Care Expenditure

We should now look at national medical care expenditure (NME, *kokumin iryōhi*) and how it relates to THE as defined above. As previously noted, this estimate produced annually by the MHW is the most commonly used measure of health spending in Japan.

NME is based on records of spending covered by social insurance. Examination of the process for compiling national accounts on health expenditures reveals that the EPA begins with this figure and then adds in categories of spending that are excluded. The EPA maintains its own statistics on childbirth expenditures (which are not directly covered by social insurance) and on the supplementary payments to cover extra hospital expenses offered to patients by many local governments. Other categories that are not included in NME are services provided by national-government-owned medical facilities that are not reimbursed by social insurance and subsidies provided by local governments to make up deficits (costs in excess of social insurance reimbursement) in the hospitals they run.

Confusingly, in most years the estimate of NME by the MHW is quite similar to the estimate of PHE calculated by the OECD methodology based on national accounts. This is just a coincidence. Note that NME includes the patient's copayment (11–12% of the total), which is not part of PHE. However, this amount happens to be roughly balanced by the various subsidies and other miscellaneous expenditures by national and local government agencies that are included in PHE but not in NME.

Specifically, in the 1990 fiscal year, subsidies to national hospitals and national sanatoriums totaled approximately ¥84.5 billion and ¥97.2 billion, respectively. The amount of subsidies provided by the MHW out of the general budget to local governments totaled approximately ¥2 billion. Therefore, total subsidies amounted to ¥183.7 billion. This amount was roughly 86% of the general government's "subsidies for medical health purposes" (which totaled ¥214.8 billion) in the 1990 national economic accounting figure.

Of the actual 1990 general government final consumption expenditure according to cost-composition and purpose, which amounts to general cost-sharing transfers from the national to the local level, expenditures for health purposes accounted for ¥1.6781 trillion. This includes, for example, local subsidies to hospitals. When ¥214.8 billion for the above-mentioned subsidies is added to this figure, the result is approximately ¥1.8929 trillion. These subsidies amount to about 80% of the difference between PHE and NME. The rest of the difference can be explained by the flexible definition of "subsidy" in the system of national accounts.

## Adjusting Total Health Expenditure for Comparability

We may now compare our estimate of national accounts THE, with its clear definitions, to THE in the United States (the OECD designation, the same as

HCFA's "national health expenditure"). The U.S. statistics clearly include a wider range of expenses.

The main items that are included in the United States but not in Japan are listed in table 3, with (in most cases) estimates for the 1980–90 period. Some details on how the estimates were compiled are included in the notes to the table. In general, these are either items that Japanese have not thought to categorize as health expenditure, such as nursing homes (which developed from old-age homes in welfare rather than health care administration), or are items that get left out of statistics because they are not covered by health insurance.

Note that various assumptions were necessary to estimate these expenditures, and in the case of the last three items so few data were available that rough estimates only for 1989 are provided. Also, in some cases the possibility of some double-counting cannot be excluded, particularly with regard to R & D and to construction expenditures in private facilities (since a portion may already have been included in THE). Nonetheless, we believe these data represent the first systematic attempt to estimate Japanese health spending in truly comparable terms, and they should be useful for other researchers until more precise studies can be carried out.

It will be observed that the largest of these items is over-the-counter drugs, followed by nursing homes and elective dental care. All of these adjustments together raise our estimate of adjusted THE for Japan by about 6%, or less than one-half a point of GDP. This ratio appears to be quite consistent across the decade of the 1980s.

### Under-the-Table Payments

A final adjustment is necessary to make Japanese THE comparable with U.S. statistics. As is well known, health-care financing in Japan has long included informal or under-the-table payment for services. Such payments run from the nonauthorized, in that they are not specified in regulations, to the clearly illegal. They are widespread, well known, and usually tolerated, but since records of such payments are not kept or at least not aggregated and published, they are difficult to estimate. Incidentally, partly for that reason, their size has often been exaggerated in journalistic accounts.

There are two important categories of these under-the-table payments. First, patients in the hospital often give gifts to the doctors who treat them, and in particular, patients who enter a leading hospital (usually a university hospital) and are treated by a well-known physician will offer a substantial "gift." It is given after discharge, and therefore only after treatment is successfully completed, but it is nonetheless a precondition for such privileged treatment. Anecdotal evidence indicates that currently such gifts range from $200–$300 to $3,000 or more.

We can make a rough estimate by assuming that all patients in regular hospital beds give ¥30,000, and that those in extra-charge beds give ¥100,000 in general hospitals and ¥300,000 in university hospitals. Extra-charge beds are 10%

of general hospital beds and 32% of university hospital beds. In 1990, there were 848,113 discharges per month from general hospitals and 67,593 from university hospitals; multiplying out produces an annual figure of ¥269.6 billion (about $1.5 billion in PPP terms).

Second, there is a shortage of geriatric hospitals that provide anything more than custodial care, and, moreover, the health insurance benefits specified in the fee schedule for inpatient geriatric care are inadequate for patients with more than minimal needs. As a result, hospitals often levy "extra" service charges, nominally for diapers and the like, that can add up to a substantial monthly out-of-pocket charge. The MHW has conducted surveys of this practice, but by all accounts its estimates are much too low. We have relied on a study by Niki (1993, 226) that found that the typical payment is ¥65,744 per month. Multiplied by twelve months and 191,905 geriatric beds in 1990, the total expenditure is ¥119.8 billion (about $660 million).

We could also add in estimates for gifts to personal physicians for providing outpatient care, but in reality these generally amount to the year-end presents of salad oil or a bottle of whiskey that are common throughout Japanese society. Potentially more important as an informal "expenditure" is the care provided to patients by relatives rather than by paid health care personnel, in the hospital or at home. Although families often do provide some care as well as laundry and other services in many hospitals, the extent of this practice has declined considerably over the years and is often exaggerated. Moreover, it should not be forgotten that due to the very rapid discharges from hospitals in the United States, many patients are returned to their families in a very weakened condition, which does not happen often in Japan. As for care at home, many frail older people in Japan live with their children, when they would be on their own and receiving paid home health services in the United States. However, statistics on health expenditures are exactly that, and in common with other national accounts calculations they cannot take unpaid family labor into account.

And note also that, with regard to both categories of under-the-table payments estimated above, we have been generous in multiplying the amount of what is called a typical payment in a given situation by the total number of patients in that situation. In fact, what is called typical often approximates a ceiling, and a substantial number of patients will pay less or nothing at all. Our estimates therefore should be seen as the maximum theoretical amount for such expenditures, almost certainly a larger amount than reality. Even so, the total for under-the-table payments of both types is about ¥390 billion ($2.2 billion in PPP) for 1990—not a trivial amount, but it increases the figure of the adjusted THE using U.S. definitions that was calculated above (¥29,664 billion) by just 1.3%.

The result of the adjustments we made, including under-the-table payments, to the health expenditure is summarized in table 4. While it is true that the NME is only about two-thirds of this total, the total amount still constitutes only 6.9% of the GDP in 1990.

Table 3. Japanese health expenditure comparable to U.S. health expenditure

| Expense category | 1980 | 1981 | 1982 | 1983 | 1984 | 1985 | 1986 | 1987 | 1988 | 1989 | 1990 |
|---|---|---|---|---|---|---|---|---|---|---|---|
| Japan THE (from table 2) | 15,376,600 | 16,720,000 | 17,978,900 | 18,995,500 | 19,420,300 | 21,319,300 | 22,628,400 | 24,005,900 | 24,956,000 | 26,258,900 | 27,906,600 |
| Nursing homes | 133,119 | 157,321 | 185,043 | 202,683 | 220,772 | 244,218 | 271,012 | 295,228 | 319,904 | 349,816 | 385,855 |
| Medical care in schools | 7,000 | 7,700 | 8,500 | 9,000 | 9,200 | 10,300 | 10,900 | 11,000 | 10,900 | 11,000 | 11,300 |
| Medical care in correctional institutions | 889 | 920 | 952 | 1,012 | 1,042 | 1,072 | 1,047 | 1,131 | 1,159 | 1,232 | 1,308 |
| Medical research, private institutions | 13,266 | 17,165 | 21,835 | 25,456 | 26,756 | 34,258 | 30,522 | 31,321 | 32,611 | 33,951 | 35,293 |
| Construction, private hospitals and clinics | 47 | 44 | 33 | 30 | 29 | 31 | 42 | 54 | 52 | 52 | 55 |
| Over-the-counter drugs | 503,740 | 543,436 | 573,717 | 593,490 | 597,503 | 618,096 | 630,890 | 683,577 | 749,634 | 825,815 | 875,103 |
| Eyeglasses | 47,362 | 49,716 | 47,720 | 48,733 | 63,675 | 68,096 | 72,077 | 78,177 | 79,382 | 79,162 | 81,918 |
| Elective dental care | 225,400 | 248,700 | 264,700 | 273,900 | 286,100 | 298,600 | 320,300 | 281,700 | 290,900 | 270,700 | 280,900 |
| Private duty aides, patient share | 9,574 | 11,283 | 12,811 | 16,885 | 19,896 | 22,242 | 23,179 | 30,141 | 35,563 | 42,875 | 48,525 |
| Health facility for the elderly, patient share | — | — | — | — | — | — | — | — | — | 16,100 | 36,900 |
| Advanced technologies, patient share | | | | | | | | | | 2,900 | |
| Massage, accupuncture, moxa | | | | | | | | | | 315,800 | |
| Adjusted Japan THE (Total) | 16,316,997 | 17,756,285 | 19,094,212 | 20,166,690 | 20,645,273 | 22,616,214 | 23,988,369 | 25,418,228 | 26,476,105 | 28,208,304 | 29,663,757 |

Nursing homes: Total expenses for nursing homes (called tokubetsu yōgo rōjin hōmu, "special care old-age homes"). A 100-bed facility in the A geographical zone was used as a model in estimating annual expenses. This annual expense was multiplied by the number of patients. Note that the amount paid by patients is included.

Medical care in schools: Total amount paid for the treatment of injuries and illness, based on "Saigai kyōsai kyufu no jyokyō" (Status of payments for accidents) by the Niho Taiku Gakkō Kenkō Sentaa (Japan Physical Education School Health Center).

Medical care in correctional institutions: An estimate of 14% of various correctional-facility-related expenses was used. (Based on the annual report of the Ministry of Justice on regional correction facilities.)

Medical research, private institutions: Estimated based on trends in research spending by various research organizations included in "Kagaku gijutsu yōran" (Indicators of science and technology), compiled by the Science and Technology Policy Bureau of the Science and Technology Agency. (Research at public institutes is included in THE as government final consumption.)

Construction, private hospitals and clinics: Estimated from Ministry of Construction reports on total planned construction in the private sector; data on hospitals and clinics supplied by Mr. Kawabuchi of the National Institute of Health Services Management. (Construction costs for public facilities are included in THE as Government Investment—Health.)

Over-the counter drugs: Estimated from production figures, from "Ippan iyakuhin to haichiyō kateiyaku no gōkei" (Total of general medical and pharmaceutical products and medications for households) in the "Yakuji kōgyō seisan dōtai nenpō" (Annual statistical report on the status of pharmaceutical industry production). No statistics on consumption are available.

Eyeglasses: Total shipments in Japan, excluding examination equipment. Also from the "Yakuji kōgyō seisan dōtai nenpō."

Elective dental care: Estimated from the dental expense component of national medical expenses and reports of dental revenue by dental clinics, including Workman's Compensation as well as out-of-pocket spending. Data from "Iryō keizai jittai chōsa" (Report on the status of the medical economy) by the Chūiko (Central Social Insurance Medical Council), plus some estimates.

Private duty aides (tsukisoi), patient's share: Estimated by using employment agency statistics to determine the difference between scheduled fees for third party payments and the amounts actually charged, multipled by the number of patients receiving private duty aides (from MHW data).

Health facilites for the elderly (rōjin hoken shisetsu), patient share: Estimated based on average usage fees, from the "Rōjin hoken shisetsu jittai chōsa rōjin hoken shisetsu hōkoku" (Report on health facilities for the elderly and their usage), multiplied by total days, from the "Rōjin iryō jigyō nenpō" (Annual report on medical care for the elderly). These are long-term-care and rehabilitation facilities, established in the late 1980s, that are mostly covered by health insurance but require a copay of several hundred dollars a month. Data only available from 1989.

Advanced technologies (kōdo senshin iryōgijutsu), patient's share: A rough estimate based on the amount paid from public sources. This system allows partial coverage for treatments not yet included in the fee schedule, carried out at designated hospitals. Because of inadequate data, this figure was estimated only for 1989.

Massage, acupuncture, moxa: No reliable statistics are available except for the small proportion of treatments covered by insurance, so expenditures were estimated roughly only for 1989.

**Table 4. Reestimate of Japan's health expenditure, 1990**

|  | Billion yen | Ratio to GDP (%) | Ratio to total (%) |
|---|---|---|---|
| A. NME | 20,607.4 | 4.7 | 68.6 |
| B. Public grants and subsidies | 3,623.8 | 0.8 | 12.1 |
| C. Expenditure not included in A, B, or D | 3,675.4 | 0.8 | 12.2 |
| D. Expenditure not accounted for in health sector | 1,757.2 | 0.4 | 5.8 |
| E. Estimated under-the-table payments | 389.4 | 0.1 | 1.3 |
| Total | 30,053.2 | 6.9 | 100.0 |

A. All expenditure paid through social insurance, including patient's copayments. Official estimate made by MHW (kokumin iryōhi).

B. Grants and subsidies provided by national and local governments (i.e., subsidies to public hospitals, PHE), excluding those provided through A.

C. Expenditure not accounted for in A, B, or D (i.e., expenditure by nonprofit organizations, extra-charge rooms, normal pregnancies). OECD's estimate is equivalent to 98.5% of A+B+C.

D. Over-the-counter drugs, social service nursing homes, construction expenditure of private sector health care facilities, R&D, and others. These categories are included in the U.S. health expenditure in the OECD Health Data but are normally excluded for other countries. The United States is unique in that the OECD obtained the data from HCFA and not from its national accounts.

E. Estimated amount of gifts given to physicians on discharge and extra payments made by patients in geriatric hospitals (based on generous estimates from available evidence).

Source: Calculations made by Katsumata from JEPA 1994 national accounts.

### Conclusion

Finally, figure 1 plots several of the data series we have discussed in this study in terms of inflation-adjusted dollars per capita, calculated on the basis of PPP. The bottom line is the most commonly used measure in Japan, the NME produced by the MHW. It is clear that this measure, which came to $932 per person in 1990, does leave out a substantial amount of spending compared with the United States.

The next line up is the national account THE as calculated by the author from EPA data. As noted above, it is calculated on the same basis as the data the OECD uses for Japan, although the numbers are slightly different for unknown reasons. It was $1,244 per person in 1990.

The third line is the new adjusted THE, following U.S. definitions but excluding under-the-table payments, calculated by supplementing the figure men-

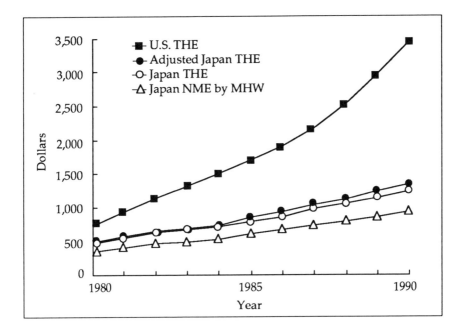

**Figure 1. Per capita health expenditure PPP conversion, NME, THE, adjusted THE, 1980–90**

tioned above with estimates of spending on items that are not included in the regular Japanese statistics. For 1990 this amounts to $1,342 per person; if we added in our generous estimate of under-the-counter payments, that would increase to $1,359 per person.

The fourth line is the U.S. THE. In 1990 this amounted to $3,449 per person. Clearly, after all these adjustments, health expenditures in Japan are still far lower than in the United States. Moreover, the gap has been widening very rapidly. In 1980 Japanese health expenditure per person in PPP terms was about two-thirds of U.S. spending; in 1985, half as much; and in 1990, the Japanese were spending less than 40% of what Americans paid for their health care.

NOTE

1. For more details of the estimates made, refer to Katsumata 1993.

REFERENCES

Haber, Susan G., and Joseph P. Newhouse. 1991. Recent revisions to recommendations for national health expenditures accounting. *Health Care Financing Review* 13.1 (Fall).

Katsumata, Yukiko. 1993. Nichibei iryōhi shishitsu no hikaku kenkyū (Comparative study of Japan–United States health expenditure). *Kōsei no shihyō* 40.8: 19–29.

Lazenby, Helen C., Katharine R. Levit, Daniel R. Waldo, Gerald S. Adler, Suzanne W. Letsch, and Cathy A. Cowan. 1992. National health accounts: Lessons from the U.S. experience. *Health Care Financing Review* 13.4 (Summer): 89–103.

Niki, Ryu. 1993. *90 nendai no iryō to shinryō hōshū* (Japan's health care in the 1990s and the reform of the fee schedule). Tokyo: Keisō Shobō.

Schieber, George J., Jean-Pierre Poullier, and Leslie M. Greenwald. 1992. U.S. health expenditure performance: An international comparison and data update. *Health Care Financing Review* 13.4 (Summer).

CHAPTER 3

# Factors in Health Care Spending: An Eight-Nation Comparison with OECD Data

*Naoki Ikegami and Yoshinori Hiroi*

SUMMARY    This paper examines trends in the supply and demand factors that should have had a major impact on health expenditure from 1960 to 1990. The data used are from the *OECD Health Data Version 1.5* (Organization for Economic Cooperation and Development [OECD] 1993), supplemented by government statistics for Japan. In Japan, the ratio of health expenditure to gross domestic product (GDP) remained constant thoughout the 1980s despite the aging of the population and the increase in the ratio of health employees to the total employed. This was reflected in the relative decline in earnings of health employees, which was especially striking for physicians. In contrast, in the United States there has been a continuous increase in the ratio of the health expenditure to GDP, an increase that was much greater than the increase in the ratio of the elderly. The reason may lie in increases in both the ratio of health employees to total employees and that of their earnings, especially that of physicians, to the earnings of others. This pattern was unique to the United States. Germany, France, the United Kingdom, Sweden, and, to a lesser extent, Canada have shown little relative increases in health expenditure in the 1980s. Of these five countries, Germany showed a pattern most similar to Japan for all the factors analyzed.

## Introduction

One of the difficulties of making international comparisons of health care data is that any observed differences may not be substantial but due to the method of statistical compilation. For example, simply comparing the average length of stay for each country has little meaning because the definition and function of a "hospital" is likely to vary considerably. In order to mitigate this problem, longitudinal analysis will be used—that is, the relative changes in the supply and demand factors that should have a major impact on health expenditure. Since the focus is on trends, as long as each country has applied a consistent methodology for the years presented, there is less need to worry about differences in the way they have compiled each set of data. Under these conditions, it becomes more feasible to analyze the factors that appear to be associated with changes in the total health expenditure. For our purpose, the factors examined are, on the demand side, the aging of the population; on the supply side, the ratios of those employed in the health sector to the total employed, their average earnings to that of the total employed, and the average earnings of physicians to that of the total employed. These supply-side factors should reflect the volume of wealth that has been transferred to the health sector. Furthermore, we looked at the changes in the average length of stay and compared that to the total number of staff per occupied bed as a crude measure of efficiency.

The data are from the 1993 *OECD Health Data Version 1.5* compiled in disk form for the years 1960–90. While the main focus will be in comparing the trends between Japan and the United States, the other major OECD countries of Canada, Germany, France, the United Kingdom, Italy, plus Sweden as a model of a welfare state, will also be analyzed to provide a broader perspective. In the case of Japan, we have added or substituted data from the official government statistics when the OECD data were either not available or clearly did not reflect the actual situation. For the other countries, we could not follow a similar process; however, we did examine whether there were any unexplained fluctuations in the time series and refrained from drawing any conclusions from that set of data.

### Growth Compared with GDP

From a public policy point of view, it is not the absolute growth in health expenditure that is important, but its relative share in the GDP.[1] Accordingly, it is first necessary to examine the relative increase of health expenditures in relation to that of the GDP on a longitudinal basis. Table 1 shows the ratio of the annual increase of health expenditure to that of GDP, averaged for five-year periods from 1960 to 1990. Since we are using ratios, the results will not be affected by fluctuations in the currency exchange rate or the use of present or constant prices.

As table 1 shows, Japan had two high-growth periods in health expenditure: one from 1960 to 1965 and the other from 1970 to 1980. The first was especially striking: health expenditure increased at an average rate that was nearly twice that of the GDP. This period has been referred to as the "first era of high health expenditure growth." The realization of universal coverage in 1961 and the general improvement in access are thought to be the main contributing factors. It slackened in the latter half of the 1960s, probably due to sustained economic growth. Although health expenditure continued to grow at an average yearly rate of 14.7%, this was offset by the growth of the GDP's rate of 14.2%. The second period occurred because health expenditure continued to increase at the same rate while that of the GDP slowed down to around 11%. This has been named the "second era of high health expenditure growth." Three factors have been held responsible for this phenomenom: (1) technology advancement, leading to a shift to drugs and diagnostic testing with higher prices (see "The 'Natural Increase' and Cost Control"); (2) increases in reimbursement fees resulting from the price and wage slide system (indexing) that was adopted in the revisions in effect from 1974

**Table 1. Ratio of the annual increase in health expenditure to that of GDP, averaged for five-year periods, 1960–90 (%)**

|         | Japan | U.S. | Canada | Germany | France | U.K. | Italy | Sweden |
|---------|-------|------|--------|---------|--------|------|-------|--------|
| 1960–65 | 1.9   | 1.6  | 1.4    | 1.7     | 1.8    | 1.6  | 1.9   | 1.9    |
| 1966–70 | 1.0   | 1.8  | 1.7    | 1.4     | 1.3    | 1.3  | 1.4   | 1.7    |
| 1971–75 | 1.5   | 1.4  | 1.0    | 1.7     | 1.4    | 1.5  | 1.3   | 1.2    |
| 1976–80 | 1.3   | 1.2  | 1.1    | 1.1     | 1.3    | 1.2  | 1.2   | 1.4    |
| 1981–85 | 1.0   | 1.2  | 1.3    | 0.8     | 1.1    | 0.9  | 1.0   | 0.6    |
| 1986–90 | 1.0   | 1.8  | 1.3    | 0.9     | 1.2    | 1.1  | 1.7   | 1.1    |

Source: Organization for Economic Cooperation and Development 1993.

to 1981; and (3) increased utilization by the elderly due to the introduction of "free" health care for those age seventy and older in 1973. However, in the 1980s, the growth of health expenditure slowed considerably, which can be attributed to the adoption of a rigorous cost-containment policy.

In contrast, in the United States the increase in health expenditure has always surpassed that of the GDP. In particular, the periods from 1965 to 1970 and from 1985 to 1990 stand out. The first can be attributed to the introduction in 1965 of Medicare and Medicaid, the first federal health care financing programs in the United States, which increased access and utilization. This could be regarded as similar to what occurred in Japan after the realization of universal health insurance in 1961. For the second period, however, it is difficult to focus on a specific reason for the increase. There were no similar expansions in coverage; if anything, the ratio of the uninsured increased. Furthermore, hospital expenditure came to be increasingly capped by Medicare and other prospective payment schemes based on the diagnostic related group (DRG) from 1983. Therefore, other reasons must be sought to explain this phenomenon.

All the other countries shared with Japan and the United States the relative high growth of health expenditure in 1960–65. Thereafter, they have followed more the pattern of Japan, except that 1965–70 was also a high-growth period. It is significant that apart from Italy and, to a lesser degree, Canada, health expenditures were relatively stable in the 1980s. In Sweden, the growth of health expenditure was significantly less than that of the GDP for the 1980–85 period.

## Aging of the Population

Demographic change should be the most important demand-side factor to explain growth in health expenditure. Unlike many others, it is quite independent of supply-side factors, such as changes in physicians' practice patterns. Figure 1 shows changes in the ratio of health expenditure to GDP in conjunction with that of the ratio of the elderly sixty-five and over to the total population, for the eight countries. If aging had occurred without any corresponding increase in health

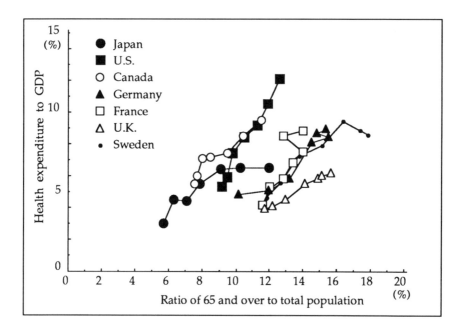

**Figure 1. Changes in the ratios of 65 and over to total population and health expenditure to GDP, 1960–90. (From OECD: *1993 OECD health data version 1.5;* MHW: *"Byōin hōkoku"* [Report from hospitals].) (Note: Data points at five-year increments.)**

expenditure, then the line would become horizontal. If health expenditure had increased without any increase in the ratio of the aged, then the line would become vertical.

In Japan, increases in health expenditure appear to be matched by that of the elderly until 1980, after which the line has become flat. Although the ratio of the elderly sixty-five and over increased from 9.1% in 1980 to 12.0% in 1990, the ratio of health expenditure to GDP has remained the same at 6.5%. In the United States, however, the ratio of health expenditure to GDP has grown much faster than the aging of the population, so that the line comes close to being vertical. While the former has more than doubled from 5.3% in 1960 to 12.1% in 1990, the latter only increased from 9.2% to 12.6%. For the other countries, the relationship tends to be somewhat more consistent, and aging and the growth in health expenditure tend to be more closely linked. The main exceptions are Germany and France in the 1980s where health expenditures increased somewhat despite the fact that the ratio of the elderly remained the same or actually temporally decreased in 1985. In Sweden, the decrease in the 1980s was mainly due to the imposition of cost-containment measures.

### Ratio of Health Employees to the Total Employed

Since roughly half of all health expenditure can be ascribed to personnel costs, the number of employees in the health sector is likely to be the most important supply-side factor related to health expenditure. Although a causal relationship is difficult to establish, an increase in health manpower would be reflected in either an increase in health expenditure or, should that be constrained, to relatively lower earnings for those working in the health sector. Alternatively, if health expenditure increases without any relative expansion in the ratio of those working in the health sector to the total employed, then it is their earnings that are likely increasing.

Although there are no clear criteria as to which occupations should be included in the "health" sector, since we are looking at trends, this does not matter so much as long as consistency is maintained. Parenthetically, the OECD appears to underestimate the number of those employed in the health sector, compared with the government data of Japan and the United States, by just over a quarter. For Japan, in 1990, according to the *Survey of Medical Facilities* (Ministry of Health and Welfare [MHW] 1992c), the number is 2,182,976, compared with the OECD's count of 1,587,000.[2] For the United States, in 1989, according to *Health United States 1992* (U.S. Department of Health and Human Services 1993a, b), the number is 9,110,000 (not counting those working in other industries) compared with 7,122,000 from the OECD. However, since the magnitude of the difference appears to be consistent over the years analyzed, and since it was necessary to compare the figures with those of other countries, the OECD data were retained.[3]

Table 2 shows the changes in the ratio of health employees to the total employed. In Japan, the ratio increased from 1.2% in 1965 to 2.4% in 1990 and was especially marked from 1970 to 1981, when it increased from 1.4 to 2.1%, reflecting the increase in the ratio of health expenditure to the GDP. However, the ratio of those employed in the health sector continued to grow in the 1980s, although to a lesser degree, from 2.1 to 2.4%, despite the constant ratio of health expenditure to GDP. In the United States, the growth in the ratio of health employees has been sustained throughout the entire period, although the increase from 6.0% in 1985 to 6.3% in 1989 was much less than that of the health expenditure to GDP ratio, which grew from 10.5% to 11.6% for the same period.

Among the other countries, Germany also showed a consistent growth in the ratio of health employees that was greater than that of the ratio of health expenditure to GDP. The data for France and Italy are suspect because there are abrupt changes in the ratio of health employees, which would point to some change in the method of statistical compilation.[4] In Italy, too, the ratio jumped from 2.5% in 1979 to 3.9% in 1980. In the United Kingdom and Sweden, the ratio decreased from 1985 to 1990, which may reflect real or statistical changes. Data for Canada were too incomplete for analysis.

**Table 2. Changes in the ratio of health employees to the total
employed, 1970–90 (%)**

|      | Japan | U.S. | Canada | Germany | France | U.K. | Italy | Sweden |
|------|-------|------|--------|---------|--------|------|-------|--------|
| 1970 | 1.4   | 3.7  |        | 2.9     |        | 3.1  | 1.6   | 6.2    |
| 1971 |       |      | 4.0    |         | 2.1    |      |       |        |
| 1975 | 1.7   | 4.9  |        | 3.7     |        | 4.3  | 2.2   | 7.8    |
| 1976 |       |      |        |         | 2.7    |      |       |        |
| 1980 |       | 5.3  |        | 4.5     |        | 4.7  | 3.9   | 9.9    |
| 1981 | 2.1   |      | 4.7    |         | 3.3    |      |       |        |
| 1984 | 2.3   |      |        |         |        |      |       |        |
| 1985 |       | 6.0  |        | 5.3     |        | 5.1  | 4.2   | 10.7   |
| 1986 |       |      | 5.2    |         | 6.7    |      |       |        |
| 1989 |       | 6.3  |        | 5.6     |        |      |       |        |
| 1990 | 2.4   |      |        |         |        | 4.6  | 4.3   | 9.9    |

Source: Organization for Economic Cooperation and Development 1993.

### Earnings of Health Workers and Physicians

Changes in the earnings of health employees expressed as ratios to the average compensation for the total employed is shown in table 3. For Japan, since this was not available in the OECD datafile, we took figures from the *Wage Census* (Ministry of Labor 1991), in which those working in the health sector have been given a separate category since 1970. For physicians, the earnings of private practitioners, who represent about one-third of the total, are not included, so the real figures would be slightly higher. It can be seen that the ratio has remained fairly constant but has declined slightly from 1.0 in 1980 to 0.9 in 1990. In contrast, in the United States there has been a consistent increase in the ratio from 0.6 in 1960 to 0.9 in 1990. Thus, not only has the ratio of those employed in the health sector increased, but their relative earnings have also increased. For the other countries in which data were available, the ratios tended to fluctuate, and no steady trend could be observed except for Sweden, where it had declined from 1.0 in 1970 to 0.8 in 1990.

The relative earnings of physicians to the total employed are shown in table 4. For Japan, since the OECD data seemed to be derived only from the *Wage Census* (Ministry of Labor 1991), we have substituted new figures by combining this data with the survey on the financial state of health care facilities made by the MHW (1990). That survey looks at the earnings of private practitioners and is available beginning in 1976. The average earnings for all physicians was calculated by figuring the average earnings of the employed and self-employed physicians according to their relative ratio. It can be seen that the ratio has decreased from 5.5 times the wage of the average worker in 1976 to 4.0 in 1989. Both employed physicians and private practitioners have witnessed a relative decline in

**Table 3. Changes in the relative earnings of health employees to that of the total employed, 1970–90 (%)**

|      | Japan | U.S. | Canada | Germany | France | U.K. | Italy | Sweden |
|------|-------|------|--------|---------|--------|------|-------|--------|
| 1970 | 1.0   | 0.7  | —      | —       | —      | 1.0  | 1.5   | 1.0    |
| 1975 | 1.0   | 0.8  | —      | 0.6     | —      | 0.8  | 1.2   | 1.0    |
| 1980 | 1.0   | 0.8  | —      | 0.6     | —      | 1.1  | 1.1   | 0.9    |
| 1985 | 0.9   | 0.9  | —      | 0.7     | —      | 1.0  | 1.2   | 0.9    |
| 1987 | —     | —    | —      | —       | —      | 1.1  | —     | —      |
| 1990 | 0.9   | 0.9  | —      | 0.6     | —      | —    | 1.2   | 0.8    |

Sources: Organization for Economic Cooperation and Development 1993; Ministry of
Labor 1991.

**Table 4. Changes in the relative earnings of physicians to that of the total employed, 1970–90 (%)**

|      | Japan | U.S. | Canada | Germany | France | U.K. | Italy | Sweden |
|------|-------|------|--------|---------|--------|------|-------|--------|
| 1970 |       | 4.7  | 5.0    |         | 3.0    |      | 1.48  | 3.7    |
| 1971 |       |      |        | 6.5     |        |      |       |        |
| 1974 |       |      |        | 5.8     |        |      |       |        |
| 1975 |       | 4.4  | 4.0    |         | 2.6    | 2.6  | 1.16  | 2.5    |
| 1976 | 5.5   |      |        |         |        |      |       |        |
| 1980 | 4.4   |      | 3.5    | 5.0     | 2.1    | 2.5  | 1.04  | 2.0    |
| 1981 |       | 4.3  |        |         |        |      |       |        |
| 1985 | 4.3   | 4.4  | 3.7    | 4.3     | 1.9    | 2.4  |       | 1.5    |
| 1989 | 4.0   | 5.2  |        |         |        |      |       |        |
| 1990 |       |      |        |         | 2.0    |      |       | 1.9    |

Source: Organization for Economic Cooperation and Development 1993; Ministry of Labor
1991; Ministry of Health and Welfare 1990.

their earnings: from 2.9 to 2.4 times for the former; from 8.2 to 6.8 times for the latter during this time period.[5] In the United States the relative earnings, after remaining fairly constant, increased from 4.4 in 1985 to 5.2 in 1990. This is in marked contrast not only to Japan, but also to Canada, Germany, France, and Italy, which showed a general pattern of decline after 1970. Sweden is unusual in that after showing a steady decline, the ratio increased from 1.5 in 1985 to 1.9 in 1990.

The only other profession whose earnings would have had a major impact on health expenditure and that could be found in the OECD datafile was qualified nurses. However, in the United States these data were available only for 1984 and 1986, the values of which were 0.96 times and 1.01 times the average of total employed. For Japan, it was 0.75 times and 0.81 times, respectively, for these two years. These ratios had increased from 0.64 in 1960 to around this level in 1975, after which it remained about the same (0.79 times in 1989). Japan's ratio was similar to that of Sweden (0.81 in 1989) but lower than Canada (1.06 in 1987) and the United Kingdom (0.87 in 1987). These figures should be treated with some caution because the definition of what constitutes a "qualified nurse" may differ according to each country.

### Relative Efficiency of Hospital Care

Efficiency of hospital care has often been measured by the average length of stay. In Japan, the long average length of stay has often been cited as an example of the health care system's inefficiency. However, this does not take into consideration the cost side of the equation. It is possible to decrease the average length of stay by increasing the intensity of care through more staffing. The corresponding increase in costs may offset any savings and could lead to a net loss of efficiency. Thus, both factors should be considered together. Figure 2 shows the changes in the relationship between the average length of stay for acute-care hospitals and the number of staff per occupied bed in somatic hospitals from 1960 to 1990 for Japan, the United States, Germany, France, and Sweden (other countries are omitted because they had incomplete data).[6] A horizontal line would imply that reductions in the average length of stay has been achieved without any corresponding increases in staffing; a vertical line, that increases in staffing have occurred without any decrease in the average length of stay.

The OECD data did not provide the average length of stay in Japan, so we have substituted the figure for general beds from the MHW's (1992b) hospital survey.[7] Japan is the only country in which there was a steady increase in the average length of stay until 1985, despite a steady increase in the staffing ratio. Thus, the average length of stay of 28 days and the staffing level of 0.54 in 1960 have increased to 39 days and 0.79 in 1985. The United States also appears to be unusual, because although staffing has steadily increased from 0.96 in 1960 to 3.35 in 1990, the average length of stay has remained largely unchanged at between 7 to 8 days. For Germany, staffing increased from 0.62 in 1960 to 1.31 in 1989, and the average length of stay decreased from 21.6 days to 12.4 days during the same period. Also, in Sweden, the average length of stay decreased from 11 days in 1970 to 7.5 days in 1985 as the staffing increased from 0.98 to 1.85. France's data are suspect because the hospital staffing jumped from 0.99 in 1975 to 1.25 in 1980 (no data are available for intervening years) but decreased abruptly from 1.37 in 1983 to 0.98 in 1985.

The above comparisons leave out changes in the function of hospitals, so they need to be treated with caution. In the case of Japan, there has been a major influx of geriatric long-stay patients after the introduction of "free" medical care in 1973 so that, at present, nearly half of the inpatients are over the age of sixty-five, of whom again nearly half have been hospitalized for over half a year (MHW 1992a). This is in marked contrast to the situation in 1970 when the ratio of

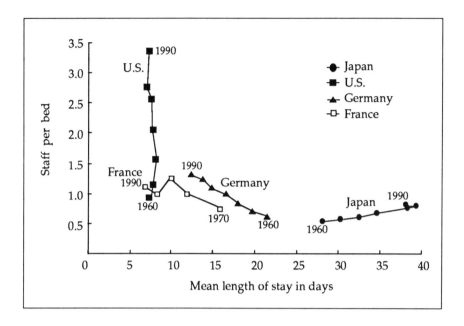

**Figure 2. Changes in the average length of stay in acute care hospitals and total staffing per occupied bed in somatic hospitals, 1960–90. (From OECD:** *1993 OECD Health data version 1.5;* **MHW:** *"Byōin hōkoku"* **[Report from hospitals].)**

patients sixty-five and over was only one-sixth. In the case of the United States, it does not take into account the growth in day surgeries and ambulatory care, which would justify increases in staffing without a commensurate decrease in the average length of stay. Improvements in the quality of care should also be taken into consideration. Nevertheless, in spite of these caveats, from the available data, neither Japan nor the United States would appear to have become more efficient in providing hospital care.[8]

**Discussion**

This analysis exposes some of the strengths and weaknesses of the OECD datafile. Although they are the best available standardized data, some inconsistencies were found in the data compilation, and, also, several key data were lacking. This confirms our concern about using it for cross-sectional comparisons. However, it becomes less of a problem when trends are analyzed. Our findings show that in Japan, the ratio of health expenditure to GDP has remained constant throughout the 1980s, despite the aging of the population and the increase in the ratio of health employees to the total employed. This was reflected in the relative decline in the earnings of health employees, which was especially large for physicians. In contrast, in the United States there has been a continuous increase in the ratio of health expenditure to GDP, which was much greater than the increase in the ratio of the elderly. The reason may lie in the increases in both the ratio of health employees and that of their earnings, especially that of physicians. In many respects, these trends are unique to the United States. In Germany, France, the United Kingdom, Sweden, and, to a lesser extent, Canada, there have been little relative increases in health expenditure in the 1980s. Of these five countries, Germany showed the trend most similar to Japan for all the factors analyzed. Sweden was close, but the relative earnings of its physicians increased again from 1985 to 1990. In the other countries, the data were too incomplete to come to any conclusion.

Based on the available evidence, we would like to emphasize the implications of the earnings of those employed in the health sector, particularly of physicians. Pauly's (1993) argument is that redistributing a lower share of the gross national product to health professionals through monopsony "does not benefit the country as a whole, or even the average citizen" because "the totality of all citizens is not made better off by having buyers gain at the expense of sellers." However, this overlooks the fact that a significant ratio of heath care is publicly financed. Even in the United States, nearly half of the health expenditure is financed by tax or social security contributions (more if the forgone revenue from making health insurance premiums tax deductible for employers is taken into consideration). Thus, if Pauly's idea were to be applied more generally, it would imply that high taxes and high incomes for government bureaucrats are justified— a position with which neither we nor Pauly himself, we conjecture, would agree.

This being the case, we are somewhat puzzled why physicians' incomes, unlike administrative costs and drugs, have not become a major target of health care reform in the United States, because in Japan, despite the fact that there has been a relative decline in their incomes, physicians' earnings have continued to be regarded as an area for further cost containment. This may be related to the high esteem that professionals enjoy in American society. It is not only physicians who earn high incomes, but also lawyers and graduates of M.B.A. programs, and this tendency to reward the symbolic analysts has intensified in the 1980s. Most Americans would probably trust their physicians more than the government, which would be unthinkable in Japan. Thus, one of the central issues in health care reform is the appropriate status and earnings for professionals, which can only be decided by a value judgment by society. This obvious but important issue appears to have been left out of the health care reform debate in the United States by all parties.

NOTES

1. Katsumata has shown that while the OECD health expenditure figures are slightly different from those she independently calculated from the national accounting figures of

Japan and the United States, the trends are very similar (see her chapter comparing health expenditure in the United States and Japan).

2. In fact, the actual number would be higher because the survey does not include those working in the public health field or other industries. If included, the total should increase by about 10%. It is not clear how the OECD figure was derived. It is slightly more than the total number employed in hospitals, which is 1,326,970.

3. Nevertheless, it is necessary to examine more closely which categories of workers are included in the health sector. For example, according to the OECD data in the eight countries observed, the ratio of qualified nurses to total employed in the health sector varied from 53.4% in Canada (1986) to 18.6% in Sweden (1990). In Japan, the rate was 47.0% (1990), and in the United States, 23.4% (1989). It is difficult to understand why Canada's ratio of qualified nurses should be twice that of the United States when the two countries have similar health care delivery systems.

4. In France the ratio suddenly jumped from 3.5% in 1982 to 6.0% in 1983. In Italy there was a similar jump from 2.5% in 1979 to 3.9% in 1980.

5. This difference between salaried physicians and private practitioners is greater than that in the United States, where it was 4.1 times average for the former versus 6.0 times for the latter in 1987. In Japan, the average for all physicians is closer to that of physicians employed in hospitals because their ratio is greater compared with the United States.

6. "Acute-care hospitals" and OECD's "somatic (nonpsychiatric) hospitals" may not be the same. However, since we are making a trend analysis, this should have less of an impact than in the case of cross-sectional analysis.

7. Hospital beds in Japan are divided into general, psychiatric, tuberculosis, communicable diseases, and leprosy beds. General beds constitute about two-thirds of the total, but this includes long-term-care beds for which there is no separate category. Thus, the average length of stay would be much longer than for acute-care beds.

8. Japan's emphasis on ambulatory care has sometimes been claimed as the secret of its low level of health expenditure. However, in point of fact, Japan's ratio of ambulatory-care expenditure to total expenditure has been steadily declining, from 48% in 1970 to 41% in 1990. At the same time, that of the United States has remained relatively stable at 27% to 29%; as has that of Germany at 27% to 29% and Canada at 22% to 24%. Data for France and Italy fluctuated without any definite pattern. Also, although the ratio of health expenditure to the GDP was about the same for Germany and France, the per capita number of physician visits differed greatly between Germany's 11.5 (1987) and France's 6.9 (1987).

REFERENCES

Ministry of Health and Welfare (MHW). 1992a. *Patient survey* (Kanyja chōsa). Tokyo: Kōsei Tōkei Kyōkai.
——. 1992b. *Byōin hōkoku* (Report from hospitals). Tokyo: Kōsei Tōkei Kyōkai.
——. 1992c. *Iryō shisetsu chōsa* (Survey of medical facilities). Tokyo: Kōsei Tōkei Kyōkai.
——. 1990. *Iryō keizai jittai chōsa* (Survey on the state of health economics). Tokyo: Kōsei Tōkei Kyōkai.
Ministry of Labor. 1991. *Chingin sensasu* (1990 Wage census). Tokyo: Ministry of Labor.
Organization for Economic Cooperation and Development (OECD). 1993. *OECD health data version 1.5*. Paris: OECD.

Pauly, M. V. 1993. U.S. health care costs: The untold true story. *Health Affairs* 12.3: 152–59.

U.S. Department of Health and Human Services. 1993a. *Health United States 1992.* Washington, D.C.: Government Printing Office.

———. 1993b. *Health people 2000 review.* Washington, D.C.: Government Printing Office.

# CHAPTER 4

# Afterword: Costs—The Macro Perspective

*William C. Hsiao*

In assessing the financial resources spent on health care, three questions should be answered: (1) How much did Japan spend on health care? (2) How does the total expenditure compare with that of the United States? (3) What are the trends in cost inflation and their underlying causes? The common analytical tool used to answer these questions is a National Health Expenditure (NHE) account. It shows how much was spent for health care, the amounts spent for different services, and who paid for these services. This information reveals how resources were allocated and whether the financial burden was shared equitably. International comparisons can provide broad indications about the efficiency of a nation's health care system and adequacy of its health care financing. In short, NHE is essential data to have.

Traditionally, physicians have been appointed as health policy makers, and they usually have had little awareness of the need for economic analysis. Consequently, economic and social information about the health sector are often inadequate. Most nations do not have a complete and accurate account of their total health expenditures; Japan is no exception. Nonetheless, the formulation of sound health policy requires the information that can be provided by an NHE. Further, in conducting international comparative analyses, the NHE has to be compiled on a consistent basis. Katsumata makes a significant contribution in developing a reliable NHE for Japan.

Compiling a national health account is not a simple matter. There are three basic issues: First, what is the definition of national health expenditure? In recent years, the Health Statistics Office of the Organization for Economic Cooperation and Development (OECD) established a common definition of health expenditure that defines it as final consumption by the government, quasi-governmental organizations, and households for health care. Final consumption is defined as expenditure paid by these bodies. Second, what are the boundaries of health care—what services and programs should be considered health care? Prevention programs, primary care, and curative services are usually considered health care. However, nations differ in their treatment of other issues, such as over-the-counter drugs, spending for medical research and education, and community and social services for the elderly and disabled. Finally, what methods should be used to compile the national health expenditure account? Different methods can produce different results. For example, the United States derives its NHE from the production side by combining the revenues received by providers. Japan compiles its NHE from the payer side by calculating the amounts spent by the government and households. Theoretically, the amounts paid by payers should equal the revenues received by the providers. But in reality that is not necessarily true. While providers usually have accurate records on their revenues, spending by households is usually gathered by household-interview surveys, and survey respondents usually understate their expenditure due to errors in recall. In making international comparisons, these three major issues in the compilation of national health expenditure accounts should be kept in mind.

Katsumata provides a detailed understanding of how the NHE account was compiled in Japan by gathering the amounts spent by the government, quasi-governmental organizations, and households. There are two major sources of information—the Economic Planning Agency and the Ministry of Health and Welfare—but she was not able to obtain the procedures and data used by the Economic Planning Agency in compiling the NHE (the figures from the two agencies do not agree). Katsumata then compared the expense items included in the U.S. national health expenditure account with those in that of Japan. She adjusted the Japanese account to consider those items in the United States NHE that were omitted in computing the Japanese NHE, including the "gifts" paid by households to senior surgeons and physicians, and she provided a detailed description of her data sources. She has made a major contribution toward aligning the national health accounts of Japan and the United States onto a comparable basis.

While Katsumata's research provides a good start, further study could improve the completeness and accuracy of the Japanese data. The methods and data used by the Economic Planning Agency in compiling the national health expenditure account should be analyzed, particularly on the estimated amount paid directly by patients. In the United States, the health expenditure compiled by the National Income Account (similar to that compiled by the Japanese Economy Agency) understates health expenditures by 12–16% because of inaccuracies, since the National Income Account focuses on the total economy rather than on just health care. The National Income Account gives less attention to the completeness and accuracy of health expenditure data. Another option is to compile a national health account independently of the government's NHE. This can be done by taking the governmental and quasi-governmental spending from the published figures (they are reliable since they are based on government accounting records), then adding household expenditure directly paid by household from household-interview surveys such as the National Household Income Expenditure Survey data. Another important area of investigation is the compiling of Japanese national health expenditure by type of service to show how resources are allocated and used in Japan.

Katsumata adjusted the official figures over the past ten years to make them more comparable with the United States data. These adjustments did not change the time trend in Japanese health care cost inflation rates. She found that Japan spent about 6.8% of its gross domestic product (GDP) for health care in 1990.

Over the ten-year period, 1980–90, health care expenditure in Japan has remained quite steady as a percentage of GDP, while the United States has increased its health expenditure from 9.5% to 12.2% of its GDP. It is equally important to consider that the United States started at a higher base in 1980, when per capita health expenditure in Japan and in the United States were $484 and $732, respectively. Two crucial questions emerge: (1) what reasons would explain the different levels of health care cost between the two nations, and (2) what caused the two countries to have different rates of increase from year to year in health expenditure, as measured by the GDP?

Ikegami and Hiroi used OECD data to analyze the trend in health care expenditure from 1960 to 1990 among the industrialized countries. They offered some plausible explanations for the two high-growth periods in health expenditure in Japan. In the first period (1960–65), they explained that perhaps the high inflation rate was due to the universalization and expanded access. By the late 1960s, however, the high rates of increase in health costs were somewhat mediated because of a very high rate of economic growth in Japan. In the second period of growth (1970–80), the rapid increase in health care costs was due to pricing policy, which induced high usage of drugs and new technology.

For later years, Ikegami and Hiroi found that Japan was able to moderate its health care cost inflation by reducing the relative wages of health care workers, especially physicians, as compared to general compensation levels. The authors also found that the slower rate of inflation in health care cost, as compared to the United States, was due to the Japanese capability to control the rising trend in the number of personnel per hospital bed, while the United States experienced significant increases in its personnel per bed.

Yet another approach contributes additional insight to where and why Japan's health care costs are lower. Instead of comparing trends in health care cost inflation between Japan and the United States, four major reasons why the absolute cost in health care per person differs between Japan and the United States are identified and analyzed.

### Reasons for the Differences in Health Care Costs

Japan has achieved enviable performance with its health care system. The gross health indices are the best in the world. The infant mortality rate is 0.46% of live births, and life expectancy at birth is 75.9 years for males and 81.8 for females (see Ikegami, chapter 1 of this book). There is universal insurance for all citizens; patients have free choice and equal access to all health care facilities. Other than organ transplants, Japan adopts new technology, such as CAT scans and MRIs, faster than anywhere else in the world.

Yet health care cost per capita in Japan is only 40% of the cost in the United States. The cost per capita in Japan (1990) was approximately ¥165,200, while the United States cost per capita was ¥407,100. There is no doubt that the Japanese health care system spends much less but produces equal or better health outcomes and patient satisfaction. What is Japan's secret?

There are four major reasons why Japan has achieved such outstanding performance. First, the morbidity rates differ between Japan and the United States. These differences are due to such causes as different diets, lifestyles, and social conditions. Americans have higher rates of cancer, mental illness, abuse of drugs and alcohol, violence, and AIDS, but Japan has higher rates in some illnesses, such as strokes. Second, the Japanese have different medical practice styles, which are caused partly by patient preferences and partly by the Japanese system of organizing health services. These differences in practice styles result in lower surgical rates, lower hospital admissions, longer average length of stay, and greater use of primary care services. Third, lower costs in Japan are partly due to the productive efficiency in the Japanese health care system. By comparison to the United States, it has lower hospital and personnel costs per bed, lower administration costs, and slightly lower drug costs. Finally, as framed by Professor Uwe Reinhardt, the health care system can be seen as a bazaar where patients can transfer their wealth to physicians, nurses, and technicians in exchange for their labor. The fees determine how much of a patient's wealth will be transferred. Japan, by comparison with the United States, transferred less from patients to physicians.

The following details will illustrate these four points. Medical practice styles are quite different between Japan and the United States. In the United States, there is an old saying in medicine: "When in doubt, take it out." Table 1 shows that the surgical rates in the United States are much higher than in Japan. Europeans describe the U.S. practice as the "aggressive" practice of medicine; in both Japan and European nations, there is a more conservative practice. The higher frequency of surgery does not necessarily produce better health for people. Evaluative studies conducted in the United States have found that 25% of the most frequently performed surgeries and high-technology tests were unnecessary. Patients, instead of being helped, face risks and suffer pain from these inappropriate procedures.

Table 2 indicates a difference in production methods used to produce health services. There are many fewer staff employed per bed in Japan than in the United

**Table 1. Comparison of selected surgical rates (per 100,000 population)**

|                  | Japan | U.S. |
|------------------|-------|------|
| Tonsillectomy    | 61    | 205  |
| Hysterectomy     | 90    | 557  |
| Cataract surgery | 35    | 294  |
| Appendectomy     | 244   | 130  |

Source: OECD 1989.

**Table 2. Comparison of staff per 100 beds
(by hospital size)**

|  | Hospital size | |
| --- | --- | --- |
|  | 200–499 beds | 500–899 beds |
| Japan | 75 | 82 |
| U.S. | 289 | 411 |

Sources: Hospital Report 1989 (Japan);
    AHA Report 1989 (U.S.).

States. The United States employs four times as many people as Japan for each day of hospital services produced. Part of the greater manpower input in the United States is due to the short length of stay for each admission, but that cannot explain the whole difference between two nations.

Next, how much wealth is transferred from patients to physicians in exchange for their services? Physicians in Japan, on the average, earn approximately four times the median income of full-time workers, while in the United States, physicians are earning 5.2 times the median. The U.S. figures are somewhat understated because hospital-salaried physicians receive much higher revenues from their billings than their salaries. The excess amounts are given to the deans of medical schools or heads of hospitals, who use the funds to support other activities. Thus, the comparison of physician earnings does not reflect accurately the amount of wealth transferred from patients to physicians for medical care in the United States.

In the international community, Japanese achievements with its low health care cost have been dismissed because health experts often explain that Japanese culture and lifestyle are so different—they lead to low morbidity and less demand for health services. These are only partial explanations. Japan's point system of paying health service is unique. This incentive structure influences medical practices and the supply of specialists. The holistic question is: What impact do these differences in morbidity rates, medical practice styles, and payment systems have on health care costs? To answer this question, I attempted to quantify these differences and see how they could explain differences in health care costs per capita between the two nations. The results are summarized in table 3. These crude calculations are intended to provoke discussion and stimulate new research rather than give a definite answer. They could be wrong by a large margin, but they give an approximate idea of how much of the difference in health care costs between Japan and the United States may be explained by various causes.

U.S. health expenditure data was adjusted to what they would be if the United States operated with the conditions in Japan, estimating the cost per capita from the difference in morbidity rates. For example, about 10% of U.S. health care

**Table 3. Estimates of the difference in average
NHE between Japan and the U.S. (1990, in yen)**

| | |
|---|---|
| Costs per capita in U.S. | 407,100 |
| Differences in morbidity | -59,000 (+/-25%) |
| Medical practice styles | -35,400 (+/-15%) |
| Production/efficiency | |
|   lower hospital costs | -64,900 (+/-15%) |
|   lower administrative costs | -29,500 (+/-10%) |
| Smaller transfer of wealth | |
|   between patients and physicians | -21,000 (+/-15%) |
| Subtotal | -209,800 |
| Residual: (Research, age difference, | |
|   nursing home, etc., errors) | -32,100 |
| Cost per capita in Japan | 165,200 |

Source: Hsiao 1993, comparison based on purchasing
power parity.

expenditures are for the treatment of mental illness and drug and alcohol abuse; the amounts spent in Japan are much less. The United States is spending approximately 2% to 3% of its health expenditures for the treatment of AIDS patients, again much higher than Japan. Going through the major disease categories, the estimated cost for differences in morbidity total ¥59,000 per capita in 1990 (plus or minus 20%).

The next big difference in cost is due to differences in medical practice style. For example, a study found that 40% of the total U.S. annual health care costs spent for people over age sixty-five were for the final episode of illness. In the United States, often every available medical and surgical intervention is used to keep the patient alive, even in ninety-year-old patients who have lost their mental capacity. I do not believe that is done in Japan. Furthermore, Japan does not perform organ transplants. These differences in medical practice style explain a large part of the health care cost difference.

Another difference in health care costs is in the unit cost of hospital and clinical services. It has already been shown that Japan uses fewer people to deliver hospital services. Kawabuchi's study also showed that the floor space per bed in the United States is four times that of Japan. In other words, the United States has a much more expensive production function. If disease categories are standardized, one study found that the hospital treatment of acute myocardial infarction is 60% more expensive in the United States than in Japan, although the Japanese patient stays three times longer in the hospital. Using the American Hospital

Association's data, it can be estimated that the difference in the production function and its costs count for a large part of the cost differences between the two nations.

Another reason for lower costs in Japan arises from more efficient ways of financing health care and paying claims—using a regulated all-payers system. The United States relies on market competition to finance and deliver health care. Consequently, there are many insurance companies paying many salesmen to sell their products. Also, each large insurer employs an army of people to manage and monitor how physicians practice medicine on patients so that they can control the clinical decisions and try to reduce utilization rates. Each insurance company in the United States also has its own claim forms and its own computer systems. Thus, in any state, there might be fifteen to twenty different forms that physicians have to fill out, and there would be twelve to fifteen duplicating claim-payment systems. The financing system in the United States may help to reduce unemployment rates, but it does not keep down administrative costs.

Finally, physicians' earnings differ between the two countries: salaried physicians in hospitals are paid much less in Japan than in the United States. This explains a significant part of the difference in costs per capita for physician services.

### What Methods Did Japan Use to Achieve Lower Cost?

From the narrow perspective of the economist, Japan has been successful in controlling its health care costs by adopting three measures. It has given much greater payments to primary care services than to surgery or hospital services. In other words, Japan has tilted its financial incentives to encourage primary care and discourage surgery and other invasive services. But Japan did more than that. By setting a standard fee for each service, the amount paid for each service established the resources available for that service. Thus, the fee schedule sets the standard of service in terms of how much personnel, equipment, material, and space would be used to produce that service. Finally, Japan also allocates resources specifically for health promotion and prevention, such as screening programs. Fee schedules also reward physicians who provide counseling and instruction to patients on self-care. All of these measures promote greater efficiency in delivering health care to the Japanese.

### Challenges for the Japanese System

Japan faces several challenges to its health care system. The current point system still is tilted in favor of tests. Also, physicians are allowed to prescribe and dispense drugs. The economic incentive in this point system induces physicians to overprescribe drug and overuse tests.

Japan seems to have given very little attention to quality of services. Until 1992, the point system did not differentiate the level of service or the quality of service. Although some corrections were made then, the point system still has to be revised further to address the issue of quality. Moreover, Japan must strengthen its system of quality assurance and establish procedures to monitor the quality of services rendered by hospitals and clinics.

To achieve such an outstanding outcome at such a low cost, Japan had to make a trade-off between equal access and some quality of services. It seems that primary care and hospital services have been made widely available, but the available personal services are limited, leaving many of these to the family. Does this practice meet peoples' needs when the labor participation rate of Japanese women is rising?

There is such a great deal of fragmentation in Japanese health care delivery, such as the strict separation of clinics and hospitals, which results in the duplication of services. For example, if a patient is seen at a clinic and many tests are performed, when he subsequently goes to a hospital, the same tests will be performed again. Japan needs to modernize its organization of health services by delineating the functions of clinics and hospitals and developing a referral system.

The current point system also allocates more financial resources to clinics than to hospitals. This may have inhibited the growth of hospitals and resulted in long waiting lines for hospital outpatient and inpatient services.

Another problem Japan faces is its reliance on the political system to allocate resources. Patient demand plays a small role. Clinics and hospitals have very little incentive and freedom to innovate in their organization and in the delivery of health care services. At the same time, clinics and hospitals have very little incentive to respond to patient needs.

In sum, the biggest challenge facing Japanese health policy makers is how to preserve the good parts of its current system while improving quality and giving institutions greater flexibility and rewards to respond to patient demands.

CHAPTER 5

# The "Natural Increase" and Cost Control

*Yoshinori Hiroi*

SUMMARY   In the 1970s medical expenditures in Japan were growing so rapidly that some people even believed that the nation would be destroyed by medical costs (*iryōhi bōkokuron*). However, despite rapid population aging, the ratio of Japanese national medical expenditures to national income has not increased in this decade. This low growth trend was the a result of a conscious cost-containment policy by the government in the area of medical expenditure.

The policy contained many specific tools, including usage control via copayments in 1984 and controls on hospital beds through regional planning in 1985. The most important tool was price control through fee-schedule revision beginning in 1981, including control of the "natural increase" (*shizenzō*). This paper will concentrate on explaining "natural increase" as a key concept in the Japanese policy of containing medical expenses in the 1980s.

## Health Care Expenditure in Japan

Japan's expenditure on health care as a proportion of national income is quite low, second only to that of the United Kingdom among industrialized nations, and its growth has been quite moderate since the early 1980s (see Katsumata, this volume; and Organization for Economic Cooperation and Development Health Data 1991 from Schieber et al. 1992). This point is remarkable in that population aging—a key determinate of health care cost growth—has been unusually rapid in Japan.

Table 1 shows the alternation of rapid growth and stability of health care costs relative to national income in Japan. Rapid growth from 1960–65 was due to the full Citizens Health Insurance coverage in 1961, which increased access to medical institutions. After a decrease in the late 1960s, relative spending increased rapidly during the 1970s because of three factors: expanded usage by the elderly due to the introduction in 1973 of free medical care for those aged seventy and older; increased prices resulting from the price and wage indexing in effect from 1974 to 1978; and the large "natural increase" centered around prescription drugs and diagnostic testing. Yet, as can clearly be seen from table 1, the growth of

**Table 1. Medical expenditure and national income growth (% increase)**

|  | Annual growth | | Ratio |
|---|---|---|---|
|  | National income | Medical expenditure |  |
|  | A | B | B/A |
| 1960–65 | 14.8 | 22.4 | *1.51* |
| 1965–70 | 17.9 | 17.3 | 0.97 |
| 1970–75 | 15.4 | 21.3 | *1.39* |
| 1975–80 | 10.0 | 13.2 | *1.32* |
| 1980–85 | 5.4 | 6.0 | 1.12 |
| 1985–90 | 5.8 | 5.2 | 0.89 |

Note: Italic figures indicate periods when medical expenditure was high relative to economic growth.

Source: Ministry of Health and Welfare, Statistics Department, "Heisei 3nen kokumin iryōhi" (National medical expenditure, 1992) (Tokyo: Kōsei Tōkei Kyōkai, 1992).

medical expenditures relative to the national economy dropped significantly after 1980. This can be attributed to the introduction of cost-containment policies and the subsequent slowing of the "natural increase."

Incidentally, the pattern in the United States has been similar in some respects. The periods of the highest growth of health care costs relative to national income were 1965–70 and 1980–present. The first can be attributed to the introduction in 1965 of Medicare and Medicaid, which increased access to medical institutions and, consequently, patient usage. Since 1980, however, growth largely came from increases in the price of medical care. A fixed-sum system based on diagnostic-related groups (DRGs) was introduced in 1983 to control Medicare hospital fees; however, doctors' fees continued rising, pushing up medical expenditures. Doctors' fees were impregnable to control until 1992, when the Medicare system began setting doctors' fees by a point system similar to the one used in Japan.

Two conclusions can be drawn from this rough comparison. First, Japan and the United States experienced periods of steep increases in medical expenditure caused by the introduction of public medical insurance systems. Second, after these periods of quantitative supply expansion, the influence of price on medical expenditures became more significant. It could be pointed out that the current situations have largely been determined by the implementation, or lack of implementation, of price controls by the respective governments.

## Medical Expenditures and the "Natural Increase"

The usual American formula is to break down increases in medical expenditure into four factors: (1) population increase, (2) general inflation, (3) medical cost inflation, and (4) other. Medical expenditure growth caused by factors 2 and 3 results purely from price increases. The makeup of factor 4 is unclear but includes the volume or intensity of medical service provided to a single patient. It is enlarged by (a) increases in average medical services given per patient due to increases in medical supply or medical insurance expansion, or (b) changes in the content of medical treatment due to technological advances. Recent U.S. data (Office of National Cost Estimates 1990) indicate that:

1. The amount of medical expenditure growth caused by population increase is nearly constant and occupies only a small part of the overall increase.
2. The proportion of medical expenditure increase caused by "other" factors (factor 4) was larger prior to 1980 than after 1980. For example, large increases in patient usage due to the introduction of Medicare and Medicaid are included under "other."
3. After 1981 the proportion of increases in medical expenditure caused by rising prices grew. This resulted not from general price inflation but rather from an increase in health care prices.

In short, the steep rise in U.S. medical expenditures after 1981 was caused by medical service price increases rather than substantive factors such as population aging and increases in usage. This agrees with the earlier assertion that the increase in doctors' fees, resulting from the slow development in the United States of health care price controls through the medical insurance system, was a major cause of large medical expenditures in the 1980s.

A similar framework is often used in Japan (table 2). Increases in medical expenditure are divided into four factors: (1) population increase, (2) the structure of population aging, (3) fee-schedule revisions, and (4) other. Here, demography is given two factors, and inflation (completely included within fee-schedule revisions) just one; the "other" category is similar to that of the United States. This sort of analysis indicates that the contribution of population aging is growing slowly, that inflation in terms of fee-schedule increases was kept low in the 1980s, and that the "other" category, as in the United States, is both large and vague. It includes changes in medical treatment due to technological advances, "excess" medical treatment (in the number of drug prescriptions and diagnostic tests), and more. Growth in this "other" category is sometimes called the "natural increase." We can call this definition "natural increase A."

A second framework for analyzing medical expenditures was implicitly used by critics of high health-care spending in the late 1970s. They divided expenditure increases into just two parts: increases attributable to fee-schedule revisions and increases caused by everything else, including population growth and aging as

**Table 2. Factors contributing to medical expenditure growth, 1980–90 (%)**

| Year | Spending Growth | Population Growth | Population Aging | Fee Sched. Revision | Other |
|------|------|------|------|------|------|
| 1978 | 16.8 | 0.9 | 1.0 | 8.1 | 6.0 |
| 1979 | 9.5 | 0.8 | 1.0 | 0.0 | 7.6 |
| 1980 | 9.4 | 0.8 | 1.0 | 0.0 | 7.5 |
| 1981 | 7.4 | 0.7 | 1.0 | 1.2 | 4.3 |
| 1982 | 7.7 | 0.7 | 1.2 | -0.1 | 5.8 |
| 1983 | 4.9 | 0.7 | 1.1 | -0.1 | 4.2 |
| 1984 | 3.8 | 0.6 | 1.2 | -2.0 | 4.0 |
| 1985 | 6.1 | 0.7 | 1.4 | 1.1 | 2.8 |
| 1986 | 6.6 | 0.5 | 1.3 | 0.7 | 4.0 |
| 1987 | 5.9 | 0.5 | 1.4 | 0.0 | 3.9 |
| 1988 | 3.8 | 0.4 | 1.3 | 0.5 | 1.6 |
| 1989 | 5.2 | 0.4 | 1.3 | 0.8 | 2.7 |
| 1990 | 4.5 | 0.3 | 1.6 | 1.0 | 1.5 |

Source: Ministry of Health and Welfare, Research Division, Insurance
    Bureau, unpublished data.

well as "intensity" growth. This everything else can be called "natural increase B," the broadest definition.

For our purposes, however, a third analytic framework is more helpful. Here, the increase in medical expenditure is equal to the population increase times the increase in medical expenditure per capita. Medical expenditure per capita, in turn, is equal to cases per capita, times the number of days of treatment per case, times medical expenditure per day. Finally, the increase in medical expenditure per day can be broken down into the increase due to price hikes (that is, the fee-schedule revision) plus "other." This "other," which amounts to quantity or "intensity" of care, is the change in medical expenditure independent of insurance fee-schedule revisions. It is the most narrow definition of "natural increase" and can be called "natural increase C."

**Components of Growth**

The logic of "natural increase C" will be analyzed shortly, but we should first note the contribution of "cases per capita" or usage to the growth of medical care cost. The propensity of people to use medical care reached a high point near 1970 and has fluctuated near that level ever since (although there has been a shift in out-

**Table 3. Usage per 100,000 population by age group**

|  | Inpatient | | | | Outpatient | | | |
|---|---|---|---|---|---|---|---|---|
|  | 1965 | 1975 | 1987 | 1990 | 1965 | 1975 | 1987 | 1990 |
| Total | 828 | 928 | 1,174 | 1,214 | 5,082 | 6,121 | 5,426 | 5,554 |
| 25–34 | 1,046 | 811 | 650 | 593 | 4,952 | 4,375 | 3,522 | 3,409 |
| 35–44 | 1,068 | 931 | 776 | 738 | 5,401 | 5,404 | 3,762 | 3,721 |
| 45–54 | 1,213 | 1,199 | 1,204 | 1,140 | 5,803 | 6,943 | 5,602 | 5,480 |
| 55–64 | 1,491 | 1,564 | 1,753 | 1,761 | 6,467 | 8,770 | 8,271 | 8,435 |
| 65+ | 2,142 | 2,990 | 4,607 | 4,652 | 8,978 | 13,761 | 13,497 | 13,568 |

Note: The figures that appear in the 1965 columns for the "65+" age group
   are 1970 figures.
Source: Ministry of Health and Welfare, "Kanja chōsa" (Patient study) (Tokyo: Kōsei
   Tōkei Kyōkai, 1967, 1977, 1989, 1992).

patient care from clinics to hospitals). In particular, usage by persons under age fifty has fallen since the 1960s (table 3).

At the macro level, this drop was offset in the 1970s by increased usage per capita by the elderly (as well as by the aging of the population). The introduction of free health care for the elderly in the early 1970s caused a rapid increase in usage by this age group. Yet, since the late 1970s the propensity of the elderly to use outpatient care has barely increased. It is true that rapid growth in inpatient care, including "social hospitalization," which is similar to nursing home care, did occur. However, it appears that "cases per capita" or the usage ratio among the elderly, even including inpatient care, has now reached its upper limits.

That means that growth in the aggregate per capita usage depends almost entirely on the aging of the population. If the trend toward a decreasing usage ratio among young and middle-aged people continues, even this upward pressure will be counterbalanced to some extent.

What about "days per case," or length of treatment (number of days in the hospital, or number of outpatient visits, for a given illness)? Table 4 gives an indication of these trends for employees (not their dependents) enrolled in Government-Managed Health Insurance. We can see that treatment time has steadily decreased, particularly for inpatient care. Japanese still go into the hospital for long periods compared with Americans but the time has been getting shorter.

That means, as table 4 clearly indicates, that "expenditures per day" has been the major contributor to the growth in overall medical expenditures. However, its growth rate has slowed significantly since the late 1970s. As noted above, "expen-

**Table 4. Trends in the three elements of medical expenditure
(Annual percentage growth for employees in
Government-Managed Health Insurance)**

|  | Cases per capita | Days per case | Med. expend. per day | Med. expend. per capita |
|---|---|---|---|---|
| **Inpatient** | | | | |
| 1960–64 | 23.02 | -10.43 | 133.48 | 157.07 |
| 1965–69 | 5.72 | -3.65 | 66.58 | 69.82 |
| 1970–74 | 5.06 | -11.25 | 81.42 | 69.07 |
| 1975–79 | 1.11 | -7.63 | 52.52 | 42.49 |
| 1980–84 | -3.44 | -11.64 | 8.41 | -7.53 |
| 1985–90 | 4.14 | -9.51 | 22.19 | 15.33 |
| **Outpatient** | | | | |
| 1960–64 | 1.97 | -2.68 | 76.79 | 75.48 |
| 1965–69 | -3.43 | -0.16 | 49.55 | 44.2 |
| 1970–74 | -12.22 | -1.95 | 124.5 | 93.27 |
| 1975–79 | -4.3 | -1.95 | 124.5 | 93.27 |
| 1980–84 | -6.3 | -6.37 | 12.62 | -1.17 |
| 1985–90 | -4.18 | -6.37 | 16.04 | 4.1 |

Note: Data drawn from the survey of claims filed by providers. These are
on a monthly basis so that, for outpatient care, a single case including
five visits in a two-month period would be shown as two claims of, e.g.,
two days and three days. However, days for inpatient care are
drawn from the "Kanja chōsa" (Patients survey), as in table 3.
Source: MHW, "Seikan kenpo jigyō nenpō" (Tokyo: Kōsei Tōkei Kyōkai,
various years).

ditures per day" has two components: price hikes, as determined in fee-schedule
revisions, and increases in intensity or the "natural increase C."

In the late 1960s and early 1970s "natural increase C" grew over 10%
annually (see table 5). The growth rate fell to the 5–10% range in the late 1970s
and has been below 5% since the beginning of the 1980s. Table 6 illustrates the
components of the natural increase in different periods. During the 1960s and
1970s prescription drugs fueled medical expenditure increases, but their impact
dropped precipitously after price controls were implemented. Diagnostic testing
became the new engine for medical expenditure in the late 1970s. Technological
innovation, centered around diagnostic equipment such as automatic blood
chemistry analyzers and CAT scanners, enabled new testing, necessary or not.
However, due to a slowdown in technological innovation as well as the introduc-

**Table 5. Annual growth of "natural increase C"**
**(two-year averages)**

| Year | Growth (%) | Year | Growth (%) |
|------|------------|------|------------|
| 1967–68 | 11.3 | 1979–80 | 7.8 |
| 1969–70 | 13.6 | 1981–82 | 3.8 |
| 1971–72 | 8.4 | 1983–84 | 3.1 |
| 1973–74 | 4.4 | 1985–86 | 2.4 |
| 1975–76 | 12.4 | 1987–88 | 3.0 |
| 1977–78 | 6.7 | | |

Source: See table 4.

**Table 6. Percentage contribution by medical treatment pattern to medical**
**expenditures per case**

| | 1960–65 | 1965–70 | 1970–75 | 1975–80 | 1980–85 | 1985–90 |
|---|---------|---------|---------|---------|---------|---------|
| Consultation | 8.4 | 13.5 | 28.6 | 8.1 | 33.4 | 12.7 |
| Home care | | | | | | 8.4 |
| Medication | 49.8 | 42.6 | 25.7 | 25.6 | -25.5 | 30.0 |
| Injection | 19.0 | 13.9 | 3.2 | 16.6 | -11.1 | -4.9 |
| Physiotherapy | 0.1 | 0.5 | 0.9 | 1.1 | 6.6 | -2.7 |
| Psychiatric treatment | 0.7 | 0.4 | -0.3 | 0.2 | 1.1 | 0.3 |
| Diagnostic imaging | 4.5 | 6.7 | 0.4 | 5.2 | 7.0 | 8.9 |
| Diagnostic testing | 4.6 | 10.6 | 9.5 | 15.7 | 19.7 | 12.8 |
| Treatment | 1.5 | 0.2 | 3.6 | 2.7 | 4.0 | 13.4 |
| Surgery | 0.3 | 1.3 | 4.3 | 5.4 | 10.3 | -5.8 |
| Anesthesia | – | 1.4 | 0.3 | 0.6 | 0.9 | 2.9 |
| Radiation therapy | – | – | – | – | 0.4 | 0.3 |
| Hospitalization | 10.7 | 8.6 | 23.6 | 18.3 | 50.7 | 22.2 |
| Others | 0.4 | 0.3 | 0.2 | 0.5 | 2.5 | 1.6 |

Source: MHW, "Shakai iryō shinryō kōi betsu chōsa" (Report of social insurance medical care according to procedure) (Tokyo: Kōsei Tōkei Kyōkai, 1961–91).

tion of cost containment policies, the percent of the contribution of diagnostic testing to overall medical expenditure growth has been small in recent years.

Immediately after World War II, streptomycin and other antibiotics were developed. This type of technology (what Lewis Thomas called "genuine technology") focused on understanding the structure of diseases in order to eliminate them. The process reduced costs; technology was cost reducing. (For example, tuberculosis was nearly eliminated by the development of antibiotics. In 1955 over one-quarter of medical expenditures were related to tuberculosis. Today, tuberculosis accounts for only about 1% of overall medical expenditures.) The second postwar period of technological innovation focused on developing diagnostic equipment. This technology ("half-way technology") was cost inducing.[1] In the future a new era of innovation (for example, biotechnology) may once again help to eliminate disease and thereby reduce medical expenditure, but this remains to be seen.

In essence, the natural increase had been driven by medical technological innovation, and one reason for its slowing in recent years is the lack of cost-inducing technological innovation on the scale of the earlier developments in diagnostic testing. Since major cost-inducing medical technology is not expected, rapid growth in medical expenditures caused by the natural increase is unlikely.

### The Fee Schedule: Macro Decisions

How is the natural increase taken into account in revising the fee schedule? The fee schedule itself is the table of points assigned to each medical procedure; it is established legally by a proclamation of the Minister of Welfare under the Health Insurance Law. An advisory committee called the Central Social Insurance Medical Care Council (Chūikyō) must be consulted; it represents providers and insurers (including the government) and is the formal site for the negotiations between the Ministry of Health and Welfare (MHW) and the Japan Medical Association (JMA), which usually dominate the fee-schedule revision process. The process can be divided roughly into two levels: decisions about how much to increase the fee schedule as a whole, and decisions about the fee for each item.

The first level is more political and economic and is related directly to the process of budgeting for the entire government (the final decision is made at the time of budgetary allocations in December). The main actors are the MHW, the Ministry of Finance (MOF), the JMA, the insurers, and a few politicians. The decision was extremely contentious until a new indexing formula was put in place in 1973; it was the built-in inflation of the indexing system that led to major reform in 1981.

The stage was set when Tarō Takemi, the charismatic chairman of the JMA, took office in 1957, and the present structure of the fee schedule was instituted in 1958. The Central Council soon became an arena for debate over fee-schedule increases. The confrontation was full of drama: threats to quit by all Central Council members, demands for the chairman's resignation, and even physicians' strikes. Often enough the JMA used its political clout to draw the leadership of the ruling Liberal Democratic Party into the conflict to force higher fee increases.

This conflict came to a head in 1971, when the JMA, angered by a demand for rationalization of the fee-schedule system put forward by several members of the Central Council, called for "the resignation of all designated insurance physicians"—a doctors' strike. The threat was not averted until a summit meeting of Prime Minister Satō, the Minister of Health and Welfare, and Chairman Takemi, and indeed conflict continued for another year until the JMA's demand for indexing was granted in 1973.

For some time, the physicians had argued that the fee schedule should "slide" with increases in prices and wages. From their point of view, this procedure would ensure regular and large increases in fees that could be justified on a more "scientific" basis. Under the system adopted in the 1974, 1976, and 1978 revisions, the costs of hospitals and clinics were classified into four categories: (1) the salary of physicians, (2) the salary of medical employees excluding physicians, (3) nonpersonnel costs (except for the cost of medication), and (4) the cost of medication. Cost estimates for each category were adjusted respectively in line with (1) GNP per capita, (2) average wages of employees, (3) the consumer price index, and (4) the market price of medication.

The assumption here is that increases in the income of doctors and hospitals (and therefore in national medical expenditure) are caused solely by the increases in the fee schedule. This premise, coupled with the notion that the main purpose of the fee schedule is to stabilize the financial condition of health care management, made it logical to institute indexing, in which all cost increases since the previous revision are compensated for by increasing the fee schedule.

However, in actuality, the income of medical institutions increases because of various reasons that are independent of the fee-schedule revision, such as an increase of the entire population, an increase of the aged population, or advances in medical technology leading to higher intensity of treatment. These really constitute "natural increase B" as explained above. When the fee-schedule increase is added on top of the natural increase, costs rise quite rapidly (see table 7).

In 1978–81, there was a clear demonstration that the underlying assumptions of indexing were incorrect. The income of medical institutions (as well as the income of medical workers including physicians) increased dramatically from February 1978 to June 1981, even though there was no fee-schedule revision in this period. It was this realization, together with increasing pressure from the MOF to cut costs, that led to the reform of 1981.

In 1981 and thereafter, "natural increase B" has in effect been deducted from the increase that would seem to be necessary in the light of wage or price trends. The underlying logic is that doctors and hospitals should be able to maintain their real income. The fee-schedule hike should therefore cover only the portion of their increased costs that are not offset by higher incomes. The underlying logic here is that if their income (in the aggregate) goes up because they are serving more patients (for example, due to population growth or population aging) or because they are giving better services (higher quantity or quality), then they will not need as much in the way of fee increases.

This process is certainly not scientific. In fact, the MHW has not published its formula for calculating the overall fee increase since abandoning indexing in 1981. The real process is more one of political negotiation than arithmetic, and in the political climate of the 1980s it has been possible for the government side to prevail and keep costs down.

**Table 7. Fee-schedule revision based on price/wage slide procedure (%)**

|      |          | Revision rate | | |
|------|----------|---------|--------|----------------|
|      |          | Medical | Dental | Pharmaceutical |
| 1974 | February | 19.0    | 19.0   | 8.5            |
|      | October  | 16.0    | 16.2   | 6.6            |
| 1976 | April    | 9.0     | –      | 4.9            |
|      | August   | –       | 9.6    | –              |
| 1978 | February | 11.5    | 12.7   | 5.6            |

Source: MHW, "Hoken to nenkin no dōkō" (Trend of health insurance and pension) (Tokyo: Kōsei Tōkei Kyōkai, 1991), p. 6.

There is some similarity between indexing in Japan and the implementation of a fee schedule based on the Resource Based Relative Value Scale in Medicare part B in the United States. That is, both adopted an objective and neutral approach for calculation in order to avoid political controversies concerning revision. Usually in such cases, however, revisions may well lead to a temporary boost of medical costs because the calculation tends to ratify current cost trends. This is precisely what happened in Japan with the slide. In fact, the idea that the income of medical institutions (or national medical expenditures) can be dealt with by subtracting the amount of "natural increase" in deciding the overall increase may be applicable to the United States as well.

**The Fee Schedule: Micro Decisions**

After the overall percentage increase is determined at the end of the year, a different process determines how the points should be distributed within this framework. Based on data about frequencies of each procedure given by the "Shakai iryō shinryō kōi betsu chōsa" (Report of social insurance medical care according to procedure) that is carried out every year, an "impact table" is constructed. That table shows the increase in total medical costs that would result from a one-point increase in a given procedure. It is used to make adjustments so that the total increase in points will match the overall growth rate decided in the first stage. Since the second stage focuses more on technical matters, the main actors are just officials of the MHW (mainly from the Health Insurance Bureau's Medical Section) and the JMA.

The two stages of fee-schedule revision correspond to an economic distinction between the overall finances of the medical care system and the "relative value" of medical skills. Because Japan has universal health insurance in which nearly all the income of medical institutions comes from the public insurance system, the first stage functions to "appropriately compensate medical practice management as a whole" and to "permit the appropriate health care management by adjusting medical costs to compensate for the rise in prices and wages" (the expressions used in legislative debates). The second stage is in principle a matter of evaluating the skills involved as "relative values."

These two dimensions could be handled separately, by raising the money value of each point based on the growth of prices and wages, and then adjusting the level of points (or "relative value") per procedure. In fact, the procedure that was instituted in Medicare part B in the United States is precisely this formula: revision of the conversion factor for the former, and revision of the Relative Value Scale for the latter. However, as the value of a single point has been fixed at ¥10 since 1958 in Japan's fee schedule, both dimensions are handled by reevaluation of the points of individual items; that is, responses to wage-price hikes and skills evaluations are carried out at the same time.

In a sense, this is a shrewd approach. The impact of wage-price increases is not transferred directly into the value of each point but is combined with reevaluations of skills plus government policy initiatives. As a result, even when the amount of the overall fee-schedule revision is decided at a given percentage increase, it is not clear how the "impact table" will be affected by changes in treatment patterns. Moreover, because the new point allocation must be based on a forecast of future treatment patterns, it is problematical whether it will actually result in the given overall increase. The resulting ambiguity is useful politically, since it tends to diffuse conflict.

In any case, it is clear that there are no set rules for deciding the number of points for a given procedure. The usual elements are evaluation of skill, or extent of difficulty; achievement of certain policy goals; and compensation for costs. Evaluation of skill is similar to the way fees are determined in other nations, and in fact allows the insertion of governmental policy goals into the process. For example, the fee-schedule revision of April 1992 included such policy-based allocations as an increase for inpatient nursing service and a differentiation in payment for initial examinations to encourage patients to go to clinics rather than hospitals. However, using fee-setting to respond to technological change is more distinctive to Japan. That is, particularly in the 1980s, officials of the MHW have been able to adjust the fees of individual items to discourage overuse. This has been an important measure in keeping providers from compensating for limitations on price by increasing quantity. Some detailed examples will be needed to illustrate this technique.

### Controlling the Impact of Technology via Price

Pharmaceuticals, identified as "over-prescribed drugs" throughout the 1970s, and medical tests, such as the blood biochemical auto analyzer, became the major cause of cost increases from the late 1970s into the 1980s. But the "natural increase" controls instituted in the 1981 revision of the fee schedule actually worked to control overuse.[2]

**Table 8. Average points per case by procedure**

| | Average points per case | | | Increase rate (%) | |
|---|---|---|---|---|---|
| | 1978 | 1981 | 1982 | 81/78 | 82/81 |
| Examination | 220.5 | 200.3 | 239.2 | -9.2 | 19.4 |
| Drug administration | 364.8 | 432.2 | 385.3 | 18.5 | -10.9 |
| Injection | 160.9 | 193.2 | 176.6 | 20.1 | -8.6 |
| Physical therapy | 11.8 | 13.2 | 23.8 | 11.9 | 80.3 |
| Psychiatric therapy | 1.6 | 1.6 | 2.7 | 0.0 | 68.8 |
| X-ray diagnosis | 44.1 | 52.8 | 51.7 | 19.7 | -2.1 |
| Medical tests | 120.7 | 166.1 | 173.9 | 37.6 | 4.7 |
| Treatment | 40.1 | 42.4 | 39 | 5.7 | -8.0 |
| Operation | 77.5 | 60.3 | 67.2 | -22.2 | 11.4 |
| Anesthesia | 7.0 | 6.7 | 8.1 | -4.3 | 20.9 |
| Inpatient | 275 | 265.8 | 302.6 | -3.3 | 13.8 |
| Others | 2.4 | 7.3 | 8.4 | 204.2 | 15.1 |
| Total number | 1,326.80 | 1,441.80 | 1,478.90 | 8.7 | 2.6 |

Source: Same as table 6.

As there were no revisions of the fee schedule between 1978 and 1981, the "natural increase" applied to specific procedures independently of any revisions. More accurately, this refers to the Q dimension (quantity—volume or intensity) of an increase in "medical cost per case" that is not simply a product of price P, and that is independent of fee revision. It was the 1981 revision of the fee schedule that first tried to control "natural increase" by means of point-system reform. Therefore, by comparing the data of the "Shakai iryō shinryō kōi betsu chōsa" of 1978, 1981, and 1982, the impact of the revision, including how it contributed to control of the "natural increase," can be determined.[3]

Table 8 displays the average points per case broken down by procedure across this period. Since one point equals ¥10, the average case in 1978 cost ¥13,268 (about $50 at the contemporary purchasing power parity of $1 = ¥277), of which ¥2,205 went for examinations, ¥3,648 for dispensed pharmaceuticals, and ¥1,609 for injected pharmaceuticals. Tests, injections and drug administration (including medication costs), and X-ray diagnosis had the highest growth between 1978 and 1981. They were central components of the "natural increase" in this period. However, by bundling multiple tests and reducing the drug tariff based on market prices, their costs were reduced in the 1981 revision.

It is interesting, however, that when broken down from points per case into instances per case and points per instance, drugs and tests show a contrasting

**Table 9. Average points for pharmaceutical tests (1978–81)**

| | Prescriptions | | | Injections | | | Medical tests | | |
|---|---|---|---|---|---|---|---|---|---|
| | 1978 | 1981 | % increase | 1978 | 1981 | % increase | 1978 | 1981 | % increase |
| Points per case | 364.80 | 432.20 | 18.5 | 160.90 | 199.50 | 24.0 | 120.70 | 166.10 | 37.6 |
| Instances per case | 17.00 | 17.40 | 2.4 | 1.95 | 1.73 | -11.0 | 2.73 | 3.45 | 26.4 |
| Points per instance | 21.40 | 24.90 | 16.4 | 82.70 | 115.20 | 39.2 | 44.10 | 48.20 | 9.3 |
| Pharmaceutical cost | 19.80 | 23.40 | 18.2 | 59.90 | 86.60 | 44.6 | – | – | – |

Source: See table 6.

pattern (table 9). For medications, what increases is points per instance. It is not an increase in the number of times that a physician dispensed or injected medication but an increase in spending each time that increases medical costs. This results from a shift both in the P dimension to more expensive new medication, and in the Q dimension toward more drugs. The latter led to a controversy over excessive drug usage.

For medical tests what increases the points per case is not points per instance but instances per case—an increase in the frequency of tests. Underlying this trend was a technological development in diagnostic procedures called "testing automation." For example, according to the "Iryō shisetsu chōsa" (Medical facilities survey), the number of hospitals with a biochemical analyzer that had more than twelve channels increased nearly threefold, from 604 in 1978 to 1,763 in 1981.

Looking first at medications, the main cause of the cost increases was the drug cost gap between the official drug tariff that providers receive from social insurance and the market price that providers actually pay to pharmaceutical companies or their agents. This stimulates shifting to high-profit medications where the gap is widest. Countering this behavior requires an investigation of market prices, leading to reductions in the official tariff on a medication-by-medication basis. In the 1981 fee-schedule revision, the drug tariff was reduced by a weighted average of 18.6%, an unprecedented amount. As a result, the rapid growth of dispensing and injection points per instance was replaced by minus growth between 1981 and 1982, as shown on table 10.

The change in the share of medication costs to total medical costs is shown on table 11. Medication costs that once occupied almost half of all medical costs have now stabilized at approximately 30%. Most noteworthy is a significant reduction from 38.7% to 30.9% between 1981 and 1984. The two fee-schedule revisions of June 1981 and March 1984 played a significant role in this reduction by decreasing the drug tariff.

Such controls can also be applied to individual items. For example, among injections, intravenous drip increased sharply from 1978 to 1981 (its share of injections among hospitalized patients rose from 29.4% to 35.9%). Much of this excessive use of intravenous drip was to save labor. Prior to the 1981 revision, the fee schedule for injections was set by the following rules: for a one-time injection over 100 cc, 35 points; when it exceeds 500 cc, 25 points additional for each 500 cc, plus 15 points when intravenous. However, with the 1981 revision, when the quantity given in one day exceeds 550 cc, only 75 points are added. As a result of this new regulation, the share of intravenous drip injections decreased dramatically, from 12.9% in 1981 to 5.1% in 1982.

Table 12 shows total points for all medical tests and the various categories in 1978 and 1981; for example, in 1978, Japan spent about ¥7.3 billion (about $26 million at contemporary PPP) on blood testing. There was a rapid increase in costs, 48.7%, from 1978 to 1981. Since there was no revision of the fee schedule (P), this increase was definitely a "natural increase" (Q). By categories of tests, the biggest increases occurred in blood tests, immunology tests, physiological exam-

**Table 10. Average points for dispensed medication and injections**

|  | 1978 | 1981 | 1982 | 81/78 | 82/81 |
|---|---|---|---|---|---|
| Dispensed medication |  |  |  |  |  |
| Points per case | 364.80 | 432.20 | 385.30 | 18.5 | -10.9 |
| Instances per case | 17.00 | 17.40 | 17.10 | 2.4 | -1.7 |
| Points per instance | 21.40 | 25.90 | 22.50 | 16.4 | -9.6 |
| Drugs per instance | 19.80 | 23.40 | 21.10 | 18.2 | -9.8 |
| Injections |  |  |  |  |  |
| Points per case | 160.90 | 193.20 | 176.60 | 20.1 | -8.6 |
| Instances per case | 1.95 | 1.73 | 1.61 | -11.3 | -6.9 |
| Points per instance | 82.70 | 111.60 | 110.00 | 34.9 | -1.4 |
| Drugs per instance | 59.90 | 86.60 | 89.10 | 44.6 | 2.9 |
| Drugs per case | – | 150.00 | 143.10 | – | -4.6 |

Source: See table 6.

**Table 11. Tests and medication
spending as a share of total
spending per case**

|  | Medical tests | Medication |
|---|---|---|
| 1960 | 2.7 | – |
| 1965 | 3.8 | – |
| 1970 | 6.6 | 45.8 * |
| 1975 | 8.0 | 37.8 |
| 1980 | 11.0 | 38.2 |
| 1981 | 11.5 | 38.7 |
| 1982 | 11.8 | 34.1 |
| 1983 | 12.5 | 35.1 |
| 1984 | 12.6 | 30.9 |
| 1985 | 12.2 | 29.1 |
| 1986 | 11.6 | 28.2 |
| 1987 | 12.4 | 29.6 |
| 1988 | 12.1 | 29.9 |
| 1989 | 12.0 | 30.8 |
| 1990 | 12.2 | 28.2 |

* 1971 figure.
Source: See table 6.

**Table 12. Total points for medical test categories**

| | Test points (1,000 points) | | | Contribution rate |
|---|---|---|---|---|
| | 1978 | 1981 | % increase | of increase (%) |
| Urine test | 75,185 | 102,410 | 36.2 | 3.50 |
| Stool test | 2,596 | 2,806 | 8.1 | 0.02 |
| Blood test | 727,162 | 1,115,726 | 53.4 | 49.90 |
| Fluid test | 1,423 | 1,197 | -15.9 | -0.03 |
| Virus test | 68,353 | 79,456 | 16.2 | 1.40 |
| Immunology related test | 81,483 | 121,785 | 49.5 | 5.20 |
| Physiological exam | 478,098 | 724,983 | 51.6 | 31.70 |
| Diagnostic function | 3,552 | 5,481 | 54.3 | 0.20 |
| Pathological exam | 48,733 | 58,369 | 19.8 | 1.20 |
| Endoscopic test | 30,668 | 49,802 | 62.4 | 2.50 |
| Total number | 1,596,849 | 2,375,138 | 48.7 | 100.00 |

Source: See table 6.

inations, diagnostic functions, and endoscopic tests. However, in terms of impact on total test spending, blood tests and physiological examinations, which occupied almost 80% of total test expenditure, exceeded all the rest.

Blood tests can be separated into "biochemical tests" and "other blood tests," and further divided into subitems. The categories that allow numerous tests simultaneously by use of a blood autoanalyzer increased sharply from 1978 to 1981. In other words, since there was no adjustment in the fee schedule to deal with technological development in diagnostic procedures, the instances of tests grew very rapidly, leading to a strong "natural increase." Similarly, for physiological examinations, the instances and cost of radioisotope tests increased sharply compared with a decrease in the relative frequency of eye examinations. This too resulted from the automation of tests.

To respond to the "natural increase" that resulted from these increased instances caused by technological improvement, the 1981 revision introduced "bundling" (*marume*). For example, prior to the revision every test item was reimbursed for blood chemistry tests, but after the 1981 revision, test items were bundled together above six items. Urine tests using test paper were given an inclusive fee regardless of how many chemicals were performed.

The effects of this revision is shown clearly in table 13; which indicates a significant reduction in test frequencies. For all tests, the number of tests per case decreased by more than 40%. As a result, the growth rate of points per case was reduced. Moreover, when individual types are considered (table 14), there is a

**Table 13. Trend of all tests (1978, 1981, 1982)**

|  | 1978 | 1981 | 1982 | Growth rate (%) 1978–81 | 1981–82 |
|---|---|---|---|---|---|
| Points per case | 120.70 | 166.10 | 173.90 | 37.6 | 4.7 |
| Instances per case | 2.73 | 3.45 | 1.97 | 26.4 | -42.9 |
| Points per test | 44.10 | 48.20 | 88.10 | 9.3 | 82.8 |

Source: See table 6.

**Table 14. Trend of tests by type of test**
**(The growth rate of instances and points)**

|  | Frequency | | Points | |
|---|---|---|---|---|
|  | 1978–81 | 1981–82 | 1978–81 | 1981–82 |
| Urine test | 36.3 | -53.0 | 36.2 | 22.8 |
| Stool test | 10.9 | -2.0 | 8.1 | 44.4 |
| Blood test | 47.2 | -59.3 | 53.4 | 9.2 |
| Fluid test | -6.8 | -16.7 | -15.9 | 31.4 |
| Virus test | 11.8 | -5.2 | 16.2 | 36.0 |
| Immunology related test | 46.9 | 9.8 | 49.5 | 39.0 |
| Physiological exam | 21.3 | 5.5 | 51.6 | -4.6 |
| Diagnostic function | 23.7 | 64.1 | 54.3 | 93.6 |
| Pathological test | 25.4 | -11.3 | 19.8 | 1.2 |
| Endoscopic test | 47.6 | 17.7 | 62.4 | 18.2 |

Source: See table 6.

marked reduction of frequency and point growth for blood tests, physiological examinations, and urine tests—key targets in the 1981 revision.

The 1981 fee-schedule revision therefore achieved the goal of "natural increase" control by point reformation. After 1981, as we have seen, testing costs were no longer a primary cause of medical cost increases. The 1981 revision thus marked the beginning of a new strategy of restraining quantity itself through price policy.

## Current Cost Concerns

Of course, solving one set of problems leads to other problems. The main cause of medical cost increases in recent years has been hospitalization (nursing, room and board, and medical oversights), rather than medications and medical tests (see table 6). Hospitalization costs pertain to manpower and capital costs and not so much to skill, technological change, or doctors' fees, so they are different from the drug and testing expenditures treated above. Doctors and hospitals cannot easily manipulate the quantity of physical capital and manpower, and when their quantity increases, the increase is not compensated by an increase in income so long as the fee schedule for such items is not increased.

That is, since increased manpower or capital spending cannot show up in the "natural increase" as defined above, it must be taken care of through fee-schedule revisions. For that reason, we can expect that fee-schedule revisions will account for a larger portion of the increase in overall health expenditures in the future. It appears that from now on, increases in health care spending in Japan will be driven mainly by increased manpower and capital costs.

The fee schedule revision of April 1992 had the goals of adequate pricing based on the quality of medical services and pricing based on functions of medical institutions. New methods such as setting medical oversight costs based on the number of physicians per bed and setting room costs based on room size were implemented. This was a substantial revision that provided a new direction to fee-schedule policy. With respect to labor and capital costs, the issue is now how to determine prices compatible with two policies: pricing in accord with input costs or quality and the redistribution of medical expenditure across medical institutions.

**Conclusions**

The fee-schedule policy in Japan since the revision of 1981 was successful in restraining medical spending both in terms of P (price) and Q (volume and intensity):

1. With respect to P, the price level of medical care as a whole was restrained by eliminating price/wage indexing and by adopting a new assessment procedure. Under the new system, income increases that result from factors other than changes in price—that is, the "natural increase"—are deducted from the increase of costs borne by medical institutions.
2. As for Q, increases in the frequency of medical practices (medical tests and medication, etc.) generated by technological improvement, and the "natural increase" in costs that followed, were controlled by reallocating points on the fee schedule.

In a sense, the second policy amounts to control of the "natural increase" itself and hence is a preventive policy, whereas the first can be described as an after-the-fact reactive policy that makes adjustments to prices after natural increases have occurred.

In the larger context of medical policy, the following points should be noted. Ultimately, medical cost amounts to medical expenses per case times the number of cases. Japanese cost-containment policy from the early 1980s regulated medical expenses per case through fee-schedule modifications. As briefly noted above, Japan tried to constrain the number of cases by increasing patient copayments (1984) and tried to reduce the growth of demand via restrictions on the supply of beds (1985).

Such measures cannot explain the slowdown of the rate of increase of Japanese medical costs in the 1980s. Bed supply planning had no effect until 1990 (in 1986–88, beds actually increased as hospitals rushed to beat the restrictions). Moreover, the usage rate for the population under sixty-five years old, and the outpatient usage rate even for the elderly, had actually levelled off before the increased copayments aimed at limiting usage.

To make a more general point, when basic access is provided through universal health insurance, usage will naturally level off after a certain period of time. It is rare for usage rates to change dramatically unless a radical change in policy occurs, so small changes in copayments will not cause large transformations in medical costs as a whole. Therefore, what causes fluctuations in medical costs is not the number of cases, but the medical costs per case. In Japan, the control of medical costs per case, in terms of both P and Q through fee-schedule adjustments, contributed significantly to the slow-down of the rate of increase in Japanese medical costs.

NOTES

1. For a historical account of postwar technological change in medicine, see Takeshi 1986.
2. For the descriptions of this case study, I consulted Gendai Iryō Keizai Kenkyūkai 1984.
3. The "Shakai iryō shinryō kōi betsu chōsa" (Report of social insurance medical care according to procedure) is based on evaluations of the fee-schedule receipts of June of every year. The statistics used are those of May. During the times in question, the revision occurred in February of 1978 and June of 1981. Therefore, the data for these three years (1978–81) are not influenced by any revisions.

REFERENCES

Gendai Iryō Keizai Kenkyūkai. 1983. Hoken iryō no dōkō to iryōhi tekiseika (Trends in health care under social insurance and rationalization of health care costs). *Shakai hoken kuhō* 1441–42.
———. 1984. 56-nen 6-gatsu shinryō hōshū kaitei no imi suru mono (The meaning of the June 1981 fee-schedule revision). *Shakai hoken kuhō* 1474–79.
Office of National Cost Estimates. 1990. National health expenditures, 1988. *Health Care Financing Review* 11.4 (Summer): 6.
Ministry of Health and Welfare (MHW). 1961–91. Shakai iryō shinryō kōi betsu chōsa

(Report of social insurance medical care according to procedure). Tokyo: Kōsei Tōkei Kyōkai.

Schieber, George J., Jean-Pierre Pouillier, and Leslie M. Greewald. 1992. U.S. health expenditure performance: An international comparison and data update. *Health Care Financing Review* 13.4: 1–87.

Kawakami, T. 1986. *Gijtsu shinpo to iryōhi* (Technology advancement and health care costs). Tokyo: Keisō Shobō.

CHAPTER 6

# Comparison of Capital Costs in Health Care between Japan and the United States

*Kōichi Kawabuchi*

SUMMARY   Japanese and U.S. health care costs were compared from the view-point of capital costs. The following were the main findings.

- Construction costs for health care facilities in Japan were less than 40% that of the United States, and on a per-bed basis, about 25%.
- For public hospitals, the hospitals' average age was about eight years for both the United States and Japan.
- The tangible fixed assets per bed for the United States is twice that of Japan (1989), but the real difference is greater because land constitutes a much higher ratio in Japan.
- The percentage of capital-related costs to operating expenses is only slightly higher in Japan than in the United States.
- Total floor space per bed for both general and psychiatric hospitals in the United States is four times that of Japanese hospitals.
- When the bed and board charges are compared, U.S. hospitals charge approximately five times that of Japanese hospitals.

This study is divided into two sections. The first looks at the details of construction costs in the United States and Japan from the macroeconomic viewpoint. The second compares and analyzes costs from the microeconomic viewpoint. Specifically, the following elements are compared between the two countries: average age of plant, tangible fixed assets per bed, ratios of capital-related costs to the operating expenses, total floor space per bed, and charges for single and double rooms.

## Macroeconomic Analysis of Capital Costs

Health care costs in the United States that are categorized as "construction" amounted to $10.4 billion in 1990. When the figures for 1980 and 1990 are compared, there has been a 1.8-fold increase in ten years, and the increase in the private sector is greater. Construction costs consist of costs for new construction, additions, and renovation of health care facilities, mechanical and electrical installations, and site preparation. However, maintenance and repair expenses for tangible fixed assets or furnishings and durable equipment such as X-rays and beds are not included. Health care facilities are defined as hospitals, nursing homes, long-term-care facilities, orphanages, and clinics run by medical practitioners. However, when a clinic run by a medical practitioner is located in a commercial building, its proportional division is ambiguous and is therefore excluded here.

The value of new construction includes the cost of materials and labor, contractor profit, the cost of architectural and engineering work, those overhead and administrative costs chargeable to the project that are on the owner's books, and interest and taxes paid during construction. It should be noted here that the construction costs listed under health care costs in the United States are computed based on the "stock concept," not the "flow concept."[1]

In contrast to the United States, Japan follows flow concept for construction costs. The annual expenditures for health care facility construction in Japan are estimated from the "Annual Report on Construction Statistics" published by the Construction Price Survey Foundation (1990). The health care facilities here are limited to hospitals and clinics, and the items listed are building expenditures for new construction and additions and renovation of buildings and facilities designated for health services. These expenditures do not include the cost of purchasing medical equipment or land used for these facilities nor the expenses for the maintenance or repair of these buildings. For this reason, it generally matches the definition of "construction" in the United States. The total number of buildings listed for 1990 is 3,106; the total projected construction costs amount to approximately ¥756.7 billion. If the figure for 1970 is expressed as 100, the figures have increased to 576 and 690, respectively, for 1980 and 1990. In other words, the ten-year growth during the 1970s was far greater than that in the 1980s.

The highest unit construction cost per square meter is ¥355,000 for medical facilities owned by prefectural governments, while the lowest is for the private sector (¥21,000 for those owned by private individuals and ¥268,000 for other organizations). The individuals and other organizations include many clinics, so a simple comparison may not be adequate, but it is undeniable that there is a clear difference between the "public hospitals" that depend on the transfer of funds from other accounts and the "private health care facilities" that as a rule must rely on independent sources.

When total construction costs of the United States and Japan are compared for 1990, Japan's costs of ¥756.7 billion or $3.9 billion (using the purchasing power parity [PPP] rate of ¥195.6) is less than 40% that of the United States's $10.4 billion. On a per-bed basis, the United States spends about 4.3 times as much as Japan. Moreover, since construction costs are more expensive in Japan, the same investment would result in fewer physical facilities in Japan. This clearly indicates that Japan spends much less than the United States in construction costs.

## Microeconomic Analysis of Capital Costs

The U.S. data concerning (1) average age of plant, (2) tangible fixed assets per bed, and (3) the ratio of capital-related costs to operating expenses were obtained from the "median" listed in the "Source Book" that was prepared jointly by Health Care Investment Analysts and Deloitte Touche (1991). They surveyed 4,817 hospitals in the United States (in 1990), 70% of all hospitals.

For the Japanese data, the "weighted average" of the "Survey on Financial Performance of Medical Facilities" (Central Social Insurance Medical Care Council 1987, 1989) was used as a rule (it was not possible to obtain the median). If these data were not sufficient, they were supplemented by the "average" from the "Yearbook on Public Enterprises" (Local Government Finance Foundation 1992). The former survey is conducted every other year, and in 1992, 1,221 hospitals participated, which corresponds to approximately 12% of the total number of hospitals in Japan. The latter survey was limited to the hospitals owned by prefectural and municipal governments, which totaled 990 hospitals in 1990 (including psychiatric and tuberculosis hospitals).

### Average Age of Plant

The average age of the physical plant is obtained by dividing the accumulated depreciation by current depreciation. This number serves as an index of how much the assets of each medical facility have been depreciated. A lower average age of the plant indicates that the health care facility owns newer assets.

For public hospitals, the United States and Japan were similar: in 1990, the average age of the plant was 8.06 years in the United States and 8.25 years in Japan. Furthermore, this timeframe has lengthened in both countries. A comparison of the average age of the plant between 1986 and 1990 shows an increase of 12% in the span of four years, in both the United States and Japan. Data were not available for other types of hospitals.

### Tangible Fixed Assets per Bed

Tangible fixed assets per bed is computed by calculating the sum of the tangible fixed assets and then dividing by the total number of beds in service. It constitutes a useful index that shows the amount of investment per bed. As table 1 shows, tangible fixed assets per bed in general hospitals in Japan were about half that of the United States, and this difference has widened from 1987 to 1989. The high figures for national hospitals must be discounted because, unlike others, their accounting is on a cash basis without depreciation and their assets are periodically revalued. Proprietary hospitals have low figures because they cannot obtain subsidies for capital investment and also because of their small bed capacity. The real difference between public and proprietary hospitals may be greater because, in the latter, a quarter of their assets is land, compared with only 7% in public hospitals.

**Table 1. Tangible fixed assets per bed in general hospitals (according to ownership, in 1,000 yen)**

|                           | 1987     | 1989     |
|---------------------------|----------|----------|
| Japan                     |          |          |
| National                  | 14,223   | 13,351   |
| Public                    | 10,615   | 10,466   |
| Quasi-public              | 7,400    | 6,474    |
| Social insurance etc.     | 4,064    | 6,857    |
| Other private             | 5,565    | 5,856    |
| Proprietary (corporate)   | 3,905    | 4,845    |
| Proprietary (Individual)  | 3,617    | 3,810    |
| Total (1)                 | 6,855    | 6,872    |
| U.S.                      | $64,404  | $71,606  |
| PPP rate (2)              | 13,500   | 14,308   |
| (1)/(2)                   | 0.507    | 0.48     |

For psychiatric hospitals, Japan had approximately one-sixth the fixed assets per bed as that of the United States in 1990 (¥1,561,000 for Japan). If the comparison is limited to proprietary hospitals, it was even lower at one-eighth the level of the United States.

Percentage of Capital-Related Costs to Operating Expenses

Capital-related costs include depreciation, interest, and capital leases. Operating expenses, on the other hand, are those normally incurred in association with medical activities, such as the cost for materials, wages and salaries, general expenses, consignment fees, research expenses, depreciation, and interest. The percentage of capital-related costs to operating expenses is computed by dividing the former by the latter and multiplying by 100. This percentage is an index for the percentage of capital costs to fixed cost among hospital expenses and is also an effective indicator for the financial risk of a hospital. Contrary to expectations, the percentage of capital-related costs to operating expenses is only slightly higher in the United States compared with Japan, 7.95% for the United States and 7.37% for Japan in 1989. The percentages have decreased from 1987, when they were 8.31% in the United States compared with 7.72% for Japan.

The ratios of capital-related costs to operating expenses are lower for public hospitals and higher for "private" hospitals (investor-owned hospitals in the United States and proprietary hospitals in Japan). This is due to fact that the latter two have a higher long-term debt to total assets ratio in both countries. Proprietary hospitals in Japan have increased this ratio from 1987 to 1989 because of their expansion of bed capacity. When analyzed by bed capacity (1990), in the United States, hospitals with 100 to 249 beds have the highest percentage (8.76%), and small hospitals with a bed capacity of 25 to 99, the lowest (6.98%). In Japan, small-to-medium hospitals with a bed capacity ranging from 100 to 299 showed the highest percentage, and large hospitals with a bed capacity exceeding 500 showed the lowest (6.33%). Thus, in both countries, the medium-sized hospitals showed the highest percentages.

For psychiatric hospitals, the ratios were 7.52% for the United States and 6.94% for Japan (1989). The difference between the two countries has narrowed considerably from 1987 (7.93% for the United States and 6.58% for Japan). These ratios are higher for Japanese proprietary hospitals due to the small number of employees in these facilities and the resultant low percentage of wages and salaries to operating expenses. Parenthetically, the ratio of wages to operating expenses for all psychiatric hospitals in 1989 was 58.5%, but was only 52.2% when limited to private hospitals.

Total Floor Space per Bed

The total floor space per bed is the total floor space in the hospital (excluding parking lots) divided by the approved number of beds. Data for the United States were obtained from *Health Facilities Review* (American Institute of Architects 1990); Japanese data were from the *Medical Facilities Surveys* (Ministry of Health and Welfare [MHW] 1987, 1990). As table 2 shows, both Japanese general and psychiatric hospitals have a total floor space per bed that is approximately one-quarter that of the United States. It should be noted that the difference in the average floor space for a new housing between United States and Japan is only about one-third, 83.1 square meters in Japan compared with 134.8 square meters in United States (Asahi Shinbunsha 1991). The reason for this discrepancy lies in the fact that while floor space for housing has greatly improved in Japan (increasing twofold per person between 1963 to 1988), conditions in hospitals have remained the same because there has been no change in the legal minimum

**Table 2.  Total floor space per bed,1990**
**(in square meters)**

|  | Total | General hospitals | Psychiatric hospitals |
|---|---|---|---|
| Japan (1) | 35.2 | 37.8 | 21.1 |
| U.S. (2) | 126.0 | 147.5 | 79.3 |
| (1)/(2) | 0.279 | 0.256 | 0.266 |

requirement. It has been 4.3 square meteres per bed in the hospital room since 1947.

Public hospitals had 1.7 times the floor space of proprietary hospitals, and hospitals with over 500 beds had 1.5 times that of those with 100 to 299 beds. The reason hospitals with 100 to 299 beds had the smallest floor space probably lies in the fact that this is the most common size for geriatric hospitals, which are included in general hospitals. Whereas the total foor space per bed was 48.8 square meters in nongeriatric general hospitals, it was 27.6 square meters in geriatric hospitals. The increase in the number of geriatric hospitals has probably led to a decrease in the average floor space per bed: whereas it was 31.3 square meters in 1987, it decreased to 30.0 in 1990. Of these geriatric hospitals, 80% are in the private sector.

Charges for Rooms

There are no statistics in the United States that show the average charges for all hospital rooms. However, the Health Insurance Association of America (HIAA) does conduct a *Hospital Semiprivate Room Charges Survey* of 1,414 short-term care, general hospitals (excluding federal hospitals) every January. According to this survey, the average bed-and-board charges for a semiprivate room in the United States were $297 in 1990, which was an increase of 12.5% from the past year (HIAA 1990).

In Japan, the room charges are set by the government and come to ¥3,350 per day, including meals with no therapeutic diet. This is equivalent to $17.00 using the PPP rate of exchange. To make this cost comparable with the U.S. figures, nursing charges must be added, which vary from ¥700 ($3.60) to ¥6,550 ($33.50) according to the staffing ratio. However, hospitals are allowed to levy extra charges if the room is private or semiprivate (although a small number of hospitals charge extra even if there are three or more beds). These extra-charge rooms are officially limited to less than 20% of the total bed capacity in each hospital. However, nationally, extra-charge rooms constituted only 10.1% of the total hospital beds in 1990, and this ratio has actually declined from 12.6% in 1981 (MHW 1991). The weighted average of all extra charges comes to ¥4,224 in 1990. If 10.1% of this amount is added to the bed-and-board charge set by the government, then the costs would total ¥3,772 ($19.20) for room and meals, and ¥4,472 to ¥10,322 ($23.00–53.00) including nursing charges.

Direct comparisons between Japan and the United States are not possible because although the semiprivate room may be the prototype for an acute-care hospital in the United States, the charges would certainly be lower in long-term care facilities, such as a nursing home. Moreover, even in an acute-care hospital, the actual amount paid may be lower than what the hospital has charged, and it would be difficult to estimate just the room and board because of the prospective payment system. However, even if the Japanese charges are based on the highest paid nurse staffing ratio, the U.S. charges still would be more than five times greater. Thus, the reason why U.S. hospitals have larger rooms may at least be partly ascribed to the difference in what is being charged to the patient.

NOTE

1. There are three criticisms against this approach in computing costs. First, health-care costs are double-counted by computing them based on the stock concept. This argument is based on the fact that capital expenditure is counted as construction expense, but interest payments for financing and possibly depreciation allowances for that capital may also be counted as operating costs. Those who criticize this double counting of health care expenses insist that listing construction expenditures as part of health care costs invites misunderstanding by users of the health care cost statistics, and, therefore, such expenditures should be excluded from health care costs. Furthermore, they maintain that treating construction costs as an operating expense (under the flow concept) is coordinated with the depreciation of fixed assets in national accounts and is therefore more logical.

Second, the critics argue that limiting assets to buildings and facilities, while excluding medical equipment, does not result in a just computation of capital costs.

Third, critics feel that the exclusion of costs for the construction of medical research and training facilities is misleading. These costs should be included in the costs of the broad category of medical facility construction.

Despite these criticisms, HCFA does not plan to alter its current framework for reasons such as: (1) a loss of coordination with past data; (2) unavailability of appropriate data; and (3) a lack of consensus among those involved concerning a change to a flow concept.

REFERENCES

American Institute of Architects. 1990. *Health facilities review.*
Asahi Shinbunsha. 1991. *Minryoku* 19.
Chūō Shakai Hoken Iryō Kyōgikai. 1987, 1989. *Iryō keizai jittai chōsa* (Survey of financial performance of medical facilities).
Kensetsu Bukka Chōsakai. 1990. *Kenchiku tōkei nenpō* (Annual report on construction statistics).
Haber, Susan G., and Joseph P. Newhouse. 1991. Special report: Recent revision to and recommendations for national health expenditures accounting. *Health Care Financing Review* 13.1: 111–16.
Health Care Investment Analyst, Inc. and Deloitte and Touche. 1991. *The comparative performance of U.S. hospitals: the sourcebook.*
Health Insurance Association of America. 1990. *Sourcebook of health insurance data.*
Chihō Zaimu Kyōkai. 1992. *Chihō kōei kigyō nenkan* (Yearbook on public enterprises).
Ministry of Health and Welfare (MHW; Koseisho). 1982, 1991. *Shitsuryō sagaku chōshū jōkyō chōsa* (Survey on extra room charges).
———. 1989, 1992. *Iryō shisetsu chōsa* (Medical facilities survey), Kōsei Tōkei Kyōkai.

CHAPTER 7

# Comparison of Administrative Costs in Health Care between Japan and the United States

*Naoki Ikegami, Jay Wolfson, and Takanori Ishii*

SUMMARY  Administrative costs for payers in Japan amounted to 2.8% of the total health care expenditures, which was about half the ratio in the United States. Within the group of payers, the government-managed health insurance had the lowest ratio (2.3%) because its nonstatutory benefits tend to be minimal, because it has economies of scale, and because its internal claims-review process is less rigorous. When the sample of four Japanese hospitals was compared to that of nine U.S. hospitals, there was a difference of two- to threefold in the ratio of administrative costs; in absolute terms, fivefold. The difference in floor space occupied by general administration was also two to three times larger in the United States. Administrative costs appear to increase as the process becomes more complex.

## Background

The high administrative costs in the United States have been regarded as the one area where savings can be made without adverse effects on the provision of health care. However, if consumer choice and competition, managed or otherwise, are to be part of the system, then both payers and providers will continue to need the administrative resources to process complicated transactions. Japan would seem to offer a middle way between the U.S.'s present fragmented system and Canada's single-payer plan with global budgets for hospitals. On the payer side, although the Japanese have very little choice in selecting their plans and all must offer the same statutory health care benefits, the various plans are allowed to differ, if only marginally so, in their benefits and premiums. On the provider side, although the nationally uniform fee schedule does set all the rates, payment is made essentially on an itemized fee-for-service basis. Thus, while Japan has a similar system of multiple payers and fee-for-service as the United States, the fact that it is more regulated and offers less choice is likely to result in lower administrative costs. Accordingly, the object of this paper is to compare the administrative cost issue for both payers and providers in Japan and the United States.

## Administrative Costs for Payers in Japan

All Japanese must join the statutory plan offered by their employers, or, if they are self-employed, the plan administered by their local governments or occupational associations. Only those who are self-employed, such as physicians, carpenters, and barbers, and have formed their own Citizens Health Insurance (CHI) associations, can choose between the plan offered by their community and that offered by their occupational associations. However, this type of insurance plan is a historical legacy. No new CHI association has been permitted to form, and the government has discouraged the existing ones from soliciting new enrollment (Okamoto 1989). Thus, there are no administrative costs associated with selling and marketing for payers in Japan. Neither is there any need for payers to negotiate with individual providers over rates since they are all set by the government.

Administrative costs for payers can be broadly divided into two categories, internal and external. Internal costs are those of administering the plan itself, including the collection of premiums and the paying of benefits. External costs are charged by the clearinghouses that process and review claims submitted by the providers and bill the payers for the costs that they have incurred. Each prefecture has two clearinghouses: the Payer's Fund (Shiharai Kikin), which handles claims for the employee-based insurance plans, and the Central Citizens Health Insurance Organization (Kokumin Kenkō Hoken Chuōkai), which handles claims for the community-based plans.

Table 1 shows the ratio of administrative costs to the total amount of health care expenditure for each broad category of insurance schemes (Kokumin Kenkō Hoken Chuōkai 1990; Prime Minister's Office 1991; Ministry of Health and Welfare [MHW] 1991; Shakai Hoken Shinryō Hōshū Shiharai Kikin 1990). The denominator does not include the amount that goes to the pooling fund for the elderly under the Health Care for the Elderly Law or the amount allocated to the Retired Employees' Insurance, as they are block transfers. However, it does include the nonstatutory benefits that are not part of the mandatory health insurance benefits. The numerator is composed of what has been appropriated as administrative costs. There are two exceptions: for the Mutual Aid Associations (MAA), personnel and benefit expenditures of the central administrative offices are used, and for Seamen's Insurance, since administrative costs have not been separately accounted in health care and pensions, they have been appropriated according to health care's share of the combined expenditure.

The ratio of administrative costs varies from 2.31% for the government-managed health insurance to 4.77% for CHI, with a mean of 2.75%. However, municipal governments usually also handle the old-age pooling fund, thereby incurring its administrative costs (hence no internal administrative costs have been accounted for in this pooling fund in the table). If the expenditure for this were to be added to the total expenditure of CHI, then the denominator would be more than doubled, leading to a much lower administrative cost ratio of 2.28%, which would be the second lowest after the ratio for the Government-Managed Health Insurance (GMHI). Parenthetically, most municipalities collect the pre-

**Table 1. Administrative costs for payers, 1989**

| | Internal costs | | External costs | | Total costs | |
|---|---|---|---|---|---|---|
| | As ratio of expend. (%) | Amount (Billion Yen) | As ratio of expend. (%) | Amount (Billion Yen) | As ratio of expend. (%) | Amount (Billion Yen) |
| Government-Managed Health Insurance | 1.66 | 57 | 0.65 | 23 | 2.31 | 80 |
| Society-Managed Health Insurance | 3.69 | 105 | 0.64 | 18 | 4.33 | 123 |
| Seamen's Insurance | 3.47 | 2 | 0.44 | 0 | 3.91 | 2 |
| Mutual Aid Associations | 3.75 | 39 | 0.72 | 7 | 4.47 | 47 |
| Citizens Health Insurance | 4.45 | 198 | 0.32 | 14 | 4.77 | 213 |
| Pooling Fund for the Elderly | — | — | 0.26 | 15 | 0.26 | 15 |
| Total | 2.31 | 401 | 0.44 | 77 | 2.75 | 480 |

Source: Kokumin Kenkō Hoken Chūōkai 1990, Ministry of Health and Welfare 1991, Prime Minister's Office 1991,
Shakai Hoken Shinryō Hōshū Shiharai Kikin 1990.

miums for CHI in the form of CHI taxes. That is, in order to enforce a higher rate of the collection of premiums, the premiums have been technically classified as taxes. This has also lowered the cost of premium collection so that it is at the same level as that of the employees' plans, which use payroll deductions. However, it should be noted that 7% of those enrolled in CHI did not pay their premiums, and this ratio has remained constant (MHW 1992). This would seem to be an unavoidable moral hazard that is inherent in community-based plans.

The Society-Managed Health Insurance (SMHI), MAA, and Seamen's Insurance have about the same administrative cost ratios. The reasons that they have higher ratios than the others are as follows (their real costs may be slightly higher than the recorded figures because the benefits section of the parent organization sometimes provides administrative support). First, they have greater flexibility in setting the extent of benefits. Among the health insurance societies the ratio of expenditure allocated mainly in the areas of health promotion and screening (which may include the subsidizing of hotel charges for vacations) varies from 3.1% to 8.4%. They are also allowed to partially reimburse some of the copayment that their members have paid to providers, and this comprises from zero to 4.4% of their total expenditure (Ikegami 1991). These nonstatutory benefits, albeit very modest, add to the complexity of administering the plans. Second, they have a relatively small enrollment, especially in the case of some of the health insurance societies. Third, these three types of insurance tend to have more rigorous, independent internal reviews (*tenken*) of claims. In this case, higher administrative costs may result in lower total costs. In contrast, in GMHI, which has the lowest administrative cost ratio, there is less health promotion and screening, no partial reimbursement of copayments, advantages in economies of scale, and a less rigorous internal-review process.

External administrative costs vary from 0.26% for the Health Care for the Elderly Law pooling fund to 0.72% for MAA, with a mean of 0.44%. The ratios for the employee-based plans are about the same since they are all handled by the same payer's fund. Review (*shinsa*) of the claims is relatively simple and is performed by a peer-review panel that retrospectively examines claims to see whether the diagnosis justifies the itemized procedures that have been performed and the drugs that have been administered. Parenthetically, the *shinsa* has greater authority than the *tenken,* and any denials made by the *tenken* must be appealed and authorized by the peer-review panel of the *shinsa*. Local medical associations wield much power within this panel. Although the amount of time spent on reviewing each claim is very short (less than one second if averaged) and less than 1% are denied full payment, the reviews do have some effect since they tend to concentrate on the high-cost claims. Since electronic billing is still not permitted in Japan, claims that appear to require examinations by the peer-review panel are usually selected beforehand by the administrative staff. In addition, denials act as a warning to the providers because should they gain a reputation for providing excessive services, their claims would in the future be subject to more extensive review.

When compared to the United States, administrative costs for the payers are quite low in Japan. According to Thorpe (1992), American administrative costs as a percentage of spending are estimated to be 5.8% of the total, with only Medicare having a low ratio of 2.1% for the total of part A and part B. The overall U.S. ratio is well over twice the ratio in Japan, and the total amount spent on health care is almost twice as much as that spent in Japan. In absolute terms, therefore, administrative costs in the United States are four times as great as those in Japan.

The Japanese ratio is still about twice that of Canada, probably because of the fact that Japan uses an itemized billing process and has multiple payers while Canada uses global budgeting for hospitals and has a single payer. The effects of a single payer versus multiple payers can be estimated by comparing the difference in the administrative cost ratios of GMHI and that of the health insurance societies. The ratio of the former is nearly half the ratio of the latter.

The National Federation of Insurance Societies of Japan (1986) have justified the societies' existence by the fact that their workplace-based cooperative venture by management and labor enhances the feeling of solidarity and allows each society the freedom to set premium rates and the extent of nonstatutory benefits. However, this very freedom has led to considerable differences in the premium rates among the health insurance societies (varying from 5.8% to 9.5%). Moreover, this difference is largely a function of the average age and wage of the employed: rates tend to be high if the ages are high (such as in the coal mining industry) and/or the wages are low (such as in the textile industry). Whether this situation is societally justifiable or not is a matter of values. Parenthetically, it should be noted that the differences in benefits and premiums among the insurance societies have not aroused much, if any, attention in Japan, as they result from a historical legacy rather than from hard negotiation by management and labor. Yet, if these extra benefits were to be discontinued, then it is likely that there would be considerable outcry against the loss of entitlements. This is the major reason why it has not been possible to move to a single payer system in Japan.

### Administrative Costs in Japanese Hospitals

It proved exceptionally difficult to obtain cost data from providers in Japan because the data were largely nonexistent. Since the reimbursement fees are uniformly set by the government irrespective of the actual cost to the provider, there is little incentive to keep detailed costing data. In most cases, the interest in accounting data remains generally limited to efforts in the private sector to minimize profits for tax purposes (the majority of private hospitals in Japan are taxed at the corporate rate despite the fact that technically they are nonprofit) and efforts in the public sector to minimize deficits so as to avoid too much scrutiny in state and municipal assemblies. This is in contrast to the situation in the United States where cost data are routinely collected by providers to calculate their charge rates, which serve as the basis for negotiations with payers.

There are three more aspects in which Japanese hospitals differ markedly from those in the United States. First, in Japanese hospitals, all physicians are employed by hospitals. This means that clerical and management costs that arise in U.S. physicians' offices would be absorbed by hospitals in Japan. Since the ratio of administrative costs is estimated to be higher for physicians' offices than for hospitals (Woolhandler and Himmelstein 1991), it is likely that under the U.S. system the administrative cost ratio for hospitals in Japan would increase. Second, Japanese hospitals derive a much higher ratio of their revenue from outpatient services. However, the ratio of administrative to total costs is not likely to differ greatly between inpatient and outpatient care. If anything, it is likely that the higher ratio of outpatient services would lead to a greater administrative load because of the much greater number of claims generated for the same amount of revenue. Third, under Japanese law the chief executive of the hospital must be a physician who devotes the majority of his time to clinical practice. Thus, his salary must be apportioned to administrative costs based on the estimated amount of time spent on administration.

Questionnaires were mailed to four acute-care private hospitals that had close connections with the authors. Their bed capacities ranged between 102 to 377 beds. Three were located in Greater Tokyo, and the fourth in a large provincial city. The information collected consisted of individual cost items (including insurance premiums), the number of personnel (total and those engaged in general administration), and floor space (total for the entire hospital and that part occupied by general administration), for the 1991 fiscal year. The personnel and floor space percentages were used to appropriate costs to general administration. Profits were not treated as administrative costs because Japanese hospitals are not permitted to issue dividends to their investors. In actual fact, two out of the four hospitals were running at a deficit, and the other two were barely breaking even. Appropriation of each item to administrative costs was based on the principle of treating general administration as a cost center and was as follows.

## Personnel Expenditure

Personnel included those employed for such purposes as patient accounting, general accounting, central supply and purchasing, data processing, and medical records functions. The salaries of the chief executives' were appropriated on the basis of spending 30% of their time on administration and the remaining on clinical activities (this ratio reflected their notion of the relative time spent in each), except in Hospital A where the chief executive was wholly engaged in administration. The amount of time spent by all other physicians on administrative tasks was not included, but its effect will later be estimated. The time spent by the nursing, pharmacy, dietary, laboratory, and other patient-related departments on administrative tasks was not considered. However, in the case of Japan, their role in hospital management tends to be marginal, so this omission should not have much effect.

Other Expenditure

(1) General expenditures such as benefits, travel, communication, and expendables were appropriated according to the ratio of administrative to total personnel employed.
(2) Facility-related expenditures such as depreciation, rent and lease, and contracted-out service for maintenance were appropriated on the basis of floor space occupied by general administration. For our purposes, medical equipment was excluded from the facility-related expenditure.
(3) Insurance premiums were appropriated to administrative costs using the ratio of administrative personnel to total employees in the case of personal insurance, and floor space to the total in the case of nonpersonal insurance. Malpractice insurance premiums were excluded because they should be wholly appropriated to clinical expenditure.

As table 2 shows, the ratios of administrative costs were within the relatively narrow range of 5.1% for Hospital C to 7.1% for Hospital A. Personnel expenditure (including that appropriated to the chief executive) amounted to about three-quarters of the total, followed by general expenditure appropriated to administration by staff.

If the time spent by physicians on administrative tasks were to be added, this would increase the administrative costs ratios by about 2% to 3%. This is based on the assumption that physicians would be spending 20% of their time on administrative tasks, and on the fact that physicians' salaries are from 8.6% to 16.9% of total expenditure. While this ratio of physicians' time devoted to administration may seem low when compared with that estimated for the physicians in their offices in the United States, in Japan it should be noted that more of the administrative burden would be carried by the hospital staff. In fact, this ratio may still be an overestimation, because younger physicians will be spending much less time on administrative tasks.

### Composition of Administrative Personnel in Japan

The composition of administrative personnel in each hospital is shown on table 3. There is a wide difference among the four hospitals. For example, the ratio for the category "purchasing, etc." varies from 17.2% in Hospital A to 2.7% in Hospital D. For medical records, no staff was listed in Hospitals B and C, while in Hospital D nearly a quarter of the total administrative staff was listed for this function. For patient accounting and billing, staff was 29.3% in Hospital A and 18.9% in Hospital C, but in Hospitals B and D there were no staff assigned to these crucial functions. This obviously does not mean that these functions were not performed. Nor does it necessarily reflect the actual differences among the four hospitals. Although they were asked to appropriate their administrative staff on the basis of the relative time spent on each task, this was difficult to realize without a rigorous time study, and the numbers correspond to their formally assigned position.

**Table 2. Administrative expenditure, sample of four Japanese hospitals, FY1991 (in thousand Yen)**

|  | Hospital A 377 beds | Hospital B 310 beds | Hospital C 198 beds | Hospital D 102 beds |
|---|---|---|---|---|
| Revenue |  |  |  |  |
| Inpatient | 2,824,707 | 1,742,563 | 1,630,609 | 843,968 |
| Outpatient | 1,220,013 | 719,271 | 1,986,301 | 1,077,141 |
| Others | 724,494 | 121,598 | 163,895 | 53,051 |
| Total | 4,769,214 | 2,583,432 | 3,780,805 | 1,974,160 |
| Expenditure (A) | 4,807,451 | 2,351,667 | 3,822,884 | 1,941,737 |
|  |  |  |  |  |
| Administrative expenditure |  |  |  |  |
| Personnel | 277,970 | 110,937 | 147,384 | 93,460 |
| Staff appropriated* | 41,794 | 26,830 | 26,658 | 15,572 |
| Depreciation** | 2,812 | 2,899 | 3,473 | 2,437 |
| Rent and lease** | 2,195 | 1,607 | 12,035 | 5,911 |
| Insurance premiums |  |  |  |  |
| Personal* | 406 | 870 | 515 | 1,182 |
| Nonpersonal (fire, etc.)** | 67 | 225 | 125 | 958 |
| Contracted services |  |  |  |  |
| Maintenance** | 1,700 | 1,475 | 4,080 | 1,022 |
| Administration | 15,429 | 4,730 |  | 1,950 |
| Total (B) | 342,373 | 149,573 | 194,270 | 122,492 |
|  |  |  |  |  |
| Ratio B/A (%) | 7.12 | 6.36 | 5.08 | 6.31 |

*Appropriated by number of administrative personnel to total (12.0–13.0%) except for
    utilities, which is appropriated by space.
**Appropriated by the space occupied by administration to total (2.3–12.0%).

The administrative staff were not paid large salaries. Except for the full-time physician chief executive in Hospital A, none of the administrative departmental chiefs earned a yearly income exceeding ¥10 million ($56,000 at $1.00 = ¥180), and their wages were only about three to four times that of the lowest-paid clerical worker.

**Table 3. Composition of administrative personnel in four Japanese hospitals, FY1991**

| | Hospital A | | Hospital B | | Hospital C | | Hospital D | |
|---|---|---|---|---|---|---|---|---|
| | No. staff | % | No. staff | % | No. staff | % | No. staff | % |
| Patient accounting, billing | 17 | 29.3 | | | 7 | 18.9 | | |
| Admitting and outpatient | 14 | 24.1 | 24 | 75.0 | 16 | 43.2 | 15 | 57.7 |
| General accounting, financing | 3 | 5.2 | 4 | 12.5 | 5 | 13.5 | 2 | 7.7 |
| Purchasing etc. | 10 | 17.2 | 2 | 6.3 | 1 | 2.7 | 2 | 7.7 |
| Medical records | 3 | 5.2 | 0 | 0.0 | 0 | 0.0 | 6 | 23.1 |
| Hospital administration (other than above) | 11 | 19.0 | 2 | 6.3 | 8 | 21.6 | 1 | 3.8 |
| Total number of administrative personnel | 58 | 100.0 | 32 | 100.0 | 37 | 100.0 | 26 | 100.0 |

## Administrative Costs in U.S. Hospitals

Data for the U.S. hospitals were obtained from extant records maintained by the Healthcare Cost Containment Board (HCCB), which regulates hospital budgets in Florida. The first submission by the hospital consists of a budget forecast, which must be approved by the HCCB only after a lengthy and complicated analysis. When the fiscal year is over, each hospital must submit a set of actual, detailed financial data against which the budget is compared. This data source includes breakdowns for hospital cost centers as well as for central hospital administrative services. These data have been collected since 1980 and in a fairly detailed form since 1986. We assessed the state computer files for a sample of nine acute-care private hospitals (all except Hospital Z were nonprofit) having a bed capacity of between one hundred to four hundred beds. Information on floor space was obtained from the original, hard-copy data maintained for each facility by the Agency for Health Care Administration, State of Florida (1993).

We applied to the U.S. sample the same costing categories and definition of administrative costs as were used for the Japanese hospital sample. Consequently, our definition of administrative costs for U.S. hospitals may not necessarily comply with that generally used. However, we were unable to obtain detailed information about the salaries of chief executives and departmental chairs, and the number of staff assigned to each task within the administrative departments for the U.S. hospital sample. Since the disclosure of these data is not mandated, the U.S. hospitals categorically refused to provide it.

As table 4 shows, there is a wide range both in the amount and in the ratios of administrative costs to total hospital expenditure, which is from 9.1% to 20.1%. These figures appear to be generally lower than the 24.8% as reported by Woolhandler, Himmelstein, and Lewonton (1993). This partially can be ascribed to the difference in accounting for capital costs: we used the floor space ratio, which is considerably lower than appropriating by the ratio of administrative costs to the total. However, there may be more fundamental differences that need to be analyzed in the future.

When the ratio in the United States is compared to that in Japan, there is a two- to threefold difference. In absolute terms, since the total expenditure for the U.S. hospitals on a per-bed basis is about two to four times that of the Japanese hospital, the total U.S. expenditure would amount to five times that of Japan. It is clear that U.S. hospitals spend much more on general administration, not only as a ratio of total expenditures, but also in absolute terms. Parenthetically, it was not possible to compare across individual items within administrative costs because both the Japanese and U.S. data tended to differ greatly for each hospital.

## Floor Space Occupied by General Administration

Since comparison by number of personnel was not possible, the relative share of floor space occupied by general administration was compared. As table 5 shows,

**Table 4. Administrative expenditure, sample of nine U.S. hospitals, FY1991 (U.S. dollars)**

|  | Hospital R 301 beds | Hospital S 242 beds | Hospital T 213 beds | Hospital U 171 beds |
|---|---|---|---|---|
| Revenue |  |  |  |  |
|   Inpatient | 111,614,764 | 59,078,374 | 90,684,879 | 34,231,896 |
|   Outpatient | 20,692,411 | 10,070,216 | 22,187,645 | 5,756,801 |
|   Others | 3,840,947 | 15,679,344 | 2,806,465 | 273,900 |
|   Total | 144,348,142 | 84,827,936 | 115,678,909 | 40,262,597 |
|     Total deductions | 49,133,045 | 27,850,999 | 44,727,133 | 18,568,165 |
|   Net revenue | 95,215,097 | 56,976,937 | 70,951,776 | 21,694,432 |
| Expenditure (A) | 85,733,883 | 55,393,006 | 65,047,721 | 23,906,932 |
|  |  |  |  |  |
| Administrative expenditure |  |  |  |  |
|   Personnel* | 8,029,018 | 4,497,945 | 6,250,949 | 2,059,210 |
|   Depreciation** | 1,002,592 | 426,254 | 547,531 | 372,145 |
|   Rent and lease | — | — | — | — |
|   Insurance premiums |  |  |  |  |
|     Personal* | 298,204 | 260,446 | 189,741 | 112,983 |
|     Nonpersonal (fire, etc.)** | -286,257 | -198,805 | -189,741 | -94,161 |
|   Contracted services |  |  |  |  |
|     Maintenance** | 200,961 | 319,983 | 149,524 | 65,372 |
|     Administration | — | — | — | — |
| Total (B) | 9,244,518 | 5,305,823 | 6,948,004 | 2,515,549 |
|  |  |  |  |  |
| Ratio B/A (%) | 10.78 | 9.58 | 10.68 | 10.52 |

*Appropriated by number of administrative personnel to total except for utilities, which is appropriated by space.

**Appropriated by the space occupied by administration to total.

the ratio of administrative floor space to total floor space ranged between 2.3% to 11.8%, with a mean of 5.8%, in Japan, compared with 4.0% to 35.3%, with a mean of 11.8%, in the United States. Thus, the Japanese ratio was about half that of the United States. In absolute terms, because the total floor space per bed in Japanese hospitals was less than half that in the United States, the administrative floor space per bed in Japan was less than a fifth that in the United States.

| Hospital V | Hospital W | Hospital X | Hospital Y | Hospital Z |
|---|---|---|---|---|
| 112 beds | 100 beds | 400 beds | 193 beds | 204 beds |
| 18,651,751 | 12,511,019 | 71,598,384 | 60,845,554 | 85,625,710 |
| 7,445,959 | 5,145,961 | 21,046,093 | 10,814,736 | 31,463,705 |
| 1,943,468 | 404,087 | 3,672,902 | 418,767 | 416,054 |
| 28,041,178 | 18,061,067 | 96,317,379 | 72,079,057 | 117,505,469 |
| 11,636,502 | 6,242,658 | 33,419,589 | 30,342,888 | 45,576,684 |
| 16,404,676 | 11,818,409 | 62,897,790 | 41,736,169 | 71,928,785 |
| 16,142,769 | 11,479,816 | 60,107,883 | 45,171,418 | 50,621,984 |
| 2,515,362 | 834,226 | 6,738,792 | 7,512,642 | 6,489,528 |
| 177,562 | 159,102 | 1,551,329 | 1,020,590 | 507,717 |
| — | — | — | — | — |
| 75,379 | 71,612 | 622,485 | 662,916 | 290,073 |
| -47,379 | -66,108 | -467,298 | -638,908 | -283,122 |
| 77,777 | 45,695 | 386,216 | 468,349 | 113,091 |
| — | — | — | — | — |
| 2,798,701 | 1,044,527 | 8,831,524 | 9,025,589 | 7,117,287 |
| 17.34 | 9.10 | 14.69 | 19.98 | 14.06 |

## Conclusion

Administrative costs are a function of the complexity of the process. Besides the direct costs associated with billing and accounting, there are the "layered" costs associated with the need for sophisticated marketing and planning by both payers and providers as the process becomes more complex. Even in Japan, which has a uniform payment system and essentially the same benefits for all, those payers that have a more complex benefit package, a smaller enrollment, and a more elaborate review of claims tend to have higher administrative cost ratios. In the United States not only does the complexity require more resources quantitatively, but also more qualitatively with the use of sophisticated management expertise.

**Table 5. Administrative floor space, Japan-U.S. comparison**

|  | Number of beds | Administrative floor space/total (%) | Administrative floor space per bed (sq. meters) | Total floor space per bed (sq. meters) |
|---|---|---|---|---|
| **JAPAN** |  |  |  |  |
| Hospital A | 377 | 2.3 | 1.0 | 43.7 |
| Hospital B | 310 | 4.0 | 1.2 | 30.5 |
| Hospital C | 198 | 4.9 | 2.0 | 41.1 |
| Hospital D | 102 | 11.8 | 3.0 | 25.0 |
| Mean | 246.8 | 5.8 | 1.8 | 35.1 |
| **U.S.** |  |  |  |  |
| Hospital R | 301 | 7.1 | 9.4 | 132.5 |
| Hospital S | 242 | 13.0 | 12.2 | 93.7 |
| Hospital T | 213 | 4.0 | 4.3 | 97.7 |
| Hospital U | 171 | 9.0 | 5.4 | 59.8 |
| Hospital V | 112 | 7.5 | 5.1 | 68.2 |
| Hospital W | 100 | 7.4 | 5.6 | 75.8 |
| Hospital X | 400 | 11.9 | 10.2 | 85.8 |
| Hospital Y | 193 | 35.3 | 27.9 | 78.9 |
| Hospital Z | 204 | 11.2 | 10.1 | 89.6 |
| Mean | 215.1 | 11.8 | 10.0 | 86.9 |

This could only be indirectly inferred from the much larger amount of floor space occupied by general administration in the United States compared to Japan, which confirms our impression of the difference in office amenities between the two countries. Further studies should be made regarding salaries and the perceived need of formal qualifications (M.B.A.s and M.H.A.s) for health care executives.

There may be some positive feedback from the high administrative costs in the United States. Quality assurance and risk management have been implemented because of the competitive market for hospitals. Expenditure for these has been negligible in Japan, and, in two of the four hospitals observed, not one full-time staff was assigned to handle medical records. However, while it is true that U.S. hospitals do spend much more in these areas, it is clear even from this study that there is a wide range of spending among the hospitals. Moreover, it is not clear whether this puts them in a more advantageous position when negotiating with the payer, or more important, if it leads to better patient outcome. More research is needed to determine whether U.S. administrative costs are too high or

Japanese costs are too low. In addition, the time-cost to the consumer in filing claims or in choosing among the various plans should also be considered in future studies.

REFERENCES

Agency for Health Care Administration. 1993. *Florida hospital discharge data, 1991–92.* Healthcare Management Decisions, Inc.

Ikegami, N. 1991. Japanese health care: Low cost through regulated fees. *Health Affairs* 11.3: 87–109.

Kokumin Kenkō Hoken Chuōkai. 1990. *Todōfuken kokumin kenkō hoken rengō jigyō no gaikyō* (Prefectural citizens health insurance federation report). Tokyo: Kokumin Kenkō Hoken Chuōkai.

Ministry of Health and Welfare. 1991. *Rōjin iryō jigyō nenpō* (Geriatric care medical annual report). Tokyo: Kōsei Tōkei Kyōkai.

———. 1992. Hoken to nenkin no dōkō (Trend of insurance and pensions). Tokyo: Kōsei Tōkei Kyōkai.

National Federation of Health Insurance Societies. 1986. Health insurance and health insurance societies in Japan, 1986. Tokyo: National Federation of Health Insurance Societies.

Okamoto, E. 1989. *Kokumin kenkō hoken* (Citizens health insurance). Tokyo: Sanitsu Shobō, 165–200.

Prime Minister's Office. 1991. *Shakai hoshō tokei nenkan* (Social security annual report). Tokyo: Prime Minister's Office.

Shakai Hoken Shinryō Hōshu Shiharai Kikin. 1990. *Kikin nenpō* (Report of kikin). Tokyo: Shakai Hoken Shinryō Hōshu Shiharai Kikin.

Thorpe, K. E. 1992. Inside the black box of administrative costs. *Health Affairs* 10.2: 41–55.

Woolhandler, S., and D.U. Himmelstein. 1991. The deteriorating administrative efficiency of the U.S. health care system. *New England Journal of Medicine* 324.18: 1,253–58.

Woolhandler, S., D. U. Himmelstein, and J. P. Lewonton. 1993. Administrative costs in U.S. hospitals. *New England Journal of Medicine* 329.6: 400–403.

CHAPTER 8

# Afterword: Costs—The Micro Perspective

*George D. Greenberg*

*The views presented are those of the author and do not represent the positions of the U.S. Department of Health and Human Services.*

This section contains a discussion of three chapters on Japanese-United States differences in physician fee-schedule policy and the control of hospital outpatient costs; in hospital capitalization; and in administrative costs. According to William Hsiao's analysis, these three sectors may account for approximately half of the per capita cost difference between the United States and Japan.

## The Japanese Fee Schedule

The chapter by Yoshinori Hiroi gives a detailed account of the workings and evolution of the Japanese point-fee system. Hiroi contends that stability in medical expenditure growth is a structural phenomenon determined by government fee-schedule policy. He sees technology as a factor that should reduce costs, and he argues that other sources of cost growth, such as growth in the number of hospital beds, have now been brought under control. In addition, increases in outpatient visits to hospital clinics have been offset by declines in outpatient visits to the smaller doctor-owned clinics. The future sources of cost growth in Japan will be increased manpower and capital costs; however, the Japanese point-fee system does not recognize or pass through these costs because they are not explicitly recognized in the fee-schedule update.

Finally, according to Hiroi, the Japanese Ministry of Health and Welfare has regained control over the updating of the fee schedule. The historical discussion makes it clear that between 1972 and 1981 the Japanese Medical Association had gained concessions that passed through what Hiroi calls the "natural increase" in medical fees. (In the United States, what Hiroi calls "natural increase" is generally termed the volume and intensity of medical services, although Hiroi gives three alternative definitions of the term.) This pass-through was called the "price/wage slide system." However, after 1981 the Ministry deducted the "natural increase" from the total increase before recommending a fee update rather than passing it through to the medical profession by means of an objective formula.

Hiroi believes the progression in Japan will be emulated in the United States, which has just adopted a fee schedule for Medicare. In the United States, we now have a system for updating Medicare fees that is automatic and based on a formula that rewards physicians with higher fee updates if they restrain volume growth. Hiroi believes that, as in Japan, this system will be replaced by one in which the government controls the update and uses the revisions as an instrument of cost-containment policy, explicitly adjusting fees downward as volume and intensity increases. Hiroi suggests that U.S. Medicare policy is similar to Japanese fee-schedule policy prior to 1981, when the "natural increase" was not subtracted from the total increase before deciding upon fee updates. If U.S. Medicare physician payment policy follows the same evolutionary path as Japan's, the volume and intensity factor allowed to physicians in the default formula for calculating the Medicare fee update would be lowered.

Hiroi makes clear that the Japanese point-fee system works differently from the Resource-Based Relative Value Scale (RBRVS) adopted by Medicare in the United States. In Japan, what we call the conversion factor is fixed at ¥10 per point. Therefore, in order to assure that the overall budget is met, the Japanese reallocate points to fees, cutting some, increasing others, thereby rearranging the economic incentives to perform certain procedures at the same time that the total points bring the overall budget into line. In the past, the government has used these reallocations to increase the points for the visits and consultations performed by doctors in solo and clinic-based practice on the theory that rewarding them would lead to fewer expensive inpatient episodes. This tilt toward the independent, clinic-based sector has made the Japanese office-based practitioner one of the highest-paid medical practitioners in the world. Nevertheless, newly trained physicians have been electing to accept salaried positions in teaching hospitals where there is greater prestige, even though they are paid less than half as much. Over 55% of Japanese physicians are now salaried, and the clinic-based doctor represents an increasingly older generation of physicians. Moreover, Japanese patients appear to be voting with their feet as they wait for over several hours to see a physician in the outpatient department of one of the prestigious teaching hospitals. This phenomenon in turn may be a future cost-increasing factor for Japan as hospitals compete with clinics for patients by means of the outpatient department, and as the outpatient department becomes the point of entry to expensive inpatient care. (According to Hiroi's data, Japanese inpatient admission rates are currently approximately half those in the United States.)

Another aspect of the Japanese point-fee system that is very different from the RBRVS is that the Japanese consciously lower the points for procedures that are increasing in volume in order to contain costs. (See, for example, Hiroi's discussion of the government's reaction to the "excessive use of intravenous drip" in 1981.) Moreover, there does not appear to be a volume response to lower fees in Japan as there is in the United States. The response to cutting the fees for intravenous drip was a rapid decline in volume of the procedure. Why do the laws of classical economics seem to work on one side of the Pacific Ocean and not the other?

The answer appears to be that the Japanese government is able to cut prices below marginal costs, while price cuts in the United States have reduced profit margins but still leave positive returns. In Japan, payments for surgery are often below the costs of doing surgery (at least in urban hospitals), and this is one reason that surgery rates are much lower in Japan than in the United States. (Other reasons include an emphasis on drug and holistic therapies and the lack of a legal definition of brain death, which makes most transplants impossible to perform.) This aggressive government behavior was colorfully described at an earlier conference as "mole-bashing," in reference to a popular Japanese arcade game where a puppet pops up from a board and the player must quickly smash it back down with a hammer in order to score points. By contrast, the emphasis in the United States is on "scientifically" establishing the relative values of procedures in order to set their appropriate relationship. Surgical procedures were cut by the RBRVS by as much as 40%, but Medicare still pays over $2,000 for a cataract operation that requires forty-five minutes of physician work. Cataract surgeons in the United States still can earn substantial fees by increasing the number of surgeries they perform.

The Japanese are also able to set fees for technologies such as MRI imaging at rates sufficiently low so that it is difficult for the physician or hospital to recover their capital costs quickly. According to Hiroi, labor and capital are not included in the fee schedule, and the chapter by Hisashige on MRI in the next section tells us that the Japanese pay one-fifth of the fee that is charged in the United States for each MRI procedure. Nevertheless, there are as many MRI units in total in Japan as in the United States, albeit even more greatly underutilized. Japanese physicians and hospitals appear to be willing to invest in these technologies, despite their lack of profitability, for reasons of prestige and the competitive desire to appear to offer the highest quality of care. By contrast, payment policy in the United States allows the cost of these machines to be captured several times over since overhead payments do not decline once a machine is fully capitalized.

The aggressive Japanese government behavior in setting prices below the physician's cost for a procedure, if attempted by the United States government, would probably be regarded as improperly skewing the economic incentives of physicians, at best, and as government interference in the practice of medicine, at worst. Nevertheless, pricing surgical and MRI services below cost in Japan makes it clear why the Japanese do not appear to have a "volume and intensity" response to fee-schedule cuts. The Japanese government's ability to aggressively set prices in part relates to the Japanese parliamentary system, the centralized governmental system, and Japanese cultural norms.

Although the Japanese point-fee system has worked well as a cost-containment tool in the past, it is unclear that this policy instrument will be useful in addressing some of the problems the Japanese health-care system faces. Although the Japanese government has deliberately tilted the fees toward the office-based physicians and away from tertiary care procedures, these physicians are declining in numbers despite their greater incomes. Care is fragmented in Japan as office-based physicians cannot treat their patients in hospitals. Physicians built clinics with small numbers of hospital beds in order not to lose their patients to the hospital, and expensive equipment is therefore purchased for both settings. Despite their high incomes, the office-based doctors feel squeezed by the high equipment overhead they must bear in order to compete with the growing prestige of the hospital outpatient departments where patients increasingly flow. Waiting lists are long and physicians are burdened by the heavy workloads. It is not clear that fee-schedule manipulation can address these issues effectively in the future. As other articles suggest, Japan may need to face manpower training issues, redefined relationships between office-based physicians and tertiary-care institutions, and the rationing of access to prestigious teaching hospitals through differential fees.

### Intensity of Hospital Services

When asked why he robbed banks, the mobster Willie Sutton replied, "Because that's where the money is." In health care, the money is in the hospital sector. According to a report at the conference, hospitalization represented 47% of costs in the United States and 33% in Japan. Therefore, if one is to understand the lower Japanese health care costs, one has to look to the hospital sector. According to Hsiao's analysis, lower hospital costs account for 25% of the per-capita cost difference, the single largest factor.

Kōichi Kawabuchi's chapter on capital costs illuminates one part of this difference. Kawabuchi found that (1) building construction costs in Japan were less than 40% of those in the United States; (2) the average age of the physical plant was comparable in both countries; (3) tangible fixed assets per bed were two times higher in the United States than in Japan; (4) the ratio of capital-related costs to operating expenses is slightly higher in Japan because wages and salaries increase operating expenses in U.S. hospitals; (5) floor space per bed is four times higher in the United States than in Japan; and (6) the daily room charge in U.S. hospitals is approximately five times that in Japan.

Discussion of the Kawabuchi chapter at the conference illustrated how difficult it is to make comparisons between the hospital sectors in the two countries. Concern was expressed that some of the measures used in the Kawabuchi analysis were expressed in absolute dollars rather than dollars per capita or dollars per bed, and that others were sensitive to depreciation assumptions. It was suggested, for example, that such depreciation-sensitive measures as tangible fixed assets per bed could be made more objective by looking instead at initial construction costs per bed. It was also noted that since land costs are so much higher in Japan, they should probably be removed from the analysis. Moreover, there was no consensus on the meaning of the floor space per bed and room charge differences. The inference was that these measured quality differences; however, others argued that the floor space between hospital beds was not much different than space between beds in Japanese homes and that there did not seem to be much demand for private beds in Japanese hospitals.

In the discussion it was argued that the principle reason for avoiding per capita or per-bed measures was that the combination of long-term-care beds with acute-care beds in Japanese hospitals made precise comparisons next to impossible. For example, Office of Economic Cooperation and Development (OECD) data list Japanese bed to population ratios at 15.7, compared with 4.8 in the United States in 1989, three times as high. But the Japanese figure includes both nursing home and psychiatric beds while the United States figure does not. If the latter are included in the U.S. total, the Japanese number is still higher, but not dramatically. Similarly, the Japanese length of stay is over fifty days, while the U.S. length of stay is just over nine. But Japanese length-of-stay statistics include Japanese long-term-care patients while the U.S. figures generally do not. According to OECD data for 1990, the Japanese received 4.1 inpatient days per capita, compared to 1.2 days per capita in the United States, a rate over three times as high. However, by contrast, the hospital staffing ratio in Japan was 0.79 people per bed compared with 3.35 per bed in the United States, a ratio four times as high. Given the lower hospital salaries in Japan, these comparisons suggest that the lower staffing costs in Japan outweigh the higher days per capita, producing on average lower hospital sector costs. Later in this volume, the Muramatsu and Liang paper on acute myocardial infarction indicates that the lower nurse-staffing ratios in Japanese hospitals lead to longer lengths of stay because shorter lengths of stay would require more nurses to deal with the increased patient acuity levels. In addition, the cost of care in the American hospital was 1.6 times higher than in the Japanese hospital, even though the length of stay in the American hospital was one-third as long and the length of stay in the intensive care unit (three days) was identical in both. The capital analysis is consistent with these conclusions, although capital costs represent only about 8% to 10% of hospital costs. The overall result, as noted above, is that institutional costs are 33% of Japan's health care costs and 47% of those in the United States.

## Administrative Costs

Administrative cost comparisons between the United States and Canada indicate that as much as $67 billion, or 10% of U.S. health costs, could be saved if U.S. administrative costs could be held to Canadian levels (U.S. General Accounting Office 1991). Hsiao estimates that ¥29,500, or approximately 12% of the difference in U.S. and Japanese health costs per capita, can be attributed to the more efficient administration of Japanese health care. In this volume, Ikegami, Wolfson, and Ishii estimate that insurance industry overhead in the United States is approximately twice the overhead in Japan and four times as much in absolute dollars considering that the United States spends twice what Japan spends on health care. Savings are generally estimated by substituting the lower Japanese percentage for the higher United States percentage. Such methodologies are weak because they generally neglect the functions that administration plays in different systems. Ikegami, Wolfson, and Ishii also found that U.S. administrative costs in the hospital sector are as much as two to three times those in Japanese hospitals, and five times as much in absolute dollars, again considering that the United States spends approximately twice what Japan spends on a per-bed basis.

Comparisons of administrative costs between countries generally examine the following: (1) the costs of administering health insurance; (2) billing and other costs incurred by hospitals (e.g., maintaining patient medical records); (3) billing and other costs incurred by physicians (e.g., dealing with peer review agencies); (4) costs incurred by consumers in submitting claims and dealing with denials; and (5) government costs in regulating providers and enforcing quality standards. In the GAO analysis, for example, savings to physicians and hospitals outweighed savings from reducing insurance industry transaction costs, although the latter was the single largest category of expense.

Ken Thorpe (1992) has argued persuasively that high administrative cost ratios are not necessarily bad. Administrative expenditures can be cost-effective if they lead to effective management of health outcomes, lower patient-care costs, or other desired results. For example, expenditures on maintaining medical records may be desirable if they improve care management.

The analysis by Ikegami, Wolfson, and Ishii only examines health insurance administrative costs and hospital administrative costs. The health insurance analysis compares the ratio of insurance industry overhead to total system expenditures in the two countries. As noted above, the United States ratio is twice the ratio in Japan. The analysis of hospital administrative costs is based on a sample of five hospitals in Japan and eight in Florida of similar bed size for which data were available. The average administrative costs in the Florida hospitals ran 20% and were two to three times as high as the average Japanese hospital's administrative costs. These differences are attributed to simpler billing arrangements, less need for marketing and planning, less investment in medical records, and less quality assurance and risk management activities in Japan. The conclusion appropriately notes that it is unclear whether the additional expenditures in U.S. hospitals are related to better patient outcomes. This is the key question that determines whether the higher administrative costs are simply waste or valued investments that improve outcomes. Nevertheless, the large differences indicate that there is a large potential for savings by reducing administrative overhead in U.S. hospitals.

REFERENCES

Thorpe, K. 1992. Inside the black box of administrative costs. *Health Affairs* 11.2: 41–56.
U.S. General Accounting Office. 1991. *Canadian health insurance: Lessons for the United States*. GAO/HRD 1990–91. Washington, D.C.: U.S. Government Printing Office.

CHAPTER 9

# Comparison of Hospital Admission Rates between Japan and the United States

*Toshihiko Hasegawa*

SUMMARY  Japan spends a lower percentage of its GDP on health care expenditures than does the United States. But judging from the statistical data such as number of physician visits, average length of stay in hospitals, and number of hospital beds, Japan should be spending more than the United States. One of the few exceptions is the hospital admission rate, which is much higher in the United States. Analysis of the official statistical data reveals that this is due mainly to the difference in the surgical admission rate.

## Background

According to the Organization for Economic Cooperation and Development (OECD) statistics, U.S. health care expenditures were 11.2% of GDP in 1987 versus 6.8% in Japan (OECD 1992); the ratio of the United States is 1.65 times that of Japan. However, when statistics on health care services are compared, the rate of contact or visits to physicians on an outpatient basis in 1986 was 5.3 per person per year in the United States, and 12.8 in Japan (Health Care Financing Administration 1989). Furthermore, the average length of stay in a general hospital in 1984 was 6.6 days in the United States and 40.9 in Japan (OECD 1992). Comparison of statistics on health care facilities in the two countries reveals that the number of hospitals per 100,000 people in 1987 was 2.9 in the United States and 8.0 in Japan, and that the number of hospital beds per 1,000 people in 1987 was 5.3 in the United States and 15.2 in Japan (including those beds in Japanese clinics) (Ministry of Health and Welfare [MHW] 1986a, 1989a, 1992a; U.S. Department of Health and Human Services 1992). The rate in Japan is approximately three times that of the United States. These statistical data on health care services and facilities imply that health expenditures should be higher in Japan than in the United States (table 1).

One of the few figures in which the rate is higher in the United States than in Japan is the per-capita annual hospital admission rate, which is 0.157 for non-federal short-stay hospitals in 1984 in the United States (U.S. Department of

**Table 1. Comparison of basic statistical data between Japan
and the U.S.**

|  | Japan | U.S. | Year |
|---|---|---|---|
| Total health care expenditure (% GNP) | 6.8 | 11.2 | 1987 |
| Health care service |  |  |  |
|    Physician contact or visit (annual per capita) | 12.8 | 5.3 | 1986 |
|    Average length of stay (days) | 40.9 | 6.6 | 1984 |
| Facility |  |  |  |
|    Hospitals (per 100,000 population) | 8 | 2.9 | 1987 |
|    Beds (per 100,000 population) | 15.2 | 5.3 | 1987 |

Health and Human Services 1965–86), compared with 0.094 for the total of
hospitals and clinics with beds in Japan (MHW 1986b, 1989b, 1992b). It would
therefore seem that the reason for the higher health care expenditures in the United
States should be focused in this area.

## Methodology

Data on the number of total hospital admissions, the number of surgical admissions, and the number of surgical procedures performed at nonfederal short-stay
hospitals in the United States are available from the annual nationwide estimates
derived from the sampling data of the National Hospital Discharge Survey (U.S.
Department of Health and Human Services 1965-86; 1990, 1992). Annual estimates on the total number of surgeries performed at all hospitals are reported in
Hospital Statistics, for both inpatient and outpatient surgery. No official annual
statistics are available in Japan for the total number of hospital admissions and
surgical admissions. However, one-month (September) nationwide sampling-
based estimates of hospital admissions and surgical admissions for 1984, 1987,
and 1990 were reported as part of the Patient Surveys (MHW 1986b, 1989b,
1992b). Provided the figures for September are close to the annual monthly
averages, fairly reasonable, annual nationwide estimates can be calculated by
multiplying the figures of September by 365 (or 366) and dividing by 30. However, no official nationwide statistics are available on the total number of surgical
procedures, either for inpatients or outpatients.

Nevertheless, it is possible to make an approximate comparison between the
two countries for the total number of hospital admissions and the number of
surgical admissions for 1984, 1987, and 1990. It should be noted that, in the
United States, the number of surgical admissions has been declining since 1984
due to the introduction of the diagnostic related group (DRG)-based prospective
payment system. This has led to an increase in outpatient surgeries. Since the

number of outpatient surgeries in the United States is not known, a meaningful comparison that excludes the influence of this trend can be made only for 1984.

In the United States, a surgical admission is defined as any hospitalization during which one or more surgeries are performed on a patient in an operating room; therefore, these figures may include minor surgeries. By contrast, in Japan that definition is left up to the physician at each facility. Furthermore, because the U.S. figure for surgical hospitalizations is for nongovernmental, short-term hospitals, it does not include figures for federal hospitals and other long-term hospitals. Consequently, the total estimate may be smaller than the actual figures for all hospitals. However, this difference is likely to be fairly small.

## Result and Discussion

In the United States in 1984, the rate of total hospital admission per 1,000 population was 156.8, or 1.66 times the rate in Japan, which was 99.4 (table 2) (U.S. Department of Health and Human Services 1992). Of these, the rate of surgical admission was 71.0 in the United States, or 3.1 times the rate in Japan, which was 22.9. On the other hand, the rate of nonsurgical admission was 85.7 in the United States, only 1.20 times the rate in Japan, which was 71.6. Therefore, 77.1% of the difference in the rate of total hospital admissions between the two countries is due to the difference in the rate of surgical admissions.

Subsequently, the rate of total hospital admissions per capita began declining in the United States and reached 123.5 in 1990, a decline of 21.2% from the 1984 level. On the other hand, this rate increased gradually in Japan and reached 100.5 in 1990, up 6.5% from the 1984 level. The rate of surgical admissions in the United States declined by 17.5% to 58.6 in 1990, while the rate in Japan increased by 17.0% to 26.8. As a result, in 1990, the rate of total hospital admissions in the United States was 1.23 times that of Japan, and the rate of surgical admissions in the United States was 2.18 times that of Japan, thus showing a narrowing of the gap. Most of this increase in the Japanese figures is considered to be due to the aging of its population. The population over 65 years old as a percentage of Japan's total population increased from 9.9% in 1984 to 12.1% in 1990. The total number of hospitalizations per capita in 1990 would be 96.4 when adjusted for the population structure of 1984, thus showing a slight decline from the 1984 figure, which was 99.4. On the other hand, despite the continued aging of the U.S. population, 11.8% (the population over 65 years old) in 1984 to 12.5% in 1990, the rate of total hospital admissions and the rate of nonsurgical admissions in United States all declined from the 1984 level. The reason for this decline probably lies in the U.S. policy of containing health care expenditures, including the implementation of the DRG system in 1983. It is possible that this policy had the effect of reducing both total hospital admissions and surgical admissions. Meanwhile, the ratio of outpatient surgery to the total increased from 27.8% in 1984 to 50.6% in 1990. Thus, while inpatient surgery declined, the total number of surgeries did not decline (table 2). These figures indicate that surgeons are in-

**Table 2. Comparison of admissions between Japan and the U.S.**

| | Japan Total hospitals and clinics | | | U.S. Nongovernment short-term hospitals | | |
|---|---|---|---|---|---|---|
| | Total Admission | Surgical Admission | Nonsurgical Admission | Total Admission | Surgical Admission | Nonsurgical Admission |
| 1984 Number x 1000 | 11,355 | 2,749 | 8,606 | 37,162 | 16,838 | 20,324 |
| Rate/1000 | 94.4 | 22.9 | 71.6 | 156.8 | 71.0 | 85.7 |
| Percent | 100 | 24.2 | | 100 | 45.3 | |
| 1987 Number x 1000 | 11,963 | 3,129 | 8,834 | 33,387 | 15,830 | 27,557 |
| Rate/1000 | 97.8 | 25.6 | 72.3 | 136.9 | 64.9 | 72.1 |
| Percent | 100 | 26.2 | | 100 | 47.4 | |
| 1990 Number x 1000 | 12,426 | 3,311 | 9,115 | 30,788 | 14,563 | 26,225 |
| Rate/1000 | 100.5 | 26.8 | 73.7 | 123.8 | 58.6 | 65.2 |
| Percent | 100 | 26.6 | | 100 | 47.3 | |

creasingly performing surgery on an outpatient basis. The rate of nonsurgical admission in the United States now is smaller than that in Japan.

Based on the result of the comparative analysis above, the difference in the rate of total hospital admission between the United States and Japan can be explained mostly by the difference in the rate of surgical admissions, which, in turn, may explain some of the difference in health care expenditures.

ACKNOWLEDGMENT

I would like to take this opportunity to express my sincere appreciation for the kind advice offered for this research by Professor Shuzō Nishimura of Kyoto University. This study was partially funded by a scientific research grant from Japan's Ministry of Education.

REFERENCES

Ministry of Health and Welfare (MHW). 1986a, 1989a, 1992a. *Iryō shisetsu chōsa* (Medical facilities survey). Tokyo: Kōsei Tōkei Kyōkai.
———. 1986b, 1989b, 1992b. *Kanja chōsa* (Patient survey). Tokyo: Kōsei Tōkei Kyōkai.
Organization for Economic Cooperation and Development (OECD). 1992. *Health Data File.* Paris: OECD.
U.S. Department of Health and Human Services. 1992. *Health United States 1991.* Washington, D.C.: GPO.
———. 1965-86.*Vital and health statistics. Trend in hospital utilization: United States, 1965-86.* Data from the National Health Survey No. 101. Washington, D.C.: GPO.

CHAPTER 10

# High-Cost Technology in Health Care:
# The Adoption and Diffusion of MRI in Japan

*Akinori Hisashige*

SUMMARY    The total number of installed magnetic resonance imaging (MRI) and computerized-axial tomography (CAT) units in Japan was 1,048 and 8,963, respectively, in 1991. Not only is the number of CAT units relative to population in Japan the highest in the world, but that of MRI is second only to that of the United States. The diffusion of MRI was slower than that of CAT, as was also the case in the United States, accelerating sharply beginning in 1986 onward. Fifty-five percent of MRI units were owned by private hospitals. This pattern of diffusion in Japan was mainly determined by the following factors: the technological attributes of MRI, the market situation of the medical engineering industry, the reimbursement system of health insurance, and the sociocultural background. However, the introduction of MRI in Japan was not linked to any formal assessment of its effectiveness and efficiency.

## Introduction

New technologies have generally been incorporated into the health care system with enthusiasm by both providers and consumers. This is particularly true in Japan, where the medical care system has quickly embraced sophisticated, high-technology equipment. For example, the total number of installed MRI and CAT units in Japan was 1,048 and 8,963, respectively, in 1991. Japan is the world leader in the number of CAT units relative to population, and its ratio of MRI to population is second only to that of the United States. Moreover, more than half of all hospitals have ultrasonoscopes and gastro-fiberscopes. One-third of them have auto-biochemical analyzers and bronchoscopes (Hisashige, Sakurai, and Kaihara 1991; Hisashige 1992b).

However, seldom are the effectiveness and efficiency of new health care technologies fully evaluated before their widespread implementation. It has been pointed out that dissatisfaction with many technologies grows over time as they fail in clinical settings to meet claims or expectations for benefits. A technology may fall into disuse as it is replaced by yet another new and incompletely evaluated technology. The most serious, common problem is that the quality of medical technology is neither evaluated nor assured (Hisashige, Sakurai, and Kaihara 1991; Hisashige 1992b). Moreover, there are no formal mechanisms for monitoring the quality of health care technologies.

The increasing adoption of new health care technologies is one of the primary factors contributing to the steeply rising health care expenditure in Japan (Hisashige 1992b). Therefore, a formal and rigorous evaluation of the clinical effectiveness and economic efficiency of major technologies is needed before their widespread adoption can improve performance within the health care system. However, in Japan, the introduction of new health care technologies has not been linked to any formal assessment of their effectiveness and efficiency.

To identify problems in how the present health care system evaluates and adopts new, expensive health care technologies in Japan, this study describes the pattern of the diffusion of MRI units as a typical new technology in comparison with CAT units, and it evaluates the following factors relative to that spread: the technological attributes of MRI, the market situation of the medical device industry, the regulation and reimbursement system of health care, and the sociocultural background.

## Methods

First, in order to analyze the diffusion pattern of MRI in comparison with CAT in Japan, the annual numbers of installed MRI by the type of unit, area, health care facility, and manufacturer were obtained from two sources: the annual lists of installed MRI and CAT in the *Journal of New Medicine* (*Shin iryō* 1975–92) and the *Medical Care Facilities Survey* (*Iryō shisetsu chōsa*) (Ministry of Health and Welfare [MHW] 1978–87). Data relative to the diffusion of MRI in other countries were obtained from studies by Hillman (1985; 1986) and Steinberg (1985; 1986).

Second, to examine the technological attributes of MRI compared with CAT, and whether the efficacy, effectiveness, and efficiency of MRI was evaluated during its diffusion in Japan, a Medline search for papers that examined sensitivity or specificity of MRI was conducted for the years 1983–91. In addition, all papers published in the following main radiological journals in Japan were also analyzed: *Japanese Journal of Clinical Radiology, Nippon Acta Radiologica, Image Technology & Information Display,* and the *Japanese Journal of Nuclear Medicine* from 1980 to 1990. These journals were selected because they contained most of the studies relative to MRI in Japan. After identifying all the articles, the annual change in the proportion of the type of papers, such as case reports, original articles, and reviews, was analyzed. In addition, original articles were examined for references to the sensitivity or specificity of MRI as a diagnostic test.

Third, to analyze the market of medical imaging devices including MRI, the annual change in the amount of their production was examined. Data were obtained from Pharmaceutical Production Statistics between 1972 and 1988.

Finally, to evaluate the influence of governmental regulation and reimbursement policy on the diffusion of MRI, the regulation process of approval and licensing of MRI and the application for approval for National Health Insurance was analyzed. In addition, changes in the fee schedule for MRI compared with those of CAT were analyzed from applications for insurance up to 1990 (MHW 1991).

**Results and Discussion**

Introduction and Diffusion of MRI

Figure 1 shows the diffusion of installed MRI units in Japan compared with that in the United States. The number of MRI scanners has increased rapidly since the first one was introduced to Japan in 1982; in 1991 the total number was 1,048. The rate of diffusion in Japan was slightly slower than that in the United States.

However, as shown in figure 2, the rate of diffusion of CAT in Japan has drastically increased since its introduction in 1975. In 1991, the total number of installed CAT units was 8,963. Although the rate of diffusion in Japan was greater than that in the United States eight years after the first unit was introduced, the pattern was similar to that in the United States. Yet, the diffusion was obviously more rapid in Japan and the United States than in other countries, such as France. The diffusion pattern of MRI and CAT in Japan is the same as that in the United States (Hillman and Schwartz 1985, 1986; Steinberg, Sisk, and Locke 1985; Steinberg 1986). Not only is the number of CAT units per population in Japan the highest in the world, but that of MRI was second only to the United States in 1988.

One of the factors determining this rapid adoption of technology is the belief among health care professionals and consumers that sophisticated, high-technology health care is desirable because it is assumed to be effective. Further, large hospitals and university (teaching and research) hospitals, which have greater resources, adopt new technology at an early stage to maintain their prestige as well as to attract patients.

However, these factors do not fully explain the pattern of diffusion because it can be seen that the spread of innovative health care technologies such as MRI is a complex process, influenced by a variety of factors related to the technologies themselves and to the socioeconomic environments (Hillman and Schwartz 1985; Steinberg, Sisk, and Locke 1985). Therefore, although empirical data are limited, further analysis and inferences are needed to comprehensively evaluate the impact of each factor on the diffusion of MRI.

Figure 3 shows the comparison of the rates of diffusion between MRI and CAT in Japan. The increase was slower for MRI than for CAT. However, the difference in this rate gradually decreased because the growth in the number of CAT units slowed four years after their introduction.

The slight delay in the diffusion of MRI reflects the technological attributes of this scanner compared with those of CAT. MRI is an incremental or substitute imaging technology. The existing imaging technology or CAT not only has already shown a remarkable performance but also has spread widely. Moreover, although there are a number of advantages to MRI over other imaging tech-

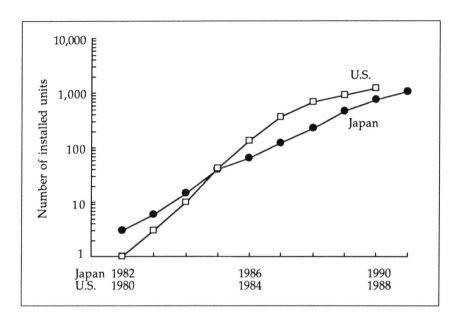

Figure 1. Diffusion of MRI since the introduction of the first unit

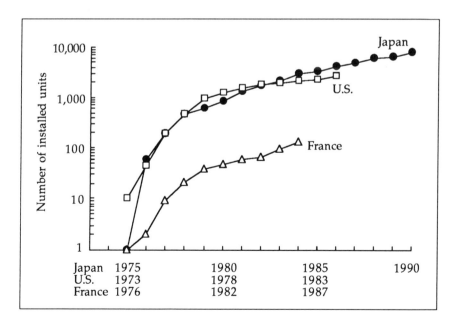

Figure 2. Diffusion of CAT scans since the introduction of the first unit

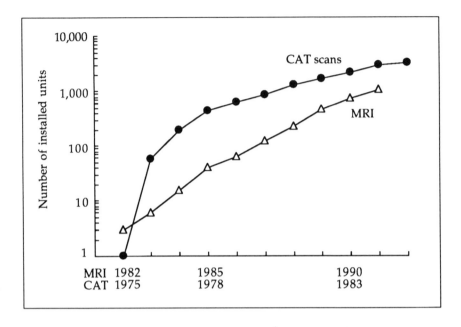

**Figure 3. Diffusion of MRI in comparison with that of CAT scans in Japan**

nologies, as well as a number of problems, the marginal efficacy of MRI over CAT and other diagnostic imaging technologies has not been established (AHTAC 1991; Guyatt and Drummond 1985; Hillman and Schwartz 1985; Steinberg, Sisk, and Locke 1985). Even in the area of the central nervous system, where MRI was expected to be superior to CAT for detection and characterization of lesions, the levels of efficacy are similar (Kent and Larson 1988; Kuhns, Thornbury, and Feryback 1989).

There was a marked change in the diffusion of the type of magnet. The earliest MRI units were resistive magnets. While the diffusion of this type has gradually increased, its proportion to all units installed decreased from 75.4% (1986) to 13.1% (1990). During the same period, the proportion of superconducting magnets sharply increased from 21.5% to 68.1%. Although the proportion of permanent magnets is still low, it increased from 3.1% to 18.8%.

In 1988, 20.6% of all units were owned by national and public health care facilities (i.e., hospitals and clinics); social insurance organizations owned 14.4%; and private health care facilities, individual and corporate, owned 55.1% of the units. As for the adoption of MRI by size of hospital, large (more than 300 beds) and medium-sized (100 to 299 beds) owned 43.7% and 35.6% of all units, respectively. While permanent magnets were owned mainly by clinics and small and medium-sized hospitals (less than 200 beds), superconducting magnets were owned by large hospitals, such as private and public general hospitals and university hospitals (more than 400 beds).

Similarly, diverse diffusion patterns for different types of magnet are found in the United States (Hillman and Schwartz 1985; 1986). There exist uncertainties regarding the optimal type and strength of the magnet in order to assure the actual marginal clinical benefit. Furthermore, each type substantially differs in fixed and operating costs. Despite the lower cost, yet clinical uncertainties, of permanent and resistive magnets, health care facilities in both Japan and the United States clearly prefer superconducting magnets (Hillman and Schwartz 1985, 1986; Steinberg, Sisk, and Locke 1985; Steinberg 1986). Recently, however, small hospitals have increasingly purchased low-cost, permanent magnets.

Based on the data for 1991, there were 6.1 MRI units per one million population in Japan. The geographical distribution of MRI by the forty-seven administrative divisions varied widely. The highest-ranking five regions (prefectures) were Yamaguchi (11.0), Kyoto (9.4), Yamanashi (9.4), Kumamoto (9.2), and Ehime (9.1), while the lowest-ranking five regions were Yamagata (2.4), Shimane (2.5), Tottori (3.2), Kanagawa (3.9), and Aomori (3.9). The ratio between the highest and the lowest is 5:1. Although low-ranking regions tended to be poor socioeconomic areas, it cannot be observed that high-ranking regions are concentrated in metropolitan areas or areas with a high socioeconomic level. Although this geographic variation in diffusion may hamper access to as well as availability of MRI, its influence on health outcomes has not yet been evaluated.

Many factors, such as the historical background of health care, socioeconomic conditions in each local area, and so on (Hisashige 1992b), are suspected to influence these geographic variations in the diffusion of MRI. For example, the numbers of physicians and beds per population were correlated with that of MRI units. This suggests that supplier-induced demands may play an important role. It is difficult, however, to determine the specific factors.

Evaluation of the Effectiveness of MRI

MRI is a complex, sophisticated new technology producing images of the human body. Since the advantages of MRI over other imaging modalities include the absence of ionizing radiation, cross-sectional views in any plane, lack of a required contrast injection, and minimal patient discomfort, the possibilities of clinical effectiveness for MRI are impressive (Guyatt and Drummond 1985; Hillman and Schwartz 1985). These attributes play an important role in determining its spread.

Despite these promising features, however, important clinical and technological issues remain unsolved. MRI shares many technological attributes with CAT as an existing diagnostic test that showed remarkable performance (AHTAC 1991; Guyatt and Drummond 1985; Hillman and Schwartz 1985). Its effectiveness must be evaluated incrementally. Since MRI is an evolving technology, it is hampered by more technological uncertainty than was CAT at a similar stage of development; for example, there is great uncertainty over the relative advantages and disadvantages of the different types and sizes of MRI magnets.

A Medline search revealed the number of reports that evaluated the sensitivity or specificity for MRI in all languages during the period 1983–91. The number of these reports increased rapidly and has maintained a level of more than forty since 1987. Among them, only two papers were reported by Japanese researchers, and the quality of their study design and evaluation was poor (Nakajima et al. 1989; Nishimura et al. 1988). Although the number of papers relative to MRI in Japanese medical journals increased rapidly from 1987, almost all the papers consisted of case reports or introductory reviews. None of them evaluated the diagnostic efficacy of MRI.

Critical appraisal of the early evaluations of MRI (published in the first four years after its introduction) using commonly accepted criteria such as sensitivity, specificity, and so on showed that these papers were flawed by a lack of proper evaluation (Cooper, Charlmers, McCally et al. 1988). Furthermore, although MRI already has been shown to be very appropriate for soft tissues, especially the brain, and appears to be also of major use in imaging the spine and cardiovascular system (AHTAC 1991; Cooper, Charlmers, McCally et al. 1988; Guyatt and Drummond 1985; Hillman and Schwartz 1985; Kent and Larson 1988), the evaluation of the demonstrated clinical efficacy of MRI in the central nervous system did not indicate that it was generally superior to that of existing imaging modalities, such as CAT (Dent and Larson 1988; Kuhns, Thornbury, and Feryback 1989). It was recommended that more rigorous clinical research studies be conducted.

In a recent consensus statement about the current concept of the clinical efficacy of MRI in Australia, it was pointed out that MRI is, at present, essentially a tertiary and complementary diagnostic-imaging modality, requested or approved by independent specialists for appropriate indications. Specific comments will require further consideration as technical developments with MRI become available (AHTAC 1991).

Moreover, the evaluation of the clinical effectiveness of MRI should not be limited to diagnostic validity. It is also necessary to examine the effects on patient management and health outcome (Guyatt and Drummond 1985), and there was no randomized clinical trial for assessing these problems. A before-and-after study showed that the introduction of MRI did not change practice patterns, such as average length of stay and number of other diagnostic tests and surgical procedures, for neurologists and neurosurgeons (Durand-Zaleski, Reizine, Duzin et al. 1991). This indicates that there has been no substitution of MRI for other tests and that MRI has been added to the existing array of neurological tests. The result of a cross-sectional questionnaire study in Japan is consistent with this result (Hisashige 1992a).

In summary, the marginal effectiveness of MRI over that of CAT and other diagnostic modalities has not been convincingly established and does not warrant the widespread adoption of MRI in general clinical settings. This situation partly explains why the diffusion of MRI has been slightly delayed in comparison with CAT. However, developed countries such as the United States have at least started the evaluation of the effectiveness at the introduction of MRI. In contrast, such an evaluation is greatly lacking in Japan due to a historical background where the quality and effectiveness of health care have not been assessed. This has hampered appropriate decision making for the adoption of MRI in Japan (Hisashige, Sakurai, and Kaihara 1991; Hisashige 1992b).

Medical Device Marketing Industry

The market for medical devices is one of the main factors that determines the diffusion pattern of MRI. The medical device industry grew remarkably quickly at the rate of 20–40% per year from 1977 to 1980 and 0–15% from 1981 to 1989 (Ministry of Health and Welfare 1972–88). In 1989, total sales of medical devices in Japan amounted to ¥1,220 billion ($6.8 billion at an appropriate PPP rate of $1.00 = ¥180); that for diagnostic imaging apparatus was ¥271 billion ($1.5 billion).

During this high-growth period, the proportion of CAT increased rapidly, while that for ultrasonic apparatus increased gradually. In this sense, CAT played an important role as the engine for rapid growth in the latter half of the 1970s (Niki 1983). Nevertheless, despite the lowering of prices since 1981, the sales of CAT have stagnated and lost their role as the leader of growth in the medical device industry.

In the latter half of the 1980s sales of MRI and its percentage of total sales of medical implements was rapidly increasing. MRI was expected to play a role in the growth of this industry by taking the place of CAT. However, sales of MRI (¥37 billion, $200 million) were still only half that of CAT (¥75 billion, $420 million) in 1989 (figure 4).

When MRI installed by manufacturers were examined, the highest-ranking three Japanese manufacturers (Toshiba, Hitachi, Shimazu) accounted for more than 60% of all units installed in Japan (*Shin iryō* 1975–92). The best-selling types of MRI were the MRP-20 (Hitachi) and MRT-50A (Toshiba). The proportion of MRI units made by foreign manufacturers in Japan remained relatively constant (32–50%) with a slight fluctuation during the period 1985–90. This percentage was lower than that (30–65%) of CAT during the period 1977–82.

It has been pointed out that the Japanese medical device industry has now been strengthened to the point that it is taking the initiative in introducing new products and commercializing new technologies. In the 1960s and early 1970s, Western industry enjoyed a six- to eight-year time lag from the introduction of products before the Japanese were able to respond (Abegglen and Stalk 1987). By the 1970s, as was shown in the case of angiography and MRI, Japanese industry was keeping pace with Western industry in new-product introduction.

In particular, although Japanese equipment achieved relatively lower performances, they were priced lower. While large or university hospitals continued to buy the higher-performance capacity of Western equipment, smaller hospitals and clinics purchased the less-effective, but much lower-priced, Japanese alternative. Moreover, as the volume of Japanese-made equipment increased, its price fell at a rapid rate. Even as prices were falling, its performance level increased. The

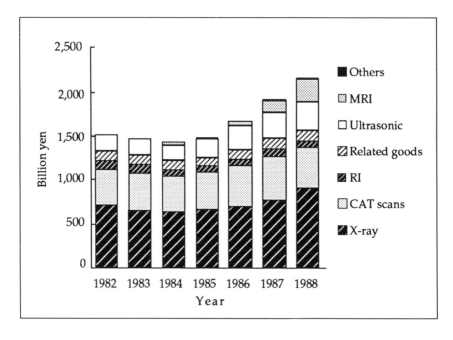

**Figure 4. The total sales for diagnostic imaging equipment**

Japanese medical device industry finds a market by developing a popular model of equipment with features that facilitate explosive sales (Abegglen and Stalk 1987; Niki 1983).

The purchase price for the main types of MRI, 1.5 T (superconducting) and 0.5 T (superconducting and resistive), decreased log-linearly (Hisashige 1992a), declining by approximately half in eight years. This decrease in price was mainly achieved by Japanese MRI, while the price of foreign MRI remained at a higher level. These phenomena have already been observed in the case of CAT (Abegglen and Stalk 1987; Niki 1983).

The strategy of the Japanese medical device industry mentioned above closely matches the characteristics of the health care system in Japan, where concern for quality or effectiveness of health care has been greatly lacking (Hisashige, Sakurai, and Kaihara 1991; Hisashige 1991b). Providers of health care are paid on a single-fee schedule (i.e., fee-for-service) regardless of their skills or the quality of their services. This financing system gives them incentives to purchase low-priced equipment and to perform diagnostic tests with high frequency to maximize profits.

The Regulation and Reimbursement System

A major factor that influences the diffusion of health care technologies is government regulation. In Japan, medical devices (instruments and apparatus) that are intended for use in the diagnosis, treatment, or prevention of diseases are subject to regulations under the Pharmaceutical Affairs Law (MHW 1991). The process of approval and licensing for medical devices under this law emphasizes safety, effectiveness, and quality. MHW officials attempt to keep up with the latest scientific standards and to respond to social demands.

However, as the pace of technological change in medical devices has recently changed and as their use has become widespread, their regulation under law has become more complex. Moreover, the regulatory process has been implicit and closed, as is most health policy decision making (Hisashige 1992b). Therefore, with MRI as with CAT, it is unclear that approval was based on scientific evidence.

Conjointly with the approval system, the reimbursement system plays an important role in the diffusion of health care technologies. In Japan, the health insurance system that covers all citizens was established in 1961. Despite various financing schemes, all prices of medical procedures are minutely defined by this nationally uniform and itemized fee schedule with the same fee paid to all providers for the same procedure regardless of skill, quality, or cost (Hisashige 1992b). This payment system has been of crucial importance in the diffusion and utilization of health care technologies. As mentioned before, such a system gives incentives to small- and medium-sized hospitals to introduce advanced technology.

The rules for approving medical devices for use and coverage by the insurance system have been enforced in accordance with Pharmaceutical Affairs Bureau (PAB) Notification No. 156, On a Rule for Introducing an Insurance System on Medical Devices (1987) (MHW 1991). A manufacturer gains official consent for Class C insurance and submits an application within a fixed period after approval. Documents providing the following information are attached to the application form: purpose, indication, effects and clinical usefulness including the results of random clinical trials, standard selling price, maintenance expenses, comparison with similar products, and literature on evidence in Japan and abroad, including control test results providing evidence of clinical usefulness. The MHW also consults with the Central Social Insurance Medical Council on the use of a medical device under the reimbursement system.

Unfortunately, the process of approval for inclusion under health insurance rules is just as implicit and closed as is that of approval and licensing. Furthermore, although the members of the council consist of experts in the appropriate scientific fields, the process is a political negotiation reflecting the relative balance of power among manufacturers. Therefore, it is unclear if clinical effectiveness and economic efficiency in terms of health care financing is actually evaluated.

Table 1 shows the time of inclusion under the insurance system and the changes in fees for selected tomography in Japan (MHW 1985–90). X-ray tomography was covered by insurance in 1958; its points rating was 100 (¥1,000, $5.60). Ultrasonography, CAT, and MRI were covered in 1973, 1978, and 1985, respectively. Their points were 330 (¥3,300, $18.00), 1,200 (¥12,000, $67.00), and 2,000 (¥20,000, $110.00), respectively. The time lag between the introduction

**Table 1. Changes of fees for selected tomography**
**(point fee: one point = ten yen)**

| Revision | X-ray | Ultrasonic | CAT (Head) | MRI |
|----------|-------|------------|------------|-----|
| 1958.10 | 100 | | | |
| 1961.7 | 110 | | | |
| 1965.1 | 120 | | | |
| 1965.11 | 150 | | | |
| 1974.2 | 150 | 330 | | |
| 1974.10 | 150 | 660 | | |
| 1976.4 | 210 | 660 | | |
| 1978.2 | 240 | 660 | 1,200 | |
| 1985.3 | 250 | 550 | 1,200 | 2,000 |
| 1988.4 | 260 | 550 | 1,000 | 2,300 |
| 1990.4 | 260 | 550 | 1,150 | 2,400 |
| 1992.4 | 264 | 500 | 1,150 | 2,450 |

to clinical settings and insurance coverage for MRI and CAT was about three years. Fee points increased about two times, from 100 to 260 for X-ray tomography and from 330 to 550 for ultrasonic tomography. Although points for MRI increased slightly from 2,000 to 2,400, points for CAT decreased from 1,200 to 1,150.

Inclusion under insurance and the revision of fees played an important role in the spread of MRI. The fee for CAT was set two to five times higher than that of existing technologies. As was shown before, this fee was reduced after the diffusion of CAT. When MRI was introduced, its fee was set two times higher than that of CAT. These fee schedules facilitated the diffusion of MRI and CAT. However, because the price of an MRI unit was more than $5 million—extremely expensive compared with that for CAT (less than $40 thousand)—the diffusion of MRI was hampered compared to CAT.

Once MRI was covered by insurance, the number of claims for reimbursement increased rapidly beginning in 1988 (table 2) (MHW 1986–90), due mainly to the increased number of units as well as to the increase in utilization per unit. The number of claims for CAT increased rapidly from 1986. Although MRI is an alternative diagnostic technology to CAT, there was no decrease in the number of claims for CAT; MRI was simply added as a new diagnostic test to the existing alternatives.

In 1989 the proportion of MRI charges in the social insurance medical care expenditure in June (¥879 billion, $4.9 billion) was 0.08% (¥720 million, $4 million) (MHW 1986–90); for CAT the proportion was 0.81% (¥7.1 billion, $40 million). The proportions of MRI and CAT to expenditure (¥36.4 billion, $200

**Table 2. Claims for reimbursement
per month (measured in June)**

| Year | MRI | CAT |
|------|------|--------|
| 1985 | 474 | 98,921 |
| 1986 | 2,130 | 334,443 |
| 1987 | 1,850 | 406,687 |
| 1988 | 15,534 | 379,253 |
| 1989 | 27,742 | 531,539 |
| 1990 | 56,653 | 612,851 |
| 1991 | 86,693 | 649,987 |

million) for all imaging tests, which mainly consisted of simple X-rays, were 2% and 19.6%, respectively. Although the total amount of expenditure for MRI is, at present, not so large, its influence on health care financing cannot be disregarded in the future, taking the trend of diffusion and utilization into consideration.

The reimbursement system affects the profitability of health care providers, another important factor affecting the decision to adopt new technology. CAT scanners achieved profitability early (Niki 1983). In contrast, the potential profitability of MRI is unclear because of the limitations of reimbursement and the uncertainty of the technology. The fees for medical procedures in Japan are much lower than those for procedures in the United States and Europe (Hisashige 1992b); MRI is no exception. The fee for its use in Japan is one-fifth of that in the United States (Hisashige 1992a).

Therefore, the profitability of MRI systems will be extremely sensitive to the volume of patients. Japanese physicians are trying to compensate for the low fee received for MRI procedures by expanding the volume of service. However, the claims review process controls at least extreme over-utilization, as does the present technological limitation of MRI (in that the procedure requires a relatively long time for each examination).

Recent technological improvements in hardware and software, as well as price reductions for units, may not only increase throughput but also ultimately reduce the charges necessary to achieve break-even performance. However, the utilization (especially scheduled hours per day) of MRI in Japan was about half that in the United States. Therefore, at present, most MRI systems, except the low-cost permanent magnet type (less than 0.5 Tesla), still fall below the break-even point of profit and loss (Arimizu 1985; Hisashige 1992a). Despite the higher cost of a superconducting MRI, large hospitals and university hospitals, which have greater resources, adopt it to maintain their prestige and competitive positions, as well as to attract patients and physicians.

These results show that the present government regulation and reimbursement system does not meet the challenge of technology assessment for new health care technologies such as MRI. Also, the government has no explicit policy to comprehensively evaluate and control the adoption of these technologies.

The appropriate diffusion and utilization of new technologies are the main policy goals. To achieve these goals in Japan, the following problems must be solved. First, there must be better evaluation of new health care technology. Earlier and more rigorous evaluation of the effectiveness and efficiency of technologies must be supported by the government as well as academic institutions.

Second, to operate regulatory and reimbursement policies appropriately, timely and accurate information is essential. This is also true in order for health care providers to adopt appropriate technologies. Scientific information based on the evaluation mentioned above needs to be assembled, synthesized, and disseminated.

Third, the process for the approval of new technologies and their inclusion under insurance are implicit and closed. At the least, the effectiveness of new technology must be extensively evaluated, and this process and information must be open and disseminated to health care providers and consumers.

Fourth, in the present health care system few incentives exist for the appropriate adoption and utilization of new technologies. To give incentives to health care providers, the regulation and reimbursement processes must be reorganized and implemented.

Fifth, a diverse regional variation is found in the average number of a particular technology per population. Planning for the optimal number and location of new technologies must be examined from the standpoint of the equity and efficiency.

Finally, there is no explicit achievement goal for health policy and no systematic evaluation of decision making and its impact after implementation. An active approach to medical technology assessment must be established. Moreover, it needs to be included in the determination of health policy.

In conclusion, since the process of policy decision making has traditionally been implicit and closed, the attempts to improve the diffusion and utilization of new technologies face serious constraints. Reform of the Japanese health care system is an urgent policy consideration, due to continuously increasing health care expenditure, a rapidly aging population, and the rights movement of patients and consumers (Hisashige 1992b). In this context, medical technology assessment has become increasingly necessary, and there have been several movements for its diffusion (Hisashige, Sakurai, and Kaihara 1991; Hisashige 1992a). Although technology assessment is still at an early stage, it will be a useful experiment to improve the spread and utilization of new technologies in Japan.

REFERENCES

Abegglen, J. C., and G. Stalk, Jr. 1987. *Kaisha: The Japanese corporation.* Tokyo: Tuttle.
Arimizu, N. 1985. Xsen CT MRI no keizaigakuteki kōritsu (Economic efficiency of X-ray CT and MRI). *Shin iryō* (Journal of new medicine) 12:25–30.

Australian Health Technology Advisory Committee (AHTAC). 1991. *Consensus statement on clinical efficacy of magnetic resonance imaging.* Canberra: Australian Institute of Health.

Cooper, L. S., T. C. Charlmers, and M. McCally, et al. 1988. The poor quality of early evaluations of magnetic resonance imaging. *Journal of the American Medical Association* 10:3,277–80.

Durand-Zaleski, I., D. Reizine, D. Puzin, et al. 1991. Economic assessment of magnetic resonance imaging. In C. Flagle, et al., eds., *Assessment of medical informatics technology.* Cedex: ENSP, 259–67.

Evens, R. G., and R. G. Evens, Jr. 1991. Analysis of economics and use of MR imaging in the United States in 1990. *American Journal of Radiology* 157:603–7.

Guyatt, G., and M. Drummond. 1985. Guidelines for the clinical and economic assessment of health technologies: The case of magnetic resonance. *International Journal of Technology Assessment in Health Care* 1:551–66.

Hillman, A. L., and J. S. Schwartz. 1985. The adoption and diffusion of CT and MRI in the United States. *Medical Care* 11:1,283–94.

———. 1986. The diffusion of MRI: Patterns of siting and ownership in an era of changing incentives. *American Journal of Radiology* 146:963–69.

Hisashige, A. 1992a. *MRI no riyō gyōkyō to keizaisei no bunsekei kōsei kagaku kenkyū* (Analysis of economic and use of MRI in Japan: The research report supported by the Health Policy Bureau). Tokyo: MHW.

———. 1992b. Health care delivery, financing system and aging in Japan. *Journal of the Japanese Association of Radiology Technology* (English issue).

———, T. Sakurai, and S. Kaihara. 1991. Medical technology assessment and medical information technology in Japan: Present and future. In C. Flagle, et al., eds., *Assessment of Medical Informatics Technology.* Cedex: ENSP.

Iglehart, J. K. 1988. Japan¥s medical care system, part 2. *New England Journal of Medicine* 319:1,166–72.

*Image Technology and Information Display* 17–27 (1980–90).

*Japanese Journal of Clinical Radiology* 25–35 (1980–90).

*Japanese Journal of Nuclear Medicine* 17–27 (1980–90).

Kent, D. L., and E. B. Larson. 1988. Magnetic resonance imaging of the brain and spine. *Annals of Internal Medicine* 108:402–24.

Kuhns, L. R., J. R. Thornbury, D. Feryback, eds. 1989. *Decision making in imaging.* Chicago: Year Book.

Ministry of Health and Welfare (MHW). 1978–87. *Iryō shisetsu chōsa* (Medical survey facilities). Tokyo: Kōsei Tōkei Kyōkai.

———. (Medical Device Division). 1991. *Iryō yōgu seizō shinsei no tebiki* (Guide to medical device registration). 6th ed. Tokyo: Yakuji Nippo.

———. (Pharmaceutical Affairs Bureau). 1972–88. *Yakugai kōgyō seisan dōtai nenpō* (Pharmaceutical industries production statistics). Tokyo. Yakugyou Keizai Kenkyūsho.

———. 1985–90. *Kaitei tensuhyō* (Revised point fees). Tokyo: Shakai Hoken Kenkyūsho.

———. 1986–90. *Shakai iryō shinryōkōi betsu chōsa* (Report of social insurance medical care according to procedure). Tokyo: Kōsei Tōkei Kyōkai.

Nakajima, Y., et al. 1989. *Teijiki MRI niyoru haishuryu byohen no shindan to sono yuyōsei ni tsuite* (The use of low magnet MRIs in the diagnosis of pulmonary tumor lesions). *Rinshō hōshasen* 34:19–25.

Niki, R. 1983. *CT sukyanaa no shakai keizaigaku* (Socioeconomics of CT scanner). *Shizen,* 44–51.

*Nippon Acta Radiologica* 40–50 (1980–1990).

Nishimura, K., et al. 1988. The validity of magnetic resonance imaging in the staging of bladder cancer. *Japanese Journal of Clinical Oncology* 18:217–26.

*Shin iryō* (Journal of new medicine). The list of installed MRI and CT. 1975–92.

Steinberg, E. P. 1986. The status of MRI in 1986: Rates of adoption in the United States and worldwide. *American Journal of Radiology* 147:453–55.

———, J. E. Sisk, and K. E. Locke. 1985. The diffusion of magnetic resonance imagers in the United States and worldwide. *International Journal of Technology Assessment in Health Care* 1:499–514.

Historical Background

Under the traditional *kanpō* (Chinese medicine), many drugs were taken on a prophylactic basis, that is, to maintain the balance between the two opposing elements of *ying* and *yang*. Moreover, it was the norm to prescribe several drugs in combination (sometimes those that have counteracting reactions) in order to obtain the right pharmacological balance. It should also be noted that the role of the physician and the pharmacist was inseparable because it was regarded as unethical to receive payment for medical services that should be provided as a humane duty. Thus, physicians could only receive payment for the drugs they dispensed, which, after all, had to be purchased by them from the wholesalers. When the point-fee system was introduced in 1927, the original point was the price of the per-diem price of a drug in the private practitioner's ambulatory setting (Ikegami 1995).

The United States has a tradition of heroic medicine and of the use of violent purging practices dating from the nineteenth century. There has also been an early separation of prescribing and dispensing, with the latter becoming equated with selling drugs and lowering the dignity of the physician. When health insurance was introduced, it was to pay for inpatient services.

## Are Prices Higher in Japan?

Comparison of Actual Prices

As table 1 shows, when the price of the top-selling drugs that are common to Japan and United States are compared (Japan Pharmaceutical Manufacturers Association 1992), U.S. prices were invariably higher: 2 to 6 times when the PPP rate was used, and 1.2 to 5 times when the exchange rate was used. While it is true that the prices listed here are not likely to be the price paid by the provider, discounts would apply for both countries, and whether they will be greater in either of the countries has yet to be researched. Nevertheless, it is very unlikely that discounts in the United States would offset the much lower Japanese list prices.

It should also be noted that while the prices of individual drugs have been going down in Japan, they have increased in the United States. This situation is unique to the United States when compared to the United Kingdom, France, and Germany (Japan Pharmeceutical Manufacturers Association 1991). Whether it will continue to do so is uncertain. Manufacturers may increase prices to offset the loss that will be incurred from the progressive enactment of rebate provisions for Medicaid (U.S. General Accounting Office 1993).

Confounders that Need to Be Considered

While prices are lower for the same brand-name drug in Japan, the following confounding factors need to be investigated. The first is the greater use of generics in the United States. This will have an effect of lowering the average prices of drugs having the same formula. In 1989, generics were estimated to amount to only 11% of total sales in Japan (Committee on the Role of Small to Medium

**Table 1. Price of drugs, Japan-U.S. comparison, 1989**

| Generic name | Brand name | Unit | Common dosage | Price* | Price** |
|---|---|---|---|---|---|
| Nifedipin | Japan: Adalat | 10mg | 30mg | 138 | 138 |
| | U.S.: Procardia | 10mg | 30–60mg | 317–635 | 223–447 |
| Captryl | Japan: Captryl | 25mg | 37.5–75mg | 136–272 | 136–272 |
| | U.S.: Capoten | 25mg | 50–75mg | 235–352 | 165–248 |
| Diltiazem | Japan: Herbessar | 60mg | 90mg | 62 | 62 |
| | U.S.: Cardizem | 60mg | 180–360mg | 441–882 | 311–621 |
| Cimetidine | Japan: Tagamet | 200mg | 800mg | 264 | 264 |
| | U.S.: Tagamet | 200mg | 800–1,200mg | 627–941 | 441–662 |
| Ranitidine | Japan: Zantac | 150mg | 300mg | 286 | 286 |
| Hydrochloride | U.S.: Zantac | 150mg | 300mg | 725 | 510 |
| Cefaclor | Japan: Kefral | 250mg | 750mg | 419 | 419 |
| | U.S.: Ceclor | 250mg | 750mg | 1,182 | 832 |
| Cefadroxyl | Japan: Camacef | 250mg | 750mg | 278 | 278 |
| | U.S.: Ultracef | 250mg | 1,000–2,000mg | 1,172–2,344 | 825–1,650 |
| Piroxicam | Japan: Feldene | 20mg | 20mg | 112 | 112 |
| | U.S.: Feldene | 20mg | 20mg | 456 | 321 |
| Sulindac | Japan: Clinoril | 100mg | 300mg | 103 | 103 |
| | U.S.: Clinoril | 150mg | 300–400mg | 447–596 | 315–412 |
| Mitomycin | Japan: Mitomycin | 2mg | | 591 | 591 |
| | U.S.: Mutamycin | 5mg | | 18,195 | 12,811 |

* Per daily common dosage, in yen; U.S. at PPP rate: $1 U.S. = ¥196 (rate used in original source).
** Per daily common dosage, in yen; U.S. at exchange rate: $1 U.S. = ¥138.
Price as listed in Insurance Tariff (Japan) and Red Book (U.S.).
Source: Japan Pharmaceutical Manufacturers Association 1992.

Pharmaceutical Companies 1990) compared to 30% in the United States (U.S. Department of Commerce 1990). The reasons why generics are used less in Japan are the following:

1. Prices are set by the brand name, so that using the lower-priced drug will not necessarily result in a greater profit to the provider. (However, it is estimated that despite the small share of generics, the profits derived from them amount to about a third of the total.)

2. The equivalents of generics are produced by small-scale manufacturers and are referred to disparagingly as *zoro* (from *zoro zoro,* meaning coming in droves).
3. Most of the dispensing is done by physicians who have brand loyalty (especially those physicians in teaching and public hospitals who do not have to worry about maximizing the profit on drugs).
4. Patients have little interest in obtaining low-priced drugs because of the low copayment rate, and there is a general reluctance to question the physician's decision.

The second confounding factor is the greater use of newly introduced drugs in Japan. These drugs tend to be more expensive than old drugs for any given clinical condition. The marginal benefit of using the new drug may not necessarily justify the increase in costs. The average number of years from the time of introduction for the twenty top-selling drugs in Japan was 8.2 years in 1982 and 5.7 years in 1989. In contrast, in the United States, it was 12.6 years and 8.3 years, respectively. Thus, the time period in Japan was shorter by 3.6 years in 1982 and 2.5 years in 1989 (Nakagawa 1991, 40–41).[2]

The more rapid turnover of drugs in Japan can best be observed for anti-infectives, which constitute a much larger share of the total drug consumption in Japan: 18.4% compared to 12.1% in the United States. As table 2 shows, the share of Cephalosporin (third-generation antibiotics) is higher in Japan, 51.4% compared to 45.9% in the United States. In contrast, the share of Beta-lactam and other penicillins, which were introduced earlier, is lower in Japan. It should be noted that the wide use of antibiotics has been criticized as the main reason for the growing spread of methicilin-resistant, staphylococcus, aureus nosocomial infections.

However, rapid turnover does not necessarily occur across the board for all drugs. As table 3 shows, with H2 blockers, which constitute a smaller share in Japan (Japan, 2.3%; United States, 5.6%), the share of Tagamet, introduced earlier by Smith Klein Beecham, is larger in Japan (Japan, 30.0%; United States, 24.2%). On the other hand, Zantac, marketed by Glaxo and Sankyo (under licence from Glaxo), and Gaster, marketed by Yamanouchi, have not attained the shares that they have in the United States. This would seem to imply that the rapid turnover may be more dependent on the market-penetrating ability of the manufacturer.

The economic incentive to use new drugs lies in periodic cuts in the reimbursement price for drugs in Japan, which is based on a survey of the actual prices paid by the provider. Cuts in the prices paid by insurance have been made progressively since the 1981 fee revision, and, on average, the prices have been halved. These cuts have been greater for the "me-too" drugs compared with the innovative original drug. However, it should also be noted that the difference between Japan and the United States in the average time from introduction to becoming one of the twenty top-selling drugs was of the same magnitude in 1982 as it was in 1989. Therefore, it is more likely to be due to a more fundamental reason. It should be noted that the Japanese industries in general have a tendency to market the same kind of products, once an innovative breakthrough is made, and then to try to enlarge aggressively their market share by making marginal improvements and

**Table 2. Composition of systemic anti-infectives, Japan-U.S. comparison, 1990**

| | Japan | | | | United States | | | |
|---|---|---|---|---|---|---|---|---|
| | 1988 | | 1990 | | 1988 | | 1990 | |
| | Amt* | % total | Amt* | % total | Amt* | % total | Amt* | % total |
| Cephalosporins | 5,621 | 53.2 | 5,224 | 51.4 | 1,717 | 44.4 | 2,172 | 45.9 |
| Beta-lactam | 64 | 0.6 | 33 | 0.3 | 268 | 6.9 | 529 | 11.2 |
| Broad spectrum penicillins | 816 | 7.7 | 664 | 6.5 | 351 | 9.1 | 289 | 6.1 |
| Other penicillins** | 24 | 0.2 | 13 | 0.2 | 131 | 3.4 | 95 | 2.0 |
| Others | 4,042 | 38.3 | 4,237 | 41.7 | 1,401 | 36.2 | 1,647 | 34.8 |
| Total | 10,567 | 100.0 | 10,171 | 100.0 | 3,868 | 100.0 | 4,732 | 100.0 |

* Estimated amount paid by providers (physicians, hospitals, pharmacies). Japan: ¥100 million; U.S. $1 million.
** Effective only for Gram positive bacteria; includes Pencillin G and K.
Source: Tanabe Seiyaku Co., Ltd.

**Table 3. Composition of H2 blockers, Japan-U.S. comparison, 1990**

| | | Japan | | | | | United States | | | |
| | | 1988 | | 1990 | | | 1988 | | 1990 | |
| | Introduced | Amt* | % total | Amt* | % total | Introduced | Amt* | % total | Amt* | % total |
|---|---|---|---|---|---|---|---|---|---|---|
| Tagamet | Jan. 1982 | 380 | 35.5 | 378 | 30.0 | June 1983 | 553 | 33.4 | 527 | 24.2 |
| Zantac | Nov. 1984 | 274 | 25.6 | 346 | 27.4 | Dec. 1984 | 957 | 57.7 | 1,271 | 58.4 |
| Gaster (Pepcid) | July 1986 | 416 | 38.8 | 524 | 41.5 | Nov. 1986 | 127 | 7.7 | 280 | 12.9 |
| Nisatidin (Axid) | Sep. 1990 | – | – | 14 | 1.1 | June 1988 | 21 | 1.3 | 97 | 4.5 |
| Total | | 1,071 | 100.0 | 1,262 | 100.0 | | 1,658 | 100.0 | 2,175 | 100.0 |

* Estimated amount paid by providers (physicians, hospitals, pharmacies). Japan: ¥100 million; U.S. $1 million.
Source: Tanabe Seiyaku Co., Ltd.

through nonprice competition. Thus, Japanese pharmaceutical companies may be only behaving in a manner similar to other industrial sectors in the country.[3]

Another factor that needs to be considered is the difference in the approval process. Although the average time required is about the same in Japan, applications have been processed sequentially, according to the date of application. However, in the United States the approval process is prioritized according to the degree of innovation. Also, in Japan, the efficacy of the drug is compared with that of the standard drug in current use, and approval is given if the new drug produces the same or better results. In contrast, placebos are used in the United States. These factors tend to favor the introduction of marginally improved drugs in Japan.

### Is the Quantity Greater?

It would seem to be paradoxical for Japan to use a larger quantity of drugs than the United States when the recommended dosage for any given drug tends to be smaller there (see table 1) and, in general, when there is a clinical impression that Japanese physicians tend to prescribe in smaller dosages. Nevertheless, since the per-capita production of drugs is greater in Japan, it stands to reason that the quantity used is greater. The following reasons can be put forward to explain this phenomena.

1. More polypharmacy (greater variety of drugs in the same prescription). For example, digestives are routinely prescribed in combination with antibiotics. This may come from the *kanpō* tradition of aiming for the right balance.
2. More use of mild-acting drugs. There seems to be a preference for drugs having few side effects, especially in anticancer immunomodulators: Krestine and similar drugs are top sellers in Japan, but they are not sold in the United States. (This trend may be further strengthened by the fact that the diagnosis of cancer is seldom disclosed to the patient in Japan. Thus, it is difficult to prescribe drugs with strong side effects.)
3. More use of vitamins and nutrients (share of total sales: Japan, 5.5% in 1991; United States, 2.9% in 1989) (Japan Pharmeceutical Manufacturers Association 1992, 40–41).
4. More use of anti-infectives (as already noted). Antibiotics are routinely prescribed for common colds. This is one reason why Kefral (Cefaclor) was the number one best-selling drug in Japan in 1989 (Nakagawa 1991).
5. More use of antihypertensive drugs. There is extensive mass screening for hypertension in Japan. Once diagnosed, patients will continue to be prescribed drugs for their entire lives. Adalat (nifepidin) and Perdipine (nicardipine hydrochloride) were the second and fourth best-selling drugs in Japan in 1989. Recently, there has been a rapid increase in the use of Mevalotin (lovastatin) (provastatin sodium) following the screening for hypercholesterolemia.

6. More use of cerebral metabolic activators. In Japan, most of the institutional long-term care is provided in hospitals that are paid on a fee-for-service basis. Thus, it is most likely that medical input in long-term care is more extensive in Japan as compared to the United States, where almost all care is given in nursing homes (see chapter 14 in this book on long-term care). Avan (idebenone) is the third best-selling drug in Japan.

7. More consultations and visits per capita: in Japan, 12.8; in the United States, 5.3 (Organization for Economic Co-operation and Development 1990). More frequent contacts are likely to lead to a greater use of drugs.

## Recent Policy Initiatives in Japan

### Setting the "Reasonable Zone"

In 1992, radical changes were made in the setting of prices and the distribution of drugs. For the next fee revision in 1994, the price of drugs will be calculated using a volume-adjusted mean. This is a sharp break from the former practice of simply taking the ninetieth or eighty-first percentile from the lowest-priced drug in the national survey of prices paid by providers (hospitals and private practitioners). The introduction of volume weighting means that the manufacturers cannot maintain the retail price by selling at an artificially high price to a few providers.

The difference that will be allowed between the reimbursement price and the market price paid by the provider is referred to as the "reasonable zone" ("reasonable" because it is judged to be about the amount of administrative costs arising from dispensing and maintaining inventory). This will be set initially at 15% of the reimbursement price, to be gradually decreased to 10% in 1998. If the next survey discloses the fact that the volume-weighted average price has exceeded the "reasonable zone," then the price set by insurance will be cut accordingly. This is expected to decrease the practice of price-cutting by manufacturers.

In distribution, manufacturers will not be allowed to negotiate directly with providers and may set the price only for wholesalers. This policy is aimed at prohibiting rebates based upon the volume of drugs purchased and other unclear competition that the manufacturers had practiced. It is worthwhile noting that this measure came as a result of the U.S. demands for the reform of the unfair drug distribution system in the MOSS trade negotiations (Tanaka 1992).

However, whether these measures will have the desired effect is still not clear. Providers may try to earn the same net profit from drugs by resorting to two different strategies: first, by shifting toward the more high-priced variety of drugs and thus increasing the total amount purchased, and second, by relying on the small manufacturers of generics (*zoro*), who are prepared to continue to sell at a large discount because, by the time of the next price revision, they will be prepared to withdraw the product from the market. At present, evidence from several private sources discloses that this has occurred to some extent. Nevertheless, there is unconfirmed evidence that hospitals, which were making profits in excess of 35% from drugs, have had their margins cut to 25% and, as a result, are facing a major financial crisis.

Separation of Prescribing and Dispensing

Pursuading physicians to write prescriptions to outside pharmacies instead of dispensing drugs themselves, or the separation of prescribing and dispensing as it is referred to in Japan, has long been the objective of the Japanese government as a measure to contain the excessive dispensing of medication by physicians. As the result of the gradual shrinkage of profit coming from dispensing and by setting generous fees for writing prescriptions to outside pharmacies, the government was able to obtain the support of the Japan Medical Association for this policy. So as not to antagonize physicians, it was not introduced ostensibly as a cost-saving measure (costs will actually increase at least in the short run because physicians and pharmacists will be paid more for providing essentially the same services as when the physicians dispensed drugs). Instead, the government stressed the need to establish a "home pharmacy" for every Japanese: that is, one pharmacy that dispenses all prescriptions so that records can be kept and checked for overdosage and complications. The likelihood of such hazards is quite high because many patients, especially the elderly, receive medications from several physicians who seldom have any knowledge of what the others have prescribed and dispensed.

However, this policy does not appear to have realized its objective because most of the dispensing is being done by the pharmacy adjacent to the hospital or clinic and seldom by the one "home pharmacy" as was envisioned (such pharmacies face practical difficulties in having the prescribed drugs in stock). Moreover, while the pharmacy must have a different ownership from the hospital or clinic, it is very difficult to monitor fee spliting (pharmacies may even offer rent-free office space to physicians). The growth of clinics that do not dispense has only been slowly increasing, from 18.6% in 1987 to 19.6% in 1990.

**Policy Implications for the United States**

Drugs are not likely to become as large an issue in the United States as in Japan because the United States already has mechanisms such as inclusive fees and charges to patients, which contain pharmaceutical expenditures. Thus, the opportunity-cost of drugs can be better evaluated. However, unlike Japan, prices have continued to rise and, with the greater use of practices such as cholesterol screening, it can be expected that there will be a greater need to contain pharmaceutical expenditures. Japan's experience shows that price controls do not necessarily lead to a lowering of aggregate costs. Manufacturers are likely to resort to a more rapid introduction of new drugs that will be priced at a higher level. While it may be true that the new drugs will have an improved efficacy, whether the increase in marginal costs is justifiable or not is difficult to prove or disprove. It should be noted that the rapid turnover has an adverse effect on monitoring effectiveness and side effects because by the time the Phase IV evaluation is done, the drug may no longer be marketed. This will be a major hurdle to cross in order to undertake the socioeconomic evaluation of drugs.

NOTES

1. Exceptions to the itemized fee-for-service form of payment are found only in the area of long-term care; the Health Facility for the Elderly and geriatric hospitals that have adopted the inclusive rate are paid on a per-diem basis. However, most geriatric hospitals continue to be paid on a fee-for-service basis.

2. While there has not been an increase in the introduction of new drugs since 1981 (see the next chapter on cost-cutting and pharmaceutical R & D), this may reflect a change in the quality of drugs given approval, that is, a decrease in "me-too" drugs. It is difficult to reconcile the massive decrease in reimbursement prices and the maintenance of, or at least no drastic decrease in, operating profits without the successful marketing of new drugs.

3. It may seem strange that rival pharmaceutical companies in Japan are able to market their own patent drugs shortly after the innovative drug has been introduced. However, the information concerning the development of new drugs travels very rapidly, long before its approval. It is at this point that the behavior of the Japanese companies may differ from those in the United States. When faced with the knowledge that its rival is ahead on developing a new drug, the U.S. company may more likely concede that market segment and instead try to develop its own different product, while the Japanese company may be more likely to accelerate its efforts and try to produce its own variation.

REFERENCES

Chūsho Seiyaku Kigyō no Arikatani Kansuru Kondankai. 1990. *Yakumūkyokuchō eno hōkokusho* (Report to the director of the pharmaceutical bureau). Tokyo.

Ikegami, N. 1995. Economic aspects of the doctor patient relationship in Japan—from the eighteenth century till the emergence of social insurance. In Y. Kawakita et al., ed., *History of the doctor patient relationship.* Tokyo: Ishiyaku EuroAmerica.

Japan Pharmaceutical Manufacturers Association (JPMA). 1992. *Data book 1991.* Tokyo: JPMA.

———. 1991. *Yakukano kokusai hikaku* (International comparisons of pharmaceutical prices). Tokyo: JPMA.

Kuno, M. 1992. Kaitei Iryōbōkoku (Revised: national ruin due to health care). Tokyo: Dōyukan.

Ministry of Health and Welfare. 1992. *1990 iryō shisetsu chōsa* (Survey of medical facilities, 1990). Tokyo: Kōsei Tōkei Kyōkai.

Nakagawa, H. 1991. *Iyakuhin sangyō no genjō to shōrai* (Present and future of the pharmaceutical industry). Tokyo: Yakugyo Gihōsha.

Organization for Economic Co-operation and Development (OECD). 1990. *Health care systems in transition.* Paris: OECD.

———. 1992. *Health datafile.* Paris: OECD.

Tanaka, Y. 1992. The Japanese pharmaceutical industry: changes in delivery, distribution and development. *Decision Resources,* 12 February.

U.S. Department of Commerce. 1990. *Industrial outlook 1990.* Washington, D.C.: Government Printing Office.

U.S. General Accounting Office. 1993. Medicaid changes in drug prices paid by HMOs and hospitals since enactment of rebate provisions. General Accounting Office/Human Resource Division-93-43. Washington, D.C.: Government Printing Office.

CHAPTER 12

# Sales, R&D, and Profitability in the Japanese Pharmaceutical Industry, 1981–92

*Will Mitchell, Thomas Roehl, and*
*John Creighton Campbell*[1]

SUMMARY  Public policies designed to control health care costs may have substantial, often unintended, effects on the strategy and performance of firms that provide the goods and services that help provide health care. Beginning in 1981, the Ministry of Health and Welfare (MHW) has carried out a series of severe reductions in the reimbursement prices paid for prescription drugs in Japan. There has been extensive discussion of how such price reductions have helped control health care costs (e.g., Yoshikawa 1989; Reich 1990, 1991; University Club 1992). However, whether the price controls have affected the innovativeness of pharmaceutical manufacturers and other health sector firms remains an open question.

In this study, we outline several key trends concerning profitability, R&D growth, and sales growth in the pharmaceutical industry. In addition, we report statistical estimation of relationships between cumulative firm-level price reductions and R&D growth undertaken by fourteen pharmaceutical manufacturers. Although our conclusions are tentative, we identify a possible firm-level relationship between higher price reductions and lower R&D growth during the mid 1980s. In an industry that depends on R&D investment by its members both to provide innovative goods to the domestic market and to compete in international markets,[2] such a negative relationship must concern policy makers and corporate managers.

## Health Cost Policy

Based on guidelines established by the Central Social Insurance Medical Council (often referred to by the abbreviated form of its name, *Chūikyō*), the MHW determines the insurance reimbursement price of each prescription drug in Japan. Under Japan's national health insurance system, the reimbursement price is standard for all medical institutions and patients.[3] Responding to the desire of the Ministry of Finance to reduce health care costs, the MHW toughened its policy of periodically revising the drug reimbursement price schedule downward. The first of the new round of stringent price revisions occurred in June 1981, when prices

132

**Table 1. Average MHW pharma-
ceutical price reductions, 1981–92**

| Date | Percent reduction |
|------|-------------------|
| Jun-81 | 18.60% |
| Jan-83 | 4.90% |
| Mar-84 | 16.60% |
| Mar-85 | 6.00% |
| Apr-86 | 5.10% |
| Apr-88 | 10.20% |
| Apr-90 | 9.20% |
| Apr-92 | 8.10% |

were reduced an average of 18.6%. Seven additional rounds of reductions to the schedule of prices reimbursed to medical institutions occurred by April 1992. Table 1 lists the date and average value of the price reductions.[4]

Two factors mitigate the apparent steepness of the reductions. First, the adjustments apply only to drugs on the market at the time of the revisions. Hence, firms can maintain or increase the level of their sales if they introduce new drugs. Many drugs that have been on the market for over ten years have faced price reductions of over 50%, but each new drug to enter the market starts at a new price. New drugs then move down the price schedule with each subsequent price revision. Only those drugs that have been on the price schedule since 1981 have taken the full effect of the price revisions.

The second mitigating factor is that the effect of the reductions differs among different therapeutic classes of pharmaceuticals. During the three price reductions between 1985 and 1990, for instance, the MHW reports that the prices of anti-infective drugs declined by an average of 18.6%, while prices for anti-cancer drugs declined by only 6.3%, and prices for anti-hyperintensives by 10.7%. Firms that have emphasized sales of anti-infective drugs have faced the largest price reductions. During the 1981–92 period, Shionogi and Fujisawa, two firms with high proportions of sales of anti-infective drugs, realized average reductions on the prices of their products of 11.1% and 11.6%, respectively. Daiichi and Sankyo, which have lower proportions of sales for anti-infectives, incurred 6.8% and 7.5% reductions (Merrill Lynch 1992).

### Pharmaceutical Industry Trends

Several trends in key industry-average measures of sales, performance, and strategy emerged during the 1980s.

Sales

The price reductions had an immediate impact on pharmaceutical industry revenues. Sales growth of ethical drugs declined sharply following the toughening of
the price adjustment policy: falling from a compound annual growth rate of 11.1%
between 1975 and 1981, to a 4.5% rate between 1982 and 1989.[5] Given their
effect on drug sales revenue, the price reductions might be expected to affect the
performance and strategy of the pharmaceutical manufacturers.

Profitability

Influences on performance should emerge in changes in profitability. We calculated operating profit to sales ratios for twenty-three Japanese publicly traded
pharmaceutical firms between 1978 and 1992. Together, these companies com-
prise about half of industry pharmaceutical sales and provide a representative
pattern of industry profitability trends. Operating profitability has fluctuated
sharply. Profitability grew immediately prior to the 1981 price reductions, fell
sharply in the subsequent years, rebounded during 1987–89, and then declined
again through 1992.[6] The ratio of net profit to sales, which includes investment
activities as well as operating results, follows a similar but more moderate fluctuating pattern. The profitability fluctuation is consistent with the argument that
the firms were able to adjust to the first rounds of price reductions but have not yet
adjusted their strategies to account for the more recent series of price reductions.

Firm Strategy

Strategic adjustments that the pharmaceutical manufacturers undertook in response to the price reductions between 1981 and 1992 might include changes in
the rate of new product introduction, the source of new products, marketing
expenditure, and R&D expenditure.

*Product introduction.* A common assertion by people familiar with the Japanese
pharmaceutical industry is that many manufacturers responded to the period of
ongoing price reductions by increasing the introduction of new drugs. The new
products, which start at higher prices than those of products in the market at the
time of the latest price revisions, would then contribute to continued profitability.

Trends in the number of new chemical entities and new drugs approved for
the Japanese market between 1975 and 1990 provide at best limited support for
this assertion. The number of new drugs and the chemical structures on which
they were based approved annually after 1981 was often slightly higher than the
numbers approved prior to the first year of the price reductions, but there was no
more than a slight upward trend from that in the prereduction period (Japan
Pharmaceutical Manufacturers Association 1992, 67). The minimal increase in
new drug introductions may stem from the time required to develop and test new
drugs, and the high uncertainty associated with new drug development.[7] In any

case, firms do not appear to have responded to the price reductions with a strikingly increased rate of new product introduction.

*Product sources.* The price reductions might also influence the source from which firms obtain new products. Needing new products in order to maintain sales levels, firms might increase their use of in-licensing from domestic or foreign sources in place of internally developed drugs. Such in-licensing offers a quicker way to obtain new products than by internal development. We gathered information concerning the proportion of drugs introduced from pre-and post-1983 that were developed internally, licensed in from Japanese pharmaceutical manufacturers, and licensed in from foreign-owned manufacturers (Nikko Research 1991; Salomon Brothers 1992a). The proportion of internally developed drugs did indeed decline slightly, from 57% prior to 1983 to 42% between 1983 and 1991. Most of the replacement for internally developed drugs came from domestic in-licenses (which rose from 3% to 14%), while foreign in-licenses rose slightly (from 40% to 44%).

At least three issues underlie the product source figures. First, the increased incentives stemming from the price reductions to introduce new drugs may have led to increased use of in-licensing. Second, the growing innovativeness of the domestic Japanese pharmaceutical industry (Halliday, Walker, and Lumley 1992; Hawkins and Reich 1992) provided domestic sources for new drugs. Many such sources were relatively recent entrants to the pharmaceutical industry that had strength in nontraditional drug areas such as products based on biotechnology, but had relatively small pharmaceutical product distribution systems and so had strong incentives to negotiate licenses with established companies that possessed larger distribution coverages. Third, foreign-owned pharmaceutical companies began to establish larger internally owned distribution systems in Japan during the 1980s, planning to gradually decrease the incidence of licensing their products for sale by Japanese-owned companies and increase the incidence of direct distribution. Hence, any increased incentives for Japanese companies to in-license products from foreign-owned companies after the price reductions may have been balanced by a decreased incentive for the foreign companies to negotiate out-licenses.[8]

*Marketing expenditure.* The price reductions also might influence marketing expenditure. Selling, general, and administrative sales ratio of the top fifteen drug companies increased slightly during the 1980s, from about 29% of sales in 1981 to 31.5% in 1991 (Salomon Brothers 1992a, 149). The increase might stem from a marketing attempt to increase the volume of sales in response to unit price reductions. In addition, though, the increased expenditure may also have been a response to increased foreign competition during the period.

*R&D expenditure.* The price adjustments also might affect R&D expenditures, leading either to increased expenditure as firms attempt to develop new higher-priced drugs or to decreased expenditure in the face of declining profits. We calculated R&D/sales ratios for the industry as a whole between 1976 and 1990. The research expenditure figures must be treated cautiously because companies vary in how they define R&D and because some of the company statistics include substantial expenditure for clinical human trials that take place before drugs are introduced to the market, but the trends are clear.[9]

R&D intensity rose substantially during the past fifteen years. The industry-average corporate R&D/corporate sales ratio was 5.3% of sales in 1976, rose to 6.6% in 1981, and rose again to 8.6% in 1990 (Japan Pharmaceutical Manufacturers Association 1991, 8, 48). Moreover, R&D intensity rose somewhat more quickly after 1981 than before the price adjustment policy was toughened. Indeed, most major firms had reached the R&D intensity level of their major international competitors by 1990 (Mitchell, Roehl, and Slattery 1993). Although the overall rate of growth of absolute R&D expenditure declined slightly during the 1980s, the sales growth rate declined even more than R&D so that R&D intensity increased. This increased intensity might be attributed, in part, to an increased need to develop new drugs in order to obtain higher prices and to compete with foreign-owned firms in Japan.

## Summary of Industry Trends

In summary, several industry-level trends are apparent during the period of severe pharmaceutical reimbursement reductions in the 1980s. Ethical drug sales growth rates declined sharply from growth rates achieved in the second half of the 1970s. On average, firms in the industry experienced fluctuating profitability during the 1980s. In contrast with the profitability fluctuation, R&D intensity grew steadily while selling expenses increased slightly between 1981 and the early 1990s. The firms were slightly more likely to introduce new products after the first round of price reductions and were somewhat more likely to obtain new products from other companies, particularly from domestic firms.

## Price-Cut Effects on Firm-Level R&D Growth

Industry-level trends are important but may mask important differences among individual firms. For instance, the degree of price reduction varied markedly among different firms, with differences stemming primarily from differences in the firms' product portfolios. We were able to obtain firm-level estimates for fourteen firms for the eight rounds of price reductions.[10]

We used the firm-level price cut information as explanatory variables for subsequent firm-level R&D growth. We chose R&D growth as the key dependent variable owing to the importance of research to the continuing vitality of the industry, both to provide new products and to compete with foreign-owned firms. Although one- and two-year periods represent very short horizons in the pharmaceutical industry, where R&D projects often continue for many years, short-term changes in the trend of a firm's R&D expenditure will have substantial long-term impact on the level of its R&D budget. We defined one- and two-year growth ratios equal to RDt+1/RDt and RDt+2/RDt, where RD is a firm's R&D expenditure in a given year *t*. We also estimated the effects of corporate sales and operating profits in each year *t*, which might affect the availability of funds needed for R&D investment.[11]

The estimates of the relationships between price cuts and R&D growth varied. We found no relationship between individual year price cuts and either one- or two-year growth in R&D. We found a significant relationship between R&D growth and cumulative price cuts, however, where a firm's cumulative price cut is defined as the sum of the price cuts it has incurred up to and including the year *t*. Table 2 reports the results of ordinary least squares regression estimates of relationships between R&D growth and the cumulative price cuts, while controlling for the level of a firm's sales and operating profit.[12]

The most conservative conclusion concerning the effects of price reductions reported in table 2 is that they had little immediate association with one- and two-year R&D growth. Influences between cumulative price cuts and R&D growth with even moderate statistical significance are found only for 1985–86 one-year growth and 1986–88 two-year growth. Nonetheless, although the results are weak, the price cut results in table 2 do suggest a weak negative relationship between R&D growth and cumulative price cuts during the middle period of the price-cut era.

There may be a link between these results and the earlier discussion of profitability trends. The 1985–88 period during which cumulative price cuts achieved their strongest negative association with R&D growth also was the period during which the industry average operating profit/sales ratio reached its minimum point (8.7% in 1986). Profitability tended to increase during the subsequent period, during which price cuts and R&D growth had no discernible significant relationships. In addition, the mid-1980s decline in R&D growth among firms facing the highest price reductions could represent a downward shift in their R&D budgets, which then had renewed growth during the late 1980s.

The conclusion that price reductions had some effect on firm-level R&D growth during the 1985–88 period is tentative because it is impossible to determine causality from a statistical association. In addition, the sales, profit, and price-cut variables can measure only some of the incentives to invest in research and development. However, the results do suggest a plausible interpretation. Early price cuts during the 1980s had no strong negative association with lower R&D growth, possibly because the firm's R&D expenditure plans had been established during the 1970s. In contrast with the early years, the lower growth of 1985–88 R&D expenditure was more likely to be associated with higher cumulative price cuts, possibly owing to decreasing profitability and consequent adjustment to R&D expenditure. The significant negative relationships disappeared in 1989 and later years, during which time corporate profitability rebounded substantially from the low point of 1986. Hence, there is suggestive evidence that the accumulation of price cuts may have led to some reduction in R&D expenditure during a period in which corporate profitability was lowest.

Whether renewed relationships between higher price cuts and lower R&D

**Table 2. Ordinary least square estimates of cumulative price-cut effects on R & D growth, 1983–92 (fourteen firms)**

| Year | Firm-level explanatory variable | Coefficient | Intercept* | R-square |
|------|--------------------------------|-------------|-----------|----------|
| RD84/RD83 | Cumulative price cut to 1983 | -0.167 | 1.182 | 0.448 |
|  | Sales, 1983 | 0.274 |  |  |
|  | Operating profit, 1983 | -5.144 ** |  |  |
| RD85/RD84 | Cumulative price cut to 1984 | 0.136 | 1.032 | 0.231 |
|  | Sales, 1984 | -0.523 *** |  |  |
|  | Operating profit, 1984 | 5.405 *** |  |  |
| RD86/RD85 | Cumulative price cut to 1985 | -0.322 *** | 1.229 | 0.383 |
|  | Sales, 1985 | -0.209 |  |  |
|  | Operating profit, 1985 | 1.793 |  |  |
| RD87/RD86 | Cumulative price cut to 1986 | -0.318 | 1.242 | 0.205 |
|  | Sales, 1986 | -0.005 |  |  |
|  | Operating profit, 1986 | -0.367 |  |  |
| RD88/RD86 | Cumulative price cut to 1986 | -0.980 ** | 1.686 | 0.502 |
|  | Sales, 1986 | 0.444 |  |  |
|  | Operating profit, 1986 | -5.749 |  |  |
| RD89/RD88 | Cumulative price cut to 1988 | 0.118 | 1.002 | 0.226 |
|  | Sales, 1988 | -0.198 |  |  |
|  | Operating profit, 1988 | 2.448 *** |  |  |
| RD90/RD88 | Cumulative price cut to 1988 | 0.075 | 1.100 | 0.166 |
|  | Sales, 1988 | -0.463 |  |  |
|  | Operating profit, 1988 | 4.739 |  |  |
| RD91/RD90 | Cumulative price cut to 1990 | 0.207 | 0.982 | 0.145 |
|  | Sales, 1990 | -0.216 |  |  |
|  | Operating profit, 1990 | 1.493 |  |  |
| RD92/RD90 | Cumulative price cut to 1990 | 0.323 | 1.023 | 0.060 |
|  | Sales, 1990 | -0.272 |  |  |
|  | Operating profit, 1990 | 1.900 |  |  |

* $p<.01$ (one-tailed tests); ** $p<.05$; *** $p<.10$.
Units: sales and profit = yen mln x 1 million; price cuts = sum of % annual cuts (e.g., 10% = 10).

growth will emerge in the future, especially if the current decline in profitability continues, is an open question. Changes to the reimbursement policies that became effective in April 1992 also add caution to projecting future trends from the results. The policy changes limit price reductions in cases where the difference between the company's price to a doctor and the amount reimbursed to the doctor by MHW would fall below 15%, with the zone being reduced to 10% by 1998. In addition, price premiums will be awarded for drugs that are particularly innovative, with innovation criteria including novelty, safety, and treatment contribution. It is possible that these changes will stem any incipient link between price reductions and R&D growth by raising the incentives for continued innovation.

**Conclusion**

Japanese pharmaceutical firms are on the verge of either being dominated by international competitors in Japan or being able to compete on equal terms in world markets. Many firms in the industry have become increasingly innovative during the past twenty years, marked by increased inputs of research expenditures and increased output of new drugs. Policy makers must exercise substantial care while achieving the necessary outcome of controlling health care costs, or risk blunting the research-based strength of the pharmaceutical manufacturers.

The findings in this study are only suggestive. Nonetheless, even interpreted cautiously, the results of the analysis are striking. At the minimum, they signal the need for continued monitoring of pharmaceutical R&D investment by those concerned with innovation and competition in the pharmaceutical industry.

NOTES

1. We appreciate comments from Joan Penner-Hahn, Naoki Ikegami, Ron Slattery, and Bernard Yeung.

2. For discussions of the pharmaceutical R&D, foreign competition, and the Japanese pharmaceutical market see *Economist* 1987; Grabowski 1990; James 1990; Suguro 1990; Nakamura 1991; Nikko Research 1991, 1992; Yano 1991; Industrial Bank of Japan 1992; Japan Economic Institute 1992; and Maurer 1992.

3. The reimbursement price paid by MHW usually exceeds the price charged by pharmaceutical manufacturers. Prior to regulatory revisions effective April 1992, the actual drug price was determined by a system of rebates and discounts between manufacturer, wholesaler, and customer. The difference between actual and reimbursement prices, which averaged about 20%, is known as *yakka saeki*. The effect of lowering the reimbursement price is either to reduce the *yakka saeki* or to put downward pressure on the actual price charged by pharmaceutical manufacturers. The greater the competition between firms, particularly for sales of established drugs with more substitutes, the more likely the latter outcome.

4. An across-the-board 2.4% price increase also was allowed in April 1989 to offset a value-added tax that had recently been created.

5. Ethical drugs realized sales of ¥1,242.8 billion in 1975, ¥2,332.4 billion in 1981, ¥3,108.3 billion in 1982, and ¥4,232.2 billion in 1989 (Japan Pharmaceutical Manufac-

turers Association 1992, 8). These figures represent growth from $6.9 billion to $24 billion at the approximate PPP rate of $1.00 = ¥180.

6. Average operating profit rose from 11.6% of sales in fiscal 1978 (March 1979 year end) to 13.5% in 1981, and then declined to 8.7% in 1986. The ratio rose again to 12.6% in 1989 before declining to 9.7% in 1992. The figures, which are drawn from various editions of the *Japan Company Handbook* (*Oriental Economist* 1976–92), address corporate profitability rather than pharmaceutical profitability, but the companies derived a large majority of their sales from the pharmaceutical industry (on average more than 85% in most years).

7. For discussions of the drug development process, including the need for several years of development for most new drugs, see Finch 1989; Grabowski 1990; and Jernigan, Smith, Banahan, and Juergens 1991.

8. As yet, the directly owned distribution systems of foreign-owned firms have achieved relatively little penetration of the Japanese market, reaching a market share of less than 9% in 1991 (Nakagawa 1992). Foreign-owned firms represent potential competition more than major current competition.

9. The pharmaceutical R&D process can be categorized in terms of basic biomedical research, drug discovery, and preclinical product development. Basic research identifies opportunities for pharmaceutical therapy. Drug discovery involves the identification and testing of development candidates from existing and newly synthesized chemical entities. Preclinical development requires characterizing a particular drug and carrying out toxicology studies. Following preclinical trials, drugs undergo several rounds of clinical testing on human subjects before being introduced commercially.

10. For instance, the 1990 firm-level price-cut estimates in our sample ranged from 5% to 12.5% (sample average=9.6%, industry average=9.2%). The cumulative price cuts for the fourteen firms as of 1990 ranged from 43.5 to 87.5 (sample average=64.9). We obtained the estimates from industry analysts (Merrill Lynch 1992; Nakagawa 1992; Salomon Brothers 1992b). We used the average estimate when we had estimates from more than one source.

11. The relationships between R&D expenditure and profitability, corporate size, and other factors have received extensive study. However, there is little consensus among the studies, likely because changes in R&D expenditure, sales, and profitability usually take place in the context of a changing industry and hence are likely to have changing relationships (Mitchell, Roehl, and Slattery 1995). The data for the R&D growth variables were drawn from the *Japan Company Handbook* (*Oriental Economist* 1983–92) and the Yano Research Institute (1991). The 1992 R&D figures are estimates, reported in the Winter 1992 edition of the *Japan Company Handbook* (*Oriental Economist* 1992).

12. The statistical analysis reported in table 2 controls for corporate sales and operating profits as alternative explanations for R&D expenditure growth. Although desirable in order to control for liquidity, the variables introduce a potential bias because the level of a firm's sales and profits might be a result of past price cuts, so that price reduction effects might be assigned to profits or sales incorrectly. However, the price-cut influences in statistical analyses that omitted the operating profit and sales variables were materially equivalent to those reported in table 2.

REFERENCES

*Economist.* 1987. Molecules and markets: a survey of pharmaceuticals. *The Economist,* 7 February, S3–S14.

Finch, J. E. 1989. Product innovation and the process of creative destruction in the U.S. pharmaceutical industry. *Journal of Pharmaceutical Marketing and Management* 3.4: 3–20.

Grabowski, Henry. 1990. Innovation and international competitiveness in pharmaceuticals. In *Evolving technology and market structure: studies in Schumpeterian economics,* edited by Arnold Heertje and Mark Perlman. Ann Arbor: University of Michigan Press, 167–85.

Halliday, R. G., S. R. Walker, and C. E. Lumley. 1992. R&D philosophy and management in the world's leading pharmaceutical companies. *Journal of Pharmaceutical Medicine* 2: 139–54.

Hawkins, Elma S., and Michael R. Reich. 1992. Japanese originated pharmaceutical products in the United States from 1960 to 1989: an assessment of innovation. *Clinical Pharmacology and Therapeutics* 51: 1–11.

Industrial Bank of Japan. 1992. Pharmaceutical and agricultural chemical industries. *Quarterly Survey: Japanese Finance and Industry* 1: 1-19.

James, B. 1990. *The global pharmaceutical industry in the 1990s: the challenge of change.* London: Economist Intelligence Unit.

Japan Economic Institute. 1992. UNITED STATES-Japan competition in pharmaceuticals: no contest? *JEI Report* No. 13A (3 April). Washington, D.C.: Japan Economic Institute.

Japan Pharmaceutical Manufacturers Association. 1991. *Data Book 1991.* Tokyo: Japan Pharmaceutical Manufacturers Association.

———. 1992. *Data Book 1992.* Tokyo: Japan Pharmaceutical Manufacturers Association.

Jernigan, J. M., M. C. Smith, B. F. Banahan, and J. P. Juergens. 1991. Descriptive analysis of the 15-year product life cycles of a sample of pharmaceutical products. *Journal of Pharmaceutical Marketing and Management* 6.1: 3–36.

Maurer, P. Reed. 1992. *Are the Japanese coming home?* Tokyo: U.S. Pharmaceutical Manufacturers Association.

Merrill Lynch. 1992. Japan drug industry. Merril Lynch, unpublished company document, 9 April.

Mitchell, Will, Thomas Roehl, and Ronald Slattery. 1995. Influences on R&D growth of Japanese pharmaceutical firms, 1975–1990. *Journal of High Technology Management* (Spring 1995).

Nakagawa, Hiroshi. 1992. The Japanese pharmaceutical industry. Morgan Stanley & Co., Inc., unpublished company document, July.

Nakamura, H. 1991. Problems in the Japanese pharmaceutical industry. *Capsule* 37: 8–13.

Nikko Research Center. 1991. *Pharmaceutical development joint venture relationships— 150 major Japanese, European and American firms.* Tokyo: Nikko Research Center.

———. 1992. Product development and alliances in the Japanese pharmaceutical industry. Tokyo: Nikko Research Center.

*Oriental Economist.* 1976, 1983, 1992. *The Japan Company Handbook.* Tokyo: Oriental Economist.

Reich, Michael R. 1991. Policy changes facing the pharmaceutical industry in Japan. Unpublished paper.

———. 1990. Why the Japanese don't export more pharmaceuticals: health policy as industrial policy. *California Management Review* 32 (Winter): 124–50.

Salomon Brothers. 1992a. Earnings model of Japanese drug companies. Unpublished company document, 10 July.

————. 1992b. The pharmaceutical industry: an overview. Unpublished company document, 27 March.

Slattery, Ronald J. 1992. Pharmaceutical and diagnostic imaging equipment technology development in Japan. Report to the Long-Term Credit Bank of Japan, Economics Division, Tokyo.

Suguro, T. 1990. *The Japanese pharmaceutical industry.* Tokyo: Kyōikusha.

University Club. 1992. Explaining Japan's low-cost health care: culture, system, politics. Conference held at the University Club, Washington, D.C., 9 March.

Yano Research Institute. 1991. *The Pharmaceutical Industry.* Tokyo: Yano Research Institute.

Yano, Yoshio. 1991. The competitiveness of the Japanese pharmaceutical industry in the 1990s. *California Management Review* 33: 9–14.

Yoshikawa, Aki. 1989. The other drug war: U.S.-Japan trade in pharmaceuticals. *California Management Review* 31 (Winter): 76–89.

# CHAPTER 13

# Afterword: Quality and Cost in Japanese and U.S. Medical Care

*John M. Eisenberg with Nancy Foster*

The chapters by Hasegawa, Hisashige, and Ikegami offer important insight into the practice of medicine in Japan and how it differs from medical practice in the United States. Following some preliminary comments, we will turn to the broader question of whether Japan has paid a price in quality for the lower costs of its medical system.

Hasegawa has presented fascinating information on rates of surgery that might help to explain the differences in costs between the Japanese and American systems. The same percentage of gross domestic product (GDP) is spent in Japan on ambulatory care as is spent in the United States, but there are dramatic differences in expenditures for inpatient care. About half of this difference is attributable to differences in surgical utilization rates.

These differences in utilization rates and surgical expenditure are striking and may help us to understand the differences in health care costs between the two countries. It is not clear, however, why these differences exist. A number of possibilities have been proposed, some by Hasegawa, and others might be suggested as well.

For example, some of the difference may be due to the disease burden in the two populations, either because of a different endogenous frequency of diseases that would be treated surgically or because of a difference in preventing these diseases from developing to the surgical stage. However, because Japanese rates of cancer tend to be higher than those in the United States, one would anticipate, if anything, that surgical rates would be higher rather than lower. Hasegawa suggests that early detection of disease may prevent surgery, and this postulate could be tested by evaluating the stage of disease at the time of detection. However, in many instances surgery would still be required even for disease at an earlier stage.

Another possibility is that the surgical rates are different for the population as a whole but not on a per-surgeon basis. Thus, it would be interesting to determine what the surgical rates are per surgeon to determine whether a limit on the capacity of the system to provide surgery is one of the explanations for the lower utilization rate in Japan. Also, even when individual physicians have been trained to perform surgery, they may not be able to do so in Japan because of the to perform surgery, they may not be able to do so in Japan because of the limitation of hospital privileges. Thus, major surgery or surgery that should be provided in larger hospitals as opposed to smaller clinics might not be performed unless the surgeon had privileges in the larger institution.

Also, the Japanese tend to be more noninterventionist in their approach to medical care, and this suggestion has been made by Hasegawa in his comment about "filial responsibility" to the body.

Still another set of reasons for the lower surgical rate in Japan may have to do with the financial incentives that are available. It is well known that the point system pays poorly for surgical services, and Hasegawa asserts that hospitals recover only about 80% of their costs on surgical procedures. This might suggest that the point system and its discouraging structure for surgery also influence utilization rates. However, it should be noted that most hospital-based surgeons are salaried, and thus surgery payment rates should not influence decision making in a major way.

Other barriers may exist to surgery, including waiting times or barriers to referral by physicians who are community-based and do not have networklike relationships with hospitals. Because of the difficulty of referring patients to a hospital where they would not have to wait before an evaluation could be performed, some patients may simply never come to surgery.

Regardless of the reasons for the lower surgical rates in Japan, it would be interesting, and likely informative, to study the threshold for admission for surgery and for the surgical procedure itself. Many of the reasons listed above would cause the threshold for surgery to be higher (e.g., waiting time, referral barriers, fee differences), but other factors might have no effect on the threshold; instead, they would simply change the nature of patients presented for possible surgery (e.g., early detection of disease and prevention of surgically modifiable diseases by an intensive ambulatory care program).

Therefore, Hasegawa's chapter has helped to elucidate some of the differences in health care costs between Japan and the United States, and it offers several avenues for further research.

In both Japan and the United States, health policy experts believe that the rapid and wide dissemination of medical technology is a major cause of the increase in health care expenditures. Although the images presented to clinicians with computerized-axial tomographic (CAT) and magnetic resonance imaging (MRI) are superior to those of traditional roentgenograms, the cost of performing these studies and payment levels for them are substantially higher. In his chapter on the introduction and evaluation of MRIs in Japan, Hisashige has elucidated the factors that have influenced the introduction and dissemination of CAT scans and MRIs there. He emphasizes the need for rigorous and public evaluation of the effectiveness and efficiency of new medical services such as these two dramatic and important imaging technologies.

The methodologies for technology assessment use the principles and techniques of several of the evaluation sciences, including clinical epidemiology, cost-effectiveness analysis, and decision analysis, among others. However, in

Japan as in the United States, there is a shortage of individuals who are capable of performing these studies. In particular, there is a shortage of well-trained clinical investigators who are knowledgeable in these methods. Further, the resources of financial support for technology assessment studies are limited. In the United States, the new Agency for Health Care Policy and Research has a budget slightly over one hundred million dollars, a little over 1% of the budget of the National Institutes of Health, and only part of this money goes for technology assessment. Little funding is available in either country for training investigators.

Hisashige emphasizes the importance of technology assessment before widespread diffusion of technology, so that its use may be guided by evidence of its usefulness. One approach that we advocate is to establish specialized centers of technology assessment to carry out these evaluations. When a new technology has been developed—or for that matter, any new medical service, including surgical and diagnostic procedures—it would be used first only at these centers. The service or technology would not be approved for broader use, and payment would not be made except at these centers, where experts in the evaluation sciences would carry out technology assessments. These centers could be located at major academic medical institutions but would include a large number of participating clinicians at teaching hospitals, clinics, and small hospitals, as well as in community-based outpatient practices. These networks of participating physicians would collect data on patients, clinical outcomes, and costs in order to evaluate the service or technology.

Medical technology cannot be considered absolutely effective or ineffective. Most services offer a contribution to the health of *some* individuals. The question that should be asked is not so much "Is this technology effective?" as "In what circumstances and for what types of patients is the technology useful?" One of the problems for clinicians is that there are very few studies that help to determine which clinical problems are helped by technologic advances so that clinicians may select the patients most appropriate for a particular service.

Also, the cost effectiveness of medical technology is likely to vary from patient to patient. Since the effectiveness will be different for patients with different problems, the cost effectiveness will also vary.

The cost and effectiveness of medical technology is very important, but, as Hisashige emphasizes, it is the *incremental* contribution that is more important. What does the new service cost compared to the alternative, and what does it add to the clinical impact of the alternative?

There are two ways in which new technology may be used: it may be a replacement for existing technology, or it may be an addition to (and thus complementary to) the existing technology. In the latter case, the cost to be considered is the combined cost of the two services and the combined effectiveness of the two compared to the cost and effectiveness of the one service alone. In contrast, when a new service substitutes for an old one, it is the degree to which one alone is more expensive or more effective than the other that is important in technology assessment.

Unfortunately, there is evidence that new technology is often, perhaps even usually, additive rather than substitutive. We studied five new technologies that were introduced in the United States around 1980 and found that in only one of the five was the introduction of new technology associated with a decrease in the use of old technology (gallbladder ultrasound partially substituted for oral cholecystogram).

As both of our countries deal with concerns about how to limit the capacity of our health care systems and how to use that capacity most appropriately and efficiently, we should seek collaborative evaluation of technology. Although services are provided locally, the technology is usually of global interest. It is particularly problematic that the regulatory agencies in many countries that approve new services for use or that determine whether payment coverage will be offered for them often require technology assessment to be done in that country. There are probably few differences in the effectiveness of technology among developed nations, and sharing our technology assessments could improve the efficiency of care in each country.

The observation that outmoded technology (e.g., the permanent magnet for MRI) is used in small hospitals and clinics in Japan is quite bothersome because it suggests that the relatively unregulated diffusion of technology and the substantial financial incentives for providing these services may deprive the public of optimal quality medical care. On the other hand, the evidence that there is an important difference in the quality of care using the two types of magnets is scanty. Therefore, the difference in clinical effectiveness, if it is real and important, could be offset by the lower cost of the nearly equivalent service and by the greater convenience to the patient of having the service provided closer to home and with less waiting time in many instances. Still, the effect of fee-for-service payment, especially with low levels of payment for office visits, is likely great in stimulating high use and perhaps high inappropriate use of services. Of course, along with possibly inappropriate use there is probably greater appropriate use of the technical service, and one might consider that this combination of relatively low unit prices and little control on dissemination provides the Japanese public with greater access to potentially valuable services.

The increased use of medical services by physicians who profit by their utilization is not necessarily good or bad. It depends on whether the financial motivation for the physician is consistent with the best interests of the patient. For noninvasive diagnostic services like MRI and CAT scanning, which are less likely to cause physical harm than invasive diagnostic tests or therapies, the risk of adverse health outcomes from supplier-induced demand is low. Still, such a waste of resources for health care does cause, even if inadvertently, fewer services to be available to other people who might benefit from them.

Ikegami's chapter on pharmaceutical expenditure documents the larger proportion of GDP spent on pharmaceuticals in Japan and the substantially greater percentage of total health expenditure, more than double the percentage of total health care expenditure, spent on pharmaceuticals in the United States. Actual per-capita spending is slightly higher in the United States, but because Japanese prices are much lower, the quantity of pharmaceuticals consumed per capita is substantially greater in Japan. Ikegami points out that the payment mechanisms for providers and the minimal out-of-pocket payments in Japan contribute to this high use of pharmaceuticals, as does the custom of traditional medicine. Although U.S. prices are higher, generics are used more and there is increasing interest, albeit still modest, in the evaluation of the economic impact of pharmaceuticals in the United States.

These three chapters all show us that differences in medical care costs and utilization between the two countries cannot be explained by any single factor. Some of the differences may be attributable to differences in disease burden, to ethnic or cultural differences, or simply to the nation's wealth. Others may be due to the traditional expectations that a people have for their system of health and medical care, such as whether it is aggressive or noninterventionist about diagnosis, treatment, and knowledge about one's ailment, or how much doctor-patient communication exists.

However, some differences are not so exogenous to the way the medical care system is designed and may be more amenable to change through health policy initiatives. For example, financial incentives for doctors and their patients may influence medical practice patterns. So might levels of access to care and the degree of financial coverage for the purchase of services. Differences in regulation or in the health profession work force may explain other differences. In any case, these differences may affect the quality as well as the amount of care received, and evaluations of new technology and of the outcomes of care are important to a full understanding of the differences in medical care between two countries, even two of the wealthiest countries in the world.

### Is There a Price in Quality for the Lower Cost of Medical Care in Japan?

The Japanese medical care system operates at a cost that is about one-half that of the system in the United States (General Accounting Office 1991). Yet, the systematic measures of quality of care, such as infant mortality and life expectancy, indicate high quality (Ministry of Health and Welfare [MHW] 1987, 1990; Liu et al. 1992, 105–18). In addition, all Japanese are covered by some form of health insurance, and access to care is open to all. Americans ask, "How can the Japanese provide such broad access to high quality at such a low cost?" There are many reasons, including Japan's fee schedule, its programs of prevention, and a different mix of disease. Americans also ask, "Do Japanese miss anything by spending less on medical care? Are there signs of difficulty in the future for the Japanese quality of care?"

In the United States there has been renewed interest in measuring the quality and, especially, the outcomes of medical care. Traditional measures of quality have generally used conventional biomedical definitions, including mortality rates, surgical complications, antibiotic use, and appropriateness of services. As the United States increasingly moves to new measures of quality emphasizing health outcomes, its health care quality experts find that they are learning much of the methodology for doing so from the Deming approach to quality improvement as it has been applied in Japan since World War II.

According to Deming, quality is defined by the customers' needs, wants, and expectations (Deming 1986). Deming contended that quality equals giving people what they have the right to expect. Japanese and Americans would agree that patients' needs should be the first concern, but what are the patients' needs in our two countries?

The needs of both our nations include the care of a growing number of elderly (13% of the United States is anticipated to be elderly by the year 2000, and 21% in Japan by the year 2010), but we have different disease burdens (General Accounting Office 1991). In the United States, cardiovascular disease is the leading cause of death, while in Japan, cancer remains the leading cause of death (Kimura 1988). AIDS is much more common in the United States than in Japan (43,672 deaths in the United States compared to 473 in Japan in 1992). In the United States, trauma is much more common, with black men having a death rate of almost 50 per 100,000 and white men 20 per 100,000. These different disease burdens create different patient-care needs. Our health care systems must be different to respond to the needs of our patients.

The expectations of people in both of our countries are different as well. In the United States, patients often believe that everything possible should be done for them. Americans are known to have a very interventionist philosophy of medical care, and patients expect to be involved in decisions about their care. In Japan, however, medical care tends to be more paternalistic. Our colleague at Georgetown University, Rihito Kimura, has written that, until recently, physicians in Japan have behaved in an authoritative way toward patients and their families (Kimura 1986, 22–23). And *Newsweek* magazine in "Whose Life Is It Anyway? Japan and U.S. at Opposite Poles on Patient Rights" (23 January 1986, p. 61) reported that fewer than 20% of Japanese doctors tell patients of their cancer diagnoses. It would be rare not to share such information with patients in the United States. Thus, in Japan there has been a more dependent relationship between patients and doctors. The important question, of course, is whether this is what patients want.

Patients in the United States seem to have a greater desire for privacy, while privacy seems not to be as great a concern in Japan. As Japanese culture becomes more Westernized, however, we wonder whether patients in Japan will want more privacy in the future. This emphasizes that some of the differences in health care between the two countries are cultural differences.

In the United States access to care is very important, as it is in Japan. However, patients wait to see physicians in both countries. In America, patients seem more willing to wait several days to weeks to have an appointment with a physician, but once they arrive at the physician's office, they expect to be seen promptly. In Japan, patients do not seem to want to wait for an appointment but appear willing to wait for hours in the clinic to be seen. In the United States, hospitals remain open 24 hours per day, 365 days per year. In Japan, hospitals are sometimes closed to admissions at nights or on holidays, sometimes with office physicians taking turns covering the public facility at night and on weekends.

The old saying that "time is money" is of note here, because when people are waiting for their medical care they are sometimes losing money, or at least not fulfilling what they understand is expected of them at work. This may be one of the reasons for the lower frequency of physician visits by working-age Japanese. Some large companies in Japan have recognized this problem and avoid the need for employees to wait by offering primary care in the company facility or by contracting with nearby clinics or hospitals for accessible care. In other instances, Japanese working men and women may choose not to seek medical care when they should because it would mean they would have to spend too much time away from work.

In addition, patients in the United States expect to spend a significant amount of time with their physician. In the United States the average patient spends twelve minutes with an internist compared with about five minutes in Japan (Yoshikawa, Shirouzu, and Holt 1991, 111–37). Thus access to care is more open in Japan in two ways—health insurance is universal, and patients do not have to wait for weeks before they can be seen by a physician of their choice. However, access is limited in Japan by the need to stand in line, sometimes for hours until being seen, as a walk-in patient or for a short visit with the doctor.

If we are to measure the quality of care in our two countries, we can be guided by Donabedian, who wrote that there are three different ways of measuring quality—structure, process, and outcome. We will emphasize three aspects of structure: (1) the proportion of generalists; (2) the diffusion of technology; and (3) the payment system.

**The Work Force**

There is great concern in the United States today that cost and quality in the future will be affected adversely by an inappropriate supply of physicians. Concern in both countries in the 1960s and 1970s about the number of physicians being trained led to more schools being established and a doubling in the number of graduates from medical schools in both countries.

This increase did not lead to more generalist physicians in either country, that is, physicians who provide ongoing comprehensive care, especially primary care, as opposed to specialists who concentrate on a single type of service (e.g., orthopedic surgery), a particular organ system (e.g., cardiology), or a certain mechanism of disease (e.g., infectious disease or oncology). In both countries, the supply of office-based generalists who provide primary care is aging and not growing like the supply of hospital-based specialists. Although the supply of generalist physicians in the United States has been relatively unchanged, the ratio of specialists to generalists in the United States has been increasing and students' choices suggest a further decline in the proportion of generalists in the future (Physician Payment Review Commission 1993; U.S. Department of Health and

Human Services 1992). In Japan, there has been a similar increase in the number of physicians and no substantial increase in the number of generalists. This is a very serious concern for each country, both regarding access to generalists and the cost of the technical services that are provided by specialists.

In Japan, there may be a major problem in the future if this potential structural problem of quality—the physician work force—is not addressed. From 1980 to 1990 Japan increased its number of medical schools by thirty-four and doubled the number of graduates from 4,000 to 8,000. The number of doctors is increasing, but the distribution of doctors to rural areas has not changed, and the proportion of private practitioners has decreased from 41% to 28% (Koboyashi and Takaki 1992, 1,391–93). The supply of private practice doctors in Japan is aging rapidly; in 1992 the average age of private doctors was 59.7 years. More patients in Japan are going to hospitals for their outpatient care, partially because too few community-based options for seeing well-trained physicians have been developed (Okayama 1992, 183).

We suggest several options for policy regarding the medical work force in Japan. Japan should train more physicians as generalists and, especially, train them in primary care, prevention, and the efficient care of patients. Japan would need to reform medical education to increase generalist training, develop more student programs oriented toward generalism, and especially move some medical education out of university hospitals and into ambulatory care and community settings to stimulate more students to consider generalist careers. Also, there needs to be better communication and coordination between the Ministry of Education and the Ministry of Health and Welfare in improving medical student education.

Japan should also consider establishing formal residency programs and faculty development programs that emphasize primary care and generalism. It will be necessary to develop new faculty in order to train a new type of physician for Japan. Similar initiatives are underway in the United States. Also, Japan should consider the development and promotion of boards to certify physicians in specialty areas as well as in areas of generalism. This could help to assure quality of care and help the public to identify capable, well-trained physicians who are in community practice, while controlling the number of subspecialists.

In addition to training more generalists, Japan will probably need to consider limits on the training of specialists, especially those based in hospitals. Requiring more formal criteria to establish the qualifications of these individuals (e.g., board certification) could help to limit their number. Work force reform will be necessary in the future to assure access to well-trained primary care physicians as well as to highly trained specialists, and reform of medical and residency education will be necessary to achieve this goal.

At Georgetown University we have been working with the Japanese MHW and the Yamanouchi Pharmaceutical Company for several years to develop a training program for Japanese primary care physicians. And in February 1993, Dr. Tsuguya Fukui from Saga University (now Kyoto University) and his colleagues at Tokyo Second National Hospital met to develop a new organization to help foster the career development of physicians interested in training in primary care fields.

Another concern with regard to the availability of high-quality generalist care in Japan is whether clinics and private doctors will continue to be a viable option in the future. Certainly, one alternative would be to assure access to high-quality care in hospitals through their outpatient departments, such as is happening now in many hospitals. Another option would be to establish networks of hospitals and affiliated practices. Referral networks could help clinic-based physicians send patients to the teaching hospital. They could also provide community-based training sites for ambulatory-care students and residents. Existing clinics and private practices could be included in these networks, but new sites of practice outside the hospital could also help the hospital outpatient department exist outside hospital walls. This initiative would help to develop a vertically integrated system of primary health care in Japan. Of course, there is a risk that, by providing more access to the hospital through these systems, there would be even more high-cost hospital services used in the future through this greater access.

Japan should also consider reeducating specialist physicians trained in the past so that these specialists, who are now experts in hospital care, can provide care in the community as well (Okayama 1992, 183). It will also be important to upgrade the training of nurses and other nonphysicians to help to improve the quality of care in Japan. Like the United States, Japan will also probably need to consider reducing the class size of its medical schools. But even so, the distribution of generalists and specialists will need to be seriously considered in order to assure high-quality care in the future.

**Evaluation and Payment of Service**

In addition to considering reform of its medical work force, Japan should consider the appropriate diffusion of new technology. New technology will need to be evaluated, and physicians will need to be educated to provide high-quality and appropriate use of technology. Very important in achieving this goal will be the education and the funding of researchers to carry out health services research, including the evaluation of technology and the quality of care.

The payment of physicians is very important in assuring the quality of care. The structure of Japan's payment system is a key element in the structure of care, and it does influence quality. Payment policy can offer short-term solutions, in contrast to manpower policy that takes years to influence the supply of physicians. Both of our countries have predominantly fee-for-service payment systems, where the payment scheme can be used to influence the quality of care provided. The Japanese fee structure is more favorable to primary care than that of the United States, especially with regard to the relative payment of primary care and procedures. In particular, as Hasegawa observed, low reimbursement for surgery likely leads to fewer operations and consequently lower medical care spending in Japan.

However, there are problems in the structure of Japanese payment systems that have important implications for the quality of care. There is a very low fee for office visits in Japan, and, of course, this can lead to very short and frequent visits that we call "churning." Even if the fee is low, these frequent visits are of some cost to patients, especially those who are working, because they must take time from work to see their physician. Yet, these frequent visits may improve the quality of care by assuring communication with the physician and the monitoring of patients' use of prescriptions. Still, perhaps a different fee should be considered in Japan for more complex patients, or a different fee should be provided for office visits, in order to encourage fewer visits. Of course, there is the possibility that patients may want frequent visits and that reducing the frequency of visits could decrease their satisfaction with care, which is an important measure of the quality of care.

Another problem with fees in Japan that needs to be considered is the high fees that are paid for laboratory tests and equipment and the ownership of this equipment by physicians. Recent research in the United States has demonstrated that physician ownership of laboratories and diagnostic equipment leads to more services being provided (Mitchell and Sunshine 1992, 1,497–501; Swedlow et al. 1992, 1,502–6).

Drug prescription by physicians is another important issue in medical payment that affects quality of care. Japan's fee system and its medical tradition encourage physicians to prescribe and dispense drugs. In the United States it has been estimated that 10% of all hospital admissions are due to the side effects of drugs (Ikegami 1993). In Japan, rates of infection from methicillin-resistant staphylococcus are increasing, in part as a result of widespread use of antibiotics (Ushio 1989, 1–18). Therefore, we need, in both of our countries, renewed attention to appropriate use of drugs and to the evaluation of pharmaceutical products.

These issues of the structure of the system certainly affect the quality of care. So do issues having to do with the process of care.

**Process of Care**

The process of medical care involves our practice styles. In Japan one very important element of practice style is the long length of hospital stay. Long length of stay could be good or bad for quality of care. Care could be better if the longer stay provides continuity throughout the episode of illness and if it provides less burden on the family. But long length of stay could result in worse quality if, for example, it leads to complications in the hospital or more time missed from work.

Another issue related to the process of care in Japan is the use of professionals other than physicians. Both the United States and Japan should consider upgrading the activities of nurses and other health professionals; they have much to offer to improve the quality of care, especially if they are treated as fellow professionals.

Although Japan is appropriately proud of its full access to care at all hospitals, waiting time serves as a barrier, and in a sense, as a mechanism of rationing care. Only those who are able to wait will be able to get full care; therefore, many people, such as those who are working and cannot leave work, will get less care.

Perhaps this is one of the reasons why the elderly receive so much more care in Japan than younger people do.

It is difficult in Japan for patients to seek out the physician they want to see or the one who is appropriate for a problem. A gatekeeper or case-manager system, in which a physician helps to direct patients to certain physicians through referral mechanisms, may help. This would be difficult for Japan because it has always wanted to give equal access to people, whether they have a referral or not. However, primary care physicians would be in a more favorable position if they could refer patients to hospital-based specialists and enable patients to have less waiting time. This would encourage more primary care because patients would go to their primary care physician rather than waiting in long lines at the hospital, knowing that, if they go to their primary care physician first, they may be able to get immediate access to the hospital.

Both Japan and the United States have many opportunities to improve the care they offer patients, but if we are to follow Deming's teaching on quality, we must begin by determining what our patients need and expect from us. In the United States, we have learned that patients want better communication, including responses to their questions or complaints, clearer instructions about their care, and more courteous treatment by all members of our staff. Additionally, Americans want to know that their treatment will efficiently and effectively improve their health. Japanese patients may have similar needs, but it is impossible to know unless data are collected.

To discover which treatments improve health most efficiently and effectively, the United States has developed an active program of health services research. In Japan, initial health service research efforts have helped to identify what treatments are provided, but further studies are needed if we are to know whether the Japanese health care system is delivering what Japanese patients need, want, and expect. Measuring the outcomes of care is also critical to understanding the quality of care, as are structure and process. These techniques help us to evaluate what we do and whether it is more helpful than it is harmful.

REFERENCES

Deming, W. E. 1986. *Out of the crisis.* Cambridge: Massachusetts Institute of Technology.
General Accounting Office. 1991. *Health care spending control: The experience of France, Germany and Japan.* Washington, D.C.: GPO.
Kimura, R. 1988. Law in the East and West. Invited paper for the thirtieth anniversary of the Institute of Comparative Law, Waseda University.
————. 1986. Caring for newborns: International views. *Hastings Center Report* 4: 22–23.
Koboyashi, Y., and H. Takaki. 1992. Geographic distribution of physicians in Japan. *Lancet* 340.
Liu, K., M. Moon, M. Sulvetta, and J. Chaula. 1992. International infant mortality ranking: a look behind the numbers. *Health Care Financing Review* 4.
Ministry of Health and Welfare (MHW). 1990. *Vital statistics.* Tokyo.
————. 1987. *Understanding maternal and child health in Japan.* Tokyo: Maternal and Child Health Division, Children and Families Bureau.

Mitchell, J. and J. Sunshine. 1992. Consequences of physician ownership of health care facilities: Joint venture in radiation therapy. *New England Journal of Medicine* 21.

Okayama, T. 1992. Integrating "generalist" into "specialist." *Journal of Integrated Medicine* 3.

Physician Payment Review Commission. 1993. *Annual Report to Congress.* Washington, D.C.

Swedlow, A., G. Johnson, N. Smithline, and A. Milstein. 1992. Increased costs and rates of use in the California Workers' Compensation System as a result of self-referral by physicians. *New England Journal of Medicine* 21.

U.S. Department of Health and Human Services. 1992. *Council on Graduate Medical Education: Third report—Improving access to health care through physician work force reform: Directions for the 21st century.* Washington, D.C.

Ushio, M. 1989. The system of health and medical services for the aged in Japan. *Japan Hospitals* 8.

Yoshikawa A., N. Shirōzu, and M. Holt. 1991. How does Japan do it? Doctors and hospitals in a universal health care system. *Stanford Law and Policy Review* 3: 11–37.

CHAPTER 14

# Comparison of Long-Term Care for the Elderly between Japan and the United States

*Naoki Ikegami and Takeshi Yamada*

SUMMARY   Despite commonly held beliefs to the contrary, the institutionalization rates of the elderly in Japan and the United States are identical. The severity of the disability of those institutionalized also appears to be of about the same level. The total monthly work hours of institution staff per 100 residents/patients is about 10% more in the United States due to the fact that more aides are employed. However, the costs (using the purchasing power parity [PPP] rate) are about the same because higher wages are paid to aides in Japan. There are more physicians in Japanese institutions because the hospital is the primary organization for providing long-term care (LTC), but whether this translates into better care is doubtful. The physical facilities are in general inferior to those in the United States, as are the efforts made to maintain quality control. The LTC system in Japan is a result of disjointed measures made by the government to solve an immediate problem. While the situation in the United States leaves much to be desired, the 1987 OBRA legislation and the case-mixed-based form of reimbursement can serve as models for Japan to pursue.

## Background

From the point view of the average American, one of the reasons for Japan's lower health care expenditures would appear to lie in the difference in the provision of LTC for the elderly. It is a commonly held belief in the United States that the elderly in Japan are well taken care of by their children and, as a consequence, require far less formal support. On the other hand, Americans themselves feel that the disintegration of the family has made informal care very difficult to provide in the United States. The objective of this paper is to point out not only that these assumptions are mistaken, but also that LTC may turn out to be more costly in Japan, especially when the quality of service is taken into consideration.

## Is There a Difference in the Demand for LTC?

The basis for the belief that the elderly are looked after well by their children probably comes from the idea that Japanese society is steeped in the Confucian tradition that stresses filial obligation. The three-generation patriarchal family with the dutiful daughter-in-law looking after the elderly parents is a model that still seems to be viable in Japan. When the composition of households is compared, as table 1 shows, the ratio of the elderly living alone or with their spouses amounts to only 36.6% of the population age 65 and over in 1990. While this ratio has tripled since 1960, it is still less than half that of the U.S. proportion in 1984, when the ratio of the population 65 and over was about the same as that in Japan (Bureau of Statistics 1962, 1992; Congressional Budget Office 1988).

However, these figures are deceptive. As Shanas (1979a, b) has pointed out, while "the proportion of parents and children living in the same household has declined, there has been a rise in the proportion of old people living within ten minutes distance of a child." Thus, "in 1975, three of every four persons with children living either lived in the same household or within a half hour's distance of a child."[1] Although more recent figures are not available, there is no reason to believe that there has been a fundamental change in the basic pattern. It is true that, in the United States, when the spouse is not able, it is most likely the daughter that takes care of the elderly parent and not the daughter-in-law as is the case in Japan. Nevertheless, in both countries, it is the family that is the primary provider of care. Indeed, in the United States, even when the daughter works outside of the home, she still spends a considerable amount of time in caring for the elderly parent (Brody and Schoonover 1986). Therefore, one should look beyond the difference in household structure and make a more detailed analysis of how much actual time the children devote to taking care of their parents when they have become frail, regardless of whether they live in the same house or not. This should be a major area for future analysis, especially in Japan because the maintenance of the three-generation household has been equated with the availability of family support for the elderly.

The difference in the household structure of the elderly is certainly not reflected in the institutionalization rate. As table 2 shows, when the ratios of the elderly 65 and over in institutions are compared, the figures are almost identical: 5.9% for Japan and 5.7% for the United States (although the year of the survey differed, the ratios of the population 65 and over were the same) (Ministry of Health and Welfare [MHW] 1991, 1992a, b; Census Bureau 1991). The only marked difference lies in the type of institution—whereas most of the Japanese elderly were in hospitals, in the United States, they were in nursing homes. The reason hospitals have become the major institution for LTC in Japan will be explained later. Here it should be noted that because inpatients in hospitals are usually not classified as being in institutions, and because Special Homes for the Aged (SHA) have been officially translated as "nursing homes," sometimes only the latter was counted for calculating the institutionalization rate, which has resulted in making the ratio erroneously low in Japan. If anything, the institu-

**Table 1. People 65 and over not living with children,
Japan and U.S. (in percentage)**

|  | Japan | | U.S. | |
|---|---|---|---|---|
|  | 1960 | 1990 | 1960 | 1984 |
| Ratio over 65 | 5.7 | 12.0 | 9.2 | 11.8 |
| Living alone (A) | 3.5 | 11.4 | 18.6 | 30.6 |
| Living with spouse only (B) | 9.4 | 25.2 | 36.8 | 45.0 |
| (A) + (B) | 12.9 | 36.6 | 55.4 | 75.4 |

Sources: Bureau of Statistics 1962, 1992; Congressional Budget Office 1988.

**Table 2. People 65 and over in institutions,
Japan and U.S. (in percentage)**

|  | Japan (1990) | U.S. (1985) |
|---|---|---|
| Nonpsychiatric hospitals | 4.0 | 0.7 |
| Psychiatric hospitals | 0.4 | 0.4 |
| Clinics | 0.3 | – |
| Health Facilities for Elderly | 0.2 | – |
| Special Homes for Aged | 1.0 | – |
| Nursing homes | – | 4.6 |
| Total | 5.9 | 5.7 |

Sources: Census Bureau 1991; Hing 1987; Ministry of Health
and Welfare 1991, 1992a, b.

tionalization rate can be expected to become higher in Japan as the ratio of the very old increases. For those age 85 and over, the rate is still only 13% compared with the United States's rate of 23%. In contrast, for the age group 65–69, the rate is higher in Japan, 3% compared with 1.8% in the United States.

From the point of view of cost, it is necessary to look at not only the ratio of institutionalization, but also the case-mix. For example, due to the greater prevalence of cerebrovascular diseases in Japan, the institutionalized there may be more incapacitated than in the United States. On the other hand, the more cramped housing conditions in Japan may have led to institutionalization at an earlier and

**Table 3. Degree of dependency in selected activities of daily living for the institutionalized and noninstitutionalized elderly, Japan and U.S. (in percentage)**

| | Japan | | | | U.S. | |
| | Geriatric hospitals 1987 | SHAs 1988 | HFEs 1990 | Total institution* | Non-institution 1990 | Nursing homes 1985 | Non-institution 1984 |
|---|---|---|---|---|---|---|---|
| Requires assistance in: | | | | | | | |
| Bathing | 84.7 | 84.4 | 90.2 | 84.6 | 3.6 | 91.2 | 6.0 |
| Dressing | – | 73.3 | 74.6 | – | 2.0 | 77.7 | 4.3 |
| Using toilet room | 71.1 | 62.6 | 55.0 | 69.4 | 2.2 | 63.3 | 2.2 |
| Eating | 52.7 | 33.0 | 21.6 | 48.8 | 0.5–2.0 | 40.4 | 1.1 |
| Bed bound (complete) | 34.7 | 36.4 | 32.0 | 35.0 | 0.5–2.2 | 6.5 | 3.0 |

Sources: Hing 1987; Ministry of Health and Welfare 1990, 1992b; Rōjin no Senmon Iryō o Kanagaerukai 1987;

Shanas 1979b; Tokyo Metropolitan Government 1991.

*Does not include clinics; data were not available.

hence a less severe stage of illness.[2] Since a cross-sectional survey of all the elderly requiring LTC has never been done in Japan, an attempt was made to synthesize the best available existing data to provide a total picture, using the indicies of selected activities of daily living (ADL). The results are summarized in table 3.[3] Japan's slightly higher ratios in "using toilet room" and "eating" are compensated by the somewhat lower ratios in "bathing." The one major exception was the ratio of bed-bound patients: 6.5% in the United States, compared to 35.1% in Japan. However, this has been ascribed more to the differences in caring practice (which will be examined later from the point of view of quality) rather than to any underlying organic conditions. If the latter were the reason, then the ratio of the elderly who are bed bound in the community should be equally higher in Japan. However, this is not borne out by the actual figures. Although the U.S. figures do come from an earlier 1975 study, when compared to the Japanese ratio, even when the broadest definition of bedbound is chosen ("is out of bed when feeling well and also is out for the toilet and meals"), this ratio is still lower than the corresponding U.S. definition of "bedfast."

More precise comparisons will have to wait until surveys can be made using identical scales and methodology. However, from the existing evidence, there does not seem to be much difference in the case-mix of those institutionalized between Japan and the United States. Thus, since it has already been noted that the institutionalization rate is also of the same level, it follows that the provisio of LTC is very similar in both countries despite popular notions to the contrary. The next question is, Of the two countries' systems, which one provides better care at lower cost?

## How Japan and the United States Compare on Cost and Quality

### Nursing Staff

Costs and quality are very difficult to evaluate from aggregated data. For example, since the SHA are under the social welfare administration, their costs are not even listed under health care expenditures. Therefore, this study will try to estimate by using a meta-analytic approach. The first focus will be on the nursing staff (both qualified nurses and aides). Costs will be measured by their personnel expenses and quality by their total work hours per patient/resident. This is primarily because of the availability of data, but it should be noted that the nursing staff is the most crucial factor in both costs and quality, especially in the case of LTC.

Certain bold assumptions still had to be made in order to make the comparison. In the case of Japanese hospitals, since the staffing ratio of geriatric hospitals is not known, it was decided to take the staffing ratio of the lowest required level in the new inclusive per-diem rate (*nyūin iryō kanriryō*), which is one qualified nurse and one aide for six patients (the highest grade would be one aide for four patients). It was further assumed that one-third would be full nurses (*seikan,* equivalent to RNs) and two-thirds assistant nurses (*junkan,* equivalent to

LPNs). These figures are based on empirical evidence.[4] For SHA, the data from the 1990 national survey were used (MHW 1992b). The staffing level for all institutions was calculated by combining that of hospitals with that of SHA on a 4:1 basis to reflect their relative share of the jobs (the other remaining facilities constitute less than 10% of the total, and their staffing ratios are estimated to lie between the two) (MHW 1991, 1992b). The wages and working hours for nurses, assistant nurses, and aides come from the 1991 Wage Census conducted annually in June by the Ministry of Labor that surveys all private businesses in Japan. It is likely that, since hospitals providing LTC are mostly in the private sector, the actual wages are likely to be slightly lower. However, this would be partially offset by the fact that the higher pay scales of the public sector would be applied to nearly all those working in SHA.

In the case of the United States, the staffing ratio comes from the 1985 National Nursing Home Survey (National Center for Health Statistics 1989). The wage scales and work hours are from the Bureau of Labor Statistics data of nonsupervisory workers employed in "nursing and personal care facilities" for the second quarter of the year 1991 (Donham et al. 1992). Of those employed in this category, 71.6% are in skilled nursing homes and 14% are in the intermediate care nursing home so that it is reasonable to assume that this represents the actual wages in the U.S. nursing homes (Department of Labor 1992). While it does exclude nurses in supervisory roles, since numerically they are a small fraction the effect should be marginal. The relative difference in wages among registered nurses (RNs), licensed practical nurses (LPNs), and aides was set at 2:1.5:1 from the results of the survey made by Schneider et al. (1988), and based on this ratio, the wages of each staff category were calculated from the average by weighing their number by the staffing ratio.

While the above method is by no means precise, it is possible to make an approximate comparison between the two countries. As table 4 shows, Japan has a much lower staffing level when compared to the United States, 33.2 per 100 patients and residents versus 47.2 in the United States. The reason for this difference lies in the number of aides, because while the number of qualified nurses are about the same, there are only 18.9 aides in Japan, which is about half of the United States's 33.6.

However, from the cost point of view, this lower ratio is offset by the following factors. First, as table 5 shows, the average hourly wage for the total nursing staff is higher in Japan; $10.54, using the exchange rate of ¥135 to $1, or $7.91, using our approximate PPP rate of ¥180 to $1, compared to the average hourly wage in the United States of $7.52. The higher wages in Japan apply for all the staff categories when the exchange rate is used, but when the PPP rate is used, only the aides are markedly high. This is because there is less pay-scale difference in Japan: whereas the RN:LPN:Aide ratio is 2:1.5:1 in the United States, the equivalent Japanese ratio is 1.7:1.4:1. Second, the average hours per month is longer in Japan: 176.6 compared to 137.6 in the United States (average hours per month in the United States was calculated by multiplying the average hours per week, 32, by 4 times 52/48). When these factors are taken together, Japanese

**Table 4. Staffing per 100 patients/residents, Japan and U.S.**

| | Japan | | | U.S. |
| | Geriatric | | | Nursing |
| | hospitals | SHAs | Total | homes |
|---|---|---|---|---|
| Nurse (RN) | 6.0 | 3.9 | 5.6 | 5.6 |
| Assistant nurse (LPN) | 11.0 | – | 8.8 | 8.1 |
| Aides | 17.0 | 26.3 | 18.9 | 33.6 |
| Total | 34.0 | 30.2 | 33.2 | 47.2 |

Sources: Ministry of Health and Welfare 1990; National Center for Health Statistics 1989.

**Table 5. Average hourly wages, hours worked per month, wages per month, Japan and U.S. (1991)**

| | Average hourly wages | | | Average hours per month | | Average monthly wage | | |
| | Japan | | U.S. | Japan | U.S. | Japan | | U.S. |
| | Exchange rate ($) | PPP rate($) | ($) | | | Exchange rate ($) | PPP rate($) | ($) |
|---|---|---|---|---|---|---|---|---|
| Nurse (RN) | 14.54 | 10.91 | 12.50 | 175.0 | 137.6 | 2,543 | 1,907 | 1,720 |
| Assistant nurse (LPN) | 11.89 | 8.92 | 9.38 | 179.0 | 137.6 | 2,127 | 1,595 | 1,290 |
| Aides | 8.73 | 6.55 | 6.25 | 176.0 | 137.6 | 1,536 | 1,152 | 860 |
| Total | 10.54 | 7.91 | 7.52 | 176.6 | 137.6 | 1,860 | 1,395 | 1,035 |

Sources: Donham, Maple, and Levit 1992; Ministry of Labor 1992.

monthly wages become higher than those in the United States for all staff categories even when the PPP rate was used. As a consequence, total personnel costs for the nursing staff turns out to be about the same despite the lower staffing ratio. As table 6 shows, the sum of all wages comes to $61,891 (exchange rate) or $46,418 (PPP rate) per month per 100 patients/residents compared with $48,808 in the United States.

Parenthetically, in Japan these figures would represent about one-quarter of the estimated revenue in an average geriatric hospital and about one-third in SHA

Table 6. Total hours worked and total wages per 100 patients/residents per month, Japan and U.S. (1991)

| | Total hours | | | | | | Total wages | | | | | |
|---|---|---|---|---|---|---|---|---|---|---|---|---|
| | Japan | | | | | U.S. | Japan | | | | | U.S. |
| | Geriatric hospitals | | SHAs | | Total | | Nursing homes | | Exchange rate ($) | PPP rate($) | | ($) | |
| Nurse (RN) | 1,050 | 17.5% | 683 | 12.9% | 977 | 16.6% | 764.0 | 11.8% | 14,194 | 10,645 | 22.9% | 9,556 | 19.6% |
| Assistant nurse (LPN) | 1,969 | 32.8% | – | | 1,575 | 26.8% | 1,109.0 | 17.1% | 18,722 | 14,042 | 30.3% | 10,399 | 21.3% |
| Aides | 2,992 | 49.8% | 4,629 | 87.2% | 3,319 | 56.5% | 4,617.0 | 71.1% | 28,973 | 21,730 | 46.8% | 28,854 | 59.1% |
| Total | 6,011 | 100.0% | 5,311 | 100.0% | 5,871 | 100.0% | 6,490.0 | 100.0% | 61,891 | 46,418 | 100.0% | 48,808 | 100.0% |

(the latter is an underestimation because these institutions receive extra funding for capital expenditures). In the United States, it would also represent about one-quarter of the total revenue if all sources of payment were averaged for all facilities. The fact that these ratios are similar would seem to validate the conclusions drawn from the original assumptions.

Next, when viewed from the point of quality, the total work hours of the nursing staff per 100 patients/residents comes to 5,871 hours in Japan compared with 6,490 hours in the United States. Even for the more heavily staffed geriatric hospitals, the number of hours is still only 6,011. This is entirely due to the larger number of manpower hours provided by aides in the United States, since the number of hours provided by qualified nurses is actually less than in Japan. When the total wages for the entire nursing staff are divided by the total work hours, it comes to $10.54 (exchange rate) or $7.91 (PPP rate) in Japan, compared with $7.52 for the United States. Thus, from this viewpoint, more manpower hours are provided in the United States at less cost than in Japan.

Physical Facilities

Hospitals in Japan tend to be very inadequate in their physical facilities for reasons that will be explained later. According to a survey made in 1990, only 12.5% of the rooms in geriatric hospitals were single or double; 62.2% had more than six beds and 7.7% had more than ten beds. The conditions are similar in the other types of hospitals, with 50.3% of the rooms having six or more beds (Kitagawa 1991). In addition, it should be noted that the average room per bed is also very small in Japan because hospitals are only required to provide 4.3 square meters per bed (including the space occupied by the bed and other nonremovable furniture). Dining rooms and rehabilitation facilities are usually not available. The situation is better in the SHA. The new regulations require that the number of beds per room must be four or less (although some old facilities still have six). Moreover, floor space per bed is more than 4.95 square meters per bed excluding space for closets, plus the mandatory requirement of dining rooms and rehabilitation facilities. These requirements are closer to the U.S. nursing homes except that most of the U.S. residents are in semiprivate rooms. However, since over 80% of the LTC is being provided for by hospitals in Japan, in general, the physical environment is poor compared with that in the United States.

Other Professional Manpower

There appears to be a major difference in the number of physicians in Japan and United States. In Japan, geriatric hospitals are legally required to have three physicians per 100 inpatients, and SHA must have at least one part-time physician (usually present half of the week) per facility (the usual size being 100 beds). In contrast, in the U.S. nursing homes have only 0.2 full-time equivalent physicians per 100 residents (National Center for Health Statistics 1989). Although this figure is probably too low because it does not take into account the time spent by physicians visiting the nursing homes, there is no doubt that there are more physicians in LTC facilities in Japan. However, it is doubtful whether this translates into better LTC. First, because of the fee-for-service method of reimbursement that is still used by a majority of geriatric hospitals, physicians tend to overmedicate and order too many laboratory tests. This practice not only adds to costs but also, because it requires nurses' time for executing the orders, decreases patient-care-centered activities.[5] However, the hospital needs the revenue for providing these services in order to pay, among other things, the salaries for the physicians they employ. Second, the quality of physicians employed by geriatric hospitals tends to be mixed, and very few have had any training in geriatrics.

The number of other professionals such as physical therapists and social workers appears to be of the same order, but comparable figures were not available. More research is needed in this area.

Patient Care Management

Patient care management by nurses is an area not well developed in Japan because nurses tend to play a much more subordinate role to physicians. The quality of nursing records is very uneven and care plans perfunctory. The managerial role of nurses has not been fully established, and even the floor head nurse frequently has to stand in for the aide who is absent without prior permission. According to a time study made in 1991, the ratio of working hours devoted to direct patient care in Japan was the same for fully qualified nurses and aides (both about two-thirds of their time). In contrast, in the United States the ratio was much lower for RNs (44%) when compared to aides (66%) (Ikegami et al. 1993). Together with overmedication, poor patient care management would seem to be the major factor that has led to the high ratio of bed-bound patients in Japan.

Turnover Rate

One factor that may contribute to quality in Japan is the much lower staff turnover rates—less than 10% in a year. This is in contrast to the United States, where over half of the staff is likely to change. Without a fairly stable workforce, it is very difficult to improve quality, especially of aides, most of whom have to receive on-the-job training. However, it should be noted that one of the reasons for the low turnover rate is the experience-rated wage increases. That is to say, if a worker remains with the organization, he or she would automatically receive an annual increase. This has made labor costs higher in Japan, as has been described earlier. For example, according to the 1991 Wage Census, aides in the age group 50–54 are paid six times as much as those in the youngest group, and this amounts to 1.4 times the wages of assistant nurses in the 18–19 age group. Assistant nurses in the highest-paid age group are paid 1.3 times that of the fully qualified nurses in the lowest-paid age group.

Prolongation of Life

Prolongation of life does not necessarily imply better quality in LTC. On the contrary, quality may be better measured by the extent to which the patient's/resident's wishes are taken into account. From this standpoint, the United States does better than Japan because of the more common provision of living wills and other measures to ascertain the patient's wish. On the cost side, heroic efforts to prolong life will definitely increase expenditure. It is unclear whether the pressure to prolong life is greater in Japan or the United States. From anecdotal stories, it would seem that there are different standards for acute hospitals and LTC facilities in both countries. Age may also be a factor in deciding whether efforts to prolong life should be made or not. An analysis of the monthly claims data in Japan by Fukaya (1992) has shown that the amount from inpatient claims in the months preceding death decreases as the patient becomes older. Thus, physicians may be treating older patients less aggresively, although it has not been possible to control for the case-mix in this study. Further research is needed in this area.

### Why LTC Has Not Been a Success in Japan

Historically, there were no institutions similar to almshouses in Japan, and the care of the frail and elderly used to be the sole responsibility of the family. Before the defeat in the war ending in 1945, public assistance was severely limited to those in dire circumstances. Consequently, the country was ill-prepared for the growing demand for the formal provision of LTC arising from the rapid aging of society and the increase of women working outside of their homes. It should be noted that in 1960, when the elderly 65 and over constituted 5.7% of the population, only 1.3% were institutionalized. These figures have increased to 12.0% and 6.4% in 1990 (Ikegami et al. 1993).

The present LTC system is a result of disjointed administrative responses to the immediate pressing need for care of the elderly. Originally, apart from hospitals, the only form of institutional care for the elderly were the Homes for Aged, for the destitute who had some functional disabilities. In 1963, to meet the expected increase in demand for LTC, it was decided to separate the SHA from the Homes for the Aged, because it was then thought that providing hospital care would be too expensive. Being under the social welfare administration, to this day the residents are committed by the order of municipal authorities (meaning they cannot exercise any choice in their SHA), and there are neither physicians nor qualified nurses during night and weekend hours. However, the greatest problem with SHAs is that they have been unable to meet the demand because they had to rely on public financing for both capital and operating costs.

Ironically, only ten years after the decision that hospitals were too expensive for LTC, mounting public pressure forced the government to make health care free for the elderly in 1973 (formerly, most had to pay a 50% copayment). This inadvertently opened the door for hospitals to fill the unmet need for LTC because they were able to get reimbursed from the open-budgeted health insurance fund, and also because they did not suffer from the negative image of indigent care. Some new hospitals were opened for LTC, but the majority of this care came to be provided by the smaller hospitals that were no longer able to compete with the larger, well-equipped hospitals for acute care.

Despite this change in the hospitals' role, they were not regulated to provide either the physical facilities or the manpower for LTC, and their standards tended to remain minimal. Furthermore, hospitals continued to be paid on a fee-for-service basis according to a nationally uniform fee schedule that determined the price of each procedure and material. Under this fee schedule, providing primary care services, such as dispensing drugs and ordering laboratory tests, has been financially rewarding, while nursing care has remained poorly reimbursed, especially if the ratio of fully qualified nurses is low. This has resulted from the political balance of power among the providers and also because the fee schedule was originally designed to pay for the services provided by clinic physicians who focused on primary care. The incentives have had a particularly adverse effect in LTC, not only because the utility of the former is often marginal, but also because hospitals that focus on LTC had difficulty recruiting qualified nurses. Moreover, to fill the nursing shortage, it has become the norm for hospitals to request that patients hire a private duty aide (PDA, *tsukisoi*) if they should require intensive care. Unlike in the past, the family usually cannot provide much direct care once the patient is hospitalized in an LTC facility, since by that time the family has already exhausted all its resources. Thus, although the PDAs rarely have any qualifications and provide only nonprofessional care, they have come to play an indispensable role in the Japanese LTC system as surrogates for families.

The PDAs not only have blurred the hospitals' responsibility for providing nursing care but also have imposed a major financial burden on the patient. To mitigate this situation, about two-thirds of PDA charges became reimbursable in 1981 for hospitals that had nurse-staffing ratios below prescribed standards. However, this official sanction of PDAs inadvertently led to institutionalizing their presence. Furthermore, the low reimbursement rate led hospitals that focused on LTC to demand extra payment for nonmedical "caring" (*osewaryō*) services such as laundry, diapers, and so forth, and these charges to patients have been implicitly condoned by the government. Thus, not only is the level of care questionable, but the patients must also pay quite significant out-of-pocket expenses, which amount to an average of ¥65,744 per month ($365 at our PPP rate) according to a survey done by Niki (1992).

### Recent Reforms by the Japanese Government

#### The Creation of the Health Facility for the Elderly

These factors led to the creation of the Health Facility for the Elderly (HFE) in 1988. Unlike SHA, these are medical facilities, and their directors are, as in hospitals, physicians. To inhibit the over-prescribing and over-ordering of tests,

HFEs are paid on a strictly inclusive per-diem rate under the national fee schedule. The government had originally hoped that some hospitals would be converted into HFEs. However, no hospital has so far done this because of the low reimbursement rate and the difficulty of meeting the HFE's higher standards on the physical facility (for example, the minimum floor space per bed is 8 square meters compared to 4.3 for hospitals). Consequently, the increase in HFEs has been slower than projected. Moreover, it has proved difficult for the HFEs to function as relatively short-term facilities because of the lack of home care and permanent institutional care. Theoretically, patients from HFEs are supposed to be discharged within three months, but 63% stay longer (MHW 1992a). It should be remembered that only SHAs are supposed to provide permanent institutional care, but their growth continues to be slow because of the limitations imposed by the government's general expenditure budget. In addition, the de facto main provider of LTC, hospitals, can no longer expand under the regional health planning legislation introduced in 1985, which has capped the number of hospital beds.

The Inclusive Per-Diem Rate for Hospitals

Reforms have also been attempted from the health care financing side. To tackle the inadequacies of the reimbursement system, the government introduced a new inclusive per-diem rate for hospitals in 1990, which has been adopted by about one-third of the geriatric hospitals, totalling 66,228 beds as of 30 April 1993. Under this scheme, for which hospitals may opt if their nurse/aide-to-patient staffing ratios exceed specified levels, PDAs are prohibited and additional reimbursement is restricted largely to rehabilitation treatment. The government has set relatively generous per-diem payment rates and has strongly encouraged hospitals with a high ratio of elderly patients and low levels of qualified nurses to adopt it, at the same time ignoring the practice of extra billing for nonmedical "caring" services. However, this is likely to lead to a problem that has already plagued the SHA and more recently the HFE. Since providers are paid on a fixed per-diem basis, they have a strong incentive to admit only those who require light care. (Although SHAs must theoretically admit whoever has been committed by the authorities, in reality, the facility usually has considerable discretion.) Thus, even if additional beds become available, there will always be an excess demand because these beds can easily be filled by light-care patients, while heavy-care patients will continue to find difficulties in being admitted.[6]

The Designation of LTC Beds in Hospitals

Following the revision of the Medical Service Law in 1992, hospitals may opt to designate all or part of their beds as LTC beds (*chōki ryōyō byōshōgun*). The physical space per bed has been increased from the former 4.3 square meters to 6. As an inducement to hospitals, on condition that they reduce their beds by 10%, grants will be made available for converting the beds to LTC. The reimbursement will continue to be under the same system; hospitals may opt for either the fee-for-service system or the inclusive per-diem rate. Since this legislation has only just been passed, it is not clear how hospitals will react. However, even with increased space, the physical facilities will continue to be below standard in the HFEs and most of the SHAs.

The Gold Plan

In 1989 the government announced a ten-year strategy to promote health and social services for the aged, the so-called Gold Plan. The plan calls for a major shift from institutional care to community care and has an ambitious objective of a "complete elimination of bedfastness among the elderly" through rehabilitative activities. Care by families will continue to be emphasized, but their burden will be lessened by increasing respite-care beds, day-care centers, and domicillary-care support centers. Table 7 shows the Gold Plan's objectives and accomplishments as of fiscal year 1991. Home helpers, respite-care beds, and SHAs have exceeded the projected figures, but in other areas they have fallen behind.

Again, it is too early to draw conclusions. The Gold Plan was envisioned because of the need to soften the impact of introducing the national sales tax and to placate the demands of the women's rights movement. Thus, cost effectiveness was not an issue. However, quite apart from cost considerations, there is a need to integrate the various service components and to establish a case management system. Such a triage system will be very difficult to realize given the present principle of open access to all hospitals and the mutual animosity between the health and human services. The crucial question of public/private mix in both financing and delivery is also left unanswered. On the one hand, there is a call for

**Table 7. Gold Plan objectives and accomplishments**

|  | Base year 1989 | 1991 Planned | 1991 Actual | Goal by year 2000 |
|---|---|---|---|---|
| Measures for community care |  |  |  |  |
| Home helpers | 31,405 | 40,905 | 48,591 | 100,000 |
| Respite-care beds | 4,274 | 11,674 | 13,371 | 50,000 |
| Day-care centers | 1,080 | 2,630 | 2,224 | 10,000 |
| Domiciliary-care support centers | – | 700 | 400 | 10,000 |
| Measures for institutional care |  |  |  |  |
| SHAs | 152,988 | 182,019 | 186,267 | 240,000 |
| HFEs | 13,083 | 69,311 | 56,238 | 280,000 |
| Care houses (no. living in) | 200 | 4,700 | 2,520 | 100,000 |
| Multipurpose senior centers | – | 80 | 71 | 400 |

a greater involvement by the private sector, but on the other hand, municipalities have been given formal responsibility to ensure the provision of services to the elderly and are now mandated to draw up a human services plan for them. Furthermore, rigidly egalitarian principles will continue to inhibit the infusion of private capital through user charges. Then, too, the goal of complete elimination of bedfastness is unrealistic; emphasis should be placed on comprehensive patient-care management rather than the mere provision of rehabilitation activities. Taking these factors together, major operational problems would seem to lie ahead for the Gold Plan.

## Conclusion

LTC is a major challenge for both Japan and the United States. The first lesson is that the two countries do share a common problem: both the rate of institutionalization and the relative severity of those institutionalized appear to be of the same order. The second lesson is that at least in the area of LTC, the Japanese system may be costing more and providing less services as measured by the number of manpower hours. It is true that there are probably many more physicians in LTC facilities in Japan, but their presence does not necessarily translate into improved patient outcome. The standard of physical facilities inferred from the number of beds per room also appears to be lower in Japan. The third lesson is that while the disjointed approach taken by the Japanese government may have been successful in containing total health expenditure, it has led to a chaotic situation as far as the provision of LTC is concerned, with no clear prospects for the future. While the United States's LTC system leaves much to be desired, the 1987 OBRA legislation and the case-mixed-based form of reimbursement can serve as models for Japan to pursue.

NOTES

1. According to the 1990 Tokyo survey, 61.2% of the elderly with children but living apart from them lived within thirty minutes of their children. This means that, with the 51.3% who lived together with their children, the proportion of those who lived within thirty minutes of their children is 79.6%, a figure very similar to that of the United States.

2. The cramped living conditions in Japan may not necessarily have contributed to institutionalization. According to a study made in a town in Kyushu, there was no statistically significant correlation between the institutionalization rate and the number of rooms nor the availability of a private room for the elderly when controlled for disability level (Ikegami 1982).

3. Nationally representative data were available for SHA and HFE. For hospitals, the most reliable and representative data were that from the survey made by the Rōjin no Senmon Iryō o Kangaerukai of 6,049 patients in twenty-seven hospitals throughout Japan. These results were combined on a proportionally representative basis to calculate the total for all institutions. For those in the community, the survey made by the Tokyo Metropolitan Government is listed since it is the most rigorously designed and representative.

4. The government purposely set the lowest required level in the new inclusive per-diem rate at a level that would make it fairly easy for the great majority of geriatric

hospitals, still opting for the fee-for-service schedule and relying on private-duty aides, to switch to this new fee schedule without difficulty. As such, it can be assumed that this level is representative for LTC hospitals as a whole.

5. Geriatric hospitals that have opted for the inclusive per-diem rate showed a dramatic decrease in medication and laboratory tests (see the next chapter by Takagi). Interviews with the hospital directors and nurse managers disclosed that nurses could devote more time to patient care activities. It is not clear how physicians are now utilizing their time since they are discouraged from prescribing and ordering laboratory tests.

6. Takagi's case study does show that, based on the available evidence, the hospital in question has not resorted to admitting light-care patients. However, the long-term effects have yet to be evaluated, and the situation may not be true for other hospitals.

REFERENCES

Brody, E. M., and C. B. Schoonover. 1986. Patterns of parent-care when adult daughters work and when they do not. *The Gerontologist* 26.4: 373–81.
Bureau of Statistics. 1962. *1960 Population census of Japan*, vol. 2: *Whole Japan*, table 4, p. 64. Tokyo: Nihon Tōkei Kyōkai
———. 1992. *1990 Population census of Japan*, vol. 2: *Whole Japan*, table 31, p. 401.
Census Bureau. 1991. *Health, United States, 1991*. U.S. Government Printing Office.
Congressional Budget Office. 1988. *Changes in the living arrangements of the elderly*. U.S. Government Printing Office.
Department of Labor. 1992. *Employment and earnings*. U.S. Government Printing Office. Monthly reports for December 1991.
Donham, C. S., B. T. Maple, and K. R. Levit. 1992. Health care indicators for the United States. *Health Care Financing Review* 13.4: 173–99.
Fukaya, T. 1992. Shibōsha data no bunseki (Analysis of the dead cases), Part 2. *Kōshueisei Shinkōkai Rōjin Iryōhi Shirizu* 3.2.
Hing, E. 1987. Use of nursing homes by the elderly: Preliminary data from the 1985 National Nursing Home Survey. NCHS advance data, 135. 14 May.
Ikegami, N. 1982. Institutionalized and the non-institutionalized elderly. *Social Science and Medicine* 16.23: 2001–8.
Ikegami, N. et al. 1994. Applying RUG-III in Japanese long-term care facilities. *The Gerontologist* 34.5: 628–39.
Kitagawa, S. 1991. Byōin ryōyō kankyō chōsa, iryōshisetsu no kōritsuteki unyō shishin no sakutei ni kansuru kenkyū (Survey of long-term hospital care, research on drawing effective management guidelines in medical facilities). Heisei 2 nendo kōsei kagaku kenkyū.
Ministry of Health and Welfare (MHW). 1990. *Shakai fukushi shisetsu chōsa hōkoku* (1988 Social welfare institution survey report). Tokyo: Kōsei Tōkei Kyōkai.
———. 1991. 1990 (Report from the Social Welfare Administration) Shakai fukushi gyōsei gyōmu hōkoku . Tokyo: Kōsei Tōkei Kyōkai.
———. 1992a. 1990 Kanjya chōsa (Patient survey). Tokyo: Kōsei Tōkei Kyōkai.
———. 1992b. 1990 Rōjin hoken shisetsu jittai chōsa (Health facilities for the elderly survey report). Tokyo: Kōsei Tōkei Kyōkai.
Ministry of Labor. 1992. *Chingin sensasu* (Wage census).
National Center for Health Statistics. 1989. *The national nursing home survey; 1985 summary for the United States*. U.S. Government Printing Office.

Niki, R. 1992. *90 Nendai no iryō to shinryōhōshu* (Health care in the 1990s and the fee schedule). Tokyo: Keisō Shobō.

Organization for Economic Cooperation and Development (OECD). 1992. *Health data file.* Paris: OECD.

Rōjin no Senmon Iryō o Kanagaerukai. 1987. (Inpatient survey) *Nyūinkanjya chōsa.*

Schneider, D. P. et al. 1988. Case mix for nursing home payment: Resource utilization groups, version II. *Health care financing review, annual supplement,* 39–52.

· Shanas, E. 1979a. Social myth as a hypothesis: The case of the family relations of old people. *The Gerontologist* 19.1: 3–9.

———. 1979b. The family as a social support system in old age. *The Gerontologist* 19.2: 169–74.

Tokyo Metropolitan Government. 1991. Kōreisha no seikatsu jittai—Heisei 2 nen Tokyoto shakai fukushi kiso chōsa hōkokusho (State of the lives of elderly—Tokyo Metropolitan Government 1990 basic social welfare survey report).

CHAPTER 15

# The Impact of Financing Reform: Inclusive Per-Diem Reimbursement in Geriatric Care

*Yasuo Takagi*

SUMMARY   The effect of the introduction of an inclusive per-diem reimbursement system was observed in the N Geriatric Hospital. Compared with the fee-for-service system, it reduced the cost of medication and diagnostic tests, without necessarily restraining their use in heavy-care cases. There was no evidence to indicate that the admission of heavy-care patients declined in the hospital studied.

## Introduction

An inclusive per-diem reimbursement system for geriatric inpatient care was introduced in Japan in April 1990 for the following two purposes: (1) to prevent over-utilization (e.g., drip infusion and laboratory tests) that has been associated with the fee-for-service system; and (2) to improve the nurse and aide staffing ratio so that patients would be given better care. This is a case-study conducted in N Geriatric Hospital to evaluate the effects of adopting this new reimbursement system.

### Outline of the Inclusive Per-Diem Reimbursement System

The new per-diem reimbursement system includes payment for nursing, medications, injections, and testing. The geriatric hospitals that adopt this system must be staffed by an adequate number of nursing personnel in order to get approval. The amount reimbursed differs according to the following three aide-to-patient ratios. One nurse per six patients is required for all three types.

1. One nurse-aide per four patients: ¥6,980/day
2. One nurse aide per five patients: ¥6,520/day
3. One nurse aide per six patients: ¥6,210/day

These fees range from $34.50 to $38.80 per day at our approximate purchasing power parity (PPP) rate of $1.00 = ¥180. Physician management fees, physical therapy, imaging diagnosis, and other procedure fees may still be separately billed, and with these additions, the amount usually paid for a geriatric inpatient will be approximately ¥340,000 per month ($1,900).

As of June 1992, about one-quarter of Japan's geriatric hospitals (*rōjin byōin*) had adopted the inclusive per-diem reimbursement system, covering about one-third of geriatric hospital beds. There were 1,121 geriatric hospitals in all, comprising 11.1% of the total number of hospitals (they had 147,442 beds or 8.8% of the total).

## Case Study of N Geriatric Hospital

### Ward Composition and Patient Characteristics

This hospital was first opened as a geriatric hospital with 146 beds in June 1979. Since then it has expanded to 942 beds and developed into one of the largest geriatric hospitals in Japan. This hospital adopted the type 1 inclusive per-diem rate in July 1990. It is focused on inpatient care, with a daily average of 939 inpatients (bed utilization, 99.7%) and 46 outpatients in 1991. The patient population is relatively stable (the average monthly number of new admissions, 28, and discharges, 28 [7 recovered, 8 transferred, and 13 deceased]). The average length of stay is 1,029 days (2.8 years), indicating that it serves as a terminal institution. The average age was 80.1 years for men and 82.2 years for women, and the gender composition was 27.2% men and 72.8% women.

The wards are classified into three types, according to the severity and nursing needs of individual patients. Nurses and aides are assigned according to patient's needs:

- Heavy care (309 beds): severely disabled patients who are totally dependent on nursing care and require extensive treatment and care. One nurse or aide is assigned to every two patients. Wards 1, 2, 3 are of this type.
- Intermediate care (441 beds): patients who remain in bed most of the time and require limited treatment. One nurse or aide is assigned to every 2.3 patients. Wards 4, 5, 6, 7, 8, 9 are of this type.
- Light care (192 beds): patients who are relatively independent, most in rehabilitation programs. One nurse or aide is assigned to every 2.8 patients. Wards 10, 11, 12 are of this type.

### Changes in Revenue and the Composition of Medication and Diagnostic Tests

Table 1 shows the daily average and range of revenue per patient for each of the three ward types in March 1990 before the adoption of the inclusive per-diem rate; in March 1991, nine months after adoption; and in March 1992, one year and nine months after adoption.

Under the fee-for-service system, the average revenue per day per patient

**Table 1. Changes in the mean revenue, medication, and laboratory tests after adoption of the inclusive per-diem reimbursement system in the three types of wards (per day in yen)**

| | Fee-for-service system | | | Inclusive per-diem system | | | | | | | | |
| | March 1990 | | | March 1991 | | | March 1992 | | |
| | Total | Medication | Tests | Total | Medication* | Tests* | Total | Medication* | Tests* |
|---|---|---|---|---|---|---|---|---|---|
| Heavy-care wards | 11,919 | 4,222 | 529 | 10,946 | 1,529 | 68 | 10,961 | 1,253 | 78 |
| Intermediate-care wards | 9,250 | 2,173 | 391 | 10,772 | 481 | 39 | 10,787 | 465 | 34 |
| Light-care wards | 8,364 | 11,199 | 372 | 11,039 | 552 | 18 | 10,886 | 427 | 16 |
| Total | 9,801 | 2,504 | 440 | 10,868 | 806 | 44 | 10,852 | 681 | 46 |

* The revenue that would have been realized under the fee-for-service system.

reflected the severity category of the ward type: heavy-care wards, ¥11,919; intermediate-care wards, ¥9,250; light-care wards, ¥8,364. However, following the adoption of the inclusive per-diem rate, the difference disappeared and all three types converged around the hospital average of ¥10,868. Paradoxically, light-care wards had the highest rate at ¥11,039 in March 1991, because of additional reimbursement for rehabilitation activities. This pattern remained the same for the second year of this new system (March 1992).

Medication and laboratory tests decreased dramatically. If the amount used were to be reimbursed under the fee-for-service system, medication would be one-third of the former level, and laboratory tests, one-tenth for the hospital as a whole. This decrease remained the same in the second year and, in fact, declined further for medication costs. However, it should be noted that the decrease was not the same for all wards and that the amount for heavy-care ward patients was still relatively higher. Laboratory tests became much more concentrated on heavy-care patients—five times more under the inclusive per-diem rate—whereas formerly, tests in heavy-care wards were only 1.4 times that in light-care wards. This would seem to imply that more appropriate care is being provided and that heavy-care patients have not been denied care in spite of the fact that the hospitals are not reimbursed more than the light-care patients.

Changes in Admission and Discharge Patterns

It was not possible to exactly determine whether N Geriatric Hospital changed its admissions policy and started to admit only light-care cases because of economic incentives following the adoption of the new system. However, the available evidence suggests that the contrary has occurred. Although the hospital may have changed its criteria for admission to its heavy-care wards, the ratio admitted to these wards increased from 40.4% in 1990 to 54.7% in 1991, while that for light-care decreased from 17.7% to 1.8%. It would also seem that the new payment system led to an improvement in the quality of care. The ratio of those discharged dead to total discharges decreased from 55.5% in 1990 to 50.0% in 1991.

CHAPTER 16

# Waiting Lists in Japanese Hospitals

*Naoki Ikegami and Shunya Ikeda*

SUMMARY   A survey of the waiting period for inpatients was conducted in two hospitals in Tokyo. In K Hospital, a 1,061-bed private university medical center, the average waiting period was thirty-one days. Fifty-two percent of those classified as "urgent" and 39% of those with cervical cancer waited for more than one month. In S Hospital, a 450-bed, quasi-public hospital, it was fifteen days. No one waited more than one month if classified as "urgent." In both hospitals, the waiting period lengthened when the level of urgency became less and for patients requesting rooms with no extra charges. The current situation is very difficult to change as long as the principle of unlimited access to all health care facilities is upheld in Japan.

## Background

Under the Japanese health care system, patients may visit any health care facility they wish. Most of the hospital visits are made without a referral and virtually all inpatients are admitted from the outpatient department. The copayment rate and the fee schedule are the same no matter where the patient chooses to go. Even if a private room is requested, extra charges will only apply for the room, and health care will be fully covered by insurance. Since there are no formal gatekeepers nor economic disincentives, queueing is an inevitable result in facilities that enjoy a high reputation. These are usually large hospitals in the metropolis that can provide tertiary care. While much attention has been drawn to the long waiting time and the inadequate attention in the outpatient department (it is popularly said that one waits three hours and then is seen for three minutes), since very few hospitals limit their intake by appointment systems, patients are at least seen on the same day that they choose to visit the hospital. The problem, in fact, is more serious in inpatient care because the number of patients who can be admitted is severely limited by the hospital's bed capacity. Grave consequences may arise from delayed admission, especially if the required treatment is of a nature that can be provided only in a tertiary-care setting. However, this issue has never been researched in Japan. It is for this reason that a survey of the waiting period for inpatient admissions was conducted in two hospitals in central Tokyo that can provide tertiary care.

## Method

Data from patient admission forms were directly transcribed into a personal computer. These forms are filled out by the admitting physicians in the outpatient departments, but the room grade (from suite type to regular, no extra-charge beds) is normally decided after asking the patient. The data consisted of the following: patient's age and sex, clinical department, diagnosis, level of urgency, level of room grade requested, date of application for admission, and date of admission. Of the two hospitals surveyed, the bed utilization rate is over 90% in both hospitals, and the average length of stay was twenty-nine days for K Hospital and eighteen days for S Hospital. The survey was conducted between April and September of 1992. For K Hospital, those patients who were discharged in the week that included the fifteenth of each month were chosen, and, for S Hospital, those who were admitted on the twelfth and thirteenth of each month were chosen. Patients admitted for normal deliveries and dental problems and those discharged dead were excluded. In total, 1,454 patients in K Hospital and 285 patients in S Hospital were analyzed.

## Results

The average waiting period was thirty-one days in K Hospital and fifteen days in S Hospital. As table 1 shows, this period was slightly longer for males. It was not necessarily longer for those over age 65, but in K Hospital it was more than twice as long for those less than age 15. When compared by clinical department, as table 2 shows, the waiting period was particularly long for K Hospital in plastic surgery (187 days), orthopedics (64 days), and opthalomology (57 days). While these departments tend to have a large ratio of elective surgeries, it should be noted that the waiting period in S Hospital for these departments was not necessarily long. However, in internal medicine, which is the largest department in both hospitals, the waiting periods were similar, with K Hospital being thirteen days and S Hospital being eleven days.

When compared by the urgency of admission, as table 3 shows, in K Hospital, while the average number of days waiting tended to become shorter according to the urgency level, even for "immediate," the mean was 1.4 days with 2% waiting more than four days. For "extremely urgent," the mean was twenty-one days with 71% waiting more than four days and 20% more than one month. For "urgent," the mean was forty-eight days with 95% waiting more than four days and 52% more than one month. In S Hospital, the situation was better with the mean for "immediate" being 0.2 days, and all were admitted within a week. For "urgent," the mean was six days with 44% admitted within a week and all admitted within a month.

The waiting period also differed according to the room grade. As table 4 shows, in K Hospital, while the waiting time was twenty-four days for the upper-grade extra-charge room (per-diem payment of more than ¥30,000 or $167 at our PPP rate of $1.00 = ¥180) and thirty-six days for the lower-level extra-charge

**Table 1. Waiting period according to age and sex**

| | K Hospital | | S Hospital | |
|---|---|---|---|---|
| | No. of patients | Mean (days) | No. of patients | Mean (days) |
| Total | 1,454 | 30.5 | 285 | 15.0 |
| Male | 721 | 31.9 | 142 | 15.6 |
| Female | 733 | 29.1 | 143 | 14.4 |
| Age | | | | |
| 0–14 | 156 | 66.3 | 12 | 12.0 |
| 15–64 | 940 | 24.5 | 190 | 17.5 |
| over 65 | 358 | 30.7 | 83 | 9.8 |

**Table 2. Waiting period according to clinical departments**

| | K Hospital | | S Hospital | |
|---|---|---|---|---|
| | Waiting period (days) | No. of patients | Waiting period (days) | No. of patients |
| Internal medicine | 13.4 | 434 | 11.3 | 141 |
| General surgery | 33.6 | 166 | 7.8 | 32 |
| Thoracic surgery | 8.6 | 50 | | |
| Neurosurgery | 9.1 | 43 | 18.0 | 1 |
| Orthopedics | 64.4 | 101 | 9.1 | 24 |
| Physical medicine | 3.3 | 4 | | |
| Plastic surgery | 187.0 | 37 | 15.8 | 4 |
| Pediatrics | 16.6 | 81 | 0.0 | 4 |
| Obstetrics | 1.8 | 118 | 40.5 | 13 |
| Gynecology | 41.1 | 71 | 9.5 | 20 |
| Opthalmology | 56.9 | 156 | 52.3 | 12 |
| Dermatology | 19.1 | 23 | 7.7 | 6 |
| Urology | 36.5 | 64 | 26.5 | 13 |
| ENT | 26.3 | 72 | 27.0 | 15 |
| Psychiatry | 16.7 | 15 | | |
| Nuclear medicine | 24.3 | 19 | | |
| Total | 30.5 | 1,454 | 15.0 | 285 |

**Table 3. Relationship between urgency and waiting period**

| | Mean (days) | Days waiting (in percent) | | | | | | | Total |
|---|---|---|---|---|---|---|---|---|---|
| | | Same day | 1–3 | 4–7 | 8–14 | 15–28 | 29– | | |
| K Hospital | | | | | | | | | |
| Immediate (N=449) | 1.4 | 94.66 | 2.90 | 0.45 | 0.89 | 0.22 | 0.88 | | 100 |
| Very urgent (N=412) | 20.6 | 2.18 | 26.21 | 20.15 | 16.99 | 14.56 | 19.91 | | 100 |
| Urgent (N=110) | 47.9 | 0.91 | 4.55 | 13.63 | 9.09 | 20.00 | 51.82 | | 100 |
| As listed (N=171) | 70.1 | 1.00 | 4.68 | 4.68 | 5.85 | 17.54 | 67.25 | | 100 |
| Not marked (N=312) | 57.8 | 5.45 | 8.01 | 7.69 | 9.94 | 20.51 | 48.40 | | 100 |
| S Hospital | | | | | | | | | |
| Immediate (N=68) | 0.2 | 92.65 | 5.88 | 1.47 | 0.00 | 0.00 | 0.00 | | 100 |
| Urgent (N=34) | 5.9 | 17.65 | 26.47 | 32.36 | 11.76 | 11.76 | 0.00 | | 100 |
| As listed (N=16) | 16.4 | 12.50 | 12.50 | 12.50 | 25.00 | 12.50 | 25.00 | | 100 |
| By appointment (N=105) | 23.7 | 6.67 | 9.52 | 7.62 | 15.24 | 30.48 | 30.47 | | 100 |
| Not marked (N=62) | 21.2 | 33.87 | 12.90 | 6.45 | 4.84 | 14.52 | 27.41 | | 100 |

**Table 4.  Waiting period according to room grade**

|  | K Hospital | | S Hospital | |
|---|---|---|---|---|
|  | No. of patients | Mean (days) | No. of patients | Mean (days) |
| Extra charge |  |  |  |  |
| Upper grade | 150 | 24.3 | 19 | 9.1 |
| Lower grade | 205 | 35.9 | 7 | 21.7 |
| No extra charge | 635 | 49.1 | 95 | 12.1 |
| No request | 464 | 4.7 | 162 | 17.3 |

room, it increased to forty-nine days for rooms with no extra charge. In S Hospital, the situation was more complicated. While the waiting time for the upper-grade extra-charge room was nine days, shorter than the twelve days for those with no extra charge, that of the lower-grade extra-charge room was longer at twenty-two days. This may be a reflection of the fact that K Hospital had twice the ratio of extra-charge rooms when compared with S Hospital. Parenthetically, about 90% of the patients were assigned to the level of bed that they had requested.

To further investigate whether urgent cases do get admitted sooner, three conditions that are fairly distinct and had a sufficient number of patients were chosen for analysis. These were threatened abortion, cervical cancer, and cataract. As table 5 shows, their mean waiting periods were, in the order of K Hospital and then S Hospital, for threatened abortions, two days and one day; for cervical cancers, thirty-eight days and seventeen days; for cataracts, seventy-two days and fifty-five days. It should be noted that, in K Hospital, 39% of the cervical cancer patients waited longer than a month, compared to only 20% in S Hospital.

### Discussion

Waiting lists are endemic in countries such as the U.K. where there is public ownership of hospitals and the supply of beds is severely controlled (Coid and Crome 1986). In Japan, the situation is complicated, because while there is a general surplus of beds (there are 1,357 beds to 100,000 population) and low bed utilization rates for the smaller, private hospitals (69% for hospitals with less than fifty beds compared with 82% for the total) (Ministry of Health and Welfare 1992), there is always a shortage in those hospitals that enjoy a high reputation. This could be regarded as an inevitable result coming from uncontrolled access to these hospitals. It should be noted that, unlike the U.K., for patients who choose not to be too selective and go to the less prestigious hospitals, there is hardly any waiting period. Indeed, the waiting time in S Hospital, which had a good reputation but was not a university medical center, was half that of K Hospital.

In these circumstances, the fact that the average waiting time for cataracts was seventy-two days in K Hospital could be regarded as permissible, especially

**Table 5. Waiting period according to clinical condition**

| | No. of patients | Mean (days) | Distribution (in percent) | | | | | |
| --- | --- | --- | --- | --- | --- | --- | --- | --- |
| | | | Same day | 1–7 days | 1–4 weeks | 5–8 weeks | 8+ weeks | Total |
| K Hospital | | | | | | | | |
| Threatened abortion | 38 | 2.20 | 76.32 | 21.05 | 0.00 | 0.00 | 2.63 | 100 |
| Cervical cancer | 28 | 37.90 | 0.00 | 7.14 | 32.14 | 46.43 | 14.29 | 100 |
| Cataract | 78 | 72.30 | 1.28 | 0.00 | 6.41 | 15.38 | 76.93 | 100 |
| S Hospital | | | | | | | | |
| Threatened abortion | 4 | 1.30 | 50.00 | 50.00 | 0.00 | 0.00 | 0.00 | 100 |
| Cervical cancer | 10 | 16.80 | 0.00 | 30.00 | 50.00 | 20.00 | 0.00 | 100 |
| Cataract | 10 | 54.80 | 0.00 | 20.00 | 0.00 | 20.00 | 60.00 | 100 |

as five months was the limit for even the longest waiting patient. On the other hand, although the waiting period was less for urgent cases, the fact that in K Hospital "very urgent" cases had to wait an average of twenty-one days, and 69% of those with cervical cancer for over one month, could have serious consequences. The only extenuating circumstances are that, in practice, if the attending physician does think that the case is really critical but there are no beds available even on an emergency basis, then the patient is usually referred to an affiliated hospital (and thereby does not make an application for admission). Also, since physicians are aware of the bed shortage, they tend to "upgrade" the level of urgency (there is no standard manual for grading the urgency, and this may vary among physicians).

There are basically three possible measures to shorten the waiting period. The first is to shorten the average length of stay. But in the hospitals surveyed, the average length of stay had no correlation with the waiting period. Also, while bed blocking by the elderly has been cited as a major reason for waiting lists in other countries, neither the waiting period nor the average length of stay were significantly longer for the elderly in the two hospitals. Although this may not be the case in other hospitals, it should be noted that decreasing the average length of stay will only increase the throughput. To shorten the waiting period, there is also a need to limit the number of patients applying for admission. This would only be possible when the hospital admits patients from a defined catchment area.

The second is to aim for greater functional differentiation among hospitals—that is, for hospitals with tertiary resources to concentrate only on providing tertiary care. However, this is very difficult to realize as long as unrestricted access to all facilities is assured. Only a very small fraction of the patients treated in these hospitals has a real need for tertiary care. Most patients go, not because they think they require that level of care, but because they feel that the quality of care is better. One solution would be to introduce a system of external audits that could disclose the fact that the quality of care is not dependent on hospital size. More patients may then opt for the smaller hospitals. However, such a system of peer review would be very difficult to implement in Japan. Moreover, if the names of the hospitals providing better quality care were made public, then waiting lists would automatically appear in these hospitals. It should also be noted that university medical centers are not in a position to concentrate on tertiary care because, at present, the ostensible purpose of these centers is to provide all the case-mix required in medical education, including primary care.

The third solution would be by pricing: admission would be decided by those willing to pay for the services in the hospitals that are perceived to be of high quality. This is to some extent the de facto situation. The waiting period is shorter for patients requesting high-grade rooms in K Hospital. It should be noted that, in these rooms, monetary gifts in the range of ¥300,000 (about $1,700) are given to the attending senior physician. Thus, together with cost of the room itself, a considerable burden is imposed on the patient. This should be an ideal market for private insurance schemes. However, by making this process explicit and the market open, it would become obvious that high-quality service is dependent on the willingness (and the ability) to pay. It is partly to avoid such accusations that there are regulations concerning the ratio of extra-charge beds in Japan, usually 20% of the total (40% for university medical centers).

Thus, it is very difficult to foresee any improvement in the current length of waiting lists. If anything, it is likely to worsen as the patients' expectations rise and the concentration of patients in large hospitals continues its present trend. Yet, neither rationing by medical need nor deciding by willingness to pay appear to be viable options in Japan.

ACKNOWLEDGMENT

We would like to express our thanks to Masanori Imabayashi, medical student at the Keio University School of Medicine, for his assistance in the gathering of the data.

REFERENCES

Coid, J., and P. Crome. 1986. Bed blocking in Bromely. *Br. Med. J.* 292:1253–56.
Ministry of Health and Welfare. 1992. (Medical facilities survey). *1990 Iryō shisetsu chōsa* Tokyo: Kōsei Tōkei Kyōkai.

CHAPTER 17

# Comparison of Hospital Length of Stay and Charges between Japan and the United States[1]

*Naoko Muramatsu and Jersey Liang*

SUMMARY    Samples of uncomplicated acute myocardial infarction patients in university hospitals in Japan and the United States were compared, based on reviews of medical and billing records plus interviews. The average length of stay in Japan was about three times longer than in the United States. Explanations for the difference include preferences, staffing levels, and reimbursement systems. Despite the shorter length of stay, total charges in the United States were more than double those in Japan at purchasing power parity (PPP) rates.

## Background and Significance

The average hospital length of stay (ALOS) is by far the longest in Japan of all the other Organization for Economic Cooperation and Development (OECD) countries (Schieber et al. 1992). The difference in ALOS in the United States and Japan has been both substantial and persistent over time as well as across disease categories. In 1989, the ALOS in Japanese general hospitals was 38.7 days (Health and Welfare Statistics Association 1989), while that in the United States was 6.5 days (Graves and Kozak 1992). Until recently, however, there have been no empirical comparative analyses of disease-specific hospital length of stay in the United States and Japan. Recent case studies (Ishikawa et al. 1993; Fukuhara and Norton 1993; Holt et al. 1992–93) have provided evidence that ALOS is much longer in Japan even for similar patients. However, few investigators have examined these differences by taking into account the social and cultural context within which health care is delivered. For instance, cross-cultural differences in length of stay (LOS) and charges have rarely been analyzed in relation to the roles of patients, their families, and their relationships with physicians and other health professionals. This paper describes and analyzes the difference in the hospital LOS and charges during the hospitalization based on a case study of uncomplicated acute myocardial infarction (AMI) patients at two university hospitals, one in the United States and the other in Japan. In contrast to a disease-centered, biomedical perspective, a person-centered perspective emphasizing the effects of social and cultural factors may yield some interesting insights.

## Method

Two university hospitals, one in the United States (884 beds) and the other in Japan (1,238 beds), were selected as study hospitals. Since different diseases have distinct etiologies, clinical courses, and medical interventions, the analysis of LOS and charges without adjusting for case mix is not likely to be informative. To select patients with the same characteristics in the United States and Japan, male uncomplicated AMI patients 40 to 65 years of age were chosen as subjects. They were selected by physicians in charge of the patients according to a specific set of criteria.[2] AMI was selected because heart disease is a leading cause of death both in the United States and in Japan, and the treatment of AMI is relatively standardized. In addition, the onset of AMI is generally followed by immediate hospitalization in both the United States and Japan. Thus, hospital LOS is not likely to be confounded by potential differences during the preadmission process in the two countries. Included in our data were all of the eleven patients who were discharged from the Japanese university hospital in February through July 1990 and who met the specific inclusion criteria listed above, and the eight patients who met the criteria and were discharged from the U.S. university hospital in February through June 1991. The average age of the eleven Japanese patients was 55.1, ranging from 51 to 64, while that of the eight American patients was 52.25 on average, ranging from 43 to 61.

The research strategies included a review of medical and billing records of each patient, as well as interviews with the patient, his primary caregiver (i.e., the family member or the person who takes care of him most), and physicians, nurses, and other ancillary staff who were involved in treatment and care of AMI patients. Face-to-face interviews were conducted with the patient and his primary caregivers at the hospital, its related facilities, the patient's home, or places close to their home. When a face-to-face interview was difficult because of the interviewee's inconvenience or long travel time (more than two hours one way), a telephone interview or mail survey was administered.

Efforts were made to make the data collection procedures as comparable as possible for the two countries. All the questionnaires on which interviews were conducted were first developed for the study in Japan and were subsequently translated into English for the study in the United States. However, the selection of patients had to follow different procedures due to the constraint on the study period and due to differences in accessibility to physicians and patients. In Japan ten of the eleven patients were selected from the list of patients discharged in the last five months as of July 1990, and another patient was identified while he was still in the hospital. Thus, interviews were conducted in July and August 1990, after the patients were discharged. In the United States all the patients were identified during their hospitalization. Brief interviews were conducted one day before the patients were discharged, and another interview was arranged one month later. In both countries, a consultation with the physician determined whether the patient met the inclusion criteria of the study. In both the United States and Japan, the primary caregiver of the patient was identified at the first contact with the patient. In the study all the contacted primary caregivers were wives of the patients.

**Results**

Hospital Length of Stay

The eight selected patients at the U.S. hospital stayed in the hospital, on average, for 8.75 days, ranging from 7 days to 11 days, while the eleven patients at the Japanese hospital stayed, on average, for 25 days, ranging from 19 days to 32 days. While the total length of stay was much longer at the Japanese hospital than that at the U.S. hospital, there was no difference in length of stay at a coronary care unit (CCU) between the two hospitals (3 nights at the U.S. hospital and 2.91 nights at the Japanese hospital, on average). That is, the difference in the total length of stay was due to the difference in the length of stay after the patient left a CCU.

Why do Japanese patients stay three times as long as their American counterparts? It seems that hospital LOS is largely determined directly by a medical professional's clinical judgment, and indirectly by organizational and societal factors. In addition, LOS is affected by the patient and the patient's family. There was a large difference in physicians' practice between the United States and Japanese hospitals. The physicians at the U.S. hospital said that the appropriate LOS would be five to eight days and stressed the benefit of early discharge. On the other hand, physicians at the Japanese hospital said that the appropriate LOS would be two to three weeks and expressed concerns about the disadvantages of early discharges and about the patients' acceptance of shorter LOS, while admitting that LOS could, and should, be shortened.

The demand and preference of the patient and his wife regarding a discharge date had a substantial impact on LOS at the Japanese hospital but not at the U.S. hospital. To begin with, the Japanese patients and their wives were more likely to prefer a specific date or day of discharge than their American counterparts. Eight out of eleven patients had preferences about their discharge date, and they were released from the hospital according to their preferences except for one patient. Three patients wanted to get discharged on the day that was considered to be a "good day" according to the traditional Japanese calendar. The wives of the Japanese patients expected their husbands to have recovered enough to function reasonably independently, while the wives of the U.S. patients expected their husbands to leave the hospital as soon as they had recovered enough to be taken care of at home.

Differences in resources, especially personnel, between the two hospitals seemed to be one of the important factors contributing to the difference in LOS. For example, although the nursing staff level in terms of Full-Time Equivalents (FTEs) in the intensive care unit was not significantly different at the two hospitals, the staff level at the step-down unit was very different (1.41 FTEs/bed at the U.S. hospital and 0.39 FTEs/bed at the Japanese hospital).

The difference in the insurance and reimbursement systems seems to have a major impact on the difference in LOS, partly mediated by physicians' practice patterns, patients' preference, and hospital human and material resources. In the state where the U.S. hospital is located, Medicaid and Blue Cross as well as Medicare reimburse the hospital based on Diagnosis Related Groups (DRGs). Such a prospective payment system (PPS) gives incentives for the hospital to make LOS as short as possible. In Japan, the health care insurance system and reimbursement system for the hospital do not give particular incentives to the hospital physician and management to discharge patients early. Also, the Japanese population is covered by one or another type of health insurance program under a universal health insurance system instituted in 1961, and cost sharing is minimal in any program.

Charges

Though the LOS of the patients at the U.S. hospital was about one-third of that at the Japanese hospital, the average total charges for the hospitalization at the U.S. hospital was about 2.2 times higher (based on the PPP rate of $1=¥195.60 in 1990) or 1.7 times (based on the exchange rate of $1=¥144.80 in 1990) than that of the Japanese hospital. The total charges for hospitalization (including physician fees, hospital fees, and extra room charges) at the U.S. hospital were, on average, $28,925 (ranging from $20,573 to $34,731). At the Japanese hospital, they were $12,828 based on PPP (ranging from $10,209 to $16,812), or $17,829 based on the exchange rate.

In order to examine the difference in more depth, we will describe the charges by roughly comparable categories at the two hospitals (see table 1). However, before such comparisons are made, some caveats are in order. First, we will examine charges, not costs or revenues. Charges do not necessarily reflect costs incurred in the production of hospital care as defined in an economic model. In Japan, the price of each service is subject to the standard national fee schedule. Thus, the charges for each service category reflect the price of each service and its volume, regardless of the actual cost incurred. In the United States, factors other than cost (e.g., competition from other hospitals, cross-subsidization among product lines) may determine the price for each service, and charges may not be fully recovered as revenues due to charity care, managed-care contracts, and possible write-offs from the prospective payment system for medicare patients.

Second, each charge category reported here is only roughly comparable. We regrouped the charge categories used by each hospital in order to make each category comparable. The items included in our new categories are listed below (table 1). In Japan, physicians' fees are embedded in hospital charges, and thus our

**Table 1. Hospital and physician charges by category**

| Charge Category* | U.S. | | | Japan | | |
|---|---|---|---|---|---|---|
| | Average ($) | Range ($) | % of Total | Average ($)** | Range ($)** | % of Total |
| CCU | 5,023 | 3,494–6,988 | 17.4 | 618 (834) | 216–862 | 4.8 |
| Ward/room & board | 3,594 | 2,208–5,152 | 12.4 | 1,262 (1,705) | 835–1,714 | 9.8 |
| Operation/treatment | 6,248 | 1,833–13,203 | 21.6 | 7,286 (9,842) | 5,134–10,824 | 56.8 |
| Drugs/injections | 2,254 | 369–5,491 | 7.8 | 971 (1,312) | 301–1,779 | 7.6 |
| Laboratory/tests | 4,600 | 2,371–7,066 | 15.9 | 1,433 (1,935) | 506–1,713 | 11.2 |
| X-ray | 151 | 0–465 | 0.5 | 685 (926) | 380–966 | 5.3 |
| Other | 1,470 | 7–3,184 | 5.0 | 20 (27) | 0–87 | 0.1 |
| Physician fee | 5,585 | 2,425–8,467 | 19.3 | — | — | — |
| Extra room charge | — | — | — | 554 (748) | 161–1,092 | 4.3 |
| Total*** | 28,925 | 20,573–34,731 | 99.9 | 12,828 (17,329) | 10,209–16,812 | 99.9 |

*Refer to the following chart for items included in each charge category.

**Calculated based on PPP of $1=¥195.60 (1990). Figures in parentheses are based on the exchange rate of $1=¥144.80 (1990).

***Percent of total does not add up to 100 due to rounding.

| Charge Category | U.S. | Japan |
| --- | --- | --- |
| CCU | CCU | CCU charges, plus food and patient administration fees during the patient's stay in CCU |
| Ward/room & board | Room and board | Room charges, food and patient administration fees after the patient left CCU |
| Operation/treatment | Medical surgical supply, sterile supply, OR services, blood storage and processing, respiratory services | Treatment, operation |
| Drugs/injections | Pharmacy, drugs/take home, IV therapy | Pharmacy, injections |
| Laboratory/tests | Laboratory, pathology labor, nuclear medicine, image service EKG/ECG | Tests |
| X-ray | X-ray | X-ray |
| Other | Emergency room, ambulance, TV | Charges for initial contact for an episode |
| Physician fees | Physician fees | N.A. |
| Extra room charge | N.A. | Out-of-pocket charge |

U.S. total charges include both hospital charges and actual physician fees. Third, different treatments and medical technologies were used at the two hospitals. This difference can influence the relative proportion of each category. The Japanese underwent coronary angiography (CAG) and percutaneous transluminal coronary angioplasty (PTCA) at admission, while the U.S. patients generally received intravenous thrombolytic therapy at the emergency room and stayed in the CCU. CAG or PTCA were used only when the patient had angina in the hospital after the aforementioned standard procedures. Fourth, the relative amount of charges at the two hospitals depends on the conversion of yen to dollars. Recognizing this effect, the charges at the Japanese hospital are shown based on both the 1990 PPP and the exchange rate. Fifth, the sample size in this study is small, and there is a wide variance within each country.

With these cautions in mind, let us highlight two major findings from the table. The most notable difference is the room charges, especially in the CCUs. At the U.S. hospital, CCU charges were, on average $5,023, accounting for 17.4% of the total charges. At the Japanese hospital, CCU charges were only $618 (based on PPP, or $834 based on the exchange rate), 12.3% (or 16.6%) of those at the U.S. hospital. This difference is a conservative estimate, given that, in the United States, CCU charges do not include physician fees for services rendered at the CCU. As the LOS in the CCU was almost the same at the two hospitals (3 nights at the U.S. hospital versus 2.91 nights at the Japanese hospital), the difference in the total CCU charges reflects the difference in daily charges. Room and board charges after the patient left CCU was $3,594 in the U.S. hospital but only $1,262 (based on PPP, or $1,705 based on the exchange rate) at the Japanese hospital ($1,816 [or $2,453] including the average extra room charges that the Japanese patients paid themselves). Using the latter figures, the total room and board charges at the U.S. hospital were on average 1.98 times (or 1.46 times) as much as those at the Japanese hospital. That is, the average total room and board charges for the average stay in a ward of 4.75 days at the U.S. hospital were 1.98 times (or 1.46 times) as much as that of 22 days at the Japanese hospital.

The absolute dollar amount is much higher at the U.S. hospital than at the Japanese hospital for all the charge categories in table 1 except two: operation/ treatment and X-ray. Operation/treatment fees amounted to $7,286 (or $9,842), accounting for 57% of the total charges, at the Japanese hospital, in contrast to $6,248, or 22% of the total charges, at the U.S. hospital. However, if we allocate physician fees to CCU, room and board, and operation/treatment according to the relative amount of these three charges, the dollar amount of operation/treatment in the United States becomes comparable to that in Japan.

Why are the charges of Japanese hospitals much lower than those of American hospitals despite the longer LOS in Japan? Though answering this question is beyond the scope of this paper, some preliminary hypotheses are in order. First, in Japan all hospitals are subject to the uniform national fee schedules for every service provided at the hospital. Thus, hospitals are not allowed to raise prices or to do balanced billing. On the other hand, in the United States, hospitals can determine prices as long as they are considered "reasonable." Second, hospital charges in Japan are mostly recovered due to the mandatory and universal health insurance system, but charges are not expected to be fully recovered in the United States. Thus, in order to compensate for unrecovered charges, the U.S. prices may be set higher. Third, costs for taking care of comparable patients may actually be much lower in Japan than in the United States. Japanese hospitals may have less human resources, lower wages for hospital employees and for physicians, fewer material resources, and fewer amenites.

## Conclusions

For patients with the same disease entity, the length of stay at a U.S. hospital was about one-third of that at a Japanese hospital, while the average total charge for hospitalization in the United States was about 2.2 times (PPP based) or 1.7 times (exchange-rate based) higher than that in Japan.

The relationships among hospital length of stay, cost, charges, and quality and quantity of care are complex even within a single country. Comparing two systems is even more complex, requiring studies beyond the superficial comparisons of statistics. This study, though limited in its generalizations, provides an in-depth view of the observed differences in hospital length of stay and charges in Japanese and American hospitals. In order to evaluate health care systems, further studies involving representative samples of patients and hospitals as well as thoughtful comparisons are required.

NOTES

1. This is a revised version of a paper presented at the Conference on Explaining Japan's Low-Cost, Egalitarian Health Care System, sponsored by the Center for Global Partnership, Ito City, Japan, 27–28 February 1993. Support for this research was provided by the Center for Japanese Studies, The University of Michigan, and by the Student Award Program from the Michigan Health Care Education and Research Foundation under grant 058-SAP/90-7. The authors wish to thank the staff, patients, and their family members at the two university hospitals involved in this study for their generous cooperation. Special thanks should be directed to Eva Kline, Mark McGourty, Satoshi Saito, Yasuo Tamura, Hisashi Ohmichi, Yoshimasa Umesato, Hitoshi Terasaki, and Yoshiko Kubo, who made this research possible at its initial stage. The assistance and comments provided by Cathy Fegan, Joan Bennett, and Linda Nyquist are gratefully acknowledged. Sylvester E. Berki, William Weissert, and the organizers and participants of the conference contributed useful comments on earlier versions of this paper.

2. In this study AMI is defined by the presence of at least three of the following four factors: (1) new Q waves or typical evolutionary ST segment and T-wave changes on the electrocardiogram; (2) transient elevation of total creatine phosphokinase; (3) presence of MB band of creatine phosphokinase; and (4) reversal of the normal isoenzyme of lactic dehydrogenase 1 < 2 ratio (McNeer et al. 1978). Uncomplicated AMI patients are defined as AMI patients who do not have the following: angina, defined as pain at rest lasting more than twenty minutes; congestive heart failure, as diagnosed by a new requirement for digoxin and furosemide therapy, or bilateral rales halfway up the posterior fields, or a

ventricular gallop; systolic blood pressure under 90 mm Hg; left ventricular ejection fraction less than 35% as determined by left ventriculography or radionuclide angiography; significant ventricular arrhythmia of a Lown class higher than 3; and high-grade block (adapted from Topol et al. 1988).

REFERENCES

Fukuhara, S., and E. C. Norton. 1993. The difference in hospital charges and use between Japan and the United States. Unpublished manuscript.

Graves, E. J., and L. J. Kozak. 1992. National hospital discharge survey: annual summary, 1989. National Center for Health Statistics. *Vital Health Statistics* 13.109.

Health and Welfare Statistics Association. 1989. Japanese population health trends (Kokumin-eisei no doko). Tokyo: Health and Welfare Statistics Association.

Holt, M., et al. 1992–93. Medical ivory towers and the high cost of health care: a comparison of teaching hospitals in the United States and Japan. *Comparative Health Care Policy Research Series.* Stanford: Asia/Pacific Research Center (Winter).

Ishikawa, K. B., et al. 1993. Performance, characteristics, and case mix in Japanese and American teaching hospitals. *Medical Care* 31.6: 542.

McNeer, J. F., et al. 1978. Hospital discharge one week after acute myocardial infarction. *The New England Journal of Medicine* 298.5: 229.

Muramatsu, N., and J. Liang. 1992. Hospital length of stay in the United States and Japan: comparative study of myocardial infarction patients. Paper presented at the 45th Annual Scientific Meeting of the Gerontological Society of America, 18-22 November, Washington, D.C.

Schieber, G.J., J. Poullier, and L. M. Greenwald. 1992. U.S. health expenditure performance: an international comparison and data update. *Health Care Financing Review* 13.4: 1.

Topol, E. J., et al. 1988. A randomized controlled trial of hospital discharge three days after myocardial infarction in the era of reperfusion. *The New England Journal of Medicine* 318: 1,083.

# CHAPTER 18

# Afterword: Implications for U.S. Health Care Policy Reform

*William G. Weissert*

## Why the Savings?

Thanks to some gifted and insightful researchers whose work is published in this volume, some things now seem obvious. Japanese health care costs less because: Japanese hospital admissions in general and those for surgery in particular are much lower than ours, and their hospitals are paid less for the surgeries they do perform (chapter 9); Japanese specialty care physicians are on salary and so realize little or no financial reward for performing surgeries (chapter 3); and these salaried physicians are paid substantially less than those in the United States and so leave more money for the rest of society's needs (chapter 4).

These are profoundly useful insights to be sure. And what is more, they are confirmation of the probable implications of some observations made in the United States: surgical rates vary inexplicably from area to area and physician to physician (Wennberg 1991; Wennberg, Malenka, and Ross 1989; Eisenberg 1986); mortality rates dropped when California physicians went on strike (Roemer 1979a, 1979b); and physicians performed more surgeries and other expensive procedures when their Medicare payment rates went down (Rice 1992).

## Transportability

Now all we have to do is translate these insights into reform of the U.S. health care system. Can it be done and, if so, does the Japanese approach instruct us on how?

The answer appears to be "no, yes, and maybe." "No," because we cannot transfer the Japanese phobia for invasions of the body. Americans do not like to be cut any more than Japanese do, but most Americans—thanks to our Western notions of Cartesian dualism perhaps—do not worry that somehow our souls will be violated if we are (chapter 9; chapter 22). Nor are Americans ever likely to be as accepting of physician decisions as the Japanese appear to be (medications with the labels torn off to treat an illness for which no diagnosis is given), or as willing to accept long waiting times to see a physician.

"No" again because our diets, behavior patterns, social stratification, and history differ: we eat more fat (though less salt); we inflict more injuries with guns, accidents, and sexually transmitted diseases, including AIDS; and we accept much larger gaps between the rich and poor, and more unemployment.

In addition, our health insurance industry has become predominately self-protecting (Light 1992; Grumet 1989). Japan's health insurance started as a government program intended to improve the work force. This led in Japan to community-rated, cross-subsidized premiums. Here, commercial firms, and more recently even the hospital and physician-sponsored Blue Cross and Blue Shield plans, have focused their efforts on avoiding enrollment by the 4–20% of claimants responsible for 50–80% of claims. Premiums here are risk-adjusted, and cost shifting is left to providers rather than insurers (Iglehart 1992). These are tough traditions—and political action committees—to overcome.

The answer is "yes," however, because much of what goes on in the Japanese health care system seems to be traceable to (1) a global budget cap and (2) a fee schedule that is under the control of a potentially transportable institution, the Central Social Insurance Medical Council. With the budget cap the society acknowledges the potentially unlimited demand for health care and simply says "enough!" Within that overall cap, then, the Central Council allocates what is available by use of a fee schedule (chapter 25).

The council is the equivalent of the proverbial payer of the piper getting the tune for which it pays. Paying little for surgery and more for consultation, gets little surgery and doctors who work late and fit in many consults (chapter 26); changing the payment schedule for IV dosage, it gets an immediate change in IV dosage (chapter 5); paying physicians to dispense drugs, it gets one of the highest prescribed-drug consumption rates in the world and excessive use of new, high-profit drugs (chapter 3); and paying little per office visit, it gets three-minute office visits (chapter 21). Japanese physicians appear to have resigned themselves to following the dictates of the board's payment policy. Indeed, looking at the clarity of the response to its policies, one could well worry that in Japan, clinical judgment has been all but replaced by bureaucratic payment policy.

But it has not been replaced by a single policy. Much like the U.S. Medicaid agency staff setting institutional care reimbursement policy, the members and staff of the national board appear to accept as their lot the necessity of annually or biannually acting out a series of moves in a continuous game of action and reaction in which the outcome is known beforehand. The budget cap is what is known in Japan and in many state Medicaid programs (chapter 5; Feder and Scanlon 1980). In both locales, the decision about how much to spend (on medical care in general in Japan and on Medicaid institutional care in many U.S. states) appears to have little to do with "medical need" per se. Rather, perceived affordability appears to be the controlling concern.

With the cap set, the negotiation process begins to decide how the pie will be shared. Considerations include Ministry of Health and Welfare (MHW) policy goals favoring one type of care or setting over another; relative value or input costs; and Japan Medical Association (JMA) demands (chapter 5). Absent from the negotiations are the large public teaching hospitals where specialty medicine and surgery are practiced—a historical artifact of the power of the JMA and the charisma of its long-time leader (chapter 25; chapter 26).

But the negotiations do not end with the formal session. Rather, the entire budget period is an extended negotiation session. Cutting the profitability of one procedure seems bound to produce an increase in the next most profitable one, thereby necessitating another payment rate change, and, ipso facto, inspiring another provider response that is sure to trigger another policy change, and so on. Masuyama and Campbell (chapter 25) call this process "permanent negotiation." The concept, if not the term, would be quite familiar to many Medicaid reimbursement specialists who see their jobs as keeping the target moving to avoid being taken advantage of by savvy providers who learn the weak points of policies left too long intact.

The lessons here seem to be both profound and transportable. First, a global budget cap makes sure the share of gross domestic product (GDP) devoted to health care does not continue to grow at what in this country has been called "an unsustainable rate" (Darman 1991, 6). Second, the fee schedule wielded by the Central Council works—it is a powerfully effective tool for altering medical professionals' behavior. And third, solutions, if they work at all, are likely to cease to be useful after a few months or, at best, years. The Japanese experience seems to be telling us that to work, reforms must have built into them both a fail-safe budget cap and the ability to respond quickly and decisively to the reactions (e.g., volume increases) caused by the reform.

Interestingly, although the allocation process involves some degree of technical input (e.g., an estimate of the impact of a 1% increase in any specific type of care) and the process began initially with a relative value scale, the role of data and technical analysis in the negotiation is limited (chapter 5; chapter 9). A deliberate and heavy dose of arbitrariness is accepted by all participants, in part because they know that errors of today can be fixed tomorrow—an essential aspect of the "permanent negotiation." Volume increases are responded to by arbitrarily cutting the fee payment for any procedure for which expenditures increase more than 10%. Some Japanese have called this process, delightfully, "mole bashing," after the children's arcade game in which the player simply smashes back down any mole that raises its ugly head. Is this a handy solution to the vexing problem we have experienced with fee schedules causing an increase in volume? It does seem to work in Japan.

### Managed Competition or Central Council?

These aspects of Japan's success raise an interesting question for the U.S. reform movement. Should we be thinking of a fee schedule administered by a national board empowered to control price and volume? Could state boards do those jobs, building upon their Medicaid institutional care experience?

Or can managed competition perform similar functions, with each large consumer purchasing cooperative setting its own fees and reacting to unwanted volume increases, perhaps within a global budget (set perhaps by a national board)? Or does it matter? The lesson from Japan may be that it does not matter who administers the fee schedule so long as that institution can make it stick.

And how do they do this in Japan? By playing one set of providers off against another: clinic-based, primary care doctors versus hospital-based specialists. The former hold all the power and are overwhelmingly the best paid by the Central Council, where they have great influence. The interests of the primary care and specialty doctors are distinctly different because the former have no admitting privileges to large hospitals and cannot perform surgery there. The result is less surgery, fewer hospital admissions, and much lower overall spending—not a bad tradeoff considering that the difference in U.S.-Japan surgery rates accounts for three-quarters of the difference in hospital admissions between the two countries and roughly half the difference in per-capita spending for health care (chapter 9). The conclusion is that if you want to cut health care expenditures, cut surgery. And if you want to cut surgery, put the primary care doctors in charge of policy making.

Assuming that we might want to do these things, can we replicate the Japanese model of having primary care doctors dominate our policy-making boards? It could not be easily done—the two countries' political environments are different. Japan has no specialty boards speaking with a single voice for each specialty. In the United States, hospitals and self-employed specialists with admitting privileges are formidable players in health reform movements.

However, the recent battle over physician fees under Medicare actually did something very similar to what is being proposed here: redressing the long-time imbalance that had tilted fees more in the direction of procedures and away from primary care diagnostic and medical cures. Congress passed the legislation and set up a national board to administer it. In the process, plans to shift 30% of fees from specialists to generalists were trimmed to 15% or so (Epstein and Blumenthal 1992). Moreover, Congress reserved the right to involve itself in the reallocation adjustments set to take place yearly.

Nonetheless, the precedent is set and the structure is in place for a fee-schedule-based methodology. What seems to be missing is any serious political alliance between an administration committed to using a fee schedule as an instrument for major reform and a medical association that believes them enough to join the team. Can that combination develop in the United States? Given the long history of American Medical Association (AMA) hostility toward government-sponsored health care, it may be a long time in coming. Yet the Clinton administration has shown some interest in extending the olive branch to the AMA. If it were to adopt a strategy that might be called "using a thief to catch a thief," it might see the wisdom of forming an alliance with the AMA or several of the primary care associations and using them to try to follow in the path of the Japanese in focusing on control of surgery rates and other specialty practices.

### Legislative Involvement

Congress would still need to be controlled. An important feature of the Japanese system is that the legislature seems to be held at bay by the Central Social

Insurance Medical Council. While legislators appear to play some role in setting the overall budget cap, implementing decisions of the Central Council do not appear to be questioned by the Diet. Indeed, talking with a Diet member, one gets the impression that even what gets on the agenda for policy discussion (e.g., upgrading hospital physical amenities and floor space) appears to come from the MHW rather than from the Diet to the ministry.

Conversely, the U.S. Congress has shown a much greater propensity to influence the behaviors of even the most independent bureaucratic agencies. The American political scientist James Q. Wilson (1989) describes how the U.S. Postal Service continues to be constrained by congressional whimsy even though it was deliberately set up as an independent agency with its own policy board and independent revenue sources. Bureaucratic preferences to the contrary, it has not been able to end costly and little-needed Saturday deliveries because Congress does not want it to. Responsive to constituent complaints, Congress let the Postal Service know that this action would not be appreciated. In short, even independent agencies find it in their best interests not to ignore congressional desires reflective of constituent demands.

Given this greater propensity of the Congress to intervene, could consumer cooperatives, a national board, or state boards implement the same policy actions employed by the Japanese Central Council—charging consumers copays, squeezing the length of visits to physicians, restricting access to surgery? "Maybe." If the American public can be sufficiently exercised over rising health care costs, Congress might be persuaded to keep its hands off. Our willingness to create a Japanese-style insulation of the policy board from the legislative process may be the true test of what Ikegami and Hiroi (chapter 3) refer to as the "political commitment to establish a universal health insurance system."

So, "yes," we may well be able to adopt some of the lessons of Japan's system for wringing out excessive surgery. But if we cannot, we are likely only to change the location of resource allocation decisions from hospital operating rooms to board rooms and congressional committee rooms, not to make a real difference in the outcome of these decisions.

## Long-Term Care

Largely uninstructive for our system is the way the Japanese handle long-term care. Ikegami and Yamada (chapter 14) devastate the notion that they institutionalize their elderly at a much lower rate, as has been widely believed. The Japanese simply call the institutions hospitals. They pay their staff better than we do, but they use far fewer of them. This is an imponderable finding given that in this country we tend to feel that quality cannot be achieved without substantial staffing (Institute of Medicine 1986, 98).

Since neither the Japanese nor the U.S. long-term-care system has moved from the dark ages of equating quality with structural and process indicators rather than outcomes, who can say which system is better or more efficient, or, more to the point, who cares? Both are chronically disabled. Until we give long-term care the explicit objective functions that we give to all other human endeavors except perhaps religion, we cannot complain if we have no standard against which to measure performance. Patient risks need to be assessed, the social cost of their occurrence needs to be estimated, that amount must become the long-term-care budget for that patient, and cost effectiveness must then be assessed in terms of success in reducing risk. In about twenty years we can reappraise our progress toward this goal in both countries.

In Japan, even efforts to shift hospitals out of acute care and into long-term care are not proceeding at the pace that health-care policy makers would like to see, despite changes in the payment system. These new payments have the potential to give hospitals that function as nursing homes substantial profits. But they cannot change the fact that long-term care remains unglamorous for physicians. Perhaps this is because, like primary care, it may be intellectually unrewarding to those whose training has so strongly emphasized specialty care. Instructively, in the United States, the Secretary of the Department of Veteran Affairs has been similarly unsuccessful in converting excess VA hospitals to nursing homes. VA administrators and physicians want to do acute care.

### Physician Specialization

This brings up a final lesson of the comparison: The ratio of primary care physicians to specialty care physicians in Japan is not much better than ours and, like ours, is getting no better. Evidently, broad power to control prices and volume do not necessarily result in changes in physician educational patterns or solve the problem of physician preferences to pursue one line of medicine versus another. The transportable lesson from this conclusion may be the most important observation coming from the study. Price and volume control methods are no substitute for direct attacks on the underlying causes of physician specialty imbalances; national boards or managed competition cooperatives are not the answer. Though Japanese primary care physicians are far better paid than specialists, the number of physicians choosing primary care continues to decline. Other policies are needed, which in this country probably means other state policies, such as those aimed at encouraging state medical colleges to alter their curricula, to change the location of their residencies from hospitals to clinics, and to bring more primary care physicians onto the faculty, among others (Weissert 1994).

### Comparative Studies

For a final lesson, one cannot go through the experience of this study without learning something about learning itself—that is, comparative studies are instructive. Nothing puts the problems of the U.S. health care system in clearer perspective than a brief look at another country's system. Taking such a look is also tremendous fun.

REFERENCES

Darman, Richard. 1991. Observations about the problem and alternative approaches to the solution. Office of Management and Budget, testimony to the U.S. House of Representatives Committee on Ways and Means, Washington, D.C., 10 October.

Eisenberg, John M. 1986. *Doctor's decisions and the cost of medical care: The reasons for doctor's practice patterns and ways to change them.* Ann Arbor, MI: Health Administration Press.

Epstein, Arnold M., and David Blumenthal. 1992. Physician-payment reform—unfinished business. *The New England Journal of Medicine* 326 (14 May): 1,330–4.

Feder, Judith, and William Scanlon. 1980. Regulating the bed supply in nursing homes. *Milbank Quarterly* 58.1 (Winter): 54–88.

Grumet, Gerald W. 1989. Health care rationing through inconvenience: The third party's secret weapon. *The New England Journal of Medicine* 321 (31 August): 607–11.

Iglehart, John. 1992. The American health care system: private insurance. *The New England Journal of Medicine* 326.25 (18 June): 1,715–20.

Institute of Medicine. 1986. *Improving the quality of care in nursing homes.* Washington, D.C.: National Academy Press.

Light, Paul Charles. 1992. *Forging legislation.* New York: W. W. Norton.

Rice, Thomas. 1992. Containing health care costs in the United States. *Medical Care Review* 49.1: 19–65.

Roemer, M. I. 1979a. Doctors' slowdown effects in the population in Los Angeles County. *Social Science and Medicine, Part C* 13.4: 213–18.

————. 1979b. Study of physician malpractice slowdown. *American Journal of Public Health* 69.8: 825–26.

Weissert, Carol. 1994. Education and the health professions: Explaining policy choices among the states. *Journal of Health Politics, Policy, and Law* 19.2 (Summer): 361–92.

Wennberg, John E. 1991. Unwanted variations in the rules of practice. *Journal of the American Medical Association* 265 (13 March): 1,306–7.

————, David J. Malenka, and Noralou P. Ross. 1989. Mortality and reoperation after open and transurethral resection of the prostate for benign prostatic hyperplasia. *The New England Journal of Medicine* 320 (27 April): 1,120–4.

Wilson, James Q. 1989. *Bureaucracy.* New York: Basic Books.

CHAPTER 19

# Paradoxical Comparison of Health Care Needs, Utilization, and Costs between Japan and the United States

*Hiroko Akiyama*

SUMMARY    Health care needs appear lower in Japan than in the United States, but Japanese health care utilization is higher, though health care costs are lower. This paper explores explanations of the paradox by focusing on the behavior of health care consumers based on a U.S.-Japan cross-national interview survey on illness behaviors.[1] In addition, 10% of the survey sample kept health diaries for four weeks. The data indicate that although Japanese reported fewer illness symptoms, they visited physicians more often and also engaged in a wide range of self-treatment. The diaries suggest that Japanese took such actions at earlier stages of illness than Americans. The results are discussed in the context of health care policies and health care financing and delivery systems in the two nations. The conclusion is that although excessive use of primary care services is certainly a concern, frequent physician visits might have led to early intervention (including self-treatment) in illnesses, preventing the development of serious illnesses and eventually containing the volume of more expensive, high-technology medicine in Japan.

## Introduction

A comparison of national health statistics in the United States and Japan indicates a paradoxical contrast: despite lower health care needs (self-reported morbidity) as compared with the United States, Japanese health care utilization is higher, but its health care costs are lower.

Although there is no single good measure of health care needs for a cross-national comparison, the self-reported morbidity statistics are probably the best indicator among the available measures. A comparison of the prevalence of a variety of illnesses found in the National Health Interview Surveys (United States) and the National Health Surveys and Comprehensive Survey of Living Conditions (Japan) over the years consistently indicates that, in most categories of illness, a larger proportion of Americans than Japanese reported illnesses at all ages.

Despite fewer self-reported illnesses, the Japanese, on the average, visit a physician's office two to three times as often as Americans: the average number of physician visits in 1989 was 5.3 in the United States and 12.8 in Japan. The statistics on the use of acute inpatient care also indicate that the volume of this care is significantly higher in Japan than in the United States. The number of bed days in an acute inpatient care facility was 0.9 day in the United States as compared with 3.4 days in Japan in the same year (Organization for Economic Cooperation and Development [OECD] 1992).

Therefore, the Japanese appear to consume a larger volume of medical care services than Americans, but U.S. health care expenditures are higher than Japan's by virtually all measures. Among them, per-capita health care spending in U.S. dollars and health care spending relative to the gross domestic product (GDP) are two frequently cited indicators. In 1990, Americans and Japanese spent $2,566 and $1,171 per capita (at the OECD purchasing power parity [PPP] estimate of $1.00 = ¥195.6), and 12.1% and 6.5% of GDP, respectively (OECD 1992).

## Findings

In this chapter, I will explore explanations of this paradox by focusing on the behavior of health care consumers. The data came from a cross-national personal interview survey of a stratified-probability sample of 728 Americans and 900 Japanese, aged forty-five and over. The questions were identical: in both countries respondents were asked if they had experienced any of twenty-nine symptoms of common illnesses among older adults in the past three months, and, if so, what actions they had taken in response. These included physician visit, use of prescribed or over-the-counter (OTC) drugs, and various forms of self-treatment such as dietary and nondietary home remedies, rest, exercise, stress management, and protective activities. The data also contain information on health beliefs, attitudes toward physicians and drugs, and accessibility and past experience with medical care services. In addition, 10% of the survey sample kept health diaries for four weeks.

As table 1 shows, our survey data were consistent with the government statistics of self-reported illnesses. The Japanese respondents reported significantly fewer symptoms than Americans. On average, Americans reported 4.9 symptoms, and Japanese, 1.4 symptoms. Approximately 10% of Americans and 47% of Japanese claimed they had experienced none of the twenty-nine listed symptoms for the three-month period. Among those who experienced symptoms, Americans were more likely to have reported multiple symptoms than the Japanese.

Our data also yielded statistics of health care utilization similar to those of government surveys. On average, our American and Japanese respondents visited physicians 1.2 times and 3.9 times during the three-month period, respectively. About 15% of Americans and 40% of Japanese who had experienced none of the twenty-nine symptoms reported a physician visit. Further, when we designed this study, we hypothesized that people who rely on themselves and engage in self-care would be less likely to see a physician. However, this "professional care

**Table 1. Number of symptoms experienced and physician visits in a three-month period (% of participants)**

|  | U.S. (N=728) | Japan (N=900) |
|---|---|---|
| None | 10 | 47 |
| 1 or 2 | 26 | 38 |
| 3 or 4 | 21 | 10 |
| 5 or 6 | 15 | 3 |
| 7 or 8 | 11 | 1 |
| 9 or more | 18 | 1 |
| Total | 101 | 100 |
| Total symptoms reported | 3,577 | 1,274 |
| Average number of symptoms | 4.9 | 1.4 |
| Average number of physician visits | 1.2 | 3 |

versus self-care" hypothesis proved to be groundless. We found in both countries that those who saw a physician were more likely to use OTC drugs and to engage in various forms of self-treatment.

Health diaries provided insightful information on the health problems *defined by the respondents* and the actions they took in response. In contrast to the survey data, in the diaries Americans and Japanese reported a relatively equal number of symptoms, 4.35 and 4.04, respectively. Table 2 shows the seven symptoms most frequently reported in the Japanese diaries compared to the American diaries. It is interesting to note that almost 60% of the Japanese who kept diaries reported "feeling tired" as a health problem. Having a stiff shoulder is another symptom that was frequently reported by Japanese. However, the most striking difference in the diaries between the two countries was the time during an illness episode in which people took the first action to respond to a symptom. The Japanese took some form of action—be it seeing a physician, taking aspirin, *tamagozake* (hot mixture of egg and rice wine), a hot bath, or rest—at earlier stages of illness than Americans. To our surprise, the Americans who kept diaries entirely ignored 40% of their symptoms.

## Discussion

A comparison of the number of symptoms reported in the survey and the diaries indicates that Japanese reported significantly fewer symptoms than Americans (1.9 versus 4.9 for the three months) in the survey, but the two groups reported a relatively equivalent number of symptoms (4.35 versus 4.04 for the four weeks) in the diaries. Although our data do not provide any conclusive explanation for this

**Table 2. Most frequently self-reported symptoms in Japanese and U.S. diaries (% reporting symptoms)**

| Symptom | Japan (N=100) | U.S. (N=79) |
|---|---|---|
| Feeling tired | 58 | 14 |
| Fever/Cold | 58 | 62 |
| Backache | 43 | 23 |
| Headache | 37 | 46 |
| Upset stomach | 30 | 25 |
| Joint pain | 27 | 19* |
| Stiff shoulder | 24 | 5** |

*Defined as arthritis.
**Defined as pains in shoulders.

apparent inconsistency in reporting symptoms, several explanations are plausible. One possible explanation has to do with the level of the severity of symptoms reported in the survey and the diaries and the consequence of the different illness behaviors between the two groups of people. In the survey using a structured questionnaire, the respondents were presented with a list of preselected illness symptoms and were asked to respond as to whether or not they had experienced those symptoms during the three-month period of time. In contrast, the health-diary technique, which allowed participants to define health problems, could identify all symptoms that were perceived as indicators of health problems by the individuals. Further, since diaries were kept on a daily basis, the majority of the entries both in the United States and Japan were of quite mild symptoms at the early stage of illness; most of those symptoms would not have been recalled and reported in the retrospective interview survey. Also, they do not often fit the description of symptoms in the interview questionnaire, which suggests a certain level of severity. For example, the cold symptom included in the survey questionnaire reads "Sore throat or runny nose with a fever as high as 100 degrees Fahrenheit for at least two days." This symptom description would not catch a mild symptom of a cold such as "Sneezed seven times. Felt chilly," which was recorded by one participant in the diary. Therefore, it is conceivable that the inconsistency in the cross-national comparison of the number of symptoms between the survey and the diaries indicates the following: Japanese actually experience as many symptoms as Americans, but since they respond to symptoms at an earlier stage, many symptoms are controlled before developing to the level of severity described in the survey questionnaire.

How can such differences be explained in the illness behavior of the health care consumers in the two countries? In order to address this question, we have to look at the issue from two different perspectives—that of health care providers and that of health care consumers. From the health care provider's perspective, a combination of the fee-for-service reimbursement system and the relatively low fixed-fee schedules in Japan creates a strong incentive for Japanese health care providers to increase the number of patients they see. Furthermore, the fee schedule and taxation system in Japan make primary care more profitable than secondary and tertiary care. Therefore, we can say that the government's health care policy underlying such incentives to providers has resulted in a high volume of primary care services in Japan.

From the Japanese consumers' perspective, health beliefs and government policy both appear to explain their illness behavior. First, prior studies of Japanese health beliefs and practices, particularly those by medical anthropologists, documented the "excessive" sensitivity about the body and its minor ailments and the pampering attitude toward the sick among Japanese (Ohnuki-Tierney 1984). In addition, our data indicate that, compared with Americans, Japanese are less likely to think they have the right to an autonomous relationship with a physician. They tend to think that lay persons are less able than professionals to deal with illnesses and therefore should defer to their greater skill. Second, health care delivery and financial systems in Japan make the consumers' out-of-pocket expenses and paper work minimal and make neighborhood (or workplace) doctors available and easily accessible. These factors encourage Japanese health care consumers to seek out primary care services.

We cannot evaluate the impact of primary care without knowing the nature of the services that people receive at a physician's office. One person who kept a diary wrote down every day: "Went to an orthopedic clinic to put myself on a horizontal device to straighten and stretch the spine." Another person visited a neighborhood clinic every other day to use an inhaler to clear the sinuses. These examples indicate that Japanese use professional services for certain treatments that are normally done at home in the United States, and they raise the question of an appropriate level of usage of professional services. At the same time, the diaries indicate that, in their frequent visits to physicians' offices, Japanese patients report a wide range of ailments (or more accurately "changes in body sensations"), many of which are quite minor. In response, physicians would treat and/or dispense drugs for certain conditions, but more often they would reassure their patients that the conditions were not serious and would tell them what could be done at home to prevent or alleviate the conditions. Such primary care practice could potentially control an illness in its early stages with a minimum of cost and, at the same time, provide a consumer with a personally tailored, health maintenance protocol.

To summarize, the utilization of primary care is considerably higher in Japan than in the United States. Both the health care policy of the Japanese government and the health beliefs and attitudes of Japanese consumers promote utilization of primary care. Although excessive use of primary care services is certainly a concern, frequent physician visits might have led to early intervention (including self-treatment) in illness conditions, preventing the development of serious illnesses and eventually containing the volume of more expensive high-technology medicine in Japan.

NOTE

1. This research was supported by the National Institute on Aging grants RO1-AG04733 (for the U.S. survey) and R01-AG05876 (for the Japanese survey)

REFERENCES

Ohnuki-Tierney, Emiko. 1984. *Illness and culture in contemporary Japan: An anthropological view.* Cambridge: Cambridge University Press.
Organization for Economic Cooperation and Development (OECD). 1992. Health care systems in transition. *Health Care Financing Review.* 13.4.

CHAPTER 20

# Keeping Pressures off the Japanese Health Care System: The Contribution of Middle-Aged Women

*Margaret Lock*

**SUMMARY**   Good health at low cost in Japan is not primarily due to the medical care system. Survey research and semistructured interviews show that middle-aged Japanese women make relatively few demands on the health care system and have better overall health than two comparable North American samples. One striking difference is that menopause is not as yet highly medicalized in Japan. Since middle-aged women provide extensive care for dependent family members, they constitute a "hidden welfare service" that is a further contribution to the containment of health expenditures.

## Introduction

In a recent *New York Times* article it was asserted that the universal health insurance system in Japan is "the most efficient in the world," producing "one of the healthiest societies on earth" while keeping the financial burden placed on corporations remarkably light (1992). By the usual measures there can be no argument about the health of Japanese society—the greatest longevity in the world for men and women and an infant mortality rate of 6.6 per 1,000 live births. This is all the more remarkable when it is recalled that until the 1950s Japan had a profile that resembled rather closely that of a "developing" country, and that most of the improvement in health has taken place over the past forty years. This improvement has happened, therefore, in approximately the same time span as the existence of the comprehensive, universal health care system, established in 1961.

However, it is arguable whether it is indeed the universal health care coverage that should be given all the credit for the greater longevity of the Japanese. Aside from anything else, the fact that there has been sustained and, at times, dramatic economic growth in the past forty years has undoubtedly made a contribution to the overall improvement in health. Furthermore, although easy access to medical care certainly contributes to a decline in mortality (particularly with respect to acute disease), as McKeown has shown for Europe at the turn of the century (1976) and as is evident in the majority of developing countries today (Frenk et al. 1991; Kunstadter et al. 1993), the major factors that contribute to a lowered mortality rate (and presumably morbidity rate) in any population are variables such as education, nutrition, and sanitation, and not curative medicine.

In this chapter, rather than consider health care costs per se, I will take an approach that focuses on certain indicators of individual health in Japan, as well as specific social and cultural factors that contribute to good health and therefore serve indirectly to contain medical expenditures. My basic assumption, in line with the arguments cited above, is that good health in Japan is not primarily a product of the medical system but the result of investments in other sectors of society such as education and employment, investments that function in the long run to keep health care costs relatively low.

A keen rivalry exists among the technologically advanced nations in connection with health statistics, and Japan is no exception. Their national figures for life expectancy and infant mortality are well known among the Japanese public, but despite an excellent standing internationally there are few signs of complacency; on the contrary, reports of a country riddled with "diseases of modernization" (*gendaibyō*) appear in the media daily. People read newspaper articles and view television programs about children who refuse to go to school and lie inert in bed all day, salarymen dying from overwork, and women who are becoming "kitchen drinkers." The fear, often explicitly expressed, is that the price for rapid economic development has been too high. In particular, there is a lament (usually from those of a conservative persuasion, but not limited to them) about the loss of "traditional" values and the rampant spread of the Western value of individualism, which, it is suggested, has led to an increasing spiritual and social malaise associated with rising ill health (Ikemi et al. 1980; Kyūtoku 1979).

The malaise is nothing like that in the United States, of course, and this is also well known in Japan. With the exception of alcohol, there is little substance abuse, and, related to this, relatively few infants need extensive neonatal care, nor are they usually born to very young unmarried women; injuries associated with violence are many fewer than in the United States; there are just over 550 active cases of AIDS (over half of whom are hemophiliacs); rather few people live in extreme poverty or are chronically malnourished; the unemployment rate is low (2.1%); and active support for public health is exemplified by the existence of what is probably the best mass screening program in the world. There are, as Ikegami has pointed out (1991), some strikes against Japan, the most obvious being that over 60% of Japanese men smoke, and the diet, although low in fat, is high in salt (but less so than was formally the case due to intensive public health campaigns). Overall, however, it appears that the positive side far outweighs the negative.

All of the above variables, together with many others, have an effect on morbidity and mortality figures, and therefore indirectly on health care costs. Closer examination of any one of them would reveal their intimate relationship to the organization of Japanese society and to cultural values, but this kind of data is in rather short supply. We do not know why, for example, in a society where the assumption of self-responsibility for health is a well-established tradition (Lock 1980; Ohnuki-Tierney 1984), there is rather little public pressure and individual initiative shown in connection with reducing smoking.

I will focus in this chapter on middle aged women who continue to be thought of by many in Japan as the "pillar" of the family—a stable center on whom other family members can lean for support and nurturance. In light of the results of a cross-sectional survey carried out in 1984 using a sample of over 1,300 Japanese women then aged 45 to 55 inclusively, together with additional findings from 100 semistructured follow-up interviews, supplemented by analysis of 25 life histories,[1] I want to suggest that this particular population is, comparatively speaking, exceedingly healthy and makes relatively few demands on the health care system. Moreover, this cohort of women, by providing care within the family for elderly relatives (usually their in-laws), supplies what Japanese feminists have described as a "hidden welfare service," and thus "saves" the government health care expenditure for the rapidly increasing aging population (Higuchi 1985; Hosoya 1987). Furthermore, although these women are passing through a part of the life cycle (menopause) that in North America is increasingly being medicalized (it has been described recently as the health problem of the 1990s), in Japan very few women seek medical care in connection with this transition.

In more general terms, although the malaise of modernity—the anomie associated with urbanization, mass consumption, and social isolation—indeed seems to be on the increase in Japan, thus far systematic medicalization and psychologization of these existential and lifestyle problems, and of life-cycle events (with the sole exception of childbirth), has not taken place. Nor, as yet, does the majority of the Japanese public have an expectation that these problems *should* be medicalized, although this situation has changed somewhat in recent years.

## Symptom Reporting and Health Status

In comparison with a sample of Canadian and American women aged 45 to 55,[2] Japanese women reported approximately the same number of physician visits per year. Thirty-eight percent of Japanese women had not seen a physician of any kind during the year prior to filling out the questionnaire, and another 28% had visited a doctor between one and three times. Of these visits, most were to the local family doctor; only 28% were to specialists, of which 6% were to internists and gynecologists, respectively. The other visits were distributed among a range of specialists with the exception of psychiatry, which had not been made use of by anyone.

Respondents were asked to report in the questionnaire on major health problems involving regular physician visits. Very few suffer from diabetes (1.3%), heart disease (3.3%), ulcers (2.3%), or asthma (0.7%). Rather more have arthritis (7%) and allergies and/or eczema (7%). High blood pressure is the most frequently reported problem (13%). A comparison with Massachusetts and Manitoban women is revealing: whereas in the North American samples 44% and

45%, respectively, reported a chronic health problem, this was the case for only 28% of the Japanese women.

The number of physician visits is not therefore a simple reflection of serious ill health and is no doubt explained by the fact that in Japan people with minor illnesses such as a common cold, having once gone to see a doctor, are likely to be asked to return two or three times during the course of a single simple illness episode. (This pattern of usage arises because family physicians obtain most of their income from basic examinations and the prescription of medicine.)

Women in these three studies were asked to respond to a list of common symptoms (appropriately modified for use in Japan [Lock 1993; Lock, Kaufert, and Gilbert 1988]), and check off any that they had experienced in the previous two weeks. Out of a core list of sixteen symptoms, Japanese women reported many fewer than did either Manitoban or Massachusetts women (see tables 1 and 2). Furthermore, reports of medication use reveal that, with the exception of herbal medicine and relief for an upset stomach, Japanese women make use of considerably less medication than do North Americans, despite the fact that, as a nation, the Japanese consume the most medicine worldwide (table 3).

Among Japanese respondents, 11.7% have undergone gynecological surgery, as compared to 22.9% in Manitoba and 31.2% in Massachusetts (table 4). This difference reflects a lower use of gynecological services (Lock 1993) and, in addition, a much more conservative approach in general to surgery in Japan (Ikegami 1991). Despite the fact that mass screening and the systematic use of noninvasive preventative measures are customary (Ikegami 1989a), 55% of the Japanese sample have never had a breast examination by a physician (as opposed to 6% in Manitoba and 4% in Massachusetts), and 23% have never had a pap smear (as opposed to 3% and 6% in North America). These numbers may have changed somewhat since 1984 because more urban residents receive routine checkups than was formally the case (Arai, personal communication); nevertheless, they reflect a reluctance on the part of Japanese women to take matters relating to reproductive health to a physician. They also reveal a much less active promotion of their services on the part of Japanese than North American

**Table 1. A comparison of the number of core symptoms reported, by study (in percent)**

| Number of symptoms reported | Japan | Manitoba | Massachusetts |
|---|---|---|---|
| 0 | 26.7 | 13.8 | 15.5 |
| 1–4 | 62.6 | 60.0 | 50.4 |
| 5+ | 10.7 | 26.2 | 34.1 |
| Total (100%) | 1,316 | 1,310 | 8,050 |

**Table 2. A comparison of the rates of core symptom reporting, by study**

| Symptom | Japan | Percent reporting Manitoba | Massachusetts | Chi-square (2df) |
|---|---|---|---|---|
| Diarrhea/constipation | 24.5 | 12.8 | 21.4 | 62.8* |
| Persistent cough | 4.2 | 5.2 | 10.1 | 68.4* |
| Upset stomach | 6.3 | 12.9 | 16.1 | 85.1* |
| Shortness of breath | 3.1 | 8.2 | 15.6 | 177.6* |
| Sore throat | 10.5 | 9.1 | 10.7 | 2.9 |
| Backaches | 24.2 | 26.8 | 29.6 | 17.7* |
| Headaches | 27.5 | 33.8 | 37.2 | 45.2* |
| Aches/stiffness in joints | 14.5 | 31.4 | 38.6 | 279.1* |
| Dizzy spells | 7.1 | 12.3 | 11.1 | 21.4* |
| Lack of energy | 6.0 | 39.8 | 38.1 | 503.3* |
| Irritability | 11.5 | 17.1 | 29.9 | 246.6* |
| Feeling blue/depressed | 10.3 | 23.4 | 35.9 | 365.1* |
| Trouble sleeping | 11.7 | 30.4 | 30.6 | 189.8* |
| Hot flashes/flushes | 12.3 | 31.0 | 34.8 | 246.6* |
| Cold/night sweats | 3.8 | 19.8 | 11.4 | 158.2* |

* indicates p = 0.01.


**Table 3. A comparison of the rates of medication use in the previous two weeks, by study**

| Medication group | Japan | Percent reporting Manitoba | Massachusetts | Chi-square (2df) |
|---|---|---|---|---|
| OTC pain reliever | 13.8 | 45.3 | 62.6 | 1065.1* |
| Prescription tranquilizers | 3.5 | 12.5 | 9.8 | 62.2* |
| Vitamins/minerals | 20.1 | 29.7 | 38.4 | 174.8* |
| Hormones | 2.7 | 6.4 | 8.1 | 46.8* |
| Sleeping pills | 1.6 | 7.1 | 4.3 | 46.0* |
| Herbs/teas | 16.0 | 4.0 | 3.2 | 385.3* |
| Relief for upset stomach | 22.0 | 8.6 | 11.0 | 137.9* |

* indicates p = 0.01.

**Table 4. Gynecological surgery, by study**

|  | Japan | | Manitoba | | Massachusetts | |
|---|---|---|---|---|---|---|
|  | % | N | % | N | % | N |
| No hysterectomy | 88.3 | 1,162 | 77.1 | 1,010 | 68.8 | 5,371 |
| Hysterectomy only | 2.3 | 30 | 12.1 | 159 | 8.4 | 656 |
| Hysterectomy and unilaterial oophorectomy | 3.0 | 39 | 3.6 | 47 | 4.1 | 323 |
| Hysterectomy and bilateral oophorectomy | 3.4 | 45 | 5.0 | 66 | 15.6 | 1,220 |
| Unilateral oophorectomy only | 2.6 | 35 | 2.2 | 28 | 2.5 | 197 |
| Bilateral oophorectomy only | 0.4 | 5 | 0.0 | 0 | 0.6 | 35 |
| Total | 100.0 | 1,316 | 100.0 | 1,310 | 100.0 | 7,802 |

gynecologists, at least with respect to middle-aged women. This can be accounted for in part because mortality from breast cancer is more than three times in North America what is in Japan (World Health Organization 1991), with the result that this disease does not produce the same national concern as it does in the West. Despite the widespread use of screening for many diseases, mammography has only been available since 1992, and its use is not yet routine.

### Aging as a Natural Process

More than 60% of the women in the present study have never discussed menopause (*kōnenki*) with a doctor, and only 17% have brought what they characterize as symptoms related to *kōnenki* to the attention of a physician. Whereas 75% of Manitoban women report that their doctors have been helpful with respect to menopause, less than 16% of Japanese women describe their doctors this way (Lock 1993). Only 7% of the women who had discussed *kōnenki* with a doctor had received medication, and the majority of these women, in contrast to North Americans, had been prescribed herbal medication and not hormone replacement therapy.

In interpreting these findings it must be emphasized that *kōnenki,* although usually glossed as menopause, is not the same concept as menopause. In contemporary North America, menopause is understood as an event—the end of menstruation. *Kōnenki,* by contrast, is a polysemic term with a range of meanings (Lock 1993), but for the majority of Japanese (physicians and the public alike) it indicates a gradual process of biological change commencing approximately in the late thirties or early forties and ending in the late fifties. The end of menstruation constitutes just one of many signs of aging, internal and external, which indicate passage through the mid-life transition of *kōnenki* (Lock 1986). This difference is not mere semantic quibbling. In practice, until very recently, *kōnenki* has been understood by virtually everyone as a "natural" transition that virtually all women will "ride over" with little difficulty. Thus, neither physicians nor women anticipate any need for medical assistance, and, indeed, seeking out help has often been described as indulgent and weak willed (Lock 1988).

The situation is in strong contrast to North America and Europe where, from early this century and particularly since the 1960s, there has been an ever-increasing tendency to interpret menopause in the medical literature as an endocrine deficiency. Menopause has been explicitly likened to diabetes and thyroid deficiency disease, for example (Thorneycroft 1989; Utian 1976), and the majority of gynecologists state today, in both professional and popular literature, that long-term medicalization, involving hormone replacement therapy together with the regular monitoring of its use, is in the best interest of all women (Lock 1993).

There are complex historical and cultural reasons why menopause and *kōnenki* are constructed differently (Lock 1993), but biology has also contributed to the picture. Japanese women report many fewer of the "classical" menopausal symptoms, in particular hot flushes and night sweats, than do North American women (tables 5 and 6). There is no *specific* word that glosses for a "hot flash" in Japanese, and neither Japanese women nor physicians recognize the hot flash as the most representative of menopausal symptoms (Lock 1993). There is some evidence that this difference may in part be related to diet (Aldercrutz et al. 1992).

Until recently, discomfort caused by hot flashes, including sleep loss, has been the principle reason why North American women go for a medical consultation and take replacement therapy at menopause. The lower incidence of troubling symptoms in Japan no doubt not only contributes to less physician visits and medication use than in North America but also has shaped in part the discourse about *kōnenki* in which hot flashes do not play a prominent role. It is also notable that Japanese women report feeling depressed at a much lower rate than do North American women (table 2). Irritability is typically associated with *kōnenki* (al-

**Table 5. Percentage of women reporting hot flashes in previous two weeks, by menopausal status (hysterectomy cases removed)**

| Menopausal status | Japan* | Manitoba* | Massachusetts* |
|---|---|---|---|
| Premenopause | 6.4 | 13.8 | 17.9 |
| Perimenopause | 13.5 | 39.7 | 38.1 |
| Postmenopause | 15.2 | 41.5 | 43.9 |
| Total (100%) | 1,104 | 1,039 | 5,505 |
| | $\chi2 = 15.77$ | $\chi2 = 84.17$ | $\chi2 = 269.51$ |

* indicates p = 0.00.

**Table 6. Percentage of women reporting night sweats
in previous two weeks, by menopausal status
(hysterectomy cases removed)**

| Menopausal status | Japan* | Manitoba** | Massachusetts** |
|---|---|---|---|
| Premenopause | 4.1 | 10.6 | 5.5 |
| Perimenopause | 4.0 | 27.6 | 11.7 |
| Postmenopause | 3.0 | 22.2 | 11.3 |
| Total (100%) | 1,104 | 1,039 | 5,484 |
| | $\chi2 = 0.772$ | $\chi2 = 33.71$ | $\chi2 = 31.34$ |

* indicates p = 0.68; ** indicates p = 0.01

though rather few of the women surveyed reported it, see table 2), but depression is not linked to this stage of the life cycle, in strong contrast to North America and Europe. Complex historical and cultural reasons account for this difference (Lock 1993) with the result in practice that Japanese psychiatrists, in contrast to North Americans, are very rarely involved in the treatment of this life-cycle transition.

Over the past fifteen years, spurred on by an aging population, the possible long-term effects of lowered estrogen levels associated with the end of menstruation on the health of older women, particularly the possibility of being at increased risk for heart and bone disease, has become a subject of major medical and health policy concern in North America. There is at present considerable pressure placed on gynecologists to medicate women over the age of 45 for the remainder of their lives as a "prophylactic" measure against the "killer" diseases of later life. (The epidemiological research that prompts this move is decidedly inconclusive and hotly debated; moreover, there is considerable evidence that long-term use of hormone medication places women at an increased risk for cancer [Berkvist et al. 1989].) Once on hormone replacement therapy, women are expected to receive an endometrial biopsy at least twice a year, sometimes resulting in curettage, on occasion performed under general anesthesia (Mack and Ross 1989). Cost-benefit analyses suggest that no clear economic advantage can be shown in terms of protection against chronic illness versus the ongoing expense of monitoring women on hormone replacement therapy (Weinstein and Tosteson 1990); nevertheless, medicalization proceeds apace.

The incidence of heart disease among Japanese women is about one-quarter that of North American women (World Health Organization 1991), and osteoporosis appears to be less than half (although the data are not entirely reliable, Ross et al. 1991). Thus far it is stroke that is of overwhelming concern in Japan, and that is targeted, through dietary changes, in order to reduce spiraling health care costs associated with an aging population. Thus, a combination of biological, epidemiological, cultural, and social factors accounts for the low rate of medicalization of *kōnenki* to date, and, when the good health of most middle-aged Japanese women is added to this, the result is that a rather small burden is placed on the health care system by this particular population.

What spoils the good record of middle-aged Japanese women is their use of medical services for abortion. More than 54% of the women in the survey have had one or more abortions—a total of 1,428 abortions between them over their reproductive lives. The low-dose contraceptive pill is not legal in Japan, and the high-dose pill is only available by prescription to control menstrual disorders, although this ruling is interpreted rather loosely. Among the women surveyed, 14% had made use of the pill at some time, and another 14% used an intrauterine device. The majority had relied on condoms or the rhythm method as contraceptive techniques throughout their married lives. Not surprisingly, the failure rate is rather high, resulting in abortion, especially because virtually everyone wishes to limit their family size to two children. Despite this situation, contrary to expectations, the *overall* rate of abortions per 1,000 women remains lower in Japan than North America (Health United States 1991).

Since the 1960s the abortion rate has declined steadily in Japan for every age group (probably due to more efficient use of condoms), except among those under twenty where it has steadily increased. The overall decline in the abortion rate, combined with a preferential use by women of tertiary-care facilities for giving birth, means that Japanese gynecologists, the majority of whom are in private practice, are at present finding themselves short of work. Until recently, most women gave birth in small clinics run by gynecologists, but today the majority want a full array of technological services on hand. The combined effect of a reduction in abortions and changing birthing practices on their income means that some gynecologists now take an active interest in the medicalization of menopause (Lock 1993). This new-found interest on the part of gynecologists, together with an increased exposure of *kōnenki* in both professional and popular literature, undoubtedly means that in the future more Japanese women will visit doctors at this stage of the life cycle. However, until the pill becomes legal in Japan, it is unlikely that there will be a widespread adoption of hormone replacement therapy (composed of essentially the same ingredients as the pill). There is considerable concern in Japan among most women and many physicians that the pill causes unwanted side reactions, and a similar reaction to a widespread use of hormone replacement therapy is predictable. It is highly likely, therefore, that herbal prescriptions (*kanpō*) will continue to be the medication of choice, which means that the monitoring of women will be neither invasive nor expensive, in contrast to hormone replacement therapy.

One other point is worth noting: a moralistic discourse about *kōnenki* is widespread—it is usually assumed in Japan that it is "spoiled," middle-class housewives with too much time on their hands who complain and run to doctors for help—however, the survey research shows otherwise. Working women, in particular those employed in factories, reported the most symptoms (although still well below the figures for North America). It is also they who have the highest rate of remaining unmarried, or of being separated or divorced. One study shows that single people in Japan have a life expectancy that is fifteen to twenty years shorter than their married counterparts; thus the health protection apparently offered by marriage appears to be considerable (Goldman and Hu 1993). Most women in the present study have this advantage since 88% are married (a figure that echoes national data), but among the remaining 12% a disproportionate number are employed as blue-collar laborers, and also report poorer health, a finding that supports an argument for an intimate relationship between low social and economic status and poor health.

## Culture and Expectations about Health Care

The above data indicate that middle-aged Japanese women do not burden the health care system for two reasons: first, the majority are healthy, and second, apart from delivery, they do not have the expectation that professional health care can or should attempt to solve problems other than those clearly designated as disease.

Several social and epidemiological factors that appear to contribute to good health in Japan have been pointed out by Marmot and Smith (n.d.); I alluded briefly to several of them at the beginning of the chapter and will in conclusion elaborate on others. Surveys in Japan have shown that, on the whole, middle-aged and older women are satisfied with their lives (Economic Planning Agency 1983; Pharr 1976). In comparison with the hardships endured prior, during, and immediately after the war, most middle-aged Japanese feel secure and fortunate. In addition, economic discrepancies among the population are not nearly as marked as in North America; moreover, Japan remains remarkably homogenous, and, comparatively speaking, the population is well educated.

Other factors make a direct contribution to the health status of the Japanese: although high in salt, the typical diet in Japan is considerably lower in fat than in North America; the average Japanese eats less than the average American, and obesity is unusual. This situation is changing quite rapidly among young people, and some of the protection afforded by the Japanese diet may well disappear before long. The Japanese are better exercised than North Americans, largely because extensive use is made of public transport (and people must therefore walk to and from their homes, at a mininum), and bicycles are used for local errands. Furthermore, activities such as farming continue to be relatively labor intensive, again in contrast to North America. Given the space constraints of Japan, this situation may well continue largely unchanged. Moreover, most middle-aged and older Japanese grew up without access to cars and have exercised much more than North Americans over their life span.

Preventive medicine, including mass screening, is given high priority in the Japanese health care system (Ikegami 1989b). It is difficult to estimate to what extent screening actually effects mortality and morbidity, but it seems likely that the emphasis given to self-responsibility for health from infancy onward must make a positive long-term contribution to health. Mothers are encouraged to monitor their children's bodies very closely, and from nursery school onward there is regular surveillance of bodily function and the behavior of children, which is continued throughout primary school and, to a lesser extent, into the adolescent years. Children are systematically taught, both in school and at home, about hygiene, self-care, good deportment, and emotional control (Lock 1980).

The Japanese are fortunate in that they do not suffer from major genetic disorders associated with a historical exposure of a population to malaria. Thus thalassemia, sickle cell anemia, and related hemoglobin disorders do not pose a problem, although other less common genetic diseases are present. Mass neonatal screening programs have been in place since 1977, and prenatal screening is available for high-risk families (Fujiki et al. 1992).

Widespread use continues to be made of traditional medical techniques, both in the home and in clinics run by acupuncturists, masseuses, and other alternative health care practitioners. In the hands of a skilled practitioner, acupuncture has been shown to be very effective for the relief of both acute and chronic pain, while producing feelings of well being through endorphin production. Traditional bone manipulators and chiropractitioners are also made use of extensively (in the case of the former, in connection with sports injuries). There are also about 100 M.D.s in Japan who specialize in herbal medicine, added to which the majority of physicians today make some use of herbal medicine, particularly in connection with geriatric, pediatric, obstetric, and gynecological care (Nikkei Medical 1981). Mounting scientific evidence shows the efficacy of herbal medicine, as well as confirming that, if appropriately used, there are few side effects (Otsuka 1983). Obtaining reliable figures of the extent to which alternative medicine is used in Japan is exceedingly difficult, but it seems reasonable to suggest that, even though usually turned to secondarily or as an adjunct to biomedical services, herbal medicine, acupuncture, and other indigenous therapeutic techniques reduce pressures on the formal health care system.

Although it is customary in Japan to imbibe medication rather freely and to consult with a doctor for minor physical ailments, rather few "worried well" or those who have "psychological" or family problems seek out medical care. A widely shared assumption remains that, aside from its physical components, distress should be contained by the individual or within the family and that with endurance and time problems will dissipate. Some people make visits to hot spring resorts, the facilities of one or other of the "new religions," or massage clinics, or simply undertake vigorous exercise as part of a healing regime. Underlying such behavior is the belief that mind and body are united, that physical distress frequently originates from a poor mental attitude (the usual explanation for trouble at *kōnenki*), and that reciprocally, physical activity, combined with an effort to resign oneself to the inevitable problems of daily life, is by far the best cure (Okuyama 1979).

It is also evident that the Japanese public does not, as yet, expect as much from its health care system as does the North American public. One major difference is with respect to the availability of auxiliary services that are singularly lacking in Japan both inside hospitals and in the community. Facilities such as genetic counseling do not exist, nor do the majority of other support services taken for granted in North America today, in particular, psychological counseling. There has been a concerted effort recently, as part of the government Gold Plan to improve care of the elderly, to train auxiliary workers to assist women caring for their aging relatives at home, and also to provide facilities for short-term respite care. However, the incentives to take on this type of work remain insufficient, and thus far the availability of services falls far short of the demand (Kinoshita 1994).

A recent study conducted by the Ministry of Labor showed that out of nearly 500 people nursing the elderly in their Tokyo homes, over 81% were women, and their average age was fifty-six years old. More than 60% of these women had been looking after their relatives single-handedly for three years or more, and over 16% of them had been caregiving for more than ten years (Tokyo Shinbun 1990). In another study, one ninety-year-old woman was taking care of her bedridden husband alone; over 57% of the caretakers were daughters-in-law or daughters, and many of these women were themselves in their seventies (Serizawa 1989, 37). When middle-aged respondents nursing their relatives were asked about health problems, 53% complained of lumbago (presumably from lifting immobile people), 44% suffered from lack of sleep, and 37% cited "nervousness" as a major problem (Serizawa 1989, 43). It is further estimated that one in three women have to give up work in order to nurse their relatives (Tokyo Shinbun 1990), indicating that not only is home care a physical and psychological burden, but it frequently produces economic hardship. It has also been suggested that, for all the well-meaning efforts of most middle-aged women, the quality of care may not be as good as would be the case if professional help was involved (Kobayashi and Reich 1993).

The above reports indicate that although middle-aged women apparently assist the government in avoiding health care expenditure on the elderly, this policy may to some extent rebound in that middle-aged women themselves become vulnerable to ill health and chronic distress, although the survey research reported earlier in this chapter suggested that this was not the case. Qualitative data discussed below permit a more nuanced interpretation of the survey findings.

### The Pillar of the Family

The lives of the women whom I interviewed are, not surprisingly, extremely varied. The majority report that they are happy and fortunate (*shiawase*), but a large number, working or otherwise, are decidedly not content, and many keep up a barrage of "low profile" (Scott 1990) resistance against the perceived perpetrators of their unhappiness, usually their husbands. Blue-collar women at times expressed a good deal of hostility about working conditions and in particular, when relevant, about a permanent lack of security at work. When asked to talk about care of the elders, however, although everyone agreed that it was hard work that often demanded considerable sacrifice on the part of many women, there was almost no argument that close female relatives should be primarily responsible. Those women already living with the older generation and those in line to do so, whatever their occupation, assumed, usually without hesitation, that their lives should be restructured and, if necessary, their financial contribution to the household would have to be curtailed to take on this task. This is in spite of the fact that few women today, when they in turn become infirm, expect to be looked after by their daughters-in-law.

Provided that one's parents-in-law do not become chronically ill, and above all senile, then caring for the elderly can be a satisfying and rewarding task. I found many women who had worked out an amicable and even loving relationship with their in-laws over the years and who did not feel particularly oppressed by their extended family situation. On the contrary, a good number are proud of their achievements on the domestic front. Rather than endure the punishing routines associated with white-collar work in Japan, many middle-class women actively embrace and reinforce the ideology of their worth as a "homebody," particularly so because care of the family is publicly recognized as a crucial and valued activity. Conflicts usually occur, however, when there is a major health problem in the family (and sometimes it is the daugther-in-law who is sick in addition to the elderly relative), or when the middle-aged woman has to give up work from which she derives satisfaction or financial security, or, alternatively, when the usual caregiver, the wife of the eldest son, does not step forward to fulfill her designated task. Today, geography compounds the problem because urban residents are, more often than not, completely removed from their elders who remain in the countryside. Situations such as these are, of course, by no means unusual, as the following narratives reveal.

Shiba-san, fifty-two at the time of the interview, worked for nearly thirty years in the farm co-op in the village where she lives, keeping the account books. Two years previously she had resigned from this job in order to take care of both her parents-in-law. Until she became ill, Shiba-san's mother-in-law had done all the housework and cooking while Shiba-san put in a full day at the co-op, and her husband worked their land in addition to doing a part-time office job in the nearby town. Two months after she resigned from her job her mother-in-law died, but Shiba-san could not take up outside employment again because her father-in-law is not able to take care of himself.

Her son, married to a nurse and with two small children aged two years and eight months, intimated that now that Shiba-san was at home all day she probably felt rather lonely; he went on to suggest that perhaps his family should move into the "big house." Shiba-san's husband encouraged his son with this idea with the result that for six months prior to the interview the family had been living with four generations under one roof.

"What's your day like?"

"Well, I get up at 6:30 and make breakfast for everyone. My daughter-in-law helps sometimes, but because she's a nurse she often works at nights so I pretty much do everything. After everyone leaves for work I do the cleaning and the washing. The washing has increased enormously with all these people in the house. My daughter-in-law does some of the children's things, but I help with the diapers and so on."

"How does it feel to be a housewife after working full-time most of your life?"

"Well, the best part about the work was getting out of the house each day. I really enjoyed it, and I had a lot of friends. I was giving some psychological counseling too, and I particularly liked that. Now, as a hobby, I manage to do Japanese classical dancing once a week. It's good exercise and I feel really fit afterwards. But unfortunately I can't do any practice at home because my father-in-law is here and it would disturb him."

"Do you find it constraining to live in an extended family? What was it like when you were first married?"

"When I came here my mother-in-law was only about forty-six years old. She was a very independent woman and at first it was hard. I was working in the co-op already, but I had to start looking after this huge family as well—my parents-in-law, my husband, and his four brothers.

"It's never been my intention that my daughter-in-law should experience the same kind of hardships that I had. My husband knows it's a bit hard on me at present, but he says that if we are to keep the peace in this family, then everything depends on me. So I must stay quiet and try to fit in with the younger people's needs. On Sundays, when my daughter-in-law is at home, in order to let her sleep in, I try to stay in bed as long as possible although I really want to get up. In the past, if a mother-in-law got up earlier than her daughter-in-law and fixed break-fast, then the daughter-in-law wouldn't be able to swallow the food from shame. But now young people don't take things that way any more."

"Will you live together for a long time?"

"Well, we have some land. We could build a house on one of the rice fields, but somehow I don't think that will happen for a long time."

"How do you feel about taking care of the grandchildren?"

"They go to a daycare center for a few hours each day so that helps." Here Shiba-san paused, clearly wondering whether she should go on or not. She looked down, sighed, and then contined in one long rush:

"My daughter-in-law has a good steady job, and she may be an exception, but in general I think that a mother should stay at home for a while and raise her own children; otherwise everyone suffers. Of course, if she stopped her work as a nurse she would probably never find a decent job again. I think the children are much too small to go into daycare all day, and anyway there're no facilities around here for full-time care. So it's very hard on me, but I'm still young and so I'm helping her. Sometimes I feel upset; I don't really agree with how things are working out, but I keep that to myself."

"Do you find it hard to do that?"

"Yes, but I was trained to suppress my feelings and I've had plenty of practice living with mother-in-law for so long. When I get older I'll be able to say what I want, but not yet."

Shiba-san assumes that if she becomes infirm her daughter-in-law will probably not relinquish her work in order to look after her. When pushed, Shiba-san admits that she feels caught between the generations, since she expects little recompense for a life devoted to the care of others (see also Lebra 1984, 266). In common with virtually all women of her age, Shiba-san believes that raising children is a woman's vocation. Men are usually characterized as helpless and passive onlookers at home, and Shiba-san has no expectations that her husband can ease her present burden, nor does she call on either him or her son to give even the minimum of assistance with the children. Thus far, the unhappiness that Shiba-san clearly experiences is not expressed as physical discomfort or illness.

In many other interviews the expectations placed on women and unequivocal demands made by family members were very evident. A single woman, for example, had been bullied by her brothers and their wives to give up her life-long employment with a printing company in order to look after her own parents. This woman, the youngest child in the family and therefore not normally expected to look after her parents, is now at serious risk for becoming impoverished as she grows older. Another woman, Miyata-san, is a self-employed Tokyo architect in order to avoid the discrimination she experienced in the company that formally hired her. While working at home she keeps an eye on her reasonably active mother-in-law who lives with the family. Miyata-san's husband is supportive of her work, helped convince his mother, when it was needed, that she must allow her daughter-in-law to work uninterrupted, but plays no part in the running of the household except to do a little cooking on Sundays. Miyata-san is hoping that she can persuade her sisters-in-law to help with their mother in the future, because if the full burden of nursing falls entirely into her hands, she will have to give up her work. Despite their legitimate concerns about the future, these two women remain exceedingly healthy.

In contrast, at forty-nine, Inagaki-san looks frail and tired. She lives on a Nagano farm that she used to work almost single-handedly, and is at present nursing her mother-in-law. When interviewed she was recovering from major surgery for breast cancer. During her stay in the hospital Inagaki-san's mother-in-law had also been hospitalized but, at her insistence, was discharged the same day as Inagaki-san, who resumed full care of her right away with only a little assistance from her husband and father-in-law. Inagaki-san's wound did not heal well; she had a major allergy to the chemotherapy; and she received no psychological counseling of any kind. She struggles on, surrounded by the sad remains of the largely untended farm, with some occasional help with the housework from her husband and mature children. She is still unable to look at her body in a mirror and is terrified each time she visits the doctor that he will tell her that the disease has returned. Inagaki-san made every effort to retain her composure throughout the interview, but several times was reduced to tears as she recounted her story.

This interview and others like it clearly revealed how the health and well being of some middle-aged women is sacrificed for a national ideology that makes them primarily responsible for the care of their family members. For many other women who take on this responsibility, no adverse effect can be detected on their physical health, although a good number suffer considerable distress. Yet other women are fulfilled and reasonably content with their assigned lot in life. Across a cohort of middle-aged women, the physical burden of nursing family members apparently does not have any obvious negative impact on the general state of their health. It is perhaps among women in their late sixties and seventies, and even older, who are still responsible for nursing family members, where the burden would be most apparent.

## Conclusion

Although hospital and clinic waiting rooms throughout Japan are usually packed with waiting patients, suggesting a sick population, this image can be deceptive. Patients seek out immediate care for acute medical problems both major and minor, and for serious chronic diseases, but they do not place a large burden on the system in terms of expecting a full range of supportive therapies or social services. Moreover, judicious use is made of traditional and alternative technologies for the relief of a range of mild and chronic problems. Furthermore, a considerable portion of the provision of health care is donated by the family—most women assume it is their primary responsibility to look after the mentally ill, the disabled, and the infirm elderly at home, unless the task becomes entirely overwhelming. Working women (more than 60% of mature females) expect to give up employment to perform care-giving tasks for the family. In summary, middle-aged Japanese women appear to be in good health due to a range of factors including nutrition, preventive medicine, and health education, in addition to being part of a well-educated society committed in theory to egalitarianism in terms of social benefits and health care. Furthermore, they place relatively few demands on health care facilities and, as is culturally expected of them, actually take pressure off the system by providing unpaid nursing care for dependent elderly and chronically ill family members.

When assessing health care costs it is important to consider not only the management of disease, but those social and cultural factors that contribute to the good health of a population, together with the expectations and behaviors of various segments of the population, which may burden or alternatively relieve the health care system.

ACKNOWLEDGMENT

Funding for this paper was provided by a research grant from the Social Science and Humanities Research Council of Canada.

NOTES

1. In a 1984 survey that I conducted with over 1,300 women aged forty-five to fifty-five inclusively, three occupational groups were included: farming women, factory workers, and full-time housewives.

The middle-class urban sample of housewives was selected from the register of names and addresses available at many city halls in Japan. The register used is classified according to residential areas. Two areas regarded as representative of middle-income families were selected, and women (525) between ages forty-five and fifty-five were noted and mailed a questionnaire. This was followed up by a reminder postcard and then a second mailing of the questionnaire to those who had not responded. After the first mailing, 191 usable questionnaires were returned; after the postcard, 68 more; and after the second question-naire, another 75 were returned, giving a total of 324 usable responses.

The factory workers were selected by first making contact with the director of the Kyoto Industrial Health Association who facilitated the distribution of 405 questionnaires to fifteen factory managers, who then passed out all of the questionnaires to women of the appropriate age. Replies were sent back by mail directly to the researchers. A second group of 145 women working in small, silk-weaving factories were contacted by personal distribution of the questionnaire to factory managers after receiving the support of the local union in the form of a letter of introduction. From this sample, 377 usable responses were obtained.

The final sample of 650 farm workers was selected mostly through the support of the public health department of a large country hospital. The questionnaires were distributed by public health workers traveling to the women's organizations of forty-five villages; re-sponses were mailed directly back to the researchers, and they yielded 434 usable re-sponses. A second, smaller sample of 176 usable responses was obtained through the cooperation of the local head of the department of public health, who introduced the researchers directly to the local women's organizations.

The overall response rate from the three occupational groups was 76%—very high when compared to the usual response rates to survey research conducted in Japan.

Interviews lasting between one and one-half and two hours were conducted with 105 women in their homes. Approximately one-third were Kobe housewives; one-third were factory workers in south Kyoto; and one-third lived in farming villages in southern Nagano, a fishing village in Shikoku, and a forestry village in Shiga. Names appearing in the text are fictitious. Interviews with physicians reported above were conducted in 1984 and 1986.

2. This survey was designed to be comparable with one conducted in Massachusetts using 8,000 women, and with another in Manitoba using 2,500 women aged forty-five to fifty-five, inclusively.

REFERENCES

Adlercreutz, Herman, et al. 1992. Dietary phyto-oestrogens and the menopause in Japan. *The Lancet* 339: 1233.

Avis, Nancy E., et al. 1992. The evolution of menopausal symptoms. In H. G. Burger, ed., *Ballière's clinical endocrinology and metabolism,* vol. 7. London: Harcourt, Brace, Jovanovich Publishers.

Bergkvist, Leif, et al. 1989. The risk of breast cancer after estrogen and estrogen-progestin replacement. *New England Journal of Medicine* 321:293–97.

Economic Planning Agency. 1983. *White paper on national life.* Tokyo: Okurashō Insatsu Kyoku.

Frenk, Julio, et al. 1991. Elements for a theory of the health transition. *Health Transition Review* 1:21–38.

Fujiki, N., et al. 1992. Genetic disease patterns in Japan: a review. *Human Biology* 64:855–67.

Goldman, Noreen, and Yuareng Hu. 1993. Excess mortality among the unmarried: a case study of Japan. *Social Science & Medicine* 36:533–46.

Higuchi, Keiko. 1985. Women at home. *Japan Echo* 12:51–57.

Higuchi, Yukiko, and Fukuko Sakamoto, eds. 1976. *Hataraku fujin no kenri no tatakai* (The struggle for working women's rights). Tokyo: Minshusha.

Hosoya, Tsugiko. 1987. Rōjin kango no tsuma no sutoresu (The stress of wives nursing their old folks). In *Gendai no espuri.* Tokyo: Shibundo, 151–62.

Ikegami, Naoki. 1989a. Health technology development in Japan. *International Journal of Technology Assessment in Health Care* 4:239–54.

———. 1989b. Best medical practice: the case of Japan. *International Journal of Health Planning and Management* 4:181–95.

———. 1991. Japanese health care: low cost through regulated fees. *Health Affairs* 10:87–109.

Ikemi, Yujiro, et. al. 1980. Psychosomatic mechanism under social changes in Japan. In S. B. Day, F. Lolas, and M. Kusinitz, eds., *Biopsychosocial health.* New York: International Foundation for Biosocial Development and Human Health, 65–81.

Kaufert, Patricia, Penny Gilbert, and Tom Hassard. 1988. Researching the symptoms of menopause: an exercise in methodology. *Maturitas* 10:117–31.

Kaufert, Patricia, and John Syrotuik. 1981. Symptom reporting at the menopause. *Social Science & Medicine* 184:173–84.

Kinoshita Yasuhito. 1994. The political-economy perspective of health and medical care policies for the aged in Japan. In Derek G. Gill and Stanley R. Ingman, eds., *Eldercare, distributive justice, and the welfare state.* Albany, NY: State University of New York Press, 203–32.

Kobayashi Yasuki and Michael R. Reich. 1993. Health care financing for the elderly in Japan. *Social Science & Medicine* 37:343–53.

Kunstadter, Peter, et al. 1993. Demographic variables in fetal and child mortality: Hmong in Thailand. *Social Science & Medicine* 36:1109–20.

Kyūtoku Shigemori. 1979. *Bogenbyō* (Mother-caused illness). Tokyo: Sanmaku Shuppan.

Lebra, Takie. 1984. *Japanese women: constraint and fulfillment.* Honolulu: University of Hawaii Press.

Lock, Margaret. 1980. *East Asian medicine in urban Japan: varieties of medical experience.* Berkeley: University of California Press.

———. 1986. Ambiguities of aging: Japanese experience and perceptions of menopause. *Culture, medicine, and psychiatry.*

———. 1988. New Japanese mythologies: faltering discipline and the ailing housewife in Japan. *American Ethnologist* 15:43–61.

———. 1993. *Encounters with aging: midlife and menopause in Japan and North America.* Berkeley: University of California Press.

———, Patricia Kaufert, and Penny Gilbert. 1988. Cultural construction of the menopausal syndrome: the Japanese case. *Maturitas* 10:317–32.

Mack, Thomas M. 1993. Hormone replacement therapy and cancer. In H. G. Burger, ed., *Ballière's clinical endocrinology and metabolism,* vol. 7. London: Harcourt, Brace, Jovanovich Publishers.

Mack, Thomas M., and R. K. Ross. 1989. Risks and benefits of long-term treatment with estrogens. *Schweiz.med.Wschr* 119:1811–20.

Marmot, M. G., and G.D. Smith. n.d. Why are the Japanese living longer? CIAR Population Health Working Paper #4.

McKeown, Peter. 1976. *The modern rise of populations.* New York: Academic Press.

*New York Times.* 1992. Japan's health care: cradle, grave and no frills. Monday, 28 December.

Nikkei Medical. 1981. Chōsa: daiissen rinshōi no kanpōyaku shiyō jōkyō (A survey of the use of *kanpōyaku* by clinicians) 10:28–31.

Ohnuki-Tierney, E. 1984. *Illness and culture in contemporary Japan.* Cambridge: Cambridge University Press.

Okuyama, Kenji. 1979. *Nihon no iryō* (Medical care in Japan). Tokyo: Shin Nihon Shinsho.

Otsuka, Yasuo, ed. 1983. *Tōyōigaku no Nyūmon* (An introduction to East Asian medicine). Tokyo: Shōronsha.

Pharr, Susan. 1976. *The Japanese woman.* In L. Austen, ed., *Japan: The paradox of progress.* New Haven: Yale University Press.

Ross, Philip D., et al. 1991. A comparison of hip fracture incidence among native Japanese, Japanese Americans, and American caucasians. *American Journal of Epidemiology.* 133:801–9.

Schorr, Ephraim. 1940. The menopause. *Bulletin of the New York Academy of Medicine.* 16:453–74.

Scott, James. 1990. *Domination and the arts of resistance: hidden transcripts.* New Haven: Yale University Press.

Serizawa, Motoko. 1989. Aspects of an aging society. *Review of Japanese Culture and Society* 3:37–46.

Thorneycroft, Ian Hall. 1989. The role of estrogen replacement therapy in the prevention of osteoporosis. *American Journal of Obstetrics and Gynecology* 160:1306–10.

*Tokyo Shinbun.* 1990. Rōjin kaigo josei ni zusshiri (Nursing the elderly is a burden on women). 13 September.

Utian W. H., and D. Serr. 1976. The climacteric syndrome. In P. A. Van Keep and R. B. Greenblatt, eds., *Consensus on menopause research.* Lancaster: MTP Press, 1–4.

Weinstein, Milton, and Anna Tosteson. 1990. Cost effectiveness of hormone replacement. In M. Flint, F. Kronenberg, and W. Utian, eds., *Multidisciplinary perspectives on menopause.* Annals of the New York Academy of Sciences, vol. 592. New York: New York Academy of Sciences, 162–71.

World Health Organization. 1991. *World health statistics: 1990.* Geneva: World Health Organization.

CHAPTER 21

# The Three-Minute Cure: Doctors and Elderly Patients in Japan

*Ruth Campbell*

SUMMARY    Japanese patients and doctors frequently note that the large number of outpatient visits in a clinic session results in a three-hour wait for a three-minute encounter with the physician. This observational study reports on the duration and content of outpatient visits by older adults to eight physicians in the Tokyo area. The average visit lasted from five to six minutes per patient. Content included routine physical complaints and nonmedical concerns such as living arrangements and family relationships. Most of the talking was done by the patient. Most of the patients had a return appointment in two to four weeks to the same physician, which facilitated recognition of incremental changes in functioning. The efficacy of more frequent brief visits with the physician for treatment of the elderly person with chronic health problems warrants further study.

## Introduction

It is a well-known maxim in Japan that, when you go to the doctor, you wait three hours for a three-minute visit. In most cases, there are no appointments; you go when you feel sick. Entering the waiting room of a large hospital on a typical morning is like going to the airport in the United States the day before Thanksgiving: doctors in large hospitals and small clinics can see from thirty to fifty patients in a morning. Clinic doctors see an average of sixty-four patients a day with an office visit averaging about five minutes (Yoshikawa, Shirouzu, and Holt 1991). The Tokyo Metropolitan Geriatric Hospital has a total of 850 outpatient visits a day. Tokai University Hospital, a 1,000-bed hospital, has close to 3,000.

In the United States, waiting for medical visits can also be a problem, particularly in large hospital outpatient clinics and emergency rooms. A recent survey (McGuire and Erhardt 1992) at a University of Michigan outpatient geriatric clinic found that the average visit lasts almost two hours and that 46% of that time is spent waiting. Radecki et al. (1988) found that visits to physicians with patients aged 65 to 74 lasted an average of 18.3 minutes for internists, 11.2 for general practitioners, and 12.1 for family practice specialists. The visit duration also decreased with age. People 75 and older were seen 1.2 minutes shorter by general practitioners and 2.3 minutes shorter by internists. This is interesting in light of the finding (Beisecker et al. 1992) that only in longer encounters (greater than 18 minutes) did older people ask significantly more questions than younger people. Patients are more satisfied with longer visits, but they also perceive that doctors spend at least 50% more time with them than they actually do.

Another difference between the U.S. and Japanese elderly is the frequency of visits to doctors. Americans 65 and older visit the doctor an average of 8.9 times a year; 9.9 times for people over age 75 (*Aging America: Trends and Projections*, 1991). An average Japanese over age 65 goes about three times as often, an estimated twenty-six times a year (Ikegami 1993). The insurance system that rewards an ambulatory care doctor for frequent visits is one reason for this, but another reason, as Ohnuki-Tierney (1984) pointed out, is "the relative readiness with which the Japanese both recognize departures from health and consult doctors about them." Hiroko Akiyama's data using health diaries also confirm that Japanese tend to recognize symptoms and seek treatment earlier than do Americans (see chapter 19).

Japanese have the highest life expectancy in the world and, by most measures, seem healthy. There is concern about the large numbers of bed-ridden elderly as compared to Western countries. Several reasons have been given for this:

1. There is a high incidence of stroke patients.
2. There has been a lack of attention to rehabilitation until fairly recently.
3. Since 60% of older people live with their children, often in fairly cramped housing, it is often easier for a caregiver to have an older person in bed than wandering around. (One daughter-in-law told me that she used to spend all her time following her mother-in-law around, preventing her from getting into trouble. After the mother-in-law returned from a two-month stay in the hospital, which she had entered in a diabetic coma, she was weak because she had refused rehabilitation and stayed in bed during her entire hospitalization. Now the daughter-in-law found her life was made easier by having her mother-in-law in bed, which happened to be in the middle of their living room.)
4. There is a cultural belief that older people should be treated well if they are sick, and that forcing them to do something they don't want to do— for example, exercise—is a bit cruel.

Currently, about 12% of the Japanese population is 65 and over, but by the year 2025 the percentage is predicted to be 25.4%, which will give Japan the largest percentage of elderly in the world. Similarly to the United States, only about 6% of people over age 65 are in institutions (Ikegami 1992). Therefore, how the majority of elderly who are living in the community experience medical care is of great interest. The brief visit has been described as "often superficial . . . the emphasis is on curative treatment rather than preventative care" (Yoshikawa, Shirouzu, and Holt 1991). This paper will discuss characteristics of the patient-doctor encounter in Japan as observed in practice and attitudes of Japanese physicians toward their elderly patients expressed in interviews with the author.

## Method of Study

In 1990 I was in Japan doing research on the relationship between caregivers and the elderly—usually mothers-in-law and daughters-in-law. I became interested in how professional caregivers, usually doctors, treat the elderly. I observed eight physicians in outpatient settings. Three physicians worked in the Tokyo Metropolitan Geriatric Hospital (two internists and one rehabilitation specialist); three physicians were from a large university hospital in Kanagawa (specialists in neurology, psychiatry, and rehabilitation); one general practitioner was from Tokyo; and one acupuncturist, who has a large elderly clientele, was also from Tokyo. Most of the doctors, with the exception of the general practitioner and the acupuncturist (who is not an M.D.), were Western-oriented and had had some experience in the United States or Europe doing research as well as clinical activity. My purpose was to see if the tale of the three-minute visit was accurate and what actually transpired during this short visit. I was interested in seeing how the doctor perceived the older patient and how the older patient behaved in the medical setting.

Previously, I had visited many hospitals in different parts of Japan, but these experiences were different in that this time I sat on a stool in the corner, observing the interaction and timing the visits. Sometimes I was introduced to the patient, sometimes not. A few times I was given a white jacket to wear, which passed for an explanation of my presence.

I expected Japanese doctors to direct much of the interaction, with the patients taking on a more passive, dependent role, based on respect for the doctor's expertise and the relatively brief time for communication between the patient and doctor. Despite a lot of discussion in recent years about shared medical decision making between physicians and patients, Beisecker et al. (1992) report that American medical students and physicians still hold attitudes consistent with greater physician authority in the decision making. As training and experience increase, the stronger was the tendency for the doctor to make decisions without input from the patients.

## General Findings and Impressions

### Duration of Visits

The doctors I observed spent from five to six minutes on average per patient. I saw just a few two- and three-minute visits. Psychiatry visits were the longest at about twenty minutes each. The general practitioner was the shortest, usually five minutes. In the afternoon, he made two home visits, about thirty minutes each, to two bed-ridden patients in his neighborhood.

## Lack of Privacy

In the hospital outpatient clinics, a curtain separates the exam room (or cubicle) from other doctors and from patients waiting to be seen. Sitting in the doctor's space, the patients can see the shoes of other patients who are waiting and hear voices of these patients as well as the doctors and patients in adjoining cubicles. Nurses walk in and out and sit at desks looking through papers while the patient is talking to the doctor. (Physicians do not regard this as a lack of privacy since the nurses function as an extension of the physician, not an outsider.) In the general practitioner's office there was the most privacy, with a door between the doctor's office and the waiting room; but the nurse still wandered in and out looking for things during the patient's visit. The acupuncturist's office carried lack of privacy to an art form, with patients sitting side by side with needles in them chatting about grandchildren, food prices, and unsatisfactory daughters-in-law.

## Frequency of Routine Complaints

Even though many of the doctors were specialists, people came in with relatively simple complaints—earaches, back pain, routine visits to check medications, loneliness, and colds. Part of this is due to the frequency of visits. Doctors can, by law, dispense or prescribe some medications for only two weeks; medications for chronic conditions, such as insulin, can be prescribed for four weeks. This means that patients have to come back to renew their medications. Doctors scheduled their return visits; the doctors I observed made appointments for three to four weeks later. Only one person was not given a return appointment when she left because she had to check about transportation. She came from Gunma Prefecture, which is several hours from Tokyo.

Example: A woman in her seventies sees the general practitioner. She says her cold is better. He takes her blood pressure and asks how she's eating. She says she's okay, "Don't worry, I don't eat that much." She asks him about a trip he made to New Zealand. He says her blood pressure is high today and asks the nurse to do an EKG. The next patient, also a woman in her seventies, rolls up her sleeve to get her blood pressure taken. She tells the doctor she's been taking care of her grandchildren. "You're probably tired," he says. He gives her a prescription and she leaves.

## Lack of Physical Examination

Patients do not undress, and I observed very little examination. Taking blood pressure was the most common procedure, with the patients simply rolling up their sleeves. Occasionally the doctor did an ear examination. The psychiatrist and neurologist administered the Hasegawa scale (a mini-mental-status scale) routinely. Mostly they talked, with the patient doing much of the talking. Frequently, the doctor would ask the equivalent of "How are you?" and the patient would report.

Example: A patient comes to see the endocrinologist. She says yesterday she felt bad, the morning is bad. She complains that she always has abdominal pains after breakfast. The doctor says that she is depressed and that she comes to see him weekly because she wants to. He says she lives alone and is a very strict Christian. She always complains of anxiety about the future. She frequently wants a GI examination and scope although they're always normal. He always makes the order. "Many times she became annoyed with the doctors because they didn't obey her order." She's gone to many specialists. She's on anti-depressant and anti-anxiety medication. She has visited a psychiatrist and a counselor. "Many doctors want to change her character but always fail. I always sit down with her and listen to her complaints. I just fit her pace. She comes almost every week. It's okay."

Relations with Family

Family members are seen together with the patient. Even a few patients who came with a volunteer or friend talked to the doctor with their friend sitting next to them. In the case of husband and wife, the doctor (or nutritionist) would frequently give directions to the wife, assuming she was the one who would carry them out.

In some cases, particularly with the psychiatrist or neurologist, when the patients couldn't or wouldn't come, alternate visits were made just with the caregiver, usually the daughter-in-law. In these cases, the daughter-in-law would meet with the doctor and receive a prescription at one visit, and the mother-in-law would come three weeks later to the next visit.

Example: A woman in her forties met with the psychiatrist for about twenty minutes. She spoke very fast, asking for clarification about the medication her mother was taking (Haloperidol). "She can't remember anything. When I find something she is looking for, she doesn't say thank you. She just says, 'You're a good pretender.'" She bought new sheets—her mother accused her of stealing them. When her husband speaks to his mother about admitting her to the hospital, she becomes calm for a few days and stops talking about stealing. She tells the doctor that the patient can distinguish family from other people and says bad things only to family members. She did think that the medicine had helped somewhat.

In talking to the daughter afterwards, I learned that she had gone to the city office to inquire about short-stay and other services and had applied for a home helper. The hospital social worker was also helping her, and she felt that since it was her own mother, she could hang on (*ganbatte*) a little longer. She was, however, very worried about the future. The psychiatrist did not recommend that her mother go to a regular hospital, and when she inquired about a geriatric hospital, she was told there were no psychiatric units. She said she appreciated talking to the doctor. In two weeks she would come back with her mother.

Nonmedical Treatment

Doctors frequently recommended nonmedical methods of treatment, such as *onsen* (hot-springs baths), exercise, and diet.

Example: A woman comes in and says her back hurts. "Do you go to an *onsen*?" the doctor asks. He then demonstrates an exercise running her fingers up the wall and then circling her hands. He takes her blood pressure and asks whether she's taking calcium. She tells him she also has had acupuncture.

## Nonmedical Motives

Visits are frequently made for nonmedical purposes. About 10% of older Japanese live alone, but they represented a larger proportion of the patients I observed. Physicians were very aware of the living situations of their patients and tended to equate living alone with loneliness and as a signal that future plans would have to be made for care.

Example: One woman with hypercalcemia comes in complaining about her ears. She says she has trouble eating because of her teeth. She also complains of pain in her legs. She has recently had a cold and didn't eat well. She says she doesn't need medicine. After she leaves, the doctor tells me that she lives alone and is lonely. He will refer her to a social worker to make plans for the future. Now she's okay, but since she has no children he thinks at some point they will have to arrange for a nursing home placement.

A surgeon told me about a man whose operation had gone very well, but he died because he lived alone and did not have adequate follow-up care. He had a home helper from the city but not often enough. The surgeon felt strongly that the government had to increase home-help services.

Another woman coming in for a routine visit told the doctor about how she was looking out her window at the large crowd attending a funeral at the funeral parlor across the street. She said she was thinking, "Who will come to my funeral?" "She's well prepared for death," he said. "She's ready."

## Conclusions

Clearly, this is an exploratory study. The doctors observed were not from a random sample. They were recommended to me by social workers and, in some cases, patients, because they were thought to be kind, knowledgeable, and good practitioners. It was also not easy to find a general practitioner who would allow observation, and it took me several months to do so. Also, I do not know what effect my presence had on the patient encounter. Did they ask more psychosocial questions because they know of my interest? Since the visits were generally short and they saw the same number of people they usually did, I doubt that my presence had a great effect.

A more serious problem is that I either worked with an interpreter nearby (a fellow social worker) or talked to the doctor in English afterward to confirm or clarify what I observed. Surely, my language shortcomings caused me to miss important points.

However, both the doctor-patient situation and the types of problems presented were very familiar to me, and I felt comfortable being in the office. Aside from a few women patients who giggled and said they were embarrassed by a foreigner, the patients did not focus on me at all but directed their attention to their doctor.

What surprised me was how much could occur during a five-minute visit. I did not expect that the doctor would talk less than the patient, which was the usual practice, and that so little actual physical examination would take place. I was struck by the fact that the frequency of the visits allowed the physicians to note small changes and to treat these changes. Family situations also seemed to be something these physicians considered important and were familiar with. Rather than seeing these visits as superficial and "curative," I began to see them as preventive medicine, in that both physical and emotional issues could be discussed briefly because the patient knew this was not the only visit for three months and that every detail did not have to be divulged at this time.

Doctors themselves thought that the visits were too short and that they were too busy. Most said they would like to have had more time. The patients I spoke with after their visits were mostly appreciative of their doctors. Surveys do indicate that Japanese are dissatisfied with their health care system, and frequent complaints are made about the long waits and short visits. However, more and more Japanese are bypassing their local practitioners (who tend to be older physicians whose ranks are dwindling) in favor of large hospitals with much longer waiting periods. Several patients spoke of the difficulty of getting to visit the specific doctor they wanted to.

In terms of the American experience, it's well known that the elderly, especially, are more likely to discuss psychosocial problems with their physician than with other health care providers or even their families. It also seems important with chronic illnesses to be very familiar with a patient's baseline health in order to recognize incremental changes in functioning. It would be interesting to compare the effectiveness of frequent brief visits as opposed to longer, less frequent visits on older patients' physical and psychosocial functioning. The obvious difficulties of transportation and cost would have to be studied, but in terms of older patients' nostalgia for the old familiar family doctor and frequent complaints about the impersonal nature of the current system, it might be worth a try. If more frequent visits could reduce hospitalization, as would seem to be the case in Japan, this system might also prove cost-effective.

REFERENCES

*Aging America: Trends and Projections.* 1991. U.S. Senate Special Committee on Aging, the American Association of Retired Persons, the Federal Council on the Aging, and the U.S. Administration on Aging, Washington, D.C.

Beisecker, A.E., et al. 1992. "Attitudes of medical students and primary care physicians regarding the input of older and younger patients in medical decisions." Paper presented at the 45th annual meeting of the Gerentological Society of America, Washington, D.C.

Ikegami, N. 1992. The economics of health care in Japan. *Science* 258 (23 October): 614–18.

————. 1993. Personal communication to the author.

McGuire, S., and A. Erhardt. 1992. "Turner geriatric service patient flow study." University of Michigan Hospitals, Ann Arbor, Michigan.

Ohnuki-Tierney, E. 1984. Illness and culture in contemporary Japan: an anthropological view. New York: Cambridge University Press.

Radecki, S.E., et al. 1988. Do physicians spend less time with older patients? *Journal of the American Geriatrics Society* 36.8: 713–18.

Yoshikawa, A., N. Shirouzu, and M. Holt. 1991. How does Japan do it? Doctors and hospitals in a universal health care system. *Stanford Law and Policy Review* 3: 111–37.

CHAPTER 22

# Over My Dead Body: The Enigma and Economics of Death in Japan[1]

## *Eric A. Feldman*

SUMMARY   The subject of brain death has been debated in Japan for years, but so far no unified policy has emerged and organ transplants are rare. Common explanations include distrust of physicians, Japanese culture, and the difficulty of obtaining consensus about a definition of death. Economic considerations have played little role in the debate.

## Introduction

Japan's brain death debate began on 8 August 1968 when an economics student from Komazawa University went for an afternoon swim. Pulled from the sea unconscious, he was rushed to Sapporo University Hospital and declared dead from drowning. The following morning his heart was implanted into an eighteen-year-old suffering from chronic heart disease, who died less than three months later.

From a technical perspective, the fact that the recipient lived for eighty-three days was a cause for pride. Just one year earlier, Dr. Christian Barnard of South Africa had performed the world's first heart transplant, and his patient lived for only eighteen days. But in Japan, no law or policy sanctioned the determination of death based on brain criteria, the method by which the donor was declared dead. Without legal acceptance of brain death, it was cavalier for a physician to rely upon such criteria. As a result, many observers thought that the actions of the transplant surgeon, Dr. Juro Wada, crossed the line between caring for an organ recipient and killing a donor.

The heart transplant in Sapporo was Japan's first and last. No unified policy on the determination of death has yet been implemented, nor has a national system for organ distribution been created.[2] Despite policy inaction, however, professional and political organizations have issued a multitude of reports and recommendations regarding brain death and transplantation. Together with the large volume of written commentary, they suggest three overlapping explanations for Japan's lack of policy in this area.

One is the legacy of the 1968 heart transplant, commonly called the Wada

234

case, and the way it has come to symbolize public mistrust of the medical profession. Another is roughly described as Japanese culture and is used to explain the tension between traditional Japanese views of death and the body and the mechanistic outlook required by high-technology medical interventions. Last is the need for, but current lack of, public consensus before a policy can be adopted. Emphasized to varying extents, these factors are used by both advocates and critics of policy reform to support their positions.

Largely absent from the Japanese debate is a discussion of the potential financial costs of sanctioning brain death and transplantation. Rarely in the media or in specialist reports is there detailed discussion of the costs and benefits of transplants as opposed to other treatments, the allocation of medical resources, or the wisdom of spending significant sums on extraordinary medical procedures.

Next, a brief overview of current law and policy regulating death and the use of body organs in Japan will be provided. The above three explanations will then be more thoroughly described and evaluated, and the lack of apparent concern about economic issues will be analyzed.

## Current Japanese Law and Policy on Death and Organ Transplantation

Japan has no statutory definition of death and no law that requires death to be determined with regard to any particular criteria. The medical profession relies on accepted norms of medical practice and judgment to decide when an individual is to be declared dead. These accord with what is thought of as death by the layperson—termination of heartbeat and respiration, lack of reflexes—and were not questioned until the possibility of determining death based on brain criteria emerged in the 1960s.

Two laws concerning the transplantation of organs have been enacted. The first, An Act Relating to Cornea Transplantation, was passed in 1957.[3] It stipulated that the removal of corneas be authorized by the written consent of the donor's family and only when a specific recipient was available. This law was superseded in 1979 by An Act Concerning the Transplantation of Cornea and Kidneys.[4] The act covers only kidneys and corneas, both of which can be effectively salvaged from bodies declared dead by conventional criteria. It does not require the existence of a specified recipient. Surgeons removing kidneys are specifically exempted from prosecution for damaging a corpse, a provision that signals concern over potential legal action resulting from transplant procedures.[5]

## The Wada Case: A Legacy of Physician Mistrust

The recipient of Japan's only transplanted heart survived for less than three months; the controversy created by the operation has had a far greater longevity.[6] Physicians in principle opposed to neither a brain death standard nor organ transplants were unhappy with the actions of Dr. Wada and his transplant team. Many believed that organ transplants would soon be performed in Japan once the dual obstacles of the definition of death and the ability to suppress the body's rejection of organs were overcome (Yonemoto 1988, 41). Wada, however, had jumped the gun. He did not consult outside experts and ignored the fact that a committee made up of members of the Japan Society of Transplantation, the Ministry of Health and Welfare (MHW), and the Ministry of Justice, which had convened in May 1967 to consider the creation of legislation related to organ transplants, had not yet announced its findings.

Consequently, several physicians from Wada's hospital published articles in national medical journals directly criticizing his professional judgment in undertaking the transplant (Fujimoto 1969; Miyahara 1969). More severe was a December 1968 complaint filed with the Osaka prosecutor's office accusing Wada of murdering the organ donor.[7] An elite interdisciplinary group was soon formed to discuss the Sapporo transplant publicly and with the Judicial Affairs Committee of the Diet, the MHW Deliberation Council, and the Japan Federation of Bar Associations (JFBA).[8] Prosecutors ultimately dismissed the complaint against Wada for lack of material evidence, the JFBA sent him a warning, and the affair was formally ended.

Nonetheless, the Wada incident continues to be regularly mentioned by the media and others concerned with the definition of death and organ transplants in Japan. They treat it as a loss of innocence, an event marking a turning point after which the unconditional faith in physicians was questioned. Some even believe that the Wada case alone is responsible for the continuing controversy over brain death in Japan, and, until such mistrust is overcome, no resolution of the conflict over death is possible.

But if mistrust of physicians were that powerful, one would expect a variety of other aspects of current medical practice to be under attack. For example, Japanese physicians tend to be far more paternalistic than their American counterparts. They frequently keep patients ignorant of their conditions and diagnoses and give them little power to make treatment decisions. Yet courts have affirmed this system, consistently underlining the importance of physician discretion.[9] Academics have not argued for replacing paternalism with autonomy (Higuchi 1992). There has been little public protest about the general competence of physicians to make medical decisions in the best interests of their patients. And patients give little indication of abandoning particularly paternalistic physicians and seeking care elsewhere.

It is possible that physicians are mistrusted only with regard to declaring brain death and transplanting organs. But such a conclusion lacks both logic and empirical grounding and strays from the view that the Wada case effected a general suspicion of physicians. In addition to mistrust, additional explanations for Japan's twenty-five-year debate about brain death and transplants must also be sought.

### Brain Death and Transplants: The Culture Connection

Underlying many analyses of a brain death standard and organ transplants is the idea that they are not suited to Japanese culture. Crude versions of this view refer to a monolithic Japan dominated by the values and traditions of its feudal past. Umehara Takeshi, a philosopher and a member of the most recent government committee to address the brain death issue, writes (1989, 20):

> Despite our seemingly boundless enthusiasm for things Western, we Japanese are unable to emulate the West in this one matter [organ transplants] because something in our basic ethical system resists the idea of organ transplants.

Western Cartesian dualism is also cited as a critical factor in the acceptance of brain death abroad, and social customs governing the management of the dead, as well as the lack of a tradition of altruistic giving, are viewed as obstacles to acceptance at home.[10] The validity of these cultural and religious claims is directly dependent upon the extent to which specific Japanese traditions influence contemporary attitudes toward death.

The traditional view of death and the body in Japan was influenced by Confucian, Shinto, and Buddhist thought. Various aspects of that view are particularly relevant to the current brain death/transplant debate. One is the Shinto notion of the freshly dead, a period during which the soul of the deceased was thought to "hover at the margin of nature and culture," wandering through the world and inhabiting neither the world of the living nor the world of the ancestors (Ohnuki-Tierney 1984, 70; Doerner 1977, 160). Yet treating death as ambiguous and uncertain clashes with brain death. Based upon technical medical factors, brain death makes a sharp distinction between life and death and cannot accommodate a middle ground between the two.

Another aspect is notions of ancestor worship. A central tenet of ancestor worship in Japan is the conviction that the welfare of the living is dependent upon paying homage to the dead. But declaring people dead based on brain death criteria and dissecting their bodies in order to harvest their organs may violate the respect that is their due.

A Japanese sociologist and expert in the brain death debate has argued convincingly that most of the traditions and values that once surrounded death have vanished (Nudeshima 1991a; 1991b, 1,063–64). Citing evidence about Westernization, urbanization, and the atomization of city life since World War II, he has shown that many customary ideas about funerals, burial, and ancestors have changed, and that a "Japanese" view of death can no longer be meaningfully discussed.

This view is supported by a recent summary of eleven public opinion polls conducted between 1953 and 1987 concerning Japanese attitudes toward death (Woss 1992, 73–100). What emerges from the surveys is the great variation between views of death when broken down by age and sex. For example, whereas almost 60% of people below the age of thirty profess a belief in life after death, less than 25% of those over sixty hold such a belief. Further, it seems that more people in Germany than in Japan believe in reincarnation (Woss 1992, 87–89, 96n.2). This lends support to those who argue for a pluralistic view of death in Japan and advocate individual consent as the basis of both brain death and organ donation (Seimei Rinri Kenkyūkai 1992).

Still, the idea that brain death and organ transplants are fundamentally in-compatible with Japanese culture is promoted by some anthropologists and the popular press. They argue that the locus of the Japanese self, unlike the mind-centered West, resides in some other part of the body, though there is disagree-ment as to which part it is (Ohnuki-Tierney 1986, 279; Lock and Honde 1990, 100; Akatsu 1990, 2). Evidence is presented that the heart is its home, explaining why heart transplants are taboo, or that the stomach (abdomen) is where the self can be found, accounting for the particular importance of kidneys in Japan and the reluctance to accept the death of the brain as equivalent to the death of the entire human (Ohnuki-Tierney 1986, 281; Lock and Honde 1990, 109; Akatsu 1990, 2).

While tradition and culture have an impact on contemporary Japanese views of death, ultimately they are an inadequate explanation of the complexity and depth of the debate over brain death and transplants.[11] Other factors, particularly the frequent appeals to consensus as a necessary condition for brain death and transplant policy, must also be examined.

## The Elusiveness of Consensus:
## Scientific, Legal, Medical, and Political Attempts to
## Define Death

Over the past two decades, with the specter of the Wada case still looming, a plethora of committees has debated the issue of brain death and issued reports meant to influence the controversy over how death should be defined in contem-porary Japan. Despite the visible rift between those advocating different defini-tions, these groups have operated within an atmosphere that has placed a high priority on the achievement of a consensus on a conclusive definition of death. As Lock and Honde (1990, 104–5) have stated, "[E]very discussion on the subject of brain death in Japan, even when presented by doctors eager to facilitate organ transplants, is based on the premise that any changes in medical or legal practice in this area can only come after a consensus has been established among the Japanese people as a whole." But consensus has not yet been reached, due to the difficulty of reaching widespread agreement on so complex an issue and the ease with which the achievement of consensus can be denied.

In the absence of a general agreement on how death should be defined, and with debaters confounded by the perceived need for consensus, the brain death debate is at a stalemate. Still, there has been a steady flow of proposals, reports, and studies, as the definition of death based on brain criteria has remained unsettled.

One of the first attempts to introduce a brain death definition in Japan was made by the Japan Electroencephalography Association (Nihon Nōha Gakkai; JEA) in 1974. A professional group consisting exclusively of physicians, the JEA drew up Japan's first medical criteria for determining brain death.[12]

For more than a decade, JEA guidelines remained unchallenged by other branches of the medical community and unimplemented by medical policy makers. Then, in December 1984, twenty-eight Diet members and forty-five other professionals and officials formed the Life Ethics Problem Study Parliamentarians League. The league set as its mission the determination of whether the Diet ought to enact legislation recognizing brain death, and after one year of monthly meetings it endorsed the idea of brain death legislation.

At almost the same time, the MHW, recognizing that the JEA criteria were outmoded, decided to reconsider the scientific guidelines for declaring brain death. It launched the Brain Death Advisory Council, which issued a final report on 6 December 1985 (MHW 1985). Billed as an official nonbinding reference for physicians, the Takeuchi Report (named for the council's chairman) displayed a deep ambiguity about the relationship between brain death and death. While explicating the technical standards for determining brain death, the report declared that "death cannot be judged by brain death." In an article published in the *New York Times,* 10 February 1987, Clyde Haberman reported that Chairman Takeuchi himself was equivocal, stating that "[A]ll the doctors in our hospital, myself included, feel that we should wait for the heartbeat to stop. There is no question about it." Thus, the MHW provided a medical definition of brain death authored by eight nationally known physicians. They defined the state of brain death but did not consider it equal to death.

Still, by sending a clear signal to both experts and the public that brain death was considered by the MHW to be a medically definable state, the Takeuchi Report stimulated further debate on both the scientific and social issues of brain death. Within a year of its publication, the Medico-Legal Society of Japan, the Japan Transplantation Society, the Japan Medical Association (JMA), the Heart Transplant Study Society, and the Science Council of Japan had joined the controversy.[13]

Most significant were the opinions of the Life Ethics Deliberative Council of the JMA (Nihon Ishikai Seimei Rinri Kondaukai 1987; 1988). The JMA supported recognition of a whole-brain definition of death and advocated diagnosis of brain death with reference to the Takeuchi criteria if a patient or representative consented to brain death being used as the measure of death (Katō 1988, 106–15).

While the JMA report was an important statement from a group central to medical policy making, it had no legal force and was far from the final word. Criticism was soon forwarded by various individuals and organizations, including Bai Koichi (Kato 1988, 106–15), the Japan Society of Psychiatry and Neurology (Yamauchi 1990, 507), and the JFBA (Clyde Haberman, *New York Times,* 14 January 1988; Nihon Bengoshi Bengokai 1988). They were joined by Tachibana Takashi, a prominent journalist,[14] and the Patient Rights Conference, a group of medical professionals and patients that fears the potential violation of patients' rights from a brain death definition.

In an attempt to break the brain death gridlock, the Diet in 1989 established the Nōshi Rinchō, or Ad Hoc Committee on Brain Death and Organ Transplantation, a consulting body to the prime minister.[15] On 22 January 1992 the final report of the committee was presented to Prime Minister Miyazawa (MHW 1992). Its release was considered important enough to temporarily force news of the increasingly tense U.S.-Japan relationship from the headlines. The following morning, the *Yomiuri Shimbun,* Japan's largest circulation daily, proclaimed, "Final Report Recognizes Brain Death and Organ Transplantation," while the *Asahi Shimbun* announced "Report Says that Brain Death is Death." But the simple, declarative headlines could not mask what became obvious upon reading the first few paragraphs of either article: the blue-ribbon government panel had failed to reach a consensus.

The majority opinion contained in the final report can be easily summarized: (1) brain death, defined as the loss of the ability to integrate the body's functions and determined by the Takeuchi criteria, is a valid definition of death; (2) social consensus has been reached that brain death is death; (3) an organ transplantation program ought to be established; (4) donor intent is critical for the performance of organ transplants, and when donor intent is unclear, a third party will be appointed to insure that the family is not agreeing to donate organs because of undue pressure from medical professionals; (5) it is important to secure informed consent before a transplant is undertaken; (6) laws should be enacted making the buying and selling of organs illegal, establishing an organ network and donor cards, and legalizing organ transplants from brain dead donors; and (7) organ recipients must be selected systematically and fairly. The committee was aware that passing a transplant law would involve myriad difficulties, so as a temporary measure it declared that even in the absence of a law transplants legally could be performed.

The minority opinion contained a number of differences. It argued that the acceptance of brain death would necessitate a new way of understanding life and death and would lead to social and legal confusion. Further, it claimed that no social consensus was yet established. Still, the minority was willing to approve of organ transplants where the consent of a donor was clearly and openly determined. Despite these differences, there is a sense of inevitability that brain death will come to be recognized and transplants will become available, but no timetable can yet be predicted.

As the possibility of institutionalizing brain death and transplants increases, however, their potential economic costs remain largely ignored. Advocates of brain death never root their arguments in the notion that the cost of maintaining the lives of those who could be declared brain dead is unjustifiably high.[16] The Ad Hoc Committee referred to a cost-related problem in its final report by stating that a fair and just system of organ distribution should be established. But no details were included as to what sort of system that might be. Why costs are a neglected element of the brain death and transplant debate, and the possible content of future discussion related to cost, will be the focus of the final section of this analysis.

### The Costs and Benefits of Ignoring Costs

The potential economic sacrifices or benefits of a brain death definition and an active transplant program have received widespread attention in the Western literature.[17] They have received so much attention, in fact, that in the United States, discussion of the ethical, political, and economic aspects of transplantation are inexorably intertwined. While economic data varies, there is abundant evidence to suggest that "while the costs per life-year or quality-adjusted life-year saved by transplantation are quite high, they are within the range of other accepted medical interventions"(Krueger 1989, 12). As transplants become more widely available to patients who are considered eligible but are not "model" recipients, however, the ideal of equitable access is approached but cost-effectiveness decreases (Krueger 1989, 14). Those who are uninsured or lack financial means are unlikely to obtain treatment, whatever their medical need. A spokesman for the University of Pittsburgh transplant center recently commented in an article published by *The Japan Times:* "like most other transplant centers, [The University of Pittsburgh] will not put a patient on its waiting list until it knows how the operation will be paid for" (Rebecca Newman-Peddie, "Transplant Operations Costs Sky-High," 10 February 1992).

Whether Western-style cost-benefit analysis is relevant to the Japanese case is uncertain, given its system of health care financing and its particular culture of medical sociology (Johnson 1982; Ikegami 1991, 87–188; Powell and Anesaki 1990). Still, in one of the few articles to address costs, published in the *Asahi Shimbun,* 25 January 1992, a familiar debate surfaced as to whether a general fund to cover transplant costs should be created or whether individuals should pay for their own care. In addressing the financial aspects of such a dispute, it is unfortunate that health care policy makers have at their disposal only a single published study related to the economics of transplantation in Japan.[18]

Despite the lack of public discussion, one decision already has been made concerning government payment for transplants. Articles published in *The Daily Yomiuri,* 18 July 1992, and *the Mainichi Daily News,* 30 July 1992, reported the announcement by the Central Social Insurance Medical Council of the MHW that national health insurance would soon cover 70% of the cost of partial liver transplants from live adult donors to children, a procedure not dependent upon a brain dead donor. These operations were previously paid for through university research funds and private contributions. The ministry will recognize such transplants as "high-level advanced medical treatment" (*kōdo senshin iryō*), a system introduced in 1984 to pay for expensive care not included under insurance. Coverage will be provided only for the cost of examinations and hospitalization, not for surgical procedures, which account for approximately 2 to 3 million of an estimated bill of ¥10 million. As of May 1992, forty-eight children had undergone this procedure, a figure that now is expected to increase.

In general, though, there has been little discussion regarding the cost-effectiveness or public financing of transplants. Several possible reasons for this can be hypothesized. One is connected to the cultural explanations discussed above and can be illustrated by analogy to abortion in the United States. Both debates to some extent highlight the way people's current views of life and death are linked to traditional or religious ideas of personhood. The rhetoric and passion surrounding both controversies indicate that some individuals are fighting over basic values rather than scientific truths. Similarly, viewed together, both issues illustrate the intertwining of science with society, politics, and culture, the way in which contemporary medical developments can be transformed into prolonged and rancorous social debate, and how scientific "facts" can be interpreted in radically different ways in different places.[19]

From such a perspective, it seems natural that questions of cost and insurance coverage are absent from the Japanese transplant controversy. Just as the financial costs of performing abortions versus the costs associated with the births of un-wanted children are not a significant element of the abortion debate, so too are the costs of transplant-related expenses irrelevant in Japan. They are irrelevant be-cause of a shared but unarticulated understanding that money is less important than the basic values and beliefs that shape one's culture. Economic aspects of care are important but are secondary to the fundamental concerns that define a society.

While there is some truth to the assertion that the Japanese brain death/ transplant debate has a more explicitly cultural or religious flavor than that in the West, the contrast is not glaring. It has already been demonstrated that there is far more at play than culture in the Japanese controversy, and there are a multitude of examples of ethical and cultural issues that have surfaced in discussions of trans-plants in the West. But the reality of culture's influence is less important than the perception, however wrong, that it is the key to the Japanese debate. And it is the perception of the centrality of culture that links the issue of physician mistrust to the neglect of the financial costs of a transplant program.

Advocates of a brain death and transplant policy, particularly physicians, are concerned about public acceptance of their views and do not want to perpetuate the impression of transplant surgeons as self-interested, greedy, and dishonest. They understand that if they ignore popular concerns about brain death and organ transplantation and talk instead about financial costs and benefits, they may be perceived as being imperious and insensitive and increase public mistrust of the medical profession. They have therefore chosen to ignore cost issues and address the issues most frequently raised by their critics.

In this way, advocates of a new policy have been trapped by their opponents, who have focused the controversy on intractable cultural concepts and made consideration of more practical concerns appear crass. Physicians in particular were easily cornered, since they have little interest in or capacity for the details of economic analysis. Even if they wanted to discuss costs, how could professionals, scholars, or politicians talk about distributing organs and paying for operations when brain death is attacked as an anathema to two thousand years of Japanese life? It would be contrary to the interests of those desiring to establish a new policy to appear insensitive to the metaphysical aspects of the debate and talk only of currency and organization. Both opponents and advocates of transplantation, therefore, have neglected transplant costs and concentrated on cultural factors.

The Ad Hoc Committee, for example, met for two years and discussed a wide variety of issues, but it never came to the question of finances. Members of the committee of course thought about potential costs, and that costs were a problem ripe for discussion, but there was a tacit agreement within the committee that discussion of the fiscal aspects of brain death and transplantation would be inappropriate, meaning that the public would get an unfavorable and distasteful impression of the work of the committee if it were to discuss such issues.[20]

This raises a third explanation for ignoring the financial aspects of transplants in Japan—the consensus conundrum. There is an unarticulated but prevalent feeling that once consensus is reached about brain death being death and about the desirability of transplants, all other practical details will fall into place. This may in part reflect faith in the efficiency of Japanese bureaucrats and politicians, who manage to implement effective policy when strongly motivated to do so. It also indicates the relative lack of concern with health care costs in Japan as opposed to the United States. The roughly 6% of GNP going to pay for health care in Japan is dwarfed by the bill in the United States, and there is correspondingly less worry about paying for new medical technologies. Finally, it is facilitated by the negligible impact of the medical ethics community on health policy in Japan and by the community's inability to makes issues of equity part of the policy agenda.

In different ways but with similar effects, therefore, all three factors primarily responsible for the continuing controversy over brain death and transplants in Japan—culture, physician mistrust, and consensus—have worked to limit discussion of financial concerns.

## Conclusion

Almost twenty-five years after the tragic death and failed heart transplant in Hokkaido, ambiguity and indecision continue to characterize the brain death and organ transplantation controversy in Japan. While a change in the definition of death has gained currency among some, a sufficient number of journalists, philosophers, attorneys, and others have attacked the idea to successfully block reform. They have done so by claiming that Japanese culture is inherently incompatible with the idea of brain death, that public mistrust of physicians is rampant, and that any change in policy requires consensus. By raising questions about brain death and transplants that by their nature invite varied and incompatible responses, and by effectively creating an environment in which consensus became a necessary condition for policy change, opponents of reform have forced the debate into an intellectual gridlock.

Even if consensus were suddenly achieved, various problems would remain. Chief among them is the question of whether transplants are a desirable substitute for current forms of treatment with regard to financial costs. The dearth of research in that area would necessitate a rapid and thorough investigation of cost-effectiveness before any new polices were enacted. Closely related to bare financial calculations are whether transplants should be publicly financed and how organ recipients should be selected, both of which require fundamental decisions about the relative impact of moral and market forces on a transplant program. Important changes in the doctor-patient relationship will also be required if the informed consent requirements advocated by the Ad Hoc Committee are to be realized.

None of these concerns is likely to receive much attention in the near future due to the current emphasis on culture, mistrust, and consensus. Instead, they will come to the fore when it becomes politically feasible for a powerful core of policy makers to declare "consensus" and begin implementing a transplant program. Until then, Japan's brain death and transplant debate will follow a meandering course, simultaneously fostering discussion about the metaphysical meaning of life and death while engendering disagreement and hostility between interested parties.

NOTES

1. Prepared for the Center for Global Partnership project on "Explaining Japan's Low Cost Health Care System: Culture, System, Politics." This research was supported by the Japan-U.S. Educational Commission (Fulbright), the Social Science Research Council/ American Council of Learned Societies, and the Japan Society for the Promotion of Science. A more detailed discussion of some aspects of this paper appears in the *Journal of Technology Assessment in Health Care* 10.3 (1994): 447–63.

2. National distribution systems are critical because of the limited number of donors, the need to operate quickly when organs become available, and the complex medical factors involved in matching donor organs with potential recipients.

3. "An Act Relating to Cornea Transplantation," Act #64, 17 April 1957.

4. "Act Concerning the Transplants of Cornea and Kidney," Act #63, 1979.

5. Article 190 of the Japanese Penal Code.

6. This section relies on the excellent analysis provided in Yonemoto 1988.

7. Japanese criminal law provides that in particular situations individuals not directly injured may notify investigating officials that they would like a particular matter prosecuted. This first stage, the complaint, carries no official weight and ordinarily gives rise to an investigation of the alleged offense by the police or public prosecutor. After the investigation is conducted and the evidence evaluated, a decision is made as to whether a case will be prosecuted (Dando 1965, 95, 323).

Because the criminal code does not specify a time within which investigations must be completed, the complaints filed by the Patient Rights Conference can be indefinitely prolonged if the investigating officials say that the investigations are ongoing.

8. The group was called the "Study Group on the Wada Heart Transplant Indictment" and consisted of thirteen members, including two former MHW ministers, social critics, and physicians.

9. Makino v. The Red Cross Hospital, Nagoya District Court Judgment, 29 May 1989, 1325 *Hanji* 103.

10. The different traditions of gift giving in Japan and the West have been noted by numerous authors. In Japan, the exchange of gifts is highly ritualized, with both the giver and receiver generally aware of the necessity of an exchange, the value of the exchanged items, and the importance of maintaining balance in the relationship by neither receiving nor giving too much. See, for example, Benedict 1946, passim. Extrapolated, this could be understood as a barrier to both organ donation and acceptance since the donor (or at least the family) would expect a return gift and the receipient would feel a tremendous and unpayable debt for having received the organ.

However, this view ignores two significant facts. One is the chronic shortage of organs in the West, which is at least in part attributable to uneasiness over giving away pieces of one's body. The other is Japan's recent experience with bone marrow donation. In January 1992, the MHW began recruiting and registering donors for its Bone Marrow Transplant Promotion Organization. Within a year it had registered over fifteen thousand donors, and it hopes to register one hundred thousand within five years. This experience suggests that despite the physical discomfort and hospitalization required of marrow donors, people are willing to give, and the MHW clearly believes that there are ample willing recipients to justify the expense of the program ("Bone Marrow Bank Plans 1st Transplants," *Daily Yomiuri,* 13 December 1992, p. 2).

11. Also ignored by those claiming a critical link between Japanese culture and the brain death debate is the fact that in the United States as well there has been persistent diagreement about when death occurs, what life means, and whether brain death is an appropriate standard, indicating that American culture is also uncomfortable about defining death. See Morison 1971; Kass 1971.

12. The JEA criteria were: (1) a coma in which patients exhibit no reactions; (2) dilated pupils; (3) lack of spontaneous breathing; (4) a rapid drop in blood pressure, succeeded by continuous low blood pressure; (5) flat brain waves; and (6) a continuation of conditions 1–5 for six hours.

13. For a discussion of the difficulties encountered by the Science Council of Japan in reaching an opinion on brain death, see: "Brain Death = Human Death, Science Committee Decides," *Japan Times,* 26 February 1987, p. 2; Ikeda 1987, 135; private discussion with Toshitani Nobuyuki, Director, Institute of Social Science, University of Tokyo, 30 July 1991; Nihon Gakujyutsu Kaigi 1987; "Nōshi kenkai de funkyū tsuzukeru Gakujutsu Kaigi" (Complications continue over brain death position in Science Council of Japan), *Asahi Shimbun,* 1987; "Science Council Rejects Brain Death Report," *Japan Times,* 24 April 1987, p. 2.

14. Tachibana's numerous writings on brain death include *Nōshi* (Brain death) (Tokyo: Chūō Kōron Shupansha, 1986) and *NHK Speshiaru: Nōshi* (Tokyo: Nihon Hōsō Shupan Kyōkai, 1991).

15. Rinji Nōshi oyobi Zōki Ishoku Chōsakai Setchi Hō, Law Number 70, 8 December 1989. The Ad Hoc Committee had fifteen full members and five affiliated experts, including a number of prominent transplant surgeons, the head of the JFBA Human Rights and Medicine Committee, a scholar of the history of medicine, and a former president of Tokyo University, as well as a philosopher, a novelist, and other well-known figures.

16. This point was made by Hardacre 1991, 235.

17. Krueger (1989, 1–17) reviews eighteen such studies.

18. The one available study is Gen et. al. 1986, 269–78.

19. See Luker 1984 for an excellent discussion of the idea of "worldview" and its importance in understanding the abortion debate in the United States.

20. Personal and confidential communication with a member of the Ad Hoc Committee.

REFERENCES

Akatsu, Haruko. 1990. The heart, the gut, and brain death in Japan. *Hastings Center Report* (March/April).
Benedict Ruth. 1946. *The Chrysanthemum and the Sword.* New York: Houghton Mifflin.
Dando Shigemitsu. 1965. *Japanese criminal procedure,* translated by B. J. George. South Hackensack, NJ: Fred B. Rothman & Co.

Doerner, David L. 1977. Comparative analysis of life after death in folk Shinto and Christianity. *Japanese Journal of Religious Studies* 4.2–3 (June-September).

Fujimoto Teruo. 1969 Hoken shoken kara mita shin ishoku (Heart transplants from the perspective of autopsy). *Saishin igaku* (Modern medicine) (March).

Gen Ohi, et. al. 1986. Why are cadaveric renal transplants so hard to find in Japan? An analysis of economic and attitudinal aspects. *Health Policy* 6: 269–78.

Hardacre, Helen. 1991. Japan: The public sphere in a non-Western setting. In Robert Wuthnow, ed., *Between states and markets: The voluntary sector in comparative perspective*. Princeton, NJ: Princeton University Press.

Higuchi Norio. 1992. The patient's right to know of a cancer diagnosis: A comparison of Japanese paternalism and American self-determination. *Washburn Law Journal* 31.3.

Ikeda Daisake. 1987. Nōshi mondai ni kansuru ikkosatsu (Thoughts on the problems of brain death). *Tōyōgaku kenkyū* 26.2.

Ikegami Naoki. 1991. Japanese health care: Low costs through regulated fees. *Health Affairs* (Fall): 87–108.

Johnson, Chalmers. 1982. *MITI and the Japanese miracle*. Stanford: Stanford University Press.

Kass, Leon. 1971. Death as an event: A commentary on Robert Morison. *Science* 173.

Katō Ichirō. 1988. Nōshi mondai: Shakaiteki gōi wa shinkirō (Brain death: Social consensus is a mirage). *Bungei shunju* 4: 106–15.

Krueger, Hans. 1989. Economic analysis of solid organ transplantation: A review for policy makers. *Health Policy* 13: 1–17.

Lock, Margaret, and Christina Honde. 1990. Reaching consensus about death: Heart transplants and cultural identity in Japan. In G. Weisz, ed., *Social science perspectives on medical ethics*. Dortrecht: Kluewer.

Lukev, Kristin. 1984. *Abortion and the Politics of Motherhood*. Berkeley: University of California Press.

Ministry of Health and Welfare (MHW). 1985. Kōseishō kenkyūhan ni yoru nōshi no hantei kijun (Brain death determination criteria of the MHW's Research Group). 6 December.

———. 1992. Rinji nōshi oyobi zōki ishoku chōsakai, nōshi oyobi zōki ishoku ni kansuru jūyō jikō (Important items related to brain death and organ transplantation). 22 January.

Miyahara Mitsuo. 1969. Shinzō ishoku toki ni okeru seishi hantei (Determination of life and death at the time of heart transplants). *Naika,* Special issue, *Rinshōka no tame no seishi hantei* (For clinicians, determinations of life and death).

Morison, Robert. 1971. Death: Process or event? *Science* 173.

Nihon Bengoshi Rengokai. 1988. Nihon Ishikai Seimei Rinri Kondankai "nōshi oyobi zōki ishoku nitsuite no saishū hōkoku" ni taisuru ikenshō (Opinion paper of the Life Ethics Deliberative Council regarding the JMA's final report concerning brain death and organ transplantation). July.

Nihon Gakujyutsu Kaigi. 1987. Iryō gakujyutsu to ningen no seimei tokubetsu iinkai hōkoku nōshi ni kansuru kenkai (An interpretation of brain death). 23 October.

Nihon Ishikai Seimei Rinri Kondankai (JMA Life Ethics Deliberative Council). 1987. Nōshi oyobi zōki ishoku ni tsuite chūkan hōkoku. (Interim report concerning brain death and organ transplantation). 25 March.

———. 1988. Saishū hōkoku (Final report). 12 January.

Nudeshima Jiro. 1991a. *Nōshi/zōki ishoku to Nihon shakai* (Brain death/organ transplantation and Japanese society). Tokyo: Kobundo.

———. 1991b. Obstacles to brain death and organ transplantation in Japan. *Lancet* 338.

Ohnuki-Tierney, Emiko. 1984. *Illness and culture in contemporary Japan.* New York: Cambridge University Press.

———. 1986. Socio-cultural dimensions of renal transplants in Japan. *Health Policy* 6.

Powell, Margaret, and Masahira Anesaki. 1990. *Health care in Japan.* New York: Routledge.

Tachibana T. 1986. *Nōshi* (Brain death). Tokyo: Chūō Kōron Shuppansha.

———. 1991. *NHK speshiaru: Nōshi.* Tokyo: Nihon Hōsō Shuppan Kyōkai.

Umehara Takeshi. 1989. Gendaijin no sei to shi (The life and death of contemporary people). *This Is* 6.10 (October): 20.

Woss, Fleur. 1992. When blossoms fall: Japanese attitudes towards death and the otherworld: Opinion polls 1953–1987. In Roger Goodman and Kirsten Refsing, eds., *Ideology and practice in modern Japan,* 73–100. London: Routledge.

Yamauchi Masaya. 1990. Transplantation in Japan. *British Medical Journal* 301 (15 September).

Yonemoto Shohei. 1988. *Sentan kakumei iryō* (Advanced medical revolution). Tokyo: Chūō Kōron Shuppansha.

# CHAPTER 23

# Afterword: Social, Cultural, and Behavioral Factors

*Arnold J. Rosoff*

This section's chapters focus on various aspects of the cultural differences between Japan and the United States that account for the differences in health services organization and utilization, which account in turn for the differences in health care costs between the two nations. Akiyama, Campbell, and Lock offer insight into the ways in which the Japanese seek and use health care services. Feldman, summarizing and analyzing the contemporary evolution of Japanese policy on the determination of death and organ transplantation, illuminates key factors that facilitate or impede the development and adoption of new technologies.

Hiroko Akiyama reports an interesting and useful cross-national study and reveals a number of intriguing differences between the behavior of Japanese and American health care consumers. At bottom, her conclusions provide a simple but compelling endorsement of primary and preventive care as practiced in Japan. Although the data are initially puzzling and permit alternative explanations, it seems appropriate to conclude, as Akiyama does, that the Japanese recognize illness symptoms at about the same frequency and level of severity as do Americans, but they seek professional care at a notably earlier stage, when the symptoms are of low severity and when prophylactic or preventive measures can be undertaken at minimal inconvenience and expense. Thus, Japan's health care system costs less than that of the United States even though the number of doctor-patient encounters is far greater. Her analysis reinforces the conventional wisdom that a good primary care network, emphasizing prevention and early detection and treatment of illnesses, leads to avoidance of greater acute care costs and ultimately yields better health at lower cost.

That conventional wisdom, however, was challenged years ago in the United States by studies indicating that screening and earlier detection do not necessarily reduce overall health care costs; rather, they just recruit patients into the health care system at an earlier stage and set them up to generate higher levels of care and greater cost. That is because—as Akiyama points out with regard to the Japanese—both patient and provider behaviors are influenced by the economic incentives established by the applicable health insurance schemes. Once a person in the United States becomes identified as a patient, the system has tended, historically at least, to direct that patient toward high-tech, high-cost therapies, especially surgery. That this does not happen so much in Japan is a function not just of the way primary care services are provided, paid for, and used but also of the traditional Japanese cultural aversion to invasive therapies. Applying the lessons learned in the United States to Akiyama's description of the Japanese system suggests that Japan's health care costs may be lower not because of the greater propensity to use primary services but, rather, because of the lesser propensity to use higher-tech, higher-cost services.

The lesson for America, then, is that simply increasing access to and use of primary services may not be the answer to health cost concerns. It must be combined with changes in patient and provider attitudes and the financial and structural incentives that lead to greater use of secondary and tertiary services in the United States. Fortunately, such changes are underway, and all of the recently considered national health care reforms, regardless of their specifics, had this as an important goal.

Ruth Campbell adds importantly to our understanding of how the Japanese receive primary care services by describing and documenting the interaction between elderly patients and their physicians in a typical office visit. It is a very useful adjunct to Akiyama's macro-level description, particularly as it shows the specific benefits that may accrue to Japanese patients from their frequent, albeit quite brief, interactions with physicians.

An important contribution of Campbell's analysis is the counterpoint she provides to the common perception that Japanese patients often wait three hours for a three-minute office visit and that these visits are "often superficial . . . [and] the emphasis is on curative treatment rather than preventive care" (citing Yoshikawa, Shirouzo, and Holt 1991). In fact, waiting times at clinics nowadays are far shorter, probably averaging less than fifteen minutes, and Campbell's observations of an elderly patient population suggest that the visits are, on average, about five to six minutes long, and substantially longer, about twenty minutes, in the case of psychiatric visits. Moreover, she observed that although, on the surface, physician visits are focused more on curative matters than preventive, closer analysis suggests there is a strong preventive aspect. Since patients are seen often, they and their physicians spend more of the time than Americans do on assessing subtle changes in how the patients feel and function. Medications are more "fine-tuned" to a patient's particular situation, needs, and responses. The patient does much of the talking, and the physician gathers information about the patient's home and family situation and general mental state. Often nonmedical approaches are recommended, such as a visit to the *onsen* (baths), exercise, diet, and other lifestyle changes.

As Campbell explains, "Rather than seeing these visits as superficial and 'curative,' I began to see them as preventive medicine in that both physical and emotional issues could be discussed briefly because the patient knew this was not the only visit for three months and that every detail did not have to be divulged at this one visit." Note that the frequent visits allow the physician to establish and update a "baseline" for the patient, against which future changes can be compared.

The picture that emerges from Campbell's study is that of a close, personal relationship between doctor and patient, surprising given the occasionally long waiting times, waiting room scenes that resemble impersonal U.S. clinics and emergency departments, and the relatively short visit times. This is the kind of holistic approach that many in America have advocated for years but that our health insurance system traditionally has not facilitated. One would think that this style of medical interaction would be satisfying to people who have lived with it for so long. However, the Japanese increasingly complain about long waiting times and the brevity of the visits. Perhaps general changes in the nature and pace of their daily lives account for this evolving reaction. Oddly, despite the complaints, more and more Japanese are bypassing older, local physicians and going to large hospitals and clinics with longer waiting lines. Presumably they are seeking a higher technical quality of physician (or institution) rather than a higher level of personal interaction with the physician or greater convenience (shorter travel and waiting times). Where this trend may lead is difficult to say—as, of course, it is difficult to predict the future of Japanese health care in any dimension.

Whereas Akiyama and Campbell examine how some Japanese citizens contribute to good cost statistics by the way they use available health services, Margaret Lock explores how one group in Japanese society, middle-aged women (defined as those age forty-five to fifty-five), help the statistics by *not* using services, or, more precisely, by not using them with the same frequency and intensity as do other groups in Japanese society or their counterparts in North America. In making the latter comparisons, Lock relies on a survey she conducted in 1984 of some 1,300 Japanese women. It was designed to correlate with similar studies previously done of 2,500 women in Manitoba and 8,000 in Massachusetts. Her basic point is that middle-aged Japanese women subsidize their nation's health care system in two important ways: (1) they use less of the health care resource (as compared with other groups in Japanese society and with their counterparts in North America) and (2) they provide an important element of social support services to elderly Japanese, thus freeing the health care system of this burden and contributing to the overall "wellness" of the population. By making these contributions as a matter of course and as an accepted part of their societal role, these women are the unsung heroes of the Japanese health care system.

Supporting Lock's point is her analysis of how Japanese women, their physicians, and the society in general treat the important mid-life transition Americans call menopause and the Japanese call *kōnenki*. (Actually, the English word generally is used to refer more specifically to the physiologic changes that occur as a woman ends her child-bearing years, whereas the Japanese *kōnenki* generally refers more broadly to the overall transition, more akin to what Americans refer to as "change of life.") It is fascinating to contemplate, as Lock does, the various reasons why menopause has been so much more medicalized in America than in Japan, where it is regarded as a natural, evolutionary process.

First—and the reasons for this are intriguing in themselves—Japanese women appear to experience far fewer of the symptoms and discomforts traditionally associated in our culture with menopause: flushes or hot flashes, difficulty sleeping, night sweats, and so forth. They also experience less heart disease and osteoporosis. Are Japanese women physically different from North American women? Are they simply less disposed for some reason to notice, dwell upon, or complain about their discomforts?[1] Do their physicians not draw out their female patients on these subjects as much as their professional counterparts in North America do, perhaps because they are less interested in or less motivated toward treating menopausal symptoms? In addition to these possibilities, Lock suggests that national differences in diet may account for the differential behavior.

More revealing, perhaps, than the cross-national differences with regard to menopause are the differences regarding breast cancer. The public consciousness regarding breast cancer and the issue of public support for breast cancer screening and treatment are major social and political issues in the United States, but breast cancer is much less of a concern in Japan. Lock notes that 55% of middle-aged Japanese women have never had a breast examination by a physician, whereas that is true of only 6% of such women in Manitoba and 4% in Massachusetts. But this does not necessarily mean that the needs of Japanese women are being overlooked, at least not as much as the first glance would suggest. The fact is that mortality from breast cancer is more than three times greater in North America than in Japan. The obvious lesson is that differences in national approaches to health problems can sometimes be explained simply by differences in the incidence or severity of the problems.

Summarizing the above, Lock states that "a combination of biological, epidemiological, cultural, and social factors account for the low rate of medicalization of *kōnenki* to date, and, combined with the good health of most middle-aged Japanese women, [this] means that a rather small burden is placed on the health care system by this particular population." Although she does not directly mention the influence of the Japanese health insurance system, surely it plays its part as well. Whatever the reasons, Japan's health system is, for the present at least, spared the burdens of addressing these women's needs. The nation's health cost statistics look the better for it, and Lock implicitly suggests that middle-aged Japanese women should be appreciated for the contribution they make to the society's smoother, more cost-efficient functioning.

The reluctance of Japanese women to use health care services does not apply across the board, however. Lock notes that Japanese women use abortion services much more freely than their counterparts in North America (even though the overall rate of abortions per 1,000 women is lower in Japan and has been dropping since the 1960s, except for the under-twenty age group). In part, this is because low-dose oral contraceptives are not legal in Japan and high-dose contraceptives are generally used only to treat menstrual disorders. Lacking oral contraceptives, and desiring strongly to limit family size to two children, Japanese women have a high dependence on abortion as a birth control measure. The link between this and the lower level of medicalization of *kōnenki* is quite interesting. The limitation on the use of oral contraceptives is tied to Japanese concerns about the long-term use of hormone therapy, the therapy commonly employed in North America when menopause is treated as a medical condition. As changing birthing practices and the decline of the abortion rate take their toll on the incomes of Japanese gynecologists, some of them have begun to take more of an interest in the medical treatment of menopause. This will be an area to watch for signs of an interplay between social-cultural factors and health care system factors affecting what is regarded as a medical problem and how it is treated.

Eric Feldman offers a particularly interesting view, rich in analysis, into the factors influencing the structure and evolution of the Japanese health care system. One of his key contributions is the insight he offers into the role that consensus and Japanese culture in general play in the advancement of medical technology and the development of health care policy in Japan. More directly than anyone else, he addresses the actions and reactions of health care providers and also the process of health policy formulation.

As the basis for his analysis, Feldman relates the story of the 1968 Wada case, a dramatic event that significantly framed the debate in Japan about organ transplantation and the determination of death. While focusing primarily on the development of standards for recognizing brain death in the context of securing organs for transplantation, Feldman also illuminates Japanese views on the inter-relationship of body, mind, and soul, on the sanctity of the body and related attitudes toward the use of invasive therapies, and on the Japanese process of policy development. Understanding the Wada incident and its sequel gives extremely valuable insight into how Japanese health policy is developed on a much broader level.

One of his key lessons is that the traditional Japanese desire for consensus is extremely powerful and affects the nature and pace of health policy development both directly and indirectly. Moreover, insistence on consensus can be, and often is, employed as a strategy for fending off change. Those who opposed the spread of organ transplantation called not only for professional consensus before proceeding but also for public consensus, an element notably difficult to achieve and to document. The desire for advance public acceptance of any change in medical standards and practice was intertwined with physicians' concerns that the profession might be seen as "self-interested, greedy, and dishonest" if they moved too rapidly in adopting the new technology. This concern with public acceptance of physicians' motives prompted advocates of transplantation to avoid discussing the critical subject of the economics of transplantation[2]—a subject they may not have been particularly disposed to address anyway[3]—and allowed opponents to focus the debate largely on the ways in which transplantation clashes with traditional Japanese beliefs. In this way, both advocates and opponents of transplantation neglected economic and practical factors and concentrated instead on cultural factors. Overall, Feldman's point is that "all three factors primarily responsible for the continuing controversy over brain death and transplants in Japan—culture, physician mistrust, and consensus—have worked to limit discussion of financial concerns." This is typical of how health policy, especially consideration of the appropriate pace of and limits upon the adoption of new technologies, has developed with what to Americans would seem a surprising lack of consideration of economic factors. These are important and far-reaching lessons for anyone seeking to understand the past and/or predict the future course of Japan's health care system.

For all its emphasis on the Japanese fetish for consensus, Feldman's story of the debates about organ transplantation and the criteria for determination of death shows signs that powerful, inexorable change is taking place. Japan is a nation very much in transition. Even as some elements of society cling to the past or present, others are pushing aggressively toward the future. One should never speak about contemporary Japanese public opinion and beliefs without recognizing the likelihood of broad differences between the older and younger members of the society. There is a real generation gap that pervades all dimensions of social thought and action. Even within age cohorts there are significant differences of view, reflecting, in a culture known for its homogeneity, differences between groups such as rural and urban, and commonly educated and highly educated. Japan is a country that has been in major societal transition for almost fifty years, and the conflicts between traditional and modern ideas and values are perhaps nowhere in the world more fully developed and more striking.

Returning to Feldman's point about the paucity of discussion regarding the cost-effectiveness or public financing of transplants, he notes,

> The rhetoric and passion surrounding both controversies indicates that some individuals are fighting over basic values rather than scientific truths. Similarly, viewed together both issues illustrate the intertwining of science with society, politics, and culture, the way in which contemporary medical developments can be transformed into prolonged and rancorous social debate, and how scientific "facts" can be interpreted in radically different ways in different places.

My own observations about the challenges of comparing the Japanese health system to that of the United States show that, despite increasing similarities, the two nations are still quite different. The Japanese are more sensitized to what is going on with their bodies; their sense of body awareness is highly developed. Thus, they favor health care approaches that "fine-tune" and help to maintain the delicate *yin-yang* balance. Their tradition of herbal medicine reflects and in part probably helps to explain this. Moreover, the cultural penchant for returning frequently to the doctor for prescriptions and persistent tinkering with the medication regimen is reinforced by the delivery system's structure as well as by the economic incentives that the national health insurance system places on the medical profession. It is not surprising that a social welfare system should reflect the values and predilections of the people it was designed to serve.

Another reason why it is so difficult to draw definitive conclusions from comparisons of the two systems is that so many things are changing in Japan: culture, diet, the pervasiveness and pace of urban life, employment patterns (including gender shifts), economic standards, demographics in general, and so on. The irony is that the very changes that frustrate comparison are what make it so interesting and important. The Japanese are concerned that as their society changes—and, in many cases, this means as it becomes more Western—the relative stability of their health care system may be eroded. They fear they will face the kinds of problems that plague the U.S. health care system, and they hope to avoid going down the same troubled path that we have trod. Perhaps they can, but as their society becomes more like ours, that is by no means assured.

That Japan may be following the path of the United States is signaled by apparent changes in what many Japanese want, expect, and demand from their health care providers. A key measure of a health care system's success that has traditionally worked in Japan's favor has been the level of satisfaction of its users. For years, studies showed the satisfaction of the Japanese public with their health care system to be very high relative to that of U.S. citizens. In recent years, there have been increasing indications that this may be changing. Waiting times for doctors' appointments that used to be taken for granted are now reported as a source of distress by a growing number. The physician's historical reticence about sharing information with patients is also increasingly unpopular. This is reflected in the popular press and in the growth of organizations that seek to promote patients' rights, including the American-born doctrine of "informed consent." For the last five or so years, a consistently popular seller has been a book that lists prescription drugs by lot number and allows Japanese patients to cross-check the drugs their doctors give them against the list, identify the drugs they are taking, and infer from that what their condition is. This is but one of many signs that many Japanese want to know more and take their medical destiny more in their own hands.

In sum, the ultimate challenge of cross-national comparison is that people can at the same time be so different and so alike, committed to their differences and yet moving closer all the time. In no context is this phenomenon more compelling than in comparing the health care systems of Japan and the United States.

NOTES

1. It is interesting to note that, as Lock points out, although the Japanese public perception is that spoiled, middle-aged women are the ones who complain about *kōnenki,* the data suggest that working-class women experience, or at least report, more menopause-related symptoms.

2. For example, the relative cost-effectiveness of kidney transplantation as opposed to long-term dialysis.

3. Feldman notes that Japanese physicians have little interest in or capacity for the details of economic analysis.

CHAPTER 24

# The Egalitarian Health Insurance System

*John Creighton Campbell*

SUMMARY    Although the Japanese health insurance system is fragmented, coverage is quite egalitarian in terms of burdens as well as benefits. This outcome is accomplished through an intricate set of cross-subsidization mechanisms, developed over the years as ways to resolve conflicts among social groups. Those who are disadvantaged by paying much more than they get back are consoled by receiving marginally higher benefits, so equity concerns do not lead to divisive politics.

## Background

Health care in Japan is financed by numerous insurance organizations that are formally independent. Government regulations are so pervasive, however, that these organizations really have very little scope for autonomous decisions on important issues.[1] That means it is possible to provide health care according to some overall notion of "fairness."

The fundamental problem here is that it is difficult to be "fair" about providing medical services because the people who need the most care are often the people who are least able to pay for it. The elderly are the obvious case: in Japan as in the United States, older people consume many times more medical care than the average, but their incomes tend to be fixed and to be too low to afford high insurance premiums. At the other extreme, current employees of large organizations, public or private, are likely to be more healthy and wealthy than the average.

This fact makes for deep conflicts of interest among social groups or, in a different sense, between two concepts of "fairness." One is fairness as equity: cost should be related to benefits, so that the premiums charged should be lower for the individual or group that is less likely to become ill. People who exercise and do not smoke should not have to subsidize those who lead riskier lives. The other concept is fairness as equality: everyone should be treated the same and, in particular, should have equal entitlement to health care.

The system that maximizes fairness in the first sense is straight free-market medicine without insurance, or its close relative, the individual or small-group policy with "experience-rated" premiums. Such a system could be run with minimum government intervention into health insurance itself, although inevitably large numbers of people will not be covered.

The system that maximizes fairness in the second sense is a tax-based health care system, based on the socialist principle that each should pay according to means (through progressive taxation) and should receive according to needs (unlimited free medical care). Here, clearly, strong government compulsion is needed to prevent the healthier and wealthier people, who will feel themselves "unfairly" treated in the first sense, from simply dropping out.

If a group of people or a nation would pick one or the other of these conflicting notions of fairness, it would be easy enough to devise a health care system to match. The problem is that most people believe in both concepts simultaneously. The Japanese in particular have not been attracted to a tax-based system, and in fact their health insurance system is fragmented into many small pools, so that an individual's premiums do in some sense pay for his or her own health care. Nonetheless, the Japanese health insurance system is extremely egalitarian.

**Egalitarian Mechanisms**

Of course, the most basic sense in which the Japanese system is fair is that all health insurance, by law, covers virtually the same list of products and services, and the reimbursement is the same for all providers and all patients. Patients can choose the provider they want, and providers have no reason to discriminate among patients—a truly egalitarian system in terms of benefits.

But if benefits are more-or-less equal, what about burdens? Less healthy people are bound to consume more care, and less wealthy people cannot pay as much. Assuming that these characteristics vary together, if they are unevenly distributed across health insurance pools, some pools should be in very comfortable circumstances and some in dire straits.

In fact, these characteristics do vary quite systematically across Japanese health insurance pools. A simplified picture, ignoring some smaller categories and many administrative details, would include seven separate groupings:[2]

1. Government or quasi-public employees, relatively young and well paid, in several large nationwide Mutual Assistance Associations (MAA).
2. Employees of large firms, also relatively young and well paid, in hundreds of insurance "Societies" at the company level.
3. Employees of small firms, not so young and not so well paid, in a single nationwide Government-Managed Health Insurance pool.
4. The self- or non-employed, including farmers and small shopkeepers, who with exceptions tend to be considerably older and with lower incomes, in Citizens Health Insurance (formally but misleadingly called National Health Insurance) pools in each locality.
5. Retired people not yet 70, who are given a special status within Citizens Health Insurance.

6. The elderly over 70, who are members of the other insurance pools but have their own special financing system.
7. The poor, those on public assistance (most often for reasons of mental health).

It will be easily appreciated that need rises and ability to pay diminishes as one descends this ladder of social groups.

Three egalitarian policies counteract these inequalities. First, Japan like most other industrialized nations collects health insurance premiums as a percentage of wages (up to a ceiling). Even Citizens Health Insurance, where most enrollees do not receive wages, bases its premiums on a combination of income and assets. Within each pool, therefore, the burdens of health insurance are adjusted by the ability to pay.

However, while proportional (or better yet, progressive) financing can equalize burdens in this sense across entire provincial populations in a single-payer system like that in Canada, more complicated mechanisms are necessary where there are many insurers, as in Japan. The Japanese approach is to employ two types of cross-subsidization: subsidies from general revenues, and direct transfers between insurers. Both mechanisms are illustrated in figure 1, which includes all these groups except the poor (whose financing does not come from social insurance).

The four groups on the top are the pools for public, large-firm, and small-firm employees, and the self-employed. The upper bar is revenues, with the left-hand portion representing income from premiums (shared between employee and employer for MAA, society and government-managed health insurance). The right-hand portion represents the portion covered by government subsidy from general tax revenues. This amounts only to administrative costs (about 2%) for the MAA and society pools, which comes to 14% for government-managed health insurance, and 50% for Citizens Health Insurance (here the government in effect picks up the employer's portion).

Note that for the old-age group (below left), 30% of revenues comes from the government (20% national, 5% each prefectural and municipal). If the poor were included on this chart, 100% of their medical care would be paid from general revenues.

The lower bar for each of the four groups on the top shows the direct transfer payments into the old-age system and, for the three employment-related systems, into the system for younger retirees as well.[3] This transfer amounts to a substantial sum: over ¥4.3 trillion or $24 billion (at our approximate purchasing power parity [PPP] rate of $1.00 = ¥180). For large firms and their employees, well over a trillion yen ($5.6 billion) or 28% of premiums are transferred out to subsidize the retired and elderly—even not counting the portion of the taxes they pay that goes to this purpose.

The result of these two forms of subsidy is a pattern of great variation in how much health insurance participants get for what they pay. Specifically, using 1991 figures, large-firm employees got back ¥62 in health care benefits for every ¥100

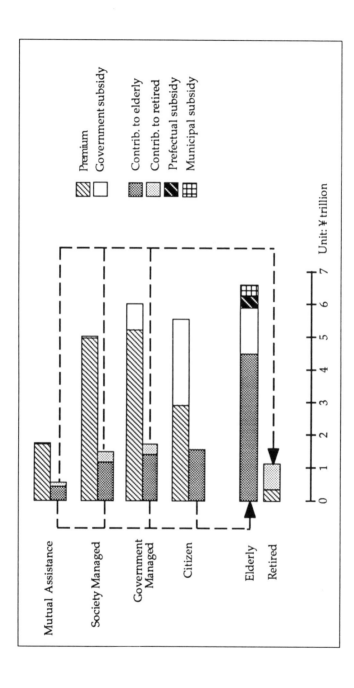

**Figure 1. Cross subsidization in health insurance, 1991. (From Social Development Research Institute: *The Cost of Social Security in Japan, FY 1991*.) (Note: For the four health insurance programs, revenues are the upper bars and expenditures on subsidies are the lower bars. The bars for the elderly and the retired are total revenues.)**

they pay in premiums (including the employer share of premiums). Small-firm employees in government-managed health insurance got back ¥84 for each ¥100 of contributions. The self- or non-employed, on the other hand, on average received ¥166 in health care benefits for every ¥100 yen of contributions.[4] This ratio cannot be calculated for the retired and elderly groups for technical reasons, but obviously they receive far more in benefits than they pay in premiums. The poor get everything for nothing.

### Minimizing Equity Protests

This pattern clearly is very fair in the sense of promoting equality—the healthy and wealthy subsidize the poor and sick. One would expect, however, that those who are paying much higher premiums than they receive in benefits would feel exploited by the system. They would believe that fairness in the sense of equity had been violated, and that others were benefitting unjustly. That should make for difficult politics.

However, the perception among Japanese is exactly the opposite. Large-firm or public employees are always seen as the most advantaged, as getting the best deal, while the self- or non-employed covered by Citizens Health Insurance are regarded as receiving poorer benefits. The main reason is that the amount of the copayment is different.

That is, regular enrollees in Citizens Health Insurance pay 30% of their medical bills directly to the doctor or hospital. Those in employment-related health insurance pay only 10% for themselves, and 20% (inpatient) or 30% (outpatient) for their dependents. Moreover, large-firm employees often have an additional benefit compared with small-firm employees in that their societies are often rich enough to cover the copayment and to provide free or subsidized health examinations (which are not covered by health insurance).[5]

It should be noted that while these differentials are real, the degree of difference in burdens is substantially mitigated by two facts. First, medical fees in Japan are quite low compared with those in the United States, so that the difference between a 10% and 30% copayment for an average doctor visit (including prescriptions and so forth) would only be about ¥900 ($5.00).[6] Second, Japan has "catastrophic" coverage, or a cap on monthly out-of-pocket spending—any copayments over ¥57,000 per month (roughly $320) are covered for members of all health insurance systems.

Because the differences in copayment and extra benefits are visible but the differential ratios of premiums to medical benefits are rarely mentioned, people naturally view large-firm employees (and government employees, who are similarly treated) as the best off. At least that is the assumption in public discourse, and when proposals are made to make the system more fair, the usual suggestion is to equalize the copayments. An official policy goal of the MHW is to have all copayments set at 20%. We might imagine, however, that the actual differences in costs and benefits are sufficiently known, or at least suspected, to mitigate feelings of unfairness on equality grounds.

One is reminded, in fact, of what is often cited as a key to political support for social security pensions in the United States: the premium or social security tax is regressive, favoring upper-income people, while the benefits are progressive, favoring lower-income people. It is difficult for participants to judge whether they are being exploited or are exploiting others. In short, a degree of confusion caused by cross-cutting principles and interests can be very helpful in maintaining support or, at least, inhibiting protest and opposition.

## Evolution

This is not to say that this system has been free of conflict. Quite the contrary: when we look at how the health insurance system developed in Japan, it is clear that, first, various social groups attained their degree of relative equality largely as the result of a political struggle and, second, that resentments about fairness as well as practical problems have led to many marginal adjustments in relative burdens.

Without treating the historical evolution of health insurance in any detail, it may be observed that, as in other countries, Japan started by covering government employees (including the military) and then provided health care to large-company employees in the prewar period (figure 2). In fact, there were steps toward a universal system even before the war, but this goal was not attained until competition between the newly formed Socialist and Liberal Democratic Parties expanded the Citizens Health Insurance system in 1959. At the start, however, the self-employed in this system had a 50% copayment, without a "catastrophic" spending cap, so their financial burdens were considerably higher than those of company employees (who at this time had a zero copayment).

This inequality was substantially redressed in the early 1970s, another period of intense political party competition, when the largest copayments were reduced to 30% and the catastrophic cap was introduced. More dramatically, "free" medical care for the elderly—coverage from general revenues of the entire copayment for most people seventy and over, and the bedridden sixty-five and over—was established by the national government in 1972. The cause was initiation of a similar program three years earlier by the progressive Minobe administration in the Tokyo Metropolitan Government, which had led to an intense campaign at the national level. Since it was clear that many older people had been prevented from seeking medical care because of its cost, this new program was a major step toward equality.

These reforms of the early 1970s marked the high point of the first form of cross-subsidization, in which the general population paid various proportions of the health care costs of needier people by means of direct payments from tax revenues. Most expensive was the subsidy for old-age medical care, which had more than doubled in the second half of the 1970s to reach nearly one trillion yen in 1980. Providing "free" medical care for the elderly became the most visible symbol for conservatives of public spending going out of control.

It was inevitable, then, that health care in general and the program for the

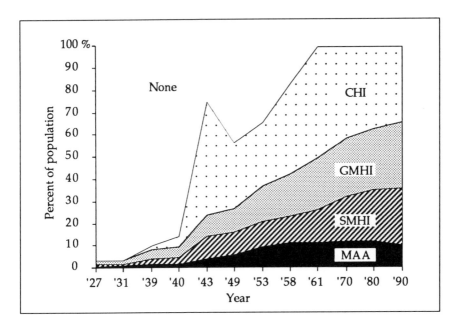

**Figure 2. Health insurance coverage, 1927–90. (From Yasuo Takagi (1994): "Kokumin kenkō hoken to chiikifukushi—Chōki nyūin no zehi to kokuho anteika taisaku no jissai to mondaiten" [The Citizens Health Insurance and the welfare in the local community—Issues of reducing the length of stay in hospitals and of strengthening the financial situation of the NHI], *Kikan Shakai Hoshō Kenkyū* 30(3):239.) (Note: Data for the wartime period are approximate.)**

elderly in particular would become targets of the "administrative reform" austerity campaign that got underway in the early 1980s. The Health Care for the Elderly Law passed in 1982 was one of the early important steps in this campaign. The interesting point is that its most significant provision was not a major cutback in expenditures but rather a new form of cross-subsidization.

That is, the old-age health care program that was created then provided that the most expensive health care would mainly be covered by direct transfer payments from employment-related insurance rather than from general revenues. The fact that society-managed health insurance for the (relatively young) employees of large firms was running large surpluses at the time made it an irresistible target. Each society contributed the amount it would pay as if it had an average number of elderly members, so it could take its fair share of supporting the increased burden of old-age health care.

It is common enough in austerity campaigns to cut government expenditures by transferring costs to consumers; increasing premiums and copayments for Medicare in the United States is an example. Such reforms make the system less egalitarian (though perhaps more equitable) because burdens tend to be increased for those with the lowest incomes and the greatest need for care, so that the burdens on the general population can be limited.

In Japan, however, this old-age health care reform, as well as the somewhat similar program for retirees created in 1985, actually made the system more egalitarian. The tax burden on the general population was lightened, but the costs were transferred not back to the elderly, but to the group that was the most healthy and wealthy, the employees of large firms.

Oddly enough, an aspect of the Health Care for the Elderly Law of 1982 that in financial terms seems a backward step away from equality, actually might be seen as a forward step in symbolic terms. This was the abandonment of "free" medical care by establishing a copayment.

The fact that elderly people had been getting health care "for free" (*tada*) and also seemed to be overusing facilities was widely resented. The elderly were seen as having unfair advantages that were not shared with the rest of the population. Introducing a copayment seemed to redress the balance, even though it was almost trivially small—initially ¥300 per day in the hospital and ¥400 per month per provider for outpatient care. (Even today both copayments are under ¥1,000, no more than a few dollars.)

Such changes, and the introduction in 1985 of a 10% copayment for employees who hitherto had been getting free care, were incremental adjustments in the balance of costs and benefits, real or symbolic, in response to perceptions of unfairness as well as to immediate financial problems. In another such move, more recently the government marginally increased its general revenue contribution to old-age health care, to provide a measure of relief for the health insurance societies, many of which were now in the red because of increased transfers.

In short, the cross-subsidization system is complicated enough and flexible enough to allow adjustments in response to immediate problems of financing or of fairness—whether equality or equity. Grievances can be assuaged without major changes in the entire system.

The key to making this system work, however, is not some Japanese willingness to cooperate, nor the political skills of MHW bureaucrats, although both characteristics are helpful. Most important is that the system is fundamentally fair. Equality is primary, and today it is accepted as natural that all Japanese are entitled to roughly the same health care at equivalent cost. Equity is secondary; to some extent the lack of strong feelings of being exploited can be attributed to clever packaging, but those who contribute more do get marginally better treatment and have no reason for severe dissatisfaction. If the allocation somehow seems to be getting unfair, appropriate adjustments can be made on an ad hoc basis.

**Lessons for Americans**

It is unlikely that the United States will move to a single-payer system. It is also unlikely that health care needs and ability to pay can be evenly distributed across insurance pools, particularly if large firms continue to self-insure their own employees. If extreme inequality of burdens is to be avoided, therefore, some form of cross-subsidization across groups will be required.

The Japanese approach is an attractive alternative to the ideas advanced by American experts. It can be summarized as follows:

1. Contributions that are proportional to income help ensure equality within insurance pools. Catastrophic coverage with a low ceiling helps ensure equality across all individuals and households in the nation.
2. Subsidies go to insurance pools, not to individual participants. Both direct subsidies from tax revenues and transfers between richer and poorer pools are provided; the formulas are renegotiated periodically to provide flexibility.
3. The complexity of the subsidization and the fact that participants in the richer pools receive marginally better benefits help obscure the inevitable "unfairness" in equity terms—better-off participants do not complain much about bearing the heavier burdens.

At a more specific level, it might also be noted that a single national pool for small business employees—or in the American context, perhaps one pool for all small business employees in each state—offers a better solution for subsidizing health insurance for this difficult population than a sliding scale based on employer characteristics.

Finally, most generally, the entire Japanese approach is based on underlying egalitarian values that up until now have not been very evident in health care in the United States. Whether a system based on such values could survive in American politics is certainly problematical.

NOTES

1. The main exceptions are that health insurance societies in large firms and Citizens Health Insurance pools run by local governments can set their own contribution rates and that the former will often spend "excess" revenues on covering the patient copayment or such services as subsidized annual physicals.

2. Groups not included in this list include seamen, with a separate employment-related system; day-laborers, with a different financing system under Government-Managed Health Insurance; and low-income households not receiving public assistance, who are granted lower premiums, copayments, and "catastrophic" ceilings under Citizens Health Insurance.

3. These retirees all belong to Citizens Health Insurance, so it has no transfer payment to this group. A health insurance society has the option of keeping its own retirees until they are seventy and thereby avoiding this subsidy.

4. Calculated from table 16-4-1 in Kōseishō Hokenkyoku Chōsaka 1991, 238. The ratio is the outlays for medical care (*hoken kyūfuhi*) divided by the income from contributions, times 100.

5. Note that ¥534 hundred billion ($3 billion) or 14% of total revenues for the health insurance societies went to "other expenditures," including such extra benefits as well as investment in various facilities and so forth. Kōseishō Hokenkyoku Chōsaka 1991.

6. The average outpatient visit cost (i.e., per day) for 1988 in government-managed health insurance was ¥4,511, which is $35 at the contemporary $1 = ¥128 exchange rate, or about $22 at the PPP rate. Table 16-6-6 in Kōseishō Hokenkyoku Chōsaka 1991, 250.

REFERENCES

Kōseishō Hokenkyoku Chōsaka, ed. 1991. *Iryōhi handobukku.* Tokyo: Hōken.
Shakai Hoshō Seido Shingikai Jimukyoku, ed. 1991. *Shakai hoshō tōkei nenpō.* Tokyo: Hōken.

CHAPTER 25

# The Evolution of Fee-Schedule Politics in Japan

*Mikitaka Masuyama and*
*John Creighton Campbell*

SUMMARY    Determination of the fee schedule is a political negotiation between payers and providers. The Ministry of Health and Welfare (MHW) Health Insurance Bureau (HIB) plays three roles: as a major payer, as the process manager, and as a policy maker with its own goals. Periods of relative equilibrium have been punctuated by intense struggles in the past, but for more than a decade the system has been quite stable and oriented toward cost control. The long battle between the government and the Japan Medical Association (JMA) has been routinized to mutual benefit.

## Introduction

The primary mechanism for controlling health care costs in Japan, as in Germany and other countries, is the fee schedule. A single fee schedule essentially applies to all physicians and hospitals in Japan. Balance-billing is prohibited; that is, no more (or less) than the prescribed fees can be charged. Nearly all medical goods and services are covered.[1] Having a mandatory fee schedule does not automatically hold costs down, and indeed in the 1970s health care spending in Japan grew rapidly, at about the same pace as in the United States. However, when the government made its mind up to hold down spending in the early 1980s, it was the fee schedule that provided the means.

Devising and maintaining a fee schedule are challenging tasks for government. The "correct" fees for each of thousands of items must be calculated, and then must be adjusted periodically to reflect economic and technological changes and, perhaps, new policies. It is a daunting intellectual enterprise. And given that powerful actors somehow have to be brought to agreement, it can be an even more difficult political enterprise.

### The Politics of Health Care Provision

The evolution of Japan's health care system can be seen as a long struggle among powerful institutions with conflicting interests. A complete tabulation of all the battles would probably show that any one of these institutions had fought with any other at some time over some issue. Without too much simplification, however, we can see the principle conflict as between two coalitions, payers and providers, over the fundamental issues of money and control.

## The Payers' Side

It is of course the Japanese people who pay for health care, as consumers, tax-payers, employees, and employers. Because Japan's health finance system is pluralistic, the people have a variety of representatives. Labor unions and Nik-keiren, the Federation of Employer Associations, are uneasy bedfellows as the chief constituents of Kenporen, the Federation of Health Insurance Societies, which provides health insurance at large firms. Small-firm employees are repre-sented by the HIB of the MHW, in charge of Government-Managed Health Insur-ance. Local governments are the insurers for the self- and non-employed under Citizens Health Insurance. Since a substantial portion of health benefits is paid directly from tax revenues, the Budget Bureau of the Ministry of Finance (MOF) is an active player on the payers' side.

All these payers differ among themselves about how the burden of medical expenses should be shared. Fights have erupted again and again over the extent of cross-subsidization from wealthy to hard-pressed systems and the amount of the treasury subsidy. However, all payers share an interest in keeping costs as low as possible. Their primary goal is to minimize fee hikes in the regular negotiations over the schedule, but they also try to control providers' behavior more directly, such as by attempting to prevent waste and fraud through payment reviews.

Leadership in this payers' coalition is taken by the MHW, which plays three roles. First, as noted, its HIB is itself a payer for the Government-Managed Health Insurance system: if that plan's costs go up, the bureau must raise more funds by increasing contribution rates or by appealing to the Budget Bureau—neither is an appealing prospect. The HIB has therefore always been concerned about costs. Second, as the organization with administrative responsibility for the system as a whole, it must manage the decision-making process well enough to avoid break-downs. In this role it must mediate between providers and the other payers.

Third, the ministry has its own ideas—perhaps its own ideology—about how health care should be provided. The traditional thinking of Japanese health officials (particularly those outside the HIB, associated with the bureaus now called Health Policy and Health Services) could be positively characterized as a public-health vision, or more negatively as paternalistic bureaucratism. These officials have long believed in a rational, efficient system of health care delivery centered on large public hospitals and salaried doctors, with an important role for local public-health centers or government-run clinics for primary care. Many have idealized the British National Health Service, with per-capita payments for outpa-tient care, direct budgeting for hospitals, and a good deal of bureaucratic policy making and special programs to meet specific medical needs.

As might be expected, these three roles can get in each other's way. In particular, the HIB's cost-cutting mission has been hampered by the policy agenda of other bureaus. The ministry therefore is not a truly credible arbitrator or broker of conflicting interests. One could argue, however, that the ministry's responsibility as a direct payer has kept its officials very practical minded and aware of grassroots problems. In any case, the MHW and particularly its HIB have long been, along with the JMA, the most active movers and shakers in the health care arena.

### The Providers' Side

Organizationally, medical care is delivered by private-practice physicians, by small privately owned hospitals, by a variety of large hospitals (including those operated by universities and by local and national governments), and by public health agencies. Less directly, one can consider drug and medical-equipment manufacturers, pharmacies, nursing homes, and others as providers. In terms of individuals, there are general practitioners, specialized physicians of various sorts, dentists, pharmacists, nurses, other medical personnel, and some public or private administrators (although in nothing like the numbers in the United States).

As with the payers, the interests of providers diverge in some areas and are shared in others. All would like to see more resources going into medical care, and most would like to keep the payers from interfering in how they do business. Their differences are about money and power among themselves. But while the payers got into frequent and relatively open skirmishes in working out their differences, battles among the various types of providers have been furtive and usually localized. The reason is that the private-practice general practitioners dominated the rest.[2]

That is, control of the JMA was closely held by private-practice physicians, and other practitioner groups were either subordinated to the JMA or excluded from much influence over health care policy, at least with regard to the fee schedule. The negotiating arena for the fee schedule is the Central Social Insurance Medical Care Council (Chūikyō; henceforth Central Council); to the extent it represents hospitals and specialists at all, it is through members named by the JMA. Dentists and pharmacists are directly represented but carry little weight beyond their own specialized concerns; other interested parties such as nurses and drug or equipment manufacturers play no role.

The privileged position of private practitioners stems from history—less a matter of their own power than the weakness of the hospitals and specialists that were such strong competitors in other nations. It is somewhat mysterious how they have stayed on top so long, but a large part of the answer is politics. For one thing, the JMA at the national and local level maintained close ties with the ruling Liberal Democratic Party (LDP) and was usually its largest single contributor of campaign funds. This relationship was carefully cultivated by the JMA's famous president from 1957 to 1982, Tarō Takemi, the exemplar of the pressure-group "emperor." Moreover, Takemi was just as skillful in insider politics among health care providers as he was in the national arena.

The ideology and rhetoric of Japanese doctors, like that of doctors elsewhere, stem from ideals of professional autonomy. In practical affairs, doctors as individuals behave much like small businessmen, and when organized much like a labor union.

### Confrontation?

As in other nations, then, the Japanese health care arena actually is crosscut by complicated conflicts among many important actors, but it is often perceived by citizens, journalists, and even the participants themselves as a simple battle between payers and providers, or more simply still, between the MHW and the JMA. The many highly publicized bouts between these two champions over the decades look like one round after another in an all-out war between incompatible enemies.

That is, to government officials, Takemi and the private practitioners who dominated the JMA looked like unscrupulous medical entrepreneurs, seeking maximum freedom to overtreat and overmedicate to maximize their incomes. To the JMA, the MHW represented "totalitarian administration," with no interest in good medical care, much less in professional values.

This confrontational rhetoric sounds like the language used by a radical union and autocratic bosses in a company, and in fact the relationship between doctors and the government most closely resembles labor-management relations. Despite the extreme language, both sides know they fundamentally depend on each other and so will ultimately make a deal. The real fight is therefore over the terms of the deal—the price at which the doctors will provide services and the amount of control government will exert over how they do their jobs. In general, the side that is most powerful at the time will get the better end of the bargain.

What determines power? Much the same factors in the doctor-government relationship as in a typical labor-management relationship: Is the supply of doctors or the supply of money plentiful or scarce? How unified and determined is either side and how skillful at strategy and tactics? How far are their allies willing to go? Which side is favored by public opinion?

These factors tend to be fairly stable over time, so as a practical matter, the entire deal is not on the table in every negotiation. Fundamental changes in the relationship therefore occur rather rarely; most negotiations are governed by a set of rules and precedents that encourage only marginal changes. Those rules and precedents amount to an institutionalized routine, with substantial inertia. They will change only in response to a major shift in the power balance between the two sides or some jarring event in the environment—or perhaps to both in combination.

In other words, the two sides in such relationships (labor-management, or doctor-government) will appear to be in equilibrium for long stretches of time, but that equilibrium will shift (or be "punctuated") on occasion.[3] We can observe two such periods of equilibrium in the recent history of Japanese medical care: roughly speaking, the years in the 1970s when the fee schedule was indexed to inflation, which favored the doctors, and the period since 1981, when the government has had the upper hand and spending has been constrained. These two periods of equilibrium were preceded by more than a decade of open conflict as the two sides felt each other out.

## Evolution

The doctors and the government have been involved with each other for many years. Japan's first fee schedule was implemented in 1927. However, a truly national system did not become possible until 1958, when "health insurance for all" (*kaihoken*) was enacted. Coincidentally, it was in the previous year that Tarō Takemi, the master strategist, had become president of the JMA.

"Health insurance for all," which meant extending mandatory coverage to nonemployees such as farmers, was essentially a political initiative, pushed by the newly amalgamated LDP as a response to electoral gains by socialists in rural areas. However, it was a policy change on which the HIB and the JMA mostly agreed, for two reasons.

First, the expansion of the medical system—more patients and more resources—clearly benefited both sides. Second, because all patients in Japan would now be covered by social insurance, the system as a whole could be rationalized through the fee schedule. In particular, until "health insurance for all," local governments could, if they wished, establish a health insurance program for their nonemployee residents, for which they could determine the level of payments to private practitioners or directly supply medical care through clinics and hospitals by hiring doctors. Neither the MHW nor the JMA cared for this degree of local initiative.[4]

### Struggle

But agreement on the idea of universal health insurance did not mean that the doctors would fall into the government's plans placidly. For example, the bureaucrats wanted to transform the fee schedule from its traditional fee-for-service basis to a new system based on cost accounting. This would favor large hospitals rather than private practitioners and was seen as a move toward per-case rather than per-service payments. Moreover, the government wanted to separate prescribing and dispensing medications and thus take away the most lucrative business of private practitioners.

The JMA vigorously resisted such efforts and gained a standoff. Irrational though it seems, the ministry introduced its new fee schedule but also kept the old one, and providers were allowed to pick between what were called the *kō* and *otsu* schedules freely.[5] The fee-for-service system that was the basis of Japanese medical care would not be transformed according to bureaucratic preferences. Government attacks on physicians selling pharmaceuticals went on for years without much change.

Yet the MHW still hoped to dominate medical care—what health providers could do and how much they would be paid for it—and the JMA was determined to resist and indeed to improve the position of private practitioners. The first decade and more from the initiation of universal health insurance thus saw constant skirmishing as both sides jockeyed for advantage. It was crucial for the MHW to get doctors to accept fees set by the schedule as payment in full; the JMA finally agreed, at the price of removing several restrictions on what would be covered by health insurance.[6] More disputes erupted over such issues as treatment guidelines, urban-rural fee differentials, how the ministry could investigate hospital and clinic finances, the amount of copayments, subsidization of financially weak local insurance pools, and simplification of reimbursement. A significant case was the attempt in 1967 by MHW officials to hold down costs and move toward their old goal of getting doctors to cut down on the amount of drugs they dispense by introducing a "temporary" extra charge for medications; a JMA counterattack ended this initiative in 1969.

These disputes over money and control were important to both sides, but still more fundamental was a long fight about process and structure, about how decisions would be made in the future. This battle centered on the Central Council. Takemi's goals were to have the JMA dominate the providers' side on the council, to limit the influence of the payers' side and even the "public interest" members vis-a'-vis the providers, to make the council's deliberations more autonomous from MHW influence, and to make the ministry go along with council recommendations (when favorable to the JMA). When these structural strategies failed, the JMA was quite willing to bypass all normal procedures and intervene at the highest levels, as by forcing a summit meeting between LDP leaders and the MHW Minister.

In all these battles, the JMA repeatedly demonstrated its willingness to disrupt the Central Council process by not attending meetings, demanding the resignation of the chairman or the dissolution of the entire council, and having the providers' representatives resign their membership. Takemi's ultimate threat was a doctors' strike (or refusal to accept health insurance reimbursement), often threatened and more than once actually ordered, if largely on a symbolic basis.[7] The ministry and the insurance carriers (particularly Kenporen) fought back as best they could, but the strong support the JMA enjoyed from the ruling LDP gave the advantage to the doctors.

Accordingly, for the most part the JMA's tactics were quite successful. The doctors usually got the better end of the bargain on the substantive issues, and for a period of eight years fee-schedule negotiations operated under the "proposal system," quite abnormal in terms of Japanese administrative procedures, in which the Central Council would make the opening bid for a price increase rather than the MHW seeking council approval for its own proposition. However, this process was both time-consuming and unpredictable and thus was increasingly problematical even from the JMA point of view.

Indexation

In the early 1970s the doctors were in an unusually favorable position. As well as holding their own in continued skirmishes over several of the issues mentioned above, they benefited from two shifts in the broader political environment. First, a threat to the LDP's political control had come in a series of victories by left-wing politicians in many urban prefectures and municipalities. Second, a new public mood favoring social welfare, particularly for the elderly, had been growing since the late 1960s—the early 1970s has been called the first "old-people boom" in Japan (Campbell 1992, chap. 5).

The government responded with several important policy expansions in health care, including "free" medical care for the elderly (the government would cover the copayments for nearly everyone over seventy), substantial reductions in copayments for Citizens Health Insurance, and enactment of "catastrophic" coverage to limit out-of-pocket costs in all health insurance plans. Among other social policy expansions, pension benefits were increased and were also indexed to prices.

Indexation was an important issue in the early 1970s because inflation had soared to double-digit levels, the result in part of high government spending. In fact, revisions of the fee schedule had long been based on an analysis of medical cost increases, but the formula was complicated and ambiguous and so left much room for argument. Much to the dislike of the JMA, it also included consideration of physicians' incomes. The doctors therefore pressed for a much simpler indexing formula: the amount charged for physicians' services would go up with GNP/capita, other personnel costs with average wages, and remaining expenses with the consumer price index.[8] This formula would lead to large fee increases on what seemed to be rational principles, without the JMA having to get into repeated battles.

Kenporen and other insurers were initially opposed to this demand, but the HIB was more ambivalent. On the one hand, accepting indexation would mean giving up the bureaucrats' discretion in setting fees, as well as risking substantial cost increases, but, on the other hand, the ministry had mostly been on the losing side in a series of quite bruising battles. Taking fee-setting out of politics had a distinct appeal. Moreover, both the JMA and the government were eager to speed the process up—the doctors so as not to delay their fee hike too much in an inflationary era, and the government partly for technical reasons. The increase had gotten to be a large enough amount to be awkward to cover in a supplementary budget, where hikes in expenditures had to be covered by reformulating earlier revenue estimates. Making the decision about the size of the increase in advance of the protracted and uncertain negotiations between the HIB and JMA would require some kind of easy and objective calculation.

From the 1974 revision, then, the Chūikyō was left to argue only about allocation among items. The overall amount of the increase was ostensibly to be decided by formula, which meant it was worked out between the MHW and the MOF, with the JMA participating only informally and behind the scenes. Procedurally that meant that the abnormal "proposal system" in which the Central Council took the initiative in fee schedule revisions was replaced by the normal "inquiry-response" process, in which council deliberations were based on plans submitted by the MHW.

A decade later this procedural reform plus two rules developed at the same time about financing Government-Managed Health Insurance would be crucial to establishing a new set of routines aimed at cost control. The first rule came about because the HIB was quite aware that indexing the fee schedule would require steady increases in revenues for Government-Managed Health Insurance, the system for small-business employees it managed directly. Since the contribution was a percentage of wages, premium revenues would be expected to rise, but not by as much as for Society-Managed Health Insurance in the large-firm sector. Until then, every year, the MHW had been forced to appeal to the MOF for a subsidy from general revenues to make up the shortfall, causing a major budget battle. MHW officials therefore induced the MOF to set the subsidy as a fixed share of expenditures (initially 10%).

The second rule resulted from the MOF's fear that it would now be vulnerable to demands that this subsidy rate be raised. It therefore insisted that the MHW agree to tying the subsidy rate to the contribution rate. Now, before taking the easy road of asking for more tax revenues, the MHW would have to get a hike in contributions approved by the legislature.[9]

Incidentally, the agreement on indexation did not end debate between doctors and the government. With its main economic goals satisfied, the JMA gave more emphasis to structural concerns, such as diminishing the power of the large-firm health insurance societies and their national federation, Kenporen. It also pushed its idea of community hospitals actually run by local medical associations, so that private practitioners could admit patients rather than losing them to regular hospitals. For its part, the MHW talked about an amendment to the Medical Care Basic Law that would strengthen the hand of prefecture-level officials in regulating health care.

In reality, these apparent battles did not amount to much more than exchanges of rhetoric. The doctors perhaps were too satisfied to fight very hard: indexation of fees plus the additional work induced by benefit improvements in the early 1970s greatly expanded health care spending, which rose in the 1970s at about the same high rate as in the United States. Most of this new money became income for health care providers, with the private practitioners who dominated the JMA getting at least their fair share.

On the government side, it appears that through much of the 1970s MHW officials were indecisive and passive. One reason was that the ministry's long-held goal of catching up with the West in social policy, including medical care, had now essentially been accomplished. It was not clear what its new mission should be. Indeed, although it was becoming increasingly clear that cost-control would have to be a high priority, there was little agreement on the implications for policy. Proponents of the ministry's traditional public-health perspective believed that the problem was overreliance on fee-for-service, private-practice medical care and hoped that moving toward more public provision of preventive care and other services would help. On the other hand, a group of younger officials within the ministry were influenced by American health policy research and looked toward market-oriented or competitive solutions.

The bargain that was made in the early 1970s thus held until 1981. The indexation formula had apparent scientific justification, and it did produce an answer to the difficult question of how much fees should be raised without creating much conflict. These advantages, plus sheer inertia and the continued perception of JMA power, were enough to inhibit serious attempts at change for some time even though the underlying conditions of health policy were changing substantially.

Cost Containment

The indexing formula was used in the fee-schedule revisions of 1974, 1976, and 1978. After 1978, there was no revision until a substantially new procedure was instituted in 1981. The negotiations since then have been conducted not by any "scientific" principle, but under a more ad hoc process driven by cost containment.[10] In each biennial negotiation, pharmaceutical prices have been reduced sharply and the fees for other services then raised by only enough to counterbalance this loss of income or, in some instances, to provide a tiny raise.

The new process may be described briefly. The starting point is a decision that amounts to a global budget for overall health care expenditures. It is mainly based on anticipated revenues for the Government-Managed Health Insurance system. Recall the rules mentioned above that fix the budget subsidy as a share of expenditures, and then tie its size to contribution rates. Since in the context of the 1980s a hike in contribution rates was seen as politically unpalatable, the HIB was severely constrained in estimating total expenditures for the Government-Managed Health Insurance system. That estimate, worked out in negotiations with the MOF during the budget process, then governs how much the fee schedule for the *entire* health insurance system can be raised.

A set of administrative rules, partly established by design and partly adapted from rules initially created for other reasons, has therefore served as an effective constraint on the growth of medical spending. Before deciding how much it can spend, the HIB has to think first about Government-Managed Health Insurance contribution revenues, which depend on how much wages will rise in the small business sector. The fiscally conservative MOF stands by to prevent overoptimistic estimates. This decision-making process looks automatic rather than discretionary; in fact, it receives far less publicity than the contentious Central Council negotiations over the details of the fee schedule itself—now limited to questions of how the pie should be divided rather than its size.

This new process for the fee-schedule negotiation was just one of several important health-policy changes in the first half of the 1980s. Others included the Health Care for the Elderly Law passed in 1982, which initiated cross-subsidization of old-age medical costs to reduce the burden on the treasury, as well as an aggressive public-health preventive-medicine campaign; increases in copayment amounts; hospital bed limitations through regional planning; new institutions for long-term care; and a variety of other innovations. All were aimed at constraining costs through bureaucratic control.

How did the government gain the upper hand in the 1980s when it had failed so often in the past? Several factors were important.

First, the perception that government spending was getting out of hand had become widespread, and social policy including health care costs (particularly for "free" medical care for the elderly) was often blamed. The idea of "reconsidering welfare" (*fukushi minaoshiron*) in reaction to the big advances of the early 1970s had gained currency since 1975 (Campbell 1992, chap. 7). More generally, this new national mood was a key factor in the broad "administrative reform campaign" of budget restraints and privatization in 1981–85.

Second, there were more specific financial pressures. The MHW had financed rising costs by raising premiums (in Government-Managed Health Insurance for small business) and by increased government subsidies. The former brought political resistance in the legislature and the latter invited pressure from the MOF. In fact, the immediate catalyst for action was a new requirement for the 1980 budget process that ministries sharply limit their budget requests. The MHW could not meet that requirement without doing something about health care costs.

Third, in the realm of politics, any cutbacks in social policy had been difficult during the 1970s because the ruling party was in electoral trouble. However, the era of *hakuchū* or near-parity in the legislature ended when the LDP finally won a big victory in the summer 1980 general election and was no longer as vulnerable to opposition party attacks.

Fourth, the MHW had gotten itself together and gained confidence. As often seems to be the case in the Japanese bureaucracy, this shift was associated with strong individual leadership. A creative and aggressive health insurance expert, Hitoshi Yoshimura, held several key positions and worked hard for more coherent ministry strategies.

Fifth, apparently, the opposition weakened. The JMA's long-term strength was vitiated by its aging core membership and its inability to enroll the younger physicians who were mostly working for hospitals. Incidentally, journalists often ascribe the JMA's loss of power to the fact that President Takemi became ill and had to resign in 1982. Note, however, that the Health Care for the Elderly Law and the new fee-schedule methodology—the two biggest changes—were already well underway before Takemi resigned, and indeed it was his agreement to cutbacks in fees that allowed the Central Council to carry out the 1981 reform.[11] This timing suggests that the important factor was the long-term weakening of the JMA's position, along with the unfavorable shifts in the policy environment noted above.

In any case, doctors did not really capitulate but changed their strategy. By 1980, their old goal of continuously increasing the national resources flowing into health care—enlarging the pie—had become untenable. The emphasis shifted to their other traditional goal, protecting the interests of private practitioners by maintaining the relative size of their slice.

That meant accepting MHW attacks on spending, including even lowering the pharmaceutical prices that were so large a part of doctors' incomes, so long as compensation (e.g., increased consultation fees) would be provided to protect the *relative* position of private practitioners. The JMA's defensive strategy can be seen even more clearly in its reaction to several specific cost-cutting measures. It formally opposed the 1985 proposals to limit the number of hospital beds, but actually cooperated since existing small hospitals (mostly owned by physicians) would be spared new competition. It also went along with a gradual erosion of the fee-for-service principle with regard to hospitals for the elderly, in exchange for stable revenues.

In fact, the guiding principle of fee-schedule revisions became a balancing act among institutions or medical specializations, so that any pains or gains would be shared more or less equally, and intense opposition thereby avoided. The key group as always was private-practice physicians. In fact, for this balancing act to succeed, it was imperative that the JMA continue to maintain order among health care providers.

## Conclusion

Here lies the largest among many ironies in Japanese health care politics. Despite the long and in many respects genuinely bitter conflict between the MHW and the JMA, they were really each other's best friends—or at least each other's closest codependents.

It is not only that practitioners get all their income from government-regulated health insurance—that is true in most nations. In Japan, the unusually high incomes of private-practice doctors are the direct result of the bias in the fee schedule that favors primary care relative to surgery and other specialties. And it is not only that ministry officials need cooperation from doctors to make the system work, which is also true everywhere. The Japanese government can actually get away with paying hospitals and specialists so little precisely because the JMA keeps them quiet.

As noted above, this system has persisted in part because fees are not set scientifically, but in a political negotiation in which dissatisfied parties can be assuaged by a bit more money. The process is ambiguous enough to obscure both compensatory political deals and government interventions for micro-policy reasons (stemming overuse or encouraging some category of health care). Global budgets can be enforced without explicit public decisions. Periodic negotiations mean the stakes are not too high, since errors can be corrected before long.

In a sense, the system is a self-correcting mechanism to minimize tension, and as such it serves to protect the status quo. This status quo is of course quite favorable to the interests of both the MHW and the JMA. At first blush, one would guess that this mechanism had been established in a cooperative deal. Our look at the evolution of the fee-schedule mechanism, however, reveals that it was the product of conflict.

Or more precisely, the *first* conflict-minimizing mechanism—the indexing formula—was directly the product of several years of struggle. The government in effect gave the doctors what they wanted to get out of fighting so many battles against so determined an opponent. Both the policy environment and the balance of skill and determination between the two contenders favored the doctors in the early 1970s.

By a decade later, the policy environment had shifted to favor an emphasis on cost containment, the MHW was more confident and capable of inventing good strategies, and the JMA was in a weakened position. When the ministry moved aggressively, the doctors assessed the power balance and capitulated—or rather, fell back into a defensive strategy of protecting what they had. Of course, private practitioners had done very well for many years, so their defensive position was quite a comfortable one.

In looking back over the more than thirty years since the establishment of universal health insurance, then, one is struck by the importance of institutional arrangements, particularly mechanisms to deal with conflict. A period of frequent battles over a wide range of issues was succeeded by a period of decisions by formula side by side with rhetorical battles, and then a period of incremental adjustments.

To return to an earlier metaphor, this evolution was similar to that of a labor-management relationship. First, a period of bitter strikes and sporadic violence as the union shows its strength. Second, management gives in to many union demands, particularly for money, in exchange for routinized negotiation rules. Third, when the power balance swings to the management side, pay raises are constrained and the rules induce cooperative behavior by workers. Indeed, it is quite common in such circumstances that a union will turn to protecting the income and job security of its existing members as they get older, with little concern for new workers or the total number of jobs. The JMA followed precisely that path in the 1980s.

In terms of health policy, the interesting point about this evolution in Japan is that a negotiated fee schedule was no guarantee of constraint in health care costs. Again, Japanese health spending grew in the 1970s at about the same high rate seen in the United States, due both to increased usage and to rising prices. However, such a mechanism may well be a *necessary* condition for effective cost containment, when the power balance shifts to the side of those interested in holding down rather than increasing spending.

NOTES

1. The principle is that social insurance covers disease and disability, so that orthodontic dentists, childbirth, abortion, birth control, plastic surgery, and the like, as well as over-the-counter drugs, many Chinese medicines, and most massage or acupuncture are not covered. Ordinary dentistry is included. Childbirth is covered by a lump-sum payment, and prenatal care and some other public-health functions are covered by public funds.

2. In fact these doctors are mostly in internal medicine plus a few other specialties, but they do not have admitting privileges to hospitals and function overwhelmingly as primary-care providers, so can be called general practitioners.

3. The term was invented by Stephen Jay Gould; see Gould and Eldredge 1977. For political science applications see Krasner 1989 and Baumgartner and Jones 1993.

4. Such systems, which in some cases resembled today's health maintenance organizations in the United States, were attractive to many academics as a cooperative enterprise to meet local needs; see, for example, Higuchi 1974, 251–74. One severe practical problem that worried national bureaucrats was coverage for members when they were out of town. Doctors opposed such plans because they were in a weak position to bargain with localities

one by one (although the JMA did often call for "regional" health insurance that would presumably be administered at the prefectural level where doctors are powerful).

5. To the everlasting confusion of researchers. Both schedules are still in effect although the differences between them have been narrowed to the point of no longer mattering much.

6. A good account by a participant in this period is Hitoshi 1985, 13–19. Recent research by Nishimura (Shakai Hoshō Kenkyūjo, forthcoming) throws new light on the evolution of fee-schedule politics.

7. For a political scientist's account of these conflicts, see Steslicke 1973.

8. In a concession to cost-control interests, pharmaceutical prices were treated differently; they would be determined after an actual survey of market prices.

9. A 0.1 percentage point hike in the contribution rate would be required to gain a 0.8 percentage point hike in the subsidy rate. Both rates were raised in 1974, 1976, and 1978, to an 8% (of covered wages) contribution rate and a 16.4% (of total benefits) subsidy rate. See Shakai Hoken Kenkyūjo 1991, 117.

10. In the 1990s, new financing procedures for geriatric hospitals, experience with Relative Value Scales in the United States, and other factors led to renewed interest in setting fees through cost accounting (see Shakai Hoshō Kenkyūjo, forthcoming).

11. Accounts vary. Some say that Takemi had, for the first time, personally taken over the negotiations for the JMA and had simply not realized what the MHW officials were up to. Others say that, knowing he had cancer, Takemi had decided to worry about the national interest. In any case, there seems to have been dismay in JMA headquarters as the process unfolded, but Takemi's long-established autocratic style made effective protest impossible.

REFERENCES

Baumgartner, Frank R., and Bryan D. Jones. 1993. *Agendas and instability in American politics.* Chicago: University of Chicago Press.

Campbell, John Creighton. 1992. *How policies change: The Japanese government and the aging society.* Princeton: Princeton University Press.

Gould, Steven J. (with Miles Eldredge). 1977. Punctuated equilibria: The tempo and mode of evolution reconsidered. *Paleobiology* 3.

Higuchi, T. 1974. Medical care through social insurance in the Japanese rural sector. *International Labour Review* 109.

Krasner, Stephen D. 1989. Approaches to the state: Alternative conceptions and historical dynamics. *Comparative Politics* 21.2.

Shakai Hoken Kenkyūjo, ed. 1991. *Shakai hoken no ayumi* (Steps to social insurance). Tokyo: Shakai Hoken Kenkyūjo.

———, ed. Forthcoming. *Iryō hoshō to iryōhi* (Health security and health expenditures). Tokyo: Tokyo University Press.

Steslicke, W. 1973. *Doctors in politics: The political life of the Japan Medical Association.* New York: Praeger.

Yoshimura Hitoshi. 1985. Iryō hoken no sanjūnen: Kaiko to tenbō (Thirty years of health insurance: retrospect and prospect). *Shakai hoken junpō* 1500–1501 (April 1 and 11).

CHAPTER 26

# The Japan Medical Association and Private Practitioners' Income

*Yasuo Takagi*

SUMMARY   (1) Medical fees have favored private practitioners (office-based physicians) who provide primary care. For this reason, hospitals have come to rely on revenue from outpatient care rather than for inpatient care, and the functional separation of hospitals and offices has not progressed.

(2) Consultation fees have been relatively high in Japan compared with surgery fees. However, the hospitals' share has increased because of their growing role in long-term care and the preference of patients for hospital outpatient care.

(3) The new fees resulting from demands by the Japan Medical Association (JMA) have added 15% to the total medical costs for office-based physicians. However, their effect has been less than expected because hospitals have also benefited to a certain extent.

## Introduction

Since universal health insurance was instituted in 1961, the point-fee system has been used for remuneration of medical care in Japan. In this system, fees are determined for individual medical procedures, such as examinations, drug dispensing, injections, tests, and surgery. The medical services provided by physicians and medical care facilities are reimbursed according to this point-fee system, and claims are submitted for payment.

This point-fee system has acted as the primary mechanism to contain health care costs. Over this fee schedule, there has been a latent conflict in the allocation of resources between hospitals and offices (private practitioners) and between internal medicine and surgery. In negotiations over the fee schedule, hospitals are not represented, and the JMA, which has traditionally backed private practitioners, has taken the leading role. As a result, outpatient treatment carried out by private practitioners has been given greater weight, while the facilities, nursing staff, and advanced medical technology of hospitals have not been fairly remunerated. Faced with this situation, hospitals, which should be concentrating on inpatient treatment, have had to rely on outpatient treatment.

In this report, we will take a historical review of the point-fee system since 1960 and analyze how the weight given to outpatient treatment has caused changes in the structure of cost allocation between hospitals and clinics. In addition, we will examine the extent to which the political influence of the JMA has increased the income of private practitioners. In particular, consultation fees, which constitute a larger share of the revenue for practitioners, have come to be given greater weight. While these favorable revisions were made partly to compensate for the reduction in drug prices (the remuneration for drugs constitutes 50% of the total in primary care), the private practitioners' share would have shrunk much more without political intervention.

## Low Surgical Fees, High Consultation Fees

In negotiations over the point-fee system, the JMA has continually opposed the Ministry of Health and Welfare (MHW) and insurers. In particular, the former president of the JMA, Tarō Takemi, wielded considerable political clout and worked toward a system of remuneration that was favorable for private practitioners. He successfully lobbied the MHW to negotiate only with the JMA in determining the point-fee system. Representatives of hospitals were not allowed to participate and he focused all of his efforts on enhancing the position of the private practitioners. The result was that reimbursement to hospitals for advanced medical technology and surgery were not proportionally increased. Ironically, his demands were in accordance with the interests of the MHW, since it was attempting to hold down total medical care costs.

Table 1 shows increases in the areas of consultation and surgery from 1960 to 1990. Initial consultation and repeat visit fees are the major source of income for private practitioners. On the other hand, surgery is provided by hospitals and is a more advanced technology compared with consultations.

Taking 1960 as an index of 100, the figures for initial visits are 250 in 1970, 694 in 1980, and 1,167 in 1990, showing a twelvefold increase over a thirty-year period. The figures for repeat visits are 300 in 1970, 1,160 in 1980, and 1,420 for hospitals, and 1,620 for clinics in 1990—increases greater than those for initial consultations. This is attributable to the fact that the MHW tries to hold down increases in initial consultation fees, as those increases directly raise medical care costs. In contrast, since repeat visit fees cannot be applied to all patients, their effect is more indirect.

Nevertheless, as repeat visit fees were increased to a greater extent than initial consultation fees, this has given rise to abuses in which physicians have patients come in for numerous consultations in order to secure their income and has contributed to the high per-capita number of visits to physicians in Japan.

Compared with consultation, remuneration for surgery has shown a smaller increase. Taking 1960 as 100, the index for 1970 was 223–208, and for 1980, 588–458 (excluding the excision of aortic aneurysms, which was 1,559). In 1990, the surgical associations requested considerable increases in the remuneration for surgery, and increases were granted for several types. However, with the excep-

**Table 1. Change in the indexed fees for selected procedures, 1960–1990**

| | Yen | | | | 1960=100 | | |
| --- | --- | --- | --- | --- | --- | --- | --- |
| | 1960 | 1970 | 1980 | 1990 | 1970 | 1980 | 1990 |
| Consultation | | | | | | | |
| Initial visit | 180 | 450 | 1,250 | 2,100 | 250 | 694 | 1167 |
| Repeat visit | 50 | 150 | 580 | 710 * | 300 | 1160 | 1420 |
| | | | | 810 ** | | | 1620 |
| Surgery | | | | | | | |
| Pneumonectomy | 13,000 | 29,000 | 62,000 | 130,000 | 223 | 477 | 1000 |
| Cleft palate surgery | 4,500 | 9,700 | 22,000 | 43,000 | 215 | 478 | 1000 |
| Gastrectomy | 12,000 | 25,000 | 70,000 | 150,000 | 208 | 583 | 1250 |
| Excision of large intestine | 12,000 | 25,000 | 55,000 | 160,000 | 208 | 458 | 1333 |
| Appendectomy | 4,000 | 8,600 | 23,500 | 48,000 | 215 | 588 | 1200 |
| Extraction of thyroid tumor | 4,000 | 8,600 | 19,000 | 39,000 | 215 | 475 | 975 |
| Glaucoma surgery | 2,500 | 5,400 | 12,500 | 15,000 | 216 | 500 | 600 |
| Mitral valve incision | 17,000 | 36,500 | 78,000 | 100,000 | 215 | 459 | 588 |
| Pericardial incision | 7,000 | 15,500 | 34,500 | 56,000 | 221 | 493 | 800 |
| Excision of aortic aneurysm | 17,000 | 36,500 | 265,000 | 500,000 | 215 | 1559 | 2941 |

* Hospitals.
** Physicians' offices.

**Table 2. Change in the relative share of
consultation, surgery, and drugs to total costs,
1960–1990 (in percent)**

|  | 1960 | 1970 | 1980 | 1990 |
|---|---|---|---|---|
| Consultation | 8.1 | 10.5 | 14.7 | 14.9 * |
| Surgery | 5.1 | 2.3 | 4.0 | 6.2 |
| Drugs | 24.2 | 56.7 | 43.1 | 32.0 |

* Consultation includes "home medical treatment" (1.0%).

tion of aortic aneurysms, these increases only kept pace with the remuneration in the area of consultation, as the following figures show: 1,333 for excision of the large intestine, 1,250 for gastrectomy, and 1,200 for straight appendectomy. The index for other types of surgery were 1,000 or less, a smaller increase than that for consultation.

Thus, it is clear that surgery has come to be given less weight than consultation. As a consequence, hospitals have ventured into long-term care in order to secure revenue. This is the main reason why the average hospital stay in Japan is 51.4 days (1989), considerably longer than in Europe and the United States. In particular, small local hospitals have come to play a central role in providing long-term care for the elderly rather than providing surgery.

Table 2 shows the change in the relative share of consultation, surgery, and drugs to total medical costs. The area of surgery showed a decrease from 5.1% in 1960 to 2.3% in 1970. The ratio for drugs peaked in 1970 at 56.7%, after which drug prices were decreased, so that the ratio decreased to 32.0% by 1990.

**New Consultation Fees**

In negotiations over the fee schedule, the JMA has been demanding that primary care services provided by private practitioners be given a preferred position. In concrete terms, this has meant increasing remuneration for outpatient care.

Table 3 shows daily medical care costs per patient. Outpatient care costs have increased considerably in both hospitals and physicians' offices, with a 31-fold increase in hospitals and a 26-fold increase in offices from 1960 to 1990. The increase in costs for inpatient care was less, 21-fold in hospitals and 14-fold in offices. The reason why hospitals have increased their outpatient care costs more than private-practice physicians is because the same fee schedule is applied to both. The result is that when the fees for primary care procedures provided by private practitioners are increased, hospital outpatient care also benefits. It should also be noted that for a given outpatient case, since the equipment and facilities in

**Table 3. Daily medical costs per patient, 1960–1990**

|                 | Yen  |       |        |        | 1960=100 |      |      |
|-----------------|------|-------|--------|--------|------|------|------|
|                 | 1960 | 1970  | 1980   | 1990   | 1970 | 1980 | 1990 |
| Hospitals total | 439  | 1,858 | 6,938  | 10,657 | 423  | 1580 | 2428 |
| Inpatient       | 705  | 2,780 | 10,902 | 14,557 | 394  | 1546 | 2065 |
| Outpatient      | 236  | 1,300 | 4,430  | 7,255  | 551  | 1877 | 3074 |
| Offices total   | 171  | 767   | 2,801  | 4,213  | 449  | 1638 | 2464 |
| Inpatient       | 649  | 2,254 | 7,739  | 9,079  | 347  | 1192 | 1399 |
| Outpatient      | 157  | 721   | 2,628  | 4,032  | 459  | 1674 | 2568 |

hospitals are more elaborate compared to that of offices, the cost per day tends to be greater. The difference between hospitals and offices has widened: whereas it was only 1.5 times in 1960 (¥236 vs ¥157), it became 1.8 times in 1990 (¥7,255 vs ¥4,032). This concentration on outpatient care by the hospitals has delayed improvement in inpatient care. The only exception is the expansion of long-term care, which has meant that hospital inpatient care has actually come to constitute the largest share of total medical care costs.

Table 4 shows the change in total medical care spending in hospitals and physicians' offices. Up to 1970, spending on outpatient care in offices was the highest, but from 1980 onward spending on hospital inpatient care became the greatest. This was not caused by fees for inpatient care becoming more expensive. Rather, from 1973 onward, when medical care for the elderly was made free of charge, there was a flood of elderly patients into inpatient care. Although fees for outpatient care were increased, since the number of patients did not increase, private practitioners' revenues did not increase as much as expected. Moreover, from 1980 onward, patients came to prefer hospitals over physicians' offices for outpatient care, and this is why total medical care costs for offices have not increased. Thus, hospitals have come to derive their revenue largely from outpatient care and long-term care.

Faced with these structural changes in medical care costs, the JMA has made efforts to establish new fees for primary care consultation in order to secure revenue for private practitioners. These are listed below in historical order.

1. 1961: Addition for infants and small children. (The fees for the initial consultation were increased when patients were infants or small children. In 1974, this was also applied to repeat visits.)
2. 1970: Addition for repeat visit consultations in internal medicine. (This was only applicable to internal medicine patients and was established to

**Table 4. Change in total medical spending, 1960–1990**

| | Y100 Million | | | | 1960=100 | | | 1960=100 (Excluding new fees) | | |
|---|---|---|---|---|---|---|---|---|---|---|
| | 1960 | 1970 | 1980 | 1990 | 1970 | 1980 | 1990 | 1970 | 1980 | 1990 |
| Hospitals total | 1,797 | 12,121 | 62,970 | 123,256 | 675 | 3504 | 6859 | 666 | 3462 | 6653 |
| Inpatient | 1,248 | 7,801 | 43,334 | 80,470 | 625 | 3472 | 6448 | 625 | 3472 | 6442 |
| Outpatient | 549 | 4,320 | 19,636 | 42,786 | 787 | 3577 | 7793 | 763 | 3470 | 7170 |
| Offices total | 1,717 | 10,392 | 42,379 | 56,507 | 605 | 2468 | 3291 | 562 | 2323 | 2811 |
| Inpatient | 179 | 998 | 5,007 | 5,082 | 558 | 2797 | 2839 | 558 | 2797 | 2836 |
| Outpatient | 1,538 | 9,394 | 37,372 | 51,425 | 611 | 2430 | 3344 | 564 | 2282 | 2816 |

**Table 5. Effect of new fees on the total medical costs for hospitals and physicians' offices, 1960–1990 (in percent)**

|  | 1970 (1–2) | 1980 (1–4) | 1990 (1–6) |
|---|---|---|---|
| Hospitals total | 1.3 | 1.2 | 3.0 |
| Inpatient |  | 0.0 | 0.1 |
| Outpatient | 3.0 | 3.0 | 8.0 |
| Offices total | 7.1 | 5.5 | 14.6 |
| Inpatient |  | 0.0 | 0.1 |
| Outpatient | 7.7 | 6.1 | 15.8 |

1. Addition of infants and small children (1961).
2. Repeat visit fee in internal medicine (1970).
3. Addition of holidays (1974).
4. Repeat visit fee for infants and small children (1976).
5. Addition for providing guidance in care and nutrition of infants and small children (1981).
6. Fee for providing guidance in chronic diseases (1981).

compensate for the decrease in income due to the reduction of drug prices.)

3. 1974: Addition for holidays. (Initial and repeat visit fees on holidays were increased.)
4. 1976: Repeat visit fees for infants and small children in internal medicine. (Repeat visit fees were increased for infants and small children in internal medicine as well.)
5. 1981: Addition for providing guidance in the care and nutrition of infants and small children. (The initial consultation fee was increased in addition to [1] for providing guidance in the care and nutrition of infants and small children by pediatricians. This fee was intended to compensate physicians for the loss of income due to the decrease in the number of children.)
6. 1981: Addition for providing guidance in chronic disease. (The fee for private practitioners was made higher than that for hospitals. The target was medical management of chronic diseases in primary care.)

Table 5 shows the percentages of total medical costs accounted for by these new fees. As can be seen, (1) and (2) accounted for 7.7% of outpatient costs in offices in 1970, clearly showing that they were a significant addition to private-practice physicians' revenue. However, in 1980, even with the addition of (1) through (4), these fees had the effect of increasing outpatient revenues for offices by only 6.1%. Thus, despite the introduction of new fees, revenue to private practitioners did not increase as much as expected, because patients preferred hospital outpatient care, and there was an increase in long-term inpatient care.

Therefore, in 1981, in order to guarantee income for private practitioners, in addition to the establishment of new fees, revisions were made so that fees for inpatient care were decreased as the length of stay increased. This had a considerable effect in reducing the hospital share of revenues, and enhanced the effect of the new fees so that they increased the amount of office outpatient revenue by 15.8%. This was equivalent to an increase of 14.6% for total spending on offices. However, for hospitals, although their outpatient care costs increased by 8% due to the effect of the new fees, in terms of total hospital costs, the increase was only 3%.

In short, revisions of the fee schedule consistently were used to compensate private-practice physicians for declines in their shared revenues. This pattern was the result of JMA political strength. However, it did not reverse the trend toward increased use of hospitals.

# CHAPTER 27

# Afterword: National Health Insurance, Cost Control, and Cross-National Lessons—Japan and the United States

*Theodore R. Marmor*

## Introduction

The very title of this commentary suggests a cautionary theme. None of the widespread discussions of medical care practices abroad is useful for purposes of drawing lessons without some understanding of the benefits, costs, and limits of comparative policy research.

Japan and the United States present an interesting picture of similarities and differences. Japan is outwardly very different from the United States: an island nation, with a significant language disparity and, until recently, strikingly different historical and cultural patterns. For purposes of direct comparisons of similar nation-states, Japan is not an obvious candidate for the United States. Yet, Japan's recent rise to be one of the world's major industrial nations and its striking move toward "Westernization" within its own cultural framework make it a fascinating object for other forms of comparative inquiry. However fascinating, the language obstacle prevents easy transfer of Japanese information. Geographical distance, too, contributes to this problem.

## The Theory of Comparative Policy Research

Broadly speaking, there are two quite different reasons for comparing social policies across nations, each of which requires a rather different research strategy. First, there is what I call *policy learning* (Klein 1983; Marmor, Bridges, and Hoffman 1978, 59–80). That is, one investigates the social policies of other countries in order to derive lessons or models that can be applied at home. This approach has a long history. Presidential bodies and European royal commissions regularly draw on the experience of other countries (see, for a telling instance, Committee on Economic Security 1935).

Second, there is what one could term *policy understanding*. Here the emphasis is not so much on learning as on explanation. For example, if we are to achieve an understanding of the factors that shape the evolution of a social security system, it is unlikely that we can do so by looking at one country in isolation. Are the key factors the level of industrialization and the political mobilization of workers? The history of Britain, examined in isolation, might suggest that they are. But comparative studies indicate otherwise (Wilensky 1975; Flora, Alber, and Kohl 1977; Carrier and Kendall 1977). Similarly, it has been argued that in Britain the power of the medical profession rests on its access to Whitehall (Eckstein 1960), while comparative studies show that the nature of that power is largely independent of the precise relationship between doctors and bureaucracy (Marmor and Thomas 1972). In short, comparative studies may be essential if misleading conclusions are not to be drawn from what are single case studies in the making, or evolution, of public policy.

The research strategy associated with the first of these two approaches would, to judge from the literature, seem to be a micro strategy (or single-issue approach) in "most similar" countries, keeping numbers down. That is, the prime concern is not with the nature of the public policy *system,* since it is implausible to assume that a total system can be transplanted from one country to another, but with a discrete area of policy. In turn, this means comparing countries judged to be roughly similar in terms of economic development, social organization, and political ideology. For if the focus of concern is the transplantability of ideas or models, then it is clearly essential that the two environments should not be too different.

The research strategy associated with the second approach is a macro strategy (or systems approach) in "most different" countries, using large numbers. In this approach, the focus of interest is on the factors that help to explain either the evolution or the behavior of the system as a whole. The nature of the analysis positively requires differences in the economic development, social organization, or political ideology of the countries being examined (for it is obviously impossible to test the significance of a specific factor if it is common to all the cases being examined). Large numbers, in as far as they allow a statistical analysis of the factors concerned, are an additional advantage.

A variant of the "different system" approach addresses an admittedly very different socio-political community, contrasts its practices with another country, and highlights the cultural and other factors that set the two societies apart. Given profound differences, one sees them more clearly by asking similar questions of the two cultures. Anthropologists do this for a living, but the practice has its own tradition of caution in drawing any policy lessons at all. The legitimate purpose of this variant is analytical illumination, not direct policy transplantation.

The inclination to use cross-national research in attempts to find solutions to the increasingly serious problems in medical care has grown in recent years. This results partly from concern about the costs of medical care in advanced industrial countries and is clearly evidenced in the choice of topic and structure for this book. Health expenditure constitutes one of the most powerful sources of strain within contemporary welfare states, making matters of change and choice both urgent and important. Increases in the proportion of public expenditure spent on social welfare policies may make a preemptive claim upon government resources or, by straining the capabilities of states to meet them, may even trigger political transformations. It is this context that lends urgency to the evident international preoccupation with the structure of public health insurance programs.

Sometimes comparative research reveals what is possible, not what is desirable or transplantable, providing illumination not indoctrination. Sometimes such research produces seemingly transplantable policies, but the effects are so hard to disentangle from other forces that learning whether such a policy would be appropriate is difficult. This is a case of temptation without satisfaction. A third lesson is that cross-national research work is difficult, costly, and time-consuming. Only compelling, expected returns justify both the costs and the difficulty of identifying comparable circumstances and similarities. When the expected benefits are policy learning, the issue is whether the policy choice is clear enough to warrant the expected costs. In other cases, the benefit will be significant tests of social science theories that would be impossible within a single-nation framework. Cross-national research in health policy suggests there is a place for both types of work.

### Learning from the Japanese Mystery

By the start of the 1980s, it was generally accepted that Japan's goal of "catching up with the West" had long since been attained, and that it had become a full-fledged member of the club of advanced, industrial nations.[1] Indeed, some writers have proclaimed Japan as "Number 1" and argued that Japanese accomplishments in a number of areas warrant close study and possible emulation in the West.[2] Many Americans are especially impressed by the way Japan produces various goods and services, as well as by the role of the Japanese state in nurturing industrial development and international trade. The notion that Americans might be able to learn *from* as well as *about* Japan now seems more acceptable than previously. Indeed, "learning from Japan" rapidly became a new, high-growth industry in the 1980s.[3]

This development has been somewhat retarded in the medical care sector. First, many Americans persist in regarding American medicine as the world's finest, though fewer businessmen and policy analysts share this view now than a decade ago. They see a chronic "medical care crisis" as troublesome, but manageable through symptomatic treatment and incremental rehabilitation. Some prescribe a larger dose of regulation, others more competition and privatization. Few elites in the 1980s felt that fundamental reform of American medicine was either necessary or possible and saw no compelling reason for looking carefully at Japanese or other foreign models. Until recently, this pervasive attitude of American medical superiority was also found in governing circles at federal and state levels. Even among medical policy experts, interest in and detailed knowledge of foreign models remains quite limited.[4] Japanese accomplishments (and concerns) are poorly appreciated, and the suggestion that investigation of medical care in Japan may reveal "lessons for America" has not been widely accepted. I am reminded of an American automobile executive's comment some years ago: "What can we learn from the Japanese about making cars? We taught them everything they know." But that attitude may well be changing. As in the auto industry, Japanese accomplishments in the medical care field are now likely to command greater attention.[5]

Many American medical professionals *are* aware that life expectancy for both males and females in Japan is the world's highest; they know that Japan compares very favorably with the United States and other advanced industrial nations with respect to other leading health status indicators. However, the fact that Japan has a system of universal, comprehensive health insurance that covers virtually the entire population and that access to medical care is readily available to most citizens and resident aliens still goes largely unnoticed. That Japanese citizens spend less of their personal and national income for a greater measure of medical security than Americans comes as something of a shock. As these and other facts become more widely known, the desire to learn more about the Japanese experience in the medical care field may grow. This book itself is, of course, premised on that development.

Unfortunately, the acquisition and dissemination of information regarding Japanese medical care, as we have noted, present problems for Americans. Few medical care analysts read or speak Japanese. Funding for study and research in Japan has been very limited. In short, there are in the United States few incentives and meager rewards for undertaking a serious investigation in Japan. Moreover, Japanese medical care specialists have not been encouraged to serve as teachers.

If American health specialists tend to be ignorant regarding Japan, their Japanese counterparts tend to be remarkably well-informed about health and medical care in the United States. In keeping with the national goal of catching up with the West during the past century, the Japanese have accepted the necessity for learning from the West—to understand and to adapt Western ideas and practices to suit their own needs and circumstances. That tradition persists. In the medical care field, Japanese continue to learn from the West in general and from the United States in particular. While much of this is haphazard, there are also systematic and concerted attempts to learn from abroad in the national interest.

But what is there to be said for drawing lessons from the Japanese experience in medical care? There is no Japanese-made panacea to cure our own medical care crisis. Scholarly testimony provided in this book demonstrates that Japan has made great progress in the health sector during the past century in keeping with its economic and social development in general. But it also suggests that Japan may have reached a critical turning point and that it will be quite difficult to maintain and improve current levels of health and welfare.[6] One scholar has provided three general observations about what medical care research might offer.

First, American analysts are unlikely to discover a "magic formula," but they may uncover some practical alternatives for dealing with generic problems. In one investigation of Japanese hospital management practices, Seth B. Goldsmith offers a five-point agenda for change in American hospital management practices. He urges American hospital managers to consider the Japanese experience from a clinical/practical standpoint and "to adapt the innovative ideas of their Japanese colleagues" (Goldsmith 1984, 134). Goldsmith points out that this need not be a purely academic exercise. "In the long run the payoff will be for the staff, the patients, and the community."[7] An open-minded but judicious examination of other specific aspects of Japanese medical care, as well as political, economic, and social developments during the 1980s, should also be of great interest to American policy makers.[8]

Second, with respect to broader issues such as national health insurance, the Japanese experience offers a relatively untapped mine of information and data. Steslicke's investigation of the Japanese experience with universal, comprehensive health insurance since 1961 led him to question the value of the social insurance model as the basis for providing medical security in contemporary America. Surely, this is one area of Japanese medical care that warrants more extensive investigation given our own partial commitment to the social insurance model and our continuing flirtation with "national health insurance." John Campbell's contribution to this book is directed precisely at this issue.

Third, how to deal with the complex problems of medical care for the aging and elderly population is one of the major issues confronting policy makers in the United States, Japan, and other advanced industrial societies. In this context, the Japanese case is especially interesting. Thus far, Japan has enjoyed a relative advantage regarding demographic factors and its high level of economic prosperity, and well-being has been facilitated by its comparatively young population. Not only has Japan had a young and healthy work force for most of the postwar period, but the burden of supporting and caring for a large elderly and dependent population has not been a major problem. In 1980, the sixty-five years of age and over portion of the population was only 9.1% as compared with 11.2% in the United States, and over 14% in France, Great Britain, West Germany, and Sweden. The Japanese situation has changed rather rapidly and dramatically so that, during the first quarter of the twenty-first century, Japan may find itself number one in the world in the proportion of its population sixty-five years of age and older.

Although this is not generally viewed as a crisis, a sense of urgency prevails. The way in which health and medical services for the aging and elderly population are organized, delivered, and financed during the coming years should be of enormous interest to Americans. The Japanese people have displayed a remarkable capacity for adapting to changing circumstances and for developing innovative responses to domestic and foreign challenges. Our greatest opportunity to learn from Japan may be provided by the challenge they are now facing, which is very similar to the demographic shifts the United States is already experiencing. The controversial Health Care for the Elderly Law of 1982 (rōjin hoken-hō) may or may not have been a major step in restructuring the Japanese health care system and integrating medical care with disease prevention/health promotion programs for the aging and elderly population.[9]

Despite all these reasons in support of learning from the Japanese approach to medical care, we must strike another note of caution. Even though Japan has done quite well in promoting the health of its population and in providing a large measure of medical security at a lower cost than most other industrial nations, the

Japanese have not developed a level of quality their experts regard as satisfactory.[10] It is of course difficult to conceive of a single "best" system—an ideal model that will work well in all or even most situations. What has been working well in Japan may not work well elsewhere. Still, it is apparent that advanced industrial nations are struggling with comparable problems in providing the kind of health care demanded by its citizenry. In that respect, comparative investigation of the Japanese experience should prove quite instructive and is long overdue.

## Recent Investigations

It is precisely to address this gap in the comparative literature that this book (and the conference on which it is based) was conceived. My brief commentary will address the cluster of chapters by Campbell, Masuyama and Campbell, and Takagi.

What these essays together show is how the Japanese system of universal health insurance has evolved in the postwar period and what factors have shaped Japan's experience with rising costs, acrimonious physician-payer bargaining over fees and incomes, and continuing struggles over who should pay what in the system's complicated financing arrangements.

The thesis of Campbell's sketch of Japan's health insurance is straightforward. Japan insures all of its citizens through a series of insurance pools in what is a hybrid of private and social insurance models. In that respect, Japan has chosen complexity over simplicity, mixing egalitarian ideas about spreading the costs of illness through cross-subsidies on the one hand with a complicated set of separate insurance programs on the other. The result, Campbell suggests, is a balance between notions of private actuarial and egalitarian notions of fairness, or as he puts it, between equity and equality. No one thinking about American medical care reform can fail to miss the complexity that such a balancing act entails.

But the more searching discussion takes place in the Masuyama and Campbell discussion of the evolution of fee-schedule politics in Japan. Here the topic is how Japanese politics have coped with the conflicting priorities of payors and providers over time. This history, while brief, is illuminating and well-informed. The authors have penetrated the rhetoric of public protestation and revealed the underlying dynamics of Japanese medical politics. And those politics are shaped not only by the resources available to the respective parties but also by changes in the broader political environment in which medical struggles take place. The story is one of the development of universal insurance in evolutionary stages, with the common pattern of rising costs and increasing resistance to those costs over time. But it is also a story of interdependence, an analog to labor-management negotiations over time where the parties come to have a stake in regularizing their disputes, adjusting deals in discrete steps, and adapting slowly to a changing environment. No one doing comparative health politics can afford to miss this synoptic treatment of what in detail would be an enormously complicated institutional history.

The Takagi research documents the distributive consequences for physicians and hospitals of the deals Masuyama and Campbell have sketched. In particular, he explains who in the world of Japanese medicine has gotten what in material rewards and deprivations from the persistently contentious bargaining. There are no surprises here but ample detail about how private practitioners came to benefit from Japanese policy choices, how the Japanese Medical Association represented their interests, and how specialists (and the medical centers in which they operate) were disadvantaged by the power struggles Campbell and his colleagues have described.

The result—from these chapters as well as others in this work—is that we now know a good deal about the costs, the financing, and the delivery of medical care in Japan. That Japan is comparatively healthy is no longer news. How its complicated system of universal health insurance protects Japanese citizens from unbudgetable medical expenses is evident from this scholarship. The politics that distributes both the financing burdens and the fiscal benefits of payment remain the most interesting story and the one most illuminated by this concluding section of the book.[11]

NOTES

1. This section of my presentation draws liberally—indeed literally—from the work of one of our acknowledged experts on Japanese medical care, William B. Steslicke. See especially "An International Perspective on Health Care: Learning from Japan," testimony before the U.S. House of Representatives Select Committee on Aging, 1 May 1984.

2. The strongest statement of the case for Japan is Vogel's (1979) controversial book, which was a bestseller in Japan.

3. For a critical review of the issue, see "Special issue: the selling of Japan," *The Nation* 234.6 (13 February 1982): 163–88.

4. Two notable exceptions are William Glaser and Vicente Navarro, who are prolific students of health care systems in various Western nations. Uwe Reinhardt, Deborah Stone, David Wilsford, Howard Leichter, Odin Anderson, and Larry Brown have also worked extensively in the comparative fields.

5. An early 1980s international review of health care statistics by Norman Macrae (1984) gives Japan high marks. Macrae writes: "Japan's unplanned medical system is proving the most economic, with the best health delivery per few dollars spent. In table 1 Japan emerges as the second lowest spender (above only Britain) but it successfully has the fewest workdays lost through workers saying they are sick." He continues: "Supporters of other countries' medical systems always wax cross with output figures like table 1 (saying, e.g., that Japan has a different method of counting live babies), but in every industry the reaction to output figures from Japan has been 'at first deny, then copy.' Other rich countries will some day suddenly imitate some features of Japan's medical system, including its emphasis on preventive medicine and extensive use of unqualified medical staff. There will be huge political and professional ructions as (*sic*) they do" (p. 18). Macrae's table 1 compares the U.S.A., West Germany, France, Britain, and Japan and is titled "Lowest input brings best output."

6. For a more detailed discussion, see Steslicke 1982, 1–35.

7. One area of Goldsmith's (1984) five-point agenda for change relates to orientation of new employees. He writes: "The orientation period in American hospitals needs a drastic overhaul. The message sent to an employee, beginning on day 1, is that the hospital does

not care about the new staff member and that the relationship will be a rather distant one. What is the message that is communicated during the four days at St. Luke's? I suggest it is a message of investment. The hospital is telling the employees that it cares about them and that they will play a significant role in the future of the organization. The presentations by the senior executives, the book discussion, the luncheons, the tour, and the final speaker create a sense of attachment rarely encountered in the American hospital" (p. 131).

8. Although Americans have not been impressed with the training of medical and health care professionals in Japan in the past, the new emphasis on community-based primary care could produce interesting innovations in health care education, as well as in the training of nonmedical care givers. Also unimpressive in the past were the limited efforts in the health planning area, but changing circumstances have led to a stronger commitment by the Japanese government to encourage regional and community health planning. Thus, new developments in health education and health planning should be of considerable interest. Although the commitment to disease prevention/health promotion is not new in Japan, the national government is placing more emphasis on the development of new programs to integrate health, medical, and welfare services. Needless to say, this is another aspect of Japanese health care that should be of great interest to Americans. Of course, Japanese efforts in the containment and rationalization of medical care costs warrant immediate attention. Although medical costs continue to rise in Japan, there has been a decline in the rate of increase since 1979 as a consequence of governmental cost containment and rationalization measures. Finally, it should be noted that, at a time when the merits of increased competition and privatization of medical care are being hotly debated in the United States, the fact that competition within and between the public and private sectors has a long history in Japan is ignored. Both friends and foes of "competition" could learn from the Japanese experience. Interestingly, competition tends to be viewed as "part of the problem" rather than "part of the solution" in contemporary Japan.

9. According to the Ministry of Health and Welfare, the 1982 law is "the first step for meeting the problems of a full-scale aging society." The aim of the new system is "to realize a comprehensive health and medical services system, from prevention to treatment and therapy at the local (city, town, and village) level, and thereby to ensure the health of the elderly. The objective is to promote mutually coordinating policies for public health, medical care, and welfare on the local level and to develop the systematized groundwork for integrated policies with regard to area medical and primary care" (Japan International Corporation for Welfare Services 1983, 18).

10. Although Japanese tend to be modest regarding their accomplishments in the health care field, the distinguished economist Shigeto Tsuru has proposed that Japan should strive to become the "health care center of the world." According to Professor Tsuru:

> Because there is still considerable room for improvement in the medical services now offered to the Japanese public, it may seem presumptuous to speak of becoming the "health care center of the world." Improvement of public medical services, of course, is an urgent matter. But planning for such improvement can be done within a wider context, encompassing the world, as suggested above. Japan has, to use an economic term, a comparative advantage in medicine. In cardiac surgery, for example, Japanese medical skill leads the world; and, though episodically, a number of patients who require especially delicate surgery come to Japan from foreign countries to receive treatment. Also, the kind and sympathetic care provided by Japanese nurses is not matched anywhere, according to the testimony of many persons who have had experiences in both domestic and foreign hospitals. The dedication, humility, and

sensitivity of the nuns who work in religious charity hospitals abroad receive frequent praise. But I feel that the keen awareness of their mission is universal among the Japanese nurses. If Japan were to become the "health care center of the world," it would be certain that the morale of medical personnel would be heightened further.

In addition, the recent development of medical equipment in Japan has been most striking. Computerized tomographic analyzers (CT scanners), for example, used in many of the nations' hospitals, presently cost about ¥150 million for the models designed for full-body analysis, and yet at the moment Japan is able to provide this equipment at the lowest price in the world. News reports now tell of the development of a computerized positron scanner for the diagnosis of brain tumors and apoplexy. This device was developed at the National Institute of Radiological Sciences of the Science and Technology Agency. Japan, as a nation of peace, should concentrate its energies on research and development in the expanding field of such medical instruments. Rather than recommend the export and technological development of "instruments of death" such as weapons, we should find our role in breaking new ground in the field of medical equipment—the "instruments of life." (Tsuru 1980, 494–95)

11. For my more extended views of Japanese medical and health developments, see Marmor 1992, 10–15.

REFERENCES

Aaron, H. J., and W. B. Schwartz. *The painful prescription: Rationing in health care.* Brookings Studies in Social Economics. Washington, D.C.: The Brookings Institution.
Carrier, J., and I. Kendall. 1977. The development of welfare states: The production of plausible accounts. *Journal of Social Policy* 6.3.
Committee on Economic Security. 1935. *Report to the President.* Washington, D.C.: U.S. Government Printing Office.
Eckstein, H. 1960. *Pressure group politics.* London: Allen and Unwin.
Flora, P., J. Alber, and J. Kohl. 1977. Zur Entwickkling des West-Europaischen Wohlfahrstsstaaten. *Politische Vierteljahresschrift* 18.4.
Goldsmith, S. B. 1984. *Theory Z hospital management: Lessons from Japan.* Rockville, MD: Aspen Systems Corp.
Japan International Corporation for Welfare Services. 1983. *Trends and policies of health services in Japan: Rationalizing medical care costs.* Tokyo.
Klein, R. 1983. Strategies for comparative social policy research. *In Health and welfare states in Britain,* edited by A. Williamson and G. Room. Heineman Educational Books.
Macrae, N. 1984. Health care international. *The Economist* 291.7339 (28 April).
Marmor, T. R. 1992. Japan: A sobering lesson. *Health Management Quarterly* 14.3.
———, A. Bridges, and W. L. Hoffman. 1978. Comparative politics and health policies: Notes on benefits, costs, limits. *In Comparing public policies: New concepts and methods,* edited by D. E. Ashford. Beverly Hills, CA: Sage Publications.
———, and D. Thomas. 1972. Doctors, politics and pay disputes. *British Journal of Political Science* 2.3.
Schwartz, W. B. 1984. The most painful prescription. *Newsweek* (12 November).
Steslicke, W. B. 1984. An international perspective on health care: Learning from Japan. Testimony before the U.S. House of Representatives Select Committee on Aging. 1 May.

————. 1982. National health policy in Japan: From the "age of flow" to the "age of stocks." *Bulletin of the Institute of Public Health* 31.1.

Tsuru, S. 1980. A positive program of nation-building in an age of uncertainty. *Japan Quarterly* 27.4.

Vogel, E. F. 1979. *Japan as number 1: Lessons for America.* Cambridge, MA: Harvard University Press.

Wilensky, H. L. 1975. *The welfare state of equality.* Berkeley: University of California Press.

# Contributors

**Hiroko Akiyama** is Assistant Research Scientist in the Institute for Social Research at the University of Michigan. Her research has focused on social relations and health behavior from a cross-cultural perspective, including participation in several cross-national survey projects. She has contributed to the journals of *Gerontology; Social Science and Medicine; Developmental Psychology;* and *Aging and Health.*

**John Creighton Campbell** is Professor of Political Science at the University of Michigan, and is the Secretary-Treasurer of the Association for Asian Studies. His interests include governmental organization and decision making as well as social policy. He wrote *How Policies Change: The Japanese Government and the Aging Society* (Princeton, 1992).

**Ruth Campbell** is Associate Director for Social Work and Community Programs, University of Michigan Geriatric Center. She has carried out research on aging in Japan for many years, in association with the Tokyo Metropolitan Institute of Gerontology and the Japan Social Work University, and is currently competing a book on that subject.

**John M. Eisenberg** is Chairman of the Department of Medicine, Physician-in-Chief, and Anton and Margaret Fuisz Professor of Medicine at Georgetown University Medical Center, and has chaired the Congressional Physician Payment Review Commission. He has published on physicians' practices, test use and efficacy, medical education, and clinical economics, and wrote *Doctors, Decisions and the Costs of Medical Care* (Health Administration Press, 1986).

**Eric A. Feldman,** who has both a J.D. and Ph.D. from the University of California, Berkeley, was a Robert Wood Johnson Scholar in Health Policy Research and recently joined the Law faculty at New York University. His current research is an interdisciplinary analysis of conflict over HIV-contaminated blood in Japan, North America, and Europe.

**Nancy Foster,** who studied at Princeton University, is the Deputy Director of the Robert Wood Johnson Foundation's Generalist Physician Faculty Scholars Program. Her research interests include payments for teaching hospitals, the costs associated with medical education, and the development of primary care curriculum and academic generalist physicians.

**George D. Greenberg,** a political scientist, is Director of the Health Financing Division in the Office of the Assistant Secretary for Planning and Evaluation at the

U.S. Department of Health and Human Services. In 1989 he helped develop the legislation that implemented a physician fee schedule in Medicare. He has published articles on public policy and bureaucratic decision making.

**Toshihiko Hasegawa** is currently Director, Department of Health Care Policy, National Institute of Health Service Management. As a physician official in the national government, he has served in the fields of public health, international health, elderly care, and hospital administration. His research interests include health transition and the application of management science to hospitals.

**Yoshinori Hiroi** is Associate Professor of Health Economics and Social Security, Chiba University. He studied at Tokyo University and MIT, and has published in the fields of health economics and policy and the philosophy of science, including *Amerika no Iryō Seisaku to Nihon* and *Seimei to Jikan* (Keisō Shobō, 1992 and 1994), and *Iryō no Keizaigaku* (Nihon Keizai Shinbunsha, 1994).

**Akinori Hisashige** is Professor and Director, Department of Preventive Medicine, University of Tokushima. He has published widely in both Japanese and English in the fields of technology assessment, clinical epidemiology, and medical decision science. He was selected for both the Mix and Yoshimura awards for outstanding research in 1994.

**William C. Hsiao** is the K. T. Li Professor of Economics at the Harvard School of Public Health. His research centers on national health insurance, cost containment measures, and payment mechanisms. He has advised the governments of Taiwan, Colombia, China, South Africa, and the United States in reforming their health systems.

**Shunya Ikeda** is a physician and a lecturer at the Department of Hospital and Medical Administration of the Keio University School of Medicine. He studied at Keio University and the Harvard School of Public Health. He is active in health services research, health economics, and medical informatics.

**Naoki Ikegami** is Professor and Chair of Hospital and Medical Administration at the School of Medicine, Keio University. His research interests are health care costs, long-term care, and comparative health care systems. He is author of *Iryō no Seisaku Sentaku* (Keisō Shobō, 1992).

**Takanori Ishii** is the chief C.P.A. of Mori Accounting Office. He has been active in the health care field and currently sits on the Japan Hospital Association's Policy Committee and the Health Economics Committee. His most recent publication is *Iryō Hōjin no Kaikei to Zeimu* (Dōbunkan, 1993).

**Yukiko Katsumata** is a Research Fellow at the Social Development Research Institute in Tokyo. She studied at Meiji Gakuin and International Christian Universities. Her field is public finance, particularly in the area of social security. Recent publications include "Users' Charges in Day Nursery Fees and Policy on Revenue Sources" (*Review of Social Policy,* 1995).

**Kōichi Kawabuchi** is a Senior Researcher at the Department of Health Care Economics, National Institute of Health Service Management. He studied at

Hitotsubashi University and the University of Chicago School of Business. His research area is health care management, including publication of *Korekara no Byōin Manejimento* (Igakushoin, 1993).

**Jersey Liang** is Professor of Health Management and Policy at the School of Public Health and Research Scientist at the Institute of Gerontology, University of Michigan. His research interests include comparative aging, health, and health care involving the United States, Japan, Taiwan, and China. Recent articles have appeared in the *Journal of Gerontology: Social Sciences* and *Social Sciences and Medicine.*

**Margaret Lock** is Professor in the Department of Social Studies of Medicine and the Department of Anthropology at McGill University. She is the author of *East Asian Medicine in Urban Japan* (California, 1980), and the prize-winning *Encounters With Aging: Mythologies of Menopause in Japan and North America* (California, 1993).

**Theodore R. Marmor,** Professor of Politics and Public Policy at Yale, is a longtime student of the major spending programs of the modern welfare state. Among his books are *The Politics of Medicare* (Aldine, 1973, 1996); *America's Misunderstood Welfare State* (Basic, 1992); and *Understanding Health Care Reform* (Yale, 1994).

**Mikitaka Masuyama** has an M.A. from Keio University and is a Ph.D. candidate in the Department of Political Science at the University of Michigan. He has researched the politics of health care and is currently working on Japanese legislative institutions.

**Will Mitchell** is Associate Professor of Corporate Strategy at the University of Michigan Business School. His research examines relationships among technology strategy, market entry, and interfirm collaboration. He recently published "Recreating and extending Japanese automobile buyer-supplier links in North America" (*Strategic Management Journal,* 1995).

**Naoko Muramatsu** is Lecturer in Gerontology at the University of Illinois at Chicago School of Public Health. She obtained her Ph.D. in Health Services Organization and Policy as well as two masters degrees at the University of Michigan. Her interests include social determinants of health, and organizational analysis of health care for the elderly in different societies.

**Thomas Roehl** is Assistant Professor of International Business at the University of Illinois at Urbana-Champaign. His interests include interfirm relationships in Japan, Japanese firm foreign investment, and the response of firms to regulatory and environmental change.

**Arnold J. Rosoff** is Professor of Legal Studies and Health Care Systems at the Wharton School and a Senior Fellow of the Leonard Davis Institute of Health Economics, University of Pennsylvania. His teaching and research on health law and policy have focused on issues of patients' rights, doctor-patient relations, and informed consent, including comparisons between the United States and Japan.

**Yasuo Takagi** is Professor of Human Life Sciences, Sendai Shirayuri University. He formerly served as Director of Reseach and Statistics at the Social Development Research Institute. His interests are in health care financing and long-term care. He is author of *Isha to Kanja no tame no Keizaigaku* (Keisō, 1983).

**William G. Weissert** is Professor of Health Management and Policy in the School of Public Health, and Research Scientist in the Institute of Gerontology, University of Michigan. He has published widely on United States long-term care policy and its effectiveness, and with his wife Carol is co-author of *Governing Health: Politics and Policy* (Johns Hopkins, forthcoming).

**Jay Wolfson** is Professor of Health Law and Finance, and Director of the Florida Public Health Information Center, College of Public Health, University of South Florida. He studies health care organizations in the public and private sectors, in Japan as well as the United States, and directs a multi-community pediatric HIV health and social services project.

**Takeshi Yamada** is Assistant Professor of Economic Policy at the Chiba University of Commerce, and a researcher at the Institute of Health Science Research. He is a candidate for the Ph.D. in health economics at Keio University. His research areas are health and public economics.

# Index